Embedded Case Study Methods

Embedded Case Study Methods

INTEGRATING QUANTITATIVE AND QUALITATIVE KNOWLEDGE

Roland W. Scholz

Olaf Tietje

Sage Publications
International Educational and Professional Publisher
Thousand Oaks ■ London ■ New Delhi

For information:

 Sage Publications, Inc.
2455 Teller Road
Thousand Oaks, California 91320
E-mail: order@sagepub.com

Sage Publications Ltd.
6 Bonhill Street
London EC2A 4PU
United Kingdom

Sage Publications India Pvt. Ltd.
M-32 Market
Greater Kailash I
New Delhi 110 048 India

English text by assistance of Daniela Urbatzka and Laura Cohen

Illustrations by Sandro Boesch

Printed in the United States of America

Library of Congress Cataloging-in-Publication Data

Scholz, Roland W.
    Embedded case study methods: Integrating quantitative and qualitative knowledge / by Roland W. Scholz and Olaf Tietje.
        p.   cm.
Includes bibliographical references and index.
    ISBN 0-7619-1945-7 (c) — ISBN 0-7619-1946-5 (p)
    1. Research—Methodology.   2. Case method.   I. Tietje, Olaf.
II. Title.
    Q180.55.M4 S365 2002
    001.4′ 32—dc21   2001002910

This book is printed on acid-free paper.

02   03   04   05   06   7   6   5   4   3   2   1

Acquisition Editor:	C. Deborah Laughton
Editorial Assistant:	Veronica Novak
Production Editor:	Sanford Robinson
Editorial Assistant:	Kathryn Journey
Typesetter:	Janelle LeMaster
Indexer:	Molly Hall
Cover Designer:	Ravi Balasuriya

CONTENTS

Part IV
Validation Perspectives

LIST OF BOXES,
FIGURES, AND TABLES

Boxes

Figures

Tables

1

INTRODUCTION

What, exactly, are case studies? First, we need to define a case. A case could be a university department, a railway company, a city, or even a child. A case is considered from a specified perspective and with a special interest. It is unique, one among others (Stake, 1995, p. 2), and always related to something general. Cases are empirical units, theoretical constructs (Ragin, 1992), and subject to evaluation, because scientific and practical interests are tied to them. They are used for purposes of demonstration and learning, both in education and in research.

The Department of Environmental Sciences at the Swiss Federal Institute of Technology (ETH Zurich), with which we are currently affiliated, can become a case. The curriculum is unique because it radically follows a system approach. The leading questions for a case study at ETH Zurich could be, Which students and professors are attracted to the program? How is learning organized? How are the outcomes (i.e., the students' performances) to be evaluated?

The Italian Railway Company may serve as a case, too. The culture and geography of Italy are unique. So is the mobility behavior—currently, Italy has the second highest number of cars per capita among the larger European countries. Because railway transportation in Italy is not as developed as in other countries, a case study could be organized from the perspective of whether the railway system has any future.

Consider Las Vegas as a case: This city could certainly become subject to research under many perspectives. Besides business, civilization, and social issues, Las Vegas is of interest from an environmental point of view. Civil engineering in Las Vegas is exceptional because it affords highly artificial water management in a rapidly growing desert city.

This book presents methods for embedded case studies. In an embedded case study, the starting and ending points are the comprehension of the case as a whole in its real-world context. However, in the course of analysis, the case will be faceted either by different perspectives of inquiry or by several subunits, and the book presents different methodological approaches to organizing this faceting process. We will use the power of the system approach in order to apply methods, which allow a scientific treatment of complex cases in a way that also will be acknowledged by the quantitative research community. We emphasize that a qualitative analysis starting from the real-world level is an indispensable part of case analysis. Thus, this book bridges the gap between two camps—quantitative and qualitative approaches to complex problems when using the case study methodology. For a scientifically sound, effective, and efficient study of cases such as those mentioned earlier, the following methods are needed:

1. *Case representation and modeling methods* to characterize the case and analyze its current problems and its development

2. *Case evaluation methods* to select one alternative that we prefer over the others, taking into consideration everything we definitely know about the case, what we consider uncertain, and what we want to risk for the case

3. *Case development and transition methods* for creating alternatives

4. *Case study team methods* for enhancing personal experience related to the case and solution-finding performance

As a fifth category, we present specific methods to analyze and assess the case that are from our specific professional background (environmental sciences). These methods may be required depending on the case and on the perspective of the investigation.

In this book, we attempt to describe the methods and to explain their effectiveness for knowledge integration within the embedded case study design. We offer a generally applicable scientific methodology for conducting embedded case studies and present an example of a case study in urban planning. The example requires, and the methodology enables, the integration of very different kinds of knowledge in a complex manner.

METHODS OF KNOWLEDGE INTEGRATION

We believe that case study skepticism arises when knowledge integration in case studies is arranged in a nontransparent manner. Most case studies require the integration of data and knowledge from various sources. Many case studies are conducted in order to improve action and make better decisions. Thus, integrative evaluation—an evaluation that integrates viewpoints from such diverse disciplines as ecology, economics, and sociology—is a crucial component of case studies. Because of the complexity of many cases, studies are conducted frequently by teams. This is especially true with embedded case studies (Yin, 1989, 1994), which apply multiple methods for data generation. Until now, however, few methods have been proposed for organizing the integration and the *synthesis* of data and of knowledge provided by diverse sources, including, for example, participants in a case study. This will be the focus and objective of this book. We will provide a methodology and a set of methods for, as well as examples of, knowledge integration.

When presenting examples, we will refer mostly to problems of urban and regional development that have been shaped by environmental issues. As will become clear with the introduction of the methodology (see Part I: Case Study Design and Synthesis), both the general methodology and the toolkit of methods can be applied in many disciplines.

The methods provide scientific procedures for integrating knowledge, particularly in case studies, that rely on both qualitative and quantitative research methods. These methods help increase the transparency, and particularly the reliability and objectivity, of a case study. By doing so, the likelihood increases that another person who applies the case study methods will end up with the same or similar conclusions.

EMBEDDED CASE STUDIES FOR COMPLEX, CONTEXTUALIZED PROBLEMS

Case studies have been used for teaching and research in many disciplines for many decades. Despite this, the case study approach is still viewed with much skepticism. This is particularly true regarding the use of case studies as a research methodology. In many disciplines, the phrase "case study" is considered a label for bad research or for studies without design.

However, a closer look reveals that the specific use of case studies in various disciplines is extremely dependent on the type of problem treated and on the discipline. The more complex and contextualized the objects of research, the more valuable the case study approach is regarded to be.

Thus, the use of case studies is becoming an increasingly respected research strategy in the following areas:

- Policy and public administration research
- Community sociology
- Management studies
- Branches of psychology and medicine, particularly neuropsychology
- Educational sciences
- Planning sciences
- Civil engineering
- Environmental sciences

Most of the time, the case study approach is chosen in research fields where the biographic, authentic, and historic dynamics and perspectives of real social or natural systems are considered. Using our approach of knowledge integration, the embedded case design is appropriate to organize different types of knowledge, such as different stakeholder or disciplinary perspectives. As this book reveals, this idea holds true in a prototypical way for environmental sciences, which addresses the quality of environmental systems and their relationship to social systems.

HISTORICAL LANDMARKS

Case studies have had a variety of applications throughout history. The French sociologist Le Play (1855) used them as a traditional research method. They were used in community sociology by scholars such as George H. Mead to explore family and worker sociology (also see Whyte, 1943), and they have also been instrumental in cultural anthropology (see Lévi-Strauss, 1955; Mead, 1923). Within the Chicago school, the case study approach was first and foremost motivated and expressed "through the primary object involved in the case studies conducted there, the social problems provoked by urbanization and immigration" (Hamel, Dufour, & Fortin, 1993, p. 15). This case study approach clearly acknowledged that the complexity of the problems to be studied not only requires a decomposed, variable-oriented, quantitative approach, but also depends on the individual case and its understanding (Abbott, 1992).

Case studies may be both descriptive and explanatory (see Yin, 1989, 1994, p. 16). They are often used as a pragmatic research tool in order to understand thoroughly the complexity of a given problem and to support decision making. Because problems do not usually end at disciplinary borders, case studies often require an interdisciplinary approach and teamwork.

Various monographs deal with crucial issues for case studies:

- Principles and designs of case study research (Yin, 1989, 1994)
- Definitions and examples of case studies (Yin, 1993)
- Recommendations for case study students, teachers, and researchers (Ronstadt, 1993)
- Perspectives on new types of theory-practice relationships for involving practitioners in the process of knowledge integration in case studies (Stake, 1995)

Furthermore, the case study approach is considered valuable as a teaching strategy in many fields. In business, for example, it provides students with valuable insights for making sound, highly skilled decisions in administrative affairs (see Barnes, Christensen, & Hansen, 1994).

Although skepticism abounds, case studies—particularly embedded case studies—are considered an appropriate approach to real, complex, current problems that cannot be treated simply by one of the known analytic methods, such as experiment, proof, or survey.

CASE STUDY DESIGN
AND SYNTHESIS

TYPES OF CASE STUDIES

The case study approach presented is an empirical inquiry that investigates a contemporary problem within its real-life context. Understanding the problem and its solution requires integrating a myriad of mutually dependent variables or pieces of evidence that are likely to be gathered at least partially by personal observation.

Although a common definition of case studies exists, one may encounter various types of case studies (see Table 2.1). In order to make clear to which type of case study the introduced methods of knowledge integration should be applied, we will briefly describe different types of case studies. A detailed review of case studies is given by Yin (1994).

DESIGN

Holistic Versus Embedded

A crucial distinction must be made between holistic and embedded case studies (Yin, 1994, p. 41). A holistic case study is shaped by a thoroughly qualitative approach that relies on narrative, phenomenological descriptions. Themes and hypotheses may be important but should remain subordinate to the understanding of the case (Stake, 1976, p. 8).

Embedded case studies involve more than one unit, or object, of analysis and usually are not limited to qualitative analysis alone. The multi-

Table 2.1   Dimensions and Classifications of Case Studies

Dimensions	Classifications
Design	Holistic or embedded Single case or multiple case
Motivation	Intrinsic or instrumental
Epistemological status	Exploratory, descriptive, or explanatory
Purpose	Research, teaching, or action/application
Data	Quantitative or qualitative
Format	Highly structured, short vignettes Unstructured or groundbreaking
Synthesis	Informal, empathic, or intuitive Formative or method driven

plicity of evidence is investigated at least partly in subunits, which focus on different salient aspects of the case. In an organizational case study, for example, the main unit may be a company as a whole, and the smallest units may be departments or even groups of individuals, such as owners and employees. In a clinical, neuropsychological case study, the units may be organized along biographically critical events in the childhood or the vocational world of the case. In case studies on regional or urban planning, the units may be different interest groups that are involved or affected by the project.

Note that an embedded case study allows for a multiplicity of methods that may be applied within the subunits. Thus, hypotheses may be formulated, quantitative data sampled, or statistical analyses applied (see Bortz & Döring, 1995; Campbell & Stanley, 1963). As the title of the book suggests, this book presents methods of embedded case studies (see Part III).

Single Case Versus Multiple Case

Another design characteristic of a case study is whether the design is single case or multiple case. There may be different reasons for choosing a single-case design. A case may be considered unique, prototypical, salient, or revelatory to the understanding of a phenomenon or problem. Analogous to Newton's *experimentum crucis,* it may even be the critical case in testing a well-formulated theory. Although there is no common understanding of how to integrate separate single-case studies into a joint multiple-case design, it is most important to note that the synthesis process between the single cases does not follow a statistical sampling rationale. As Yin (1994) notes, "Every case should serve a specific purpose within the overall scope of inquiry. Here, a major insight is to consider multiple cases as one would consider multiple experiments—that is, to follow a 'replication' logic" (p. 45).

MOTIVATION

The case study researcher often feels intrinsically motivated to investigate a certain case for nonscientific reasons. This may hold true for a new type of educational or public health program, or a specific project in urban development. If there is intrinsic interest, the study team usually takes responsibility and is accountable for the analysis and its consequences (see Gibbons et al., 1994). But if the objective of the study is something other than understanding the particular case, then the inquiry is an instrumental case study.

To illustrate the difference between these types of studies, consider the characters of two different physicians. A physician with an intrinsic motivation is personally interested in and feels responsible for the patient. A physician with an instrumental motivation is primarily interested in using anamnestic and laboratory data to further scientific or financial objectives, and is less interested in the case itself.

EPISTEMOLOGICAL STATUS

The label *case study* is most frequently associated with the exploratory case study. It usually precedes a final study, which can, itself, be a case study, but it can also have a different research design (Boos, 1992). Exploratory case studies help to gain insight into the structure of a phenomenon in order to develop hypotheses, models, or theories. An exploratory study very much resembles a pilot study; the research design and data collection methods usually are not specified in advance.

A descriptive case study differs from an exploratory study in that it uses a reference theory or model that directs data collection and case description. In some respects, a descriptive case study tests whether and in what way a case may be described when approaching it from a certain perspective. Many Formative Scenario Analyses may be considered typical of this type of study (see Chapter 9).

Explanatory case studies can also serve to test cause-and-effect relationships. Clearly, according to conventional understanding of theory testing, a single case can only falsify a theory. However, a case may also be used for theory testing, either if the case is used for quantitative data sampling (see Petermann, 1989), or, in a replication logic, if the research team investigates "whether similar causal events—within each case—produce these positive outcomes" (Yoon & Hwang, 1995, p. 12). Note that the theory testing is done in a qualitative manner. However, as in traditional hypothesis testing, specifications for the cause-impact chain have to be formulated before case analysis.

PURPOSE

A case study may be used as a method of research, teaching, or action/application. For instructional purposes, case studies are commonly used in business, law, and medical schools. The case encounter quite often changes the traditional educational approach into a discussion pedagogy. Thus, the case method is a variation on the Socratic method, which is another name for proactive interaction between teachers and students (Ronstadt, 1993). Unfortunately, when teaching by case studies (see Barnes et al., 1994), the primacy of data and of situation analysis is often not respected as a principle. This is due to the fact that a prepared, written case offers only limited access to data, and, therefore, teaching case studies are based on a virtual process of case analysis.

FORMAT

Several basic formats for case studies exist (Ronstadt, 1993, pp. 17-18). The first two types are teaching cases and are always provided in written form.

- *Highly structured cases:* The problem is well ordered, and the facts are provided in a written, condensed way. The case looks like a mathematical textbook problem. A "best solution" often exists, and one is expected to treat the case using known methods.
- *Short vignettes:* The case is well structured, has little excess information, and covers just a few pages. A best solution does not usually exist in the sense of a right or wrong answer. Often, the case is a prototype or demonstrates a key concept.
- *Unstructured cases:* In many complex cases, no best solution can be found. However, a preferred practice or even theory may exist. If the case is in writing, information about the situational context is necessary to structure the case and propose solutions. Real cases, per se, are of a limited problem scope. For instance, a patient with backache can be taken as a medical case. There can be various reasons for the backache, but the range within which rational solutions or explanations are sought is small. Although in the beginning, backache is a diffuse and unstructured phenomenon, the experienced doctor will try to structure the case by asking the patient about possible physical and behavioral causes.
- *Groundbreaking cases:* The case provides new terrain for the study team. The situation is totally new, and little, if any, knowledge exists that has been gained through structured research. The case team has to structure the case and formulate a specific perspective or theoretical framework.

DATA COLLECTION AND METHODS OF KNOWLEDGE INTEGRATION

In principle, each case study should use multiple sources of information. All methods should employ direct and participant observations, structured interviews, and surveys, and they can also include experimental design, focused interviews, open-ended interviews, archival records, documents, and scientific data from field and laboratory (see Box 2.1). (A detailed description of data gathering is given in Yin, 1994, p. 93, and Stake, 1995, p. 49.) This remains true regardless of case design. The main distinction for case studies is whether they have a holistic or embedded design.

Knowledge integration within a holistic design is ruled almost exclusively by the principles of qualitative research. The synthesis process is

> ## Box 2.1   Using Multiple Sources of Data and Evidence
>
> In all phases of the case, a wide variety of data from different sources have to be integrated (Yin, 1994, p. 91). The source and type of data depend on the case and its nature.
>
> Documents, archival records, and open-ended interviews are typical sources used in the beginning of most studies. In an embedded case design, structured or focused interviews are often used, but this design also allows for surveys, questionnaires, and even the sampling experimental data. In neuropsychological or environmental case studies, laboratory data or simulation studies are also helpful in gaining insight into the case. The following figure illustrates the potential sources of evidence and techniques for data sampling that can be integrated in case analysis.
>
>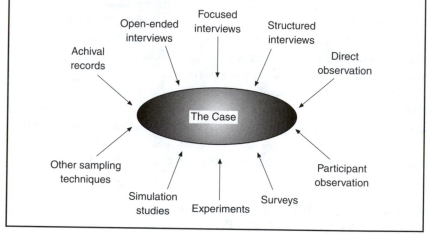

informal (avoiding reductionism and elementalism), empathic, and mostly intuitive. Thus, the research report is narrative in nature.

The embedded case design allows for both qualitative and quantitative data and strategies of synthesis or knowledge integration. The methods provided in Part III of this volume may be used to interrelate and integrate the variables, findings, evaluations, and so on from the various facets of the case or subunits of case inquiry. Thus, the methods of knowledge integration help explain the data under consideration, thereby making data and inferential processes more transparent. The global statements and conclusions are usually derived by an intuitively qualitative process based on both experiential understanding and a more or less formative synthesis process that is supported by the methods introduced.

THE USE OF CASE STUDIES
IN DIFFERENT DISCIPLINES

We want to provide insight into the use of case studies in neuropsychology, education, business, law, and environmental sciences. We will look at the characteristics of the problems treated by the case study method, and we will discuss the relationships between the case and the data, theories, study teams, and dynamics of the case. When presenting the approaches of the different disciplines, we will focus only on certain aspects of case study work and knowledge integration within each subject, because the lessons to be learned from the different disciplines overlap.

NEUROPSYCHOLOGY

Neuropsychology is a branch of both medicine and psychology that correlates the psychological and organic aspects of mental disorders. A nonmystical approach to mental disorders was first developed in the age of enlightenment. It is worth noting that, historically, scientific understanding of human psychic processes became obvious through case reports.

Many researchers in the history of science consider the 10 volumes on *Erfahrungsseelenkunde* (experiential mindography) of Karl Philipp

Moritz to be the first scientific psychology journal (see Lück, 1991). The volumes are filled with case reports from physicians, teachers, parsons, and philosophers on their own personal experiences (*Selbsterfahrung*) with mental disorders and other mental experiences. The tradition of novelistically styled case stories has accompanied the development of the theory and practice of neuropsychology from Freud to Luria to Sacks. Sacks (1973) notes that this romantic style, with its efforts to describe life holistically and the impacts of disease, has nearly disappeared since the mid-20th century.

In many subdisciplines of medicine, case studies are used as a means of teaching (see Box 3.1), but they have many other functions (Stuhr & Deneke, 1993) . Within neuropsychology, for example, case studies also serve to describe and define concepts.

A mental disease may be defined by an extensional definition when giving a list of all its features. This conveys that certain diseases cannot be defined by a set of data and phenomena. When diagnosing a mental disease, data are sampled from technical procedures such as electromyography, which is the assessment of nerve conduction velocity, or electroencephalogram (EEG). Furthermore, one may occasionally find physiological anomalies such as hormone overproduction; specific viruses; or unusual, salient symptoms such as tremors or ataxia, which is a disorder of the extremities. But as we have learned from several examples, this approach will not necessarily lead to an understanding of a disease, nor will it provide a valid diagnosis.

Sacks (1973) illustrated this when studying Parkinson's disease and encephalitis lethargica. The latter is also called European sleeping sickness and appeared as an epidemic all over Europe in 1916 and 1917, killing about 5 million people. The puzzling thing about this disease is that no two patients show the same symptoms. Hence, completely different diagnoses—epidemic delirium, epidemic Parkinson's disease, rabies—have been made in different places. Nevertheless, despite the huge variety of symptoms and phenomena, only one single disease was characterized by this structure of damage to the psychophysical equilibrium.

This also holds true for Parkinson's disease, which has to be understood as a very specific state of an individual organism. Sacks (1973) stresses that this understanding may be attained only by a theory that synthesizes observations, episodes, laboratory data, and technical medicine. Thus, a theory for integrating data and knowledge is necessary. If we stick to the mere analysis of data alone, no suitable conclusions can be drawn.

| Box 3.1 | Novelistic Case Descriptions for Exploratory, Descriptive, and Explanatory Case Studies |

Novelistic episodes and case descriptions are part of neuropsycholog-ical research and teaching. A famous example is the case of H.M. This case has been investigated for more than three decades, and dozens of journal articles have been published about H.M.

H.M. suffered from anamnestic syndrome (a severe loss of memory) after having had brain surgery for epilepsy, although his intelligence re-mained nearly unaffected. Even 10 months after his family had moved, H.M. could not find his new home. He remembered his former address perfectly, but he had no idea as to where he had left his lawn mower the day before. He was not able to recognize his new neighbors even after they had visited him continuously for 6 years. Because he had no memory of doing so, he repeatedly composed the same puzzle or read the same journal. Only half an hour after lunch, he could not recall that he had eaten, much less what. H.M. could not be left alone at home because he welcomed any strangers, assuming they were family friends. Apparently, he is conscious of his situation, as indicated by his statement, "Every day is alone, whatever enjoyment I've had, and whatever sorrow I've had."

Some rare episodes showed that the potential to remember new infor-mation was still present, but such information had to be strongly linked to emotions and feelings. H.M. was very bothered and annoyed when a gun was taken out of a collection he was very proud of.

Case studies with H.M. showed that brain damage that is anatomically limited can still cause lifelong memory malfunction. Further insights into brain structure and the differential localization of declarative and opera-tional memory were gained.

Episodes and case descriptions were decisive in both understanding and explaining the cause-and-effect relationships (see Markowitsch, 1985; Scoville & Millner, 1957; Sidman, Soddard, & Mohr, 1968) and de-scribing the limited, but definite, impact of a lost or damaged temporal lobe.

Case studies in brain research are often of an explanatory nature. The case of H.M. (see Box 3.1), for instance, has been important in both un-derstanding epilepsy and finding a structure to describe the cause-and-effect relationship of human memory. Since 1957, more than 30 scientific journal articles have dealt with this biography and the impact that brain surgery has on behavior, mental functioning, and personal identity. It is noteworthy, albeit only natural, that computer tomography and other techniques currently provide much deeper insight into human physical structure than was available in the 1950s. The need for a detailed case description and the integration of data from different sources, however, remains.

LESSONS TO BE LEARNED

▶ Hard- and software data have to be integrated. Hardware data are provided by laboratory analysis, EEG, MCT, and other "graphies" from technical medicine. Software data consist of the biography and the behavior observed. Because the case analyst has to be able to investigate both types, he or she has to consider and integrate endogene and exogene impact factors. Thus, we usually have an embedded case study design.

▶ The dynamics of a case allow for causal analysis. Sometimes, a case is observed over a long period of time. An explanatory case design describes the dynamics of a case and its cause-and-effect relationship.

▶ Real cases are unique. A real case is unique in that the phenomenology, biography, and biology of two patients will never be totally identical.

▶ The case analysis affects the case. The interaction between a case analyst and his or her case affects the state of the case. This phenomenon is called interactional resonance.

▶ Both diagnosis and therapy are targeted. The neuropsychologist is usually interested in both therapy and diagnosis. As a consequence, the case study team should also contribute to the case development.

▶ Knowledge from different roles and perspectives has to be integrated. The case analyst sequentially, and sometimes even simultaneously, takes on the role of a chronist, an objective observer, a participatory observer, an introspective observer, a predictor, an interpreter, and a therapist (Rudolph, 1993, p. 23). It must be acknowledged that different types of knowledge, and sometimes different va-lue or preference systems, have to be integrated.

▶ Mutual problem solving is needed. Both good diagnoses and good therapy will work only if both parties—the patient and the therapist—are willing to cooperate. Thus, a case is shaped by a mutual, intrinsic conception of the case analysis, both by the case and by the case analyst.

▶ A model/theory is needed for knowledge integration. Due to the complex nature of cases in neuropsychology, orienting at the phenomenology of mental diseases is not sufficient. An integrating model or theory of mental diseases based on data is needed. This should also provide an explanation of cause-and-effect relationships.

EDUCATIONAL SCIENCES

The educational sciences cover a wide field of knowledge about the processes necessary for the acquisition of knowledge, skills, competence, and other desirable qualities of behavior or habits in individuals, groups, and organizations. Some of this knowledge has been acquired by using the case study approach. In this section, however, we will take a closer look only at the use of case studies in school program evaluations, because many arguments in favor of using the case study approach for educational purposes have already been presented in the section on neuropsychology. A kind of continuum exists from neuropsychological case studies to the investigation of learning disabilities (see Grissemann & Weber, 1982; Lorenz, 1992; Luria, 1969), as well as from the investigation of subjects' knowledge acquisition in specific environments (also labeled cognitive ethnography) (see Easley, 1983; Erlwanger, 1975) to Piagetian case studies on stages of cognitive development. This Piagetian type of case study relies heavily on high-resolution protocols for the individual's behavior and thinking aloud. A synthesis process is organized either along a single theory or across a range of theories (on cognitive development, socialization, curriculum development, etc.) from different disciplines, allowing for a variety of interpretations. Note that the rise of case studies in educational sciences in the 1970s came in response to the disappointing results of the dominant statistical psychometric, quantitative approach (see Scholz, 1983b).

Program evaluation is a special branch of educational research and the major subject of Robert Stake's (1976, 1995) case study research. Typically, the desire for a new program or discomfort with the current program precedes the need for evaluation. A new program is usually motivated by "issues about which people disagree" (Stake, 1995, p. 133). For instance, the public in the United States felt dissatisfied with high school students' achievements. Teacher education was considered to be responsible for this deficiency. Traditional teacher education programs were judged to be insufficiently theoretically founded, without targets, and too conventional. Thus, 15 states developed new programs, such as the competency-based teacher education (CBTE) in Texas (see Houston & Howsam, 1974), and enforced them by law.

During the planning of the CBTE program (see Vogel, 1978), it had already been acknowledged that

> change in complex social systems is not likely to occur unless all elements are collaboratively involved. . . . Change strategies should involve colleges and universities, professional units, academic units, school districts and other employing units, administrators, teachers, public, professional associations . . . , state governmental units, teacher education students. (pp. 3-4)

Furthermore, the evaluation should encompass the pilot phase, the implementation of the program, and the regular activities after implementation.

Basically, there are three approaches that may be chosen for evaluations. First, there is a genuinely quantitative evaluation design for applying batteries of more or less sophisticated tests to assess each group's, unit's, and pupil's performance. Second, there is a holistic case design, and third, there is an embedded case design. We will discuss briefly some methodological prerequisites for and constraints of the holistic approach (see Stake, 1995).

Stake (1995) agrees that when studying a case, a specific issue or perspective is advantageous for gathering data. However, throughout a study, these issues may change such that the study may become "progressively focused" (p. 133). In the process of data gathering, the case team should minimize intrusion, particularly avoiding formal tests and "assignments characteristic of survey and laboratory study" (p. 134). To minimize misperception and invalidity, triangulation should be applied. By triangulation, Stake means the process of substantiating interpretations. The triangulation process aims to (a) have the reader gain insight into the case analysis or the construction of meaning, and (b) improve the validity of case analysis. In triangulation, one has the choice of using not only co-observers, panelists, or reviewers from alternative theoretical viewpoints, but also the standard tools of qualitative research (see Denzin & Lincoln, 1994).

Stake (1995) stresses that a qualitative, holistic case study is highly personal research. He notes that "the quality and utility of the research is not based on its reproducibility but on whether or not the meanings generated, by the researcher or the reader, are valued. Thus a personal valuing of the work is expected" (p. 135).

Although this radical constructivistic approach may not be shared, Stake stresses the role of the case study researcher as a subject. In the course of analysis, the researcher's role may change from biographer to interpreter to evaluator, and perhaps even to advocate of the case.

The embedded case design will be introduced in some detail in Chapter 5. It particularly differs from the holistic case design in that it combines qualitative and quantitative research and is conceived of almost exclusively as a collective study (i.e., a study run by a study team). Although we prefer and recommend this approach, we want to remind the reader of Stake's warnings. The case study researcher should be aware that he or she has to serve many audiences.

LESSONS TO BE LEARNED

▶ Holistic case studies allow for evaluations of complex programs. A holistic case design shaped by the principles of qualitative research may serve for the evaluation of complex programs that have not been treated effectively with quantitative designs.

▶ A case may be treated from different perspectives. For data gathering and case analysis, certain issues must be formulated in advance. The case researcher should allow, but be aware of, the shifting of these issues throughout the course of the study.

▶ The criteria of objectivity may not be applied in holistic case studies. Holistic case studies are a highly subjective affair and include the personal value system of the case study team.

LAW

Let us take a brief look at the history of law in the United States. Until the end of the 19th century, law was not an academic discipline. Entry into the legal profession could be attained primarily through apprenticeship. The investigation of real cases was the basis of education. During the deanship of Christopher Langdell at Harvard University Law School, law developed as a formalized system and became accepted as a scientific discipline. The price to be paid for this entry into the world of academic knowledge was "that all available materials of that science are contained in printed books" (Langdell, 1887, p. 123). Cases became case descriptions. A typical feature of these descriptions was that they were tailored to the systematics of the jurisprudence system. The task of the students was not to construct legal arguments for a real case, but rather to map a case into a comprehensive, complete, conceptually ordered, formal system that complied fully with statute books, rules, and regulations (Quinn, 1994, p. 12).

In the period between 1930 and 1960, there was a renaissance in the study of real cases. Classification of cases was not conceived as an end, but rather a starting point for analysis. Cases were to be grasped and analyzed, including their economic and social constraints. Thus, a Socratic style of teaching was practiced. The metaphor "clinical studies" refers to the tradition of medical studies. "Clinical legal education is to get the novice to understand rules in their true environment by involving students in real-life exercises" (Quinn, 1994, p. 119).

LESSONS TO BE LEARNED

▶ Written case studies run the risk of decontextualization. The abstraction of a legal case from its situational context creates a couple of risks. First, there is the loss of one's functional perspective, or the perspective held by the particular sector being regulated. Second, there is the inhibition of understanding the interdisciplinary constituents of legal rules and their application.

▶ Case studies should be both the end point and the starting point of further analysis. Within a formalistic treatment, case studies serve as illustrations of legal subjects as part of a formal system. Within a functionalist view, the cases are a starting point for an open process of argumentation and Socratic dialogue.

BUSINESS

A couple of famous case studies in business and organizational sciences, such as the Hawthorne study at Western Electric Company (Mayo, 1933; Röthlisberger & Dickson, 1939), resulted in findings that changed the concept of a successful business. One of the lessons learned repeatedly from many studies is that in order to be accurate, a monodisciplinary economic view has to be broadened to take the sociopsychological aspects into account. In spite of this, we will focus on teaching cases in this section. This is because the Harvard School of Business has developed the case method of instruction (Frazer, 1931).

The teaching case approach integrates different educational and epistemological concepts about learning. Clearly, the goal of teaching by case studies is to improve one's ability to solve problems. Case studies are good for problems where truth is relative, reality is realistic, and a structural relationship is contingent. Hence, case teaching focuses primarily on the development of understanding, judgment, and intuition.

The use of case studies in teaching is linked with a situation-theoretic or pragmatic approach to learning, that is, the "learning by doing" principle. A real, naturalistic empirical situation (Dewey, 1966) is needed for the initiating phase of thought. The situation should allow the problem to become the student's own and, thus, of the intrinsic study type.

Case teaching and case study research obey the principles of the Socratic method as well as those for leadership of discussions. The basic requisites are expressed well by Barnes et al. (1994): "The capacity to ask appropriate questions, to listen carefully and respond constructively, to deal with uncertainty, to reward and to punish, [and] to create learning environments of openness and trust" (p. 4).

In case studies, the traditional, hierarchical teacher-student relationship is changed into a partnership between teacher and student. The teacher becomes a guide in the process of discovery. Likewise, in case study research, the hierarchical professor-student relationship is dissolved. This is due to the multilevel, multiquality knowledge that has to be integrated for case analysis and development. As has been shown at Harvard University, case teaching is a kind of artistry that does not allow any "masquerade forms" (Barnes et al., 1994, p. 4). Thus, teaching and researching by means of case studies should be conceived of as open learning approaches that encourage community involvement—an active, democratic approach.

Box 3.2   Synthesis Moderation

Case study teams must fulfill numerous prerequisites. The subsequent text is taken almost verbatim from Ronstadt (1993, p. 11), changed only minimally, and extended. It may also hold true for study teams doing research.

1. Each person must thoroughly know the case and perform an appropriate amount of thinking and analysis before the first group meeting.
2. Each person will be expected to attend all group meetings and give these meetings scheduling priority.
3. Each person will be given the opportunity to speak at the meeting, and no one will be allowed to monopolize a meeting. Everyone tries to contribute something.
4. Useful contributions made by individual team members will be respected and rewarded.
5. Goof-offs and free-riders will not be tolerated.

Many cases are so complex that investigation by a single student or researcher does not seem promising. Furthermore, different types of knowledge have to be integrated, such as those of practitioners and theorists. Case study work has to be conceived of as a collective activity, both within the study team and between science and society. This promotes a kind of cooperative learning and collective rationality. Because of this, there is the need for effective team operations (see Box 3.2).

Finally, case studies in business are action oriented. Therefore, the analysis should always begin concretely with the case and its processes, rather than with abstract hypotheses or theoretical ideas (Towl, 1969). The case study team should be willing to accept compromise, accommodate others, and have a sense for the possible.

LESSONS TO BE LEARNED

▶ Case teaching calls for a new type of instruction. When using cases as a means of instruction, it is important to encourage open, Socratic discourse, learning, and research.

▶ Study teams need disciplined, democratic, efficient cooperation. Although study teams' degrees of knowledge and roles may vary, case team members must obey rules for effective team operation.

▶ Case studies are good for problems where truth is relative, reality is realistic, and a structural relationship is contingent. Hence, case teaching focuses primarily on the development of understanding, judgment, and intuition.

ENVIRONMENTAL SCIENCES

The environmental sciences deal with the structure and quality of natural environmental systems and their relationship to social systems. Thus, environmental studies cover a wide field of complex issues. Knowledge must be integrated from the natural and social sciences. Often, planning and engineering are a part of environmental studies, particularly in cases concerning landscape and regional development, or water management, or in cases in which there is the need for mobility or product optimization. We do not intend to provide an extensive review of environmental studies, but rather to introduce briefly three types of case studies—structure, dynamics, and qualities of natural systems—that focus on these different aspects and their relationship to social systems.

Models for regional water flux or climate dynamics must appropriately incorporate constraints and specific knowledge and data of soil science, agriculture, geology, mathematics, and other varied disciplines. Generally, an answer cannot be attained through a monodisciplinary approach, but rather is procured by fusing knowledge from physics, chemistry, biology, and the disciplines mentioned earlier. For model development, study teams often choose a case, such as a region, for a descriptive case study. But if the models rely partially on first principles, the character they exhibit is, at least in part, explanatory (Rohdenburg, 1989). Because the study is usually motivated by a desire for model development and theory verification rather than by the case itself, the study is of the instrumental type. There are usually two types of knowledge integration: the integration of knowledge from different disciplines, and the integration and scaling up of the data provided by subsystems. For example, in a case

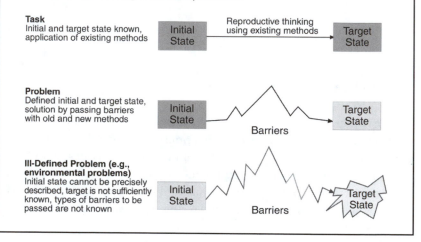

Box 3.3 Groundbreaking Case Studies for Ill-Defined Problems

Clearly, the case study methodology is suitable for ill-defined problems. This type of problem often arises in "young" sciences or in the applied sciences that deal with real-world problems. Groundbreaking cases provide the soil for generating ill-defined problems.

Task
Initial and target state known, application of existing methods

Initial State — Reproductive thinking using existing methods → Target State

Problem
Defined initial and target state, solution by passing barriers with old and new methods

Initial State — Barriers — Target State

Ill-Defined Problem (e.g., environmental problems)
Initial state cannot be precisely described, target is not sufficiently known, types of barriers to be passed are not known

Initial State — Barriers — Target State

involving water dynamics, the former might be the integration of knowledge about soil and water characteristics, and the latter the scaling up from a specific site to a catchment.

Intrinsic case studies are provided by many projects on restoring natural sites, landscape engineering, and urban development. The starting point is interest in the case and its related environmental problems. These environmental problems, such as the endangerment of certain species or the contamination of groundwater by agriculture, establish the core of the case. The study team's values usually have a strong influence on the target of the study. In studies on restoring natural sites, the teams often focus on certain species or designated land use. In groundwater conservation, the strategies vary from finding technical solutions to creating financial incentives, such as subsidies, for those who comply with conservation standards. It should be mentioned that, as in architecture, developing projects in the field of the environmental sciences is an art. One must have a special feel for it to do it well, and the importance of this should not be over-looked; in many such cases, the artistic design is a determining factor for success.

Special types of case studies are provided by sustainability projects. Sustainability may be considered a system quality. The sustainability of social systems is characterized by certain qualitative system properties. We consider three issues to be crucial for sustainability (Scholz, Mieg, Weber, & Stauffacher, 1998). First, the potential must exist for future generations to have the same opportunities that former ones did. Second, there must be a high likelihood of system maintenance (i.e., the system should not collapse). Third, there needs to be a well-adjusted balance between change and stability, which, at least to some degree, should be under human control.

Sustainable management presents a specific type of problem. Today, we do not know the properties of a sustainable target state (see Box 3.3). Furthermore, we usually do not know how sustainable an initial or current state of a system is. Finally, we do not know which barriers have to be overcome in order to attain the target state. Thus, we speak about a typical ill-defined problem (see Box 3.3). The case team may (and should) be interested in the case itself. Case studies that are run in the sustainability framework may be of an intrinsic and/or instrumental type. They are mostly of an exploratory type, because we do not have an elaborate sustainability definition or theory at our disposal. It is usually highly unstructured, of an embedded design, and should be groundbreaking, because we want to gain new insights.

Note that sustainability can be attained only if human behavior changes. Thus, an understanding of the cause-and-effect relationships between natural and social systems is important.

LESSONS TO BE LEARNED

▶ Case studies may serve for natural sciences. In the natural sciences, models for the description and prognosis of natural systems have to be developed. A case serves for developing and testing models in a real-world matrix and brings the aleatory, indeterminate nature of environmental systems to the scientist.

▶ Case engineering is value focused. In intrinsic studies, the case teams want to not only describe but also improve the case. This is a highly value-driven activity shaped by interests.

▶ Ill-defined problems may be treated with groundbreaking cases. If insight into system qualities that are not well-known, such as sustainability, is targeted, then groundbreaking cases are wanted.

THE ARCHITECTURE OF KNOWLEDGE INTEGRATION IN EMBEDDED CASE STUDIES

T he previous chapter covered a broad spectrum of types of case study research and their applications. We have shown that knowledge integration is essential for case studies, and that it can be organized in multiple ways. For many cases, the embedded case design is appropriate and favorable. This chapter outlines an epistemology of an embedded case study. First, we will make distinctions between different levels of knowledge (see Figure 4.1; see Steiner 1989, 1990) and corresponding epistemics, which are the carriers of recognition (such as a result of a statistic, a causal explanation by propositional logic, a conceptual model, or simply a pictorial representation) and have to be connected hierarchically according to these levels. Second, we will introduce various strategies of synthesis. Third, we will present the Brunswikian Lens Model, which is considered an appropriate model for the process and epistemic nature of knowledge integration in embedded case studies. Finally, we will introduce different types of knowledge integration. Although this chapter is highly theoretical, it is strongly recommended for all readers because it helps you to understand which type of method is appropriate for which case and problem.

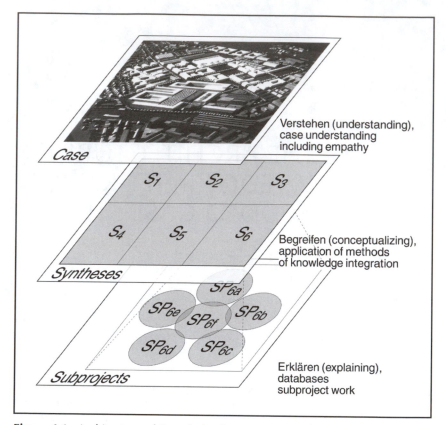

Figure 4.1. Architecture of Knowledge Integration in Embedded Case Studies

THE ARCHITECTURE OF EMBEDDED CASE STUDIES

We postulate that case analysis should be organized and structured on three levels (see Figure 4.1), each with its own, specific importance. The levels are linked to different qualities of knowledge. When referring to the theory of knowledge, we call them the levels of *Verstehen, Begreifen,* and *Erklären,* or, to express them in English terms, between understanding, conceptualizing, and explaining (see Scholz, 1998).

On the first level, there is the case as a whole. Some examples are a patient, an organization, or, as shown in Figure 4.1, a site, each with its own history, constraints, and dynamics. For each case study, it is important that the researcher develops an encompassing and empathic case understanding. The key epistemics on this level are feeling; pictorial representation; and intuitive, sometimes subconscious, comprehension. The study team should always focus only on the case and not on general questions or issues tied to the case. The case is the means to reduce the complexity of the discourse of the universe from general problems, such as mental disease, efficient organizations, or sustainable development, to one individual state of affairs.

On the second level, there is a conceptual model of the real world. We are changing from the holistic perspective of the first level to a system or model view on the second level. The key to successful work on this level is the methods of knowledge integration. These methods help to develop a more valid case understanding. They are the vehicles to the syntheses. They are tools for both organizing knowledge and managing the study team's internal cooperation. This latter point is important, because synthesis work is conducted mostly by teams. Epistemologically, this level contributes to the *Begreifen* (conceptualizing) of the case.

On the third level are scattered data and results from disciplinary subprojects. Usually, only separated compartments or fragments of the case are subjects of investigation. The *Erkenntnisform* (epistemic) on this level is *Erklären* (i.e., causal explaining by propositional logic). This is provided prototypically by the formal natural sciences. We distinguish between two types of data. The first is data from the case, such as observations, measurements, surveys, documents, expertises, and so on. The second is data from the existing body of scientific knowledge (i.e., disciplinary propositions). The data-level work is often organized in subprojects. Note that these subprojects and the data they generate have to be organized carefully according to the requirements of the synthesis level. Analytic methods of all types from every field are a part of this level.

STRATEGIES OF SYNTHESIS

In the subsequent introduction of four types of synthesis, we take an epistemological perspective, because the theory of knowledge allows for the differentiation between the foundations of knowledge. For embedded case studies, this differentiation was already introduced in Figure 4.1. Note that scientific work in general is characterized by partitioning and decomposing a subject into elements in order to attain a refined analysis. In contrast, in the context of case studies, syntheses are necessary. They can be conceived of as scientifically combining often-varied data, infor-mation, and ideas into a consistent whole. Knowledge integration in embedded case studies can be conceived of as a kind of synthesis designed specifically for such a case study type. The following classification pre-dominantly refers to the history of philosophy.

What is meant by synthesis obviously differs from one branch of sci-ence or humanities to another. However, even within a single branch, there is a considerable range of definitions. Adopting an epistemological perspective, we will introduce four different types of synthesis that illumi-nate the various strategies chosen in case study work and show how anal-ysis and synthesis link up in the methods introduced.

Synthesis as a Philosophical Strategy of Contemplation

Distinctions between analytic and synthetic methods were originally made in the age of high scholastics and are attributed to Giacomo Zabarella (see Bhatnagar & Kanal, 1992). Zabarella's differentiation en-compasses the whole field of science. On one hand, there are the syn-thetic-contemplative sciences such as philosophy, in which knowledge ac-quisition and inquiry are stimulated through intrinsic motivation and holistic consideration. On the other hand, we find the analytic sciences, particularly mathematics and the natural sciences. According to the pre-vailing interpretation, mathematics starts with axioms and derives new knowledge by method of proof. In the natural sciences, analysis reveals hidden rules, such as the natural laws that underlie the apparent cause-and-effect relationships and their phenomenology. Note that ana-lytic methods may be both inductive and deductive. The key to analytic methods lies in the principles of analytic decomposition, which make it possible to explain a new invention through what is already known. Note that René Descartes (1596-1650) considered the analytic method to be the only true method of philosophy and sciences.

Synthesis as a method of description in the contemplative philosophy is now part of the humanities and is often associated with prescientific cate-gories of knowledge and direct experience (Landgrebe, 1959). The ap-proach is linked to the medieval, clerically shaped humanity that under-stood synthesis as a philosophical approach to understanding the essence of the whole. Note that the holistic case study and the concept of empathy are related to this approach. Thus, a case study team would follow a prescientific, contemplative approach if, after surveying and inspecting the case, it would reflect and think about the case and try to gain understanding and insight of the case's true nature, essence, and meaning.

Synthesis Through a Pure Case Model

Up until Gottfried von Leibniz (1646-1716), the potential of synthetic methods was supposed to be limited to the representation of facts. However, Leibniz considered the synthetic method to be the most accomplished because it permits descending from general rules of truth to the composed. A critical issue in this argument, however, was that the rules of truth have to be found by analytic methods. The most general truths are the natural laws. As Churchman (1971) notes, the Leibnizian concept relied on the assumption that the truth is provided in the model.

An example of the pure case model is the Copernican *Himmelsmechanik*. This model made progressively complex calculations of planets and other physical bodies possible. In general, one may consider the pure case as a fictive physical environment that behaves perfectly like the model. For instance, an urn or roulette wheel may be considered a pure case for the preexisting probability model. However, any recording of a real roulette wheel will show, at least in the long run, some deviation from the model. Note that social psychology also uses the metaphor of the pure case. For instance, Kurt Lewin, one of the most renowned social psychologists, used this term when referring to Galileo's study of falling bodies (see Brunswik, 1943, p. 266). Regarding physics as a standard for science, Lewin tried to find general laws of social cognition via laboratory experiments.

The System Dynamics (see Chapter 10) approach, which is widely used in economics and environmental sciences, among other fields, also refers to the pure case model. As Bhatnagar and Kanal (1992) wrote, "A Leibnizian enquirer assumes the existence of an a priori model of the situation (the innate ideas or the theory), and attempts to configure the inputs of the situation according to this model" (p. 32). The reader should be cognizant that both descriptive and explanatory case studies may be organized according to the Leibnizian concept.

In our understanding, the Leibnizian strategy of synthesis is appropriate at least as a partial synthesis, and in particular for natural science

representations of the case. In general, however, the Leibnizian model remains on the level of explaining (see Figure 4.1), rather than leading to, a
general synthesis.

Synthesis as a Pre-Stage of
Higher Conceptual Knowledge

The complementarity between analytic and synthetic reasoning may be
compared to the complementarity between *Begriff und Anschauung* (concept and perception) by Immanuel Kant (1724-1804), in that both synthetic reasoning and perception are regarded as prerequisites for analytic
reasoning and theoretical concepts.

Bhatnagar and Kanal (1992, p. 32) point out that the Kantian type of
inquiry, in which truth is to be found partly in the data and partly in the
model, is predominant in the social sciences. The validation of hypothe-
sis-based theory testing thus shows some reference to the Kantian concept
and perception. The perceptual side is represented by the theories and
their hypotheses, and the analytical side is represented by the observed
data. Empirical data substantiates, differentiates, and refutes the theories.
Clearly, in the Kantian type of inquiry, the theory, not the case, is the point
of reference. Cases in the Kantian conception may be used instrumentally
to illustrate different aspects or notions of a theory or concept.

Synthesis as a Method for
Complex Problem Solving

For complex, real-world problems, no single unifying theory or model
exists. The problem is usually multifaceted, ill-defined (see Box 3.3), and
shaped by innumerable sets of mutually linked subsystems and impact
factors. Because the analysis of complex, real-world problems not only is
theoretically motivated, but also mostly arises out of a genuine desire for
improvement, the analysis is oriented toward effectual actions.

When facing a real-world problem, various issues are at the disposal of
the problem solver. First, there is the history of the problem and its definition. The problem usually arises from general world experience, and
sometimes, there is a specific case from which the problem originated.
Consequently, we will often have a problem that is represented by a case

and has an accompanying set of questions, statements, or issues to be raised. Second, we usually have a set of theories or models that partially illuminates the topics of interest, the problem, and its context, but lacks an integrating strategy. This strategy is given by the Hegelian model of inquiry, which "seeks to develop the ability to see the same input from different points of view" (Bhatnagar & Kanal, 1992, p. 32). Thus, an intermediate state of analysis consists of different, even seemingly contradictory, models of the problem or the case (i.e., the thesis and its antithesis). According to the Hegelian perspective, through synthesis, the inquirer approaches truth in a dialectical way. Note that synthesis incorporates certain aspects of the different world models, resulting in a new, larger model.

Choosing the Strategy for Knowledge Integration

It is important to understand that none of the types of synthesis introduced is the "right" one. For many well-defined problems in the natural sciences, there are strong models and even pure cases that allow for a close-to-model demonstration. However, let us demonstrate Hooke's Law by considering a real spiral spring of the type that might be found in cars or a physics laboratory. Robert Hooke asserted that the stress placed on an elastic solid (its compression or extension) is proportional to the strain responsible for it. This natural law can be demonstrated only at low and medium extension, and cannot be verified when the extension is maximal or minimal. One can infer from this that Hooke's Law is largely wrong. Pure cases that reliably demonstrate the theories or models are rarely found, particularly if real-world cases are considered.

For the ill-structured problem domains found in the real world, such as management, education, politics, urban planning, and environmental sciences, we consider the Hegelian type of synthesis to be appropriate.

In order to avoid misunderstandings, we want to add that we are not purporting the analytic method to be generally superior to the synthetic one. We believe that these methods contain complementary types of knowledge, and that they allow for different, but not better or worse, knowledge or epistemics. This is particularly valid for complex problems because "the true sciences are at the same time analytic and synthetic" (Bachmann, quoted in Gethmann, 1980, p. 361).

THE BRUNSWIKIAN LENS MODEL

Egon Brunswik was originally an experimental psychologist who worked in the field of perception (Brunswik, 1935). While investigating the performance of our perceptual systems, Brunswik concentrated on the question of how these systems manage to provide a reliable, valid, stable, crisp (proximal) image and judgment in the face of such biased, arbitrarily sampled, fuzzy (distal) inputs. It is a matter of fact that our image of a moving object, such as a walking child, maintains its visual crispness and robustness even though the transmission of the information to our visual cortex is done at a rather slow speed by our rods and cones, which do not provide the physical foundations for this perceptual result. In addition, the size estimation of an object is not based solely on the stimuli received. Brunswik (1943) assumed that the object under consideration provides a set of cues relating to various dimensions of the perceived world. He noted that "survival and its sub-units, which may be defined as the establishment of stable interrelationships with the environment, are possible only if the organism is able to establish compensatory balance in the face of comparative chaos within the physical environment" (p. 257).

For instance, the estimation of a person's height is not severely affected by changes in position—whether the person stands straight, runs, or lies on the floor—even though, physically, completely different information is sampled.

In an epochal lecture at the Symposium on Psychology and Scientific Methods in 1941, Brunswik revealed that human perception outperforms straight calculations based on the physical information available in the perceptual neurons. Obviously, the cognitive system is sampling different cues that are transformed, interpreted, and integrated. For instance, the context cues in size estimation are token items (e.g., a plate, or other known object, that is lying beside the person to be judged) that then become integrated into the assessment. Stimuli obviously lack "univocality." Thus, the initial focal variable produces stray causes or cues that induce stray effects or perceptions that are composed into a terminal focal variable, such as a judgment, attitude, or habit. According to the Brunswikian Lens Model (see Figure 4.2), operations within the lens framework are affected by two stray processes. One is due to the informational assemblage on the left side of the lens. There may be a multitude of stray causes, originating from either the suitability of the perspective on

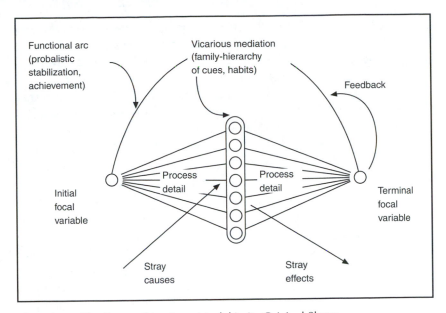

Figure 4.2. The Brunswikian Lens Model in Its Original Shape
SOURCE: Brunswik (1950)

the initial focal variable or the imperfectness of the media. For instance, the quality of light may be disturbed by additional colored light sources in the environment, or the transmission of light may be affected by humidity, pollution, or other factors. On the right side, stray effects are caused by the imprecision of the perceptors and the distortions in the internal information transmission process. The multitude of these stray processes is also the rationale for Brunswik's probabilistic approach.

The central principle of robust information processing, judgment, and decision making is called vicarious mediation, vicarious functioning, or mutual substitutability. As Brunswik (1956) notes,

Since there is no perceptual cue which would be available under all circumstances or is completely trustworthy . . ., the perceptual system of higher organisms must, for types of perceptual attainment, develop what the present writer has suggested calling "or-collective" or an "or-assemblage" of mutually interchangeable cues vicariously mediating distance or other situational circumstances to the organism. (p. 19)

The "or-assemblage" enables a robust image if at least some of the pre-ceptors are recording the information from the physical environment properly. Because Brunswik often referred to the probabilistic regression model, his theory is also called probabilistic functionalism.

Hammond, Steward, Brehmer, and Steinmann (1975) recognized that the Brunswikian Lens Model may also serve as a framework for social judgment theory. Here, the initial focal variable is a certain task or crite-rion, such as a social norm, and the terminal focal variable is a judgment. Brunswik himself had taken a more general perspective than traditional psychology and requested an in-depth analysis of the environment, which is considered the initial focal variable, in order to understand the informa-tional sampling. This analysis should be performed in at least the same depth as the analysis of the organism:

> Both organism and environment will have to be seen as systems. Each with properties of its own. . . . Each has surface and depth, or overt and covert regions. . . . It follows that, as much as psychology must be concerned with the texture of the organism or of its nervous properties and investigate them in depth, it must also be concerned with the texture of the environment. (Brunswik, 1950, p. 5)

Within the case study framework, Brunswik's admonition "to be con-cerned with the texture" of the environment may be interpreted as a request that in case analysis, as opposed to theoretical interpretation, efforts toward data gathering be increased. The closer and more multifac-eted the process of data gathering, the more sufficient the cues and the more robust the understanding and the result, which is the terminal focal variable, will be. From a more general point of view, the multifaceted pro-cess of data acquisition also may be conceived of as a kind of analytical decomposition (see Figure 4.3). Such a process is usually established if the study team defines certain perspectives on a case.

Data acquisition is followed by data interpretation, a transformational process relying on different types of methods to arrive at a perception, judgment, or evaluation. This transformation, resulting in new knowl-edge or an insight, is what is meant by synthesis (see Figure 4.3) or, to ex-press it in Brunswikian terms, "the terminal focal variable."

In order to avoid misunderstandings, we want to add two remarks. First, designing an embedded case study according to the Brunswikian

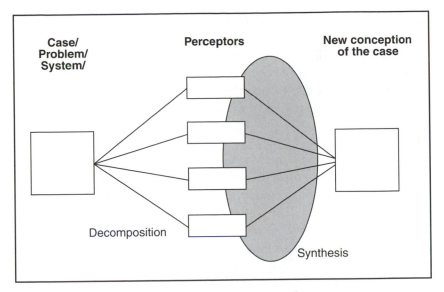

Figure 4.3. The Brunswikian Lens Model in Its Basic Shape

Lens Model does not imply optimizing cue redundancy, but rather employing the satisficing principle for cue acquisition (Simon, 1982).

> Satisficing provides an escape from the difficulty that, in a complex world, the alternatives of action are not given but must be sought out. Since the search generally takes place in a space that is essentially infinite, some stop rule must be imposed to terminate problem solving activity. The satisficing criterion provides that stop rule: search ends when a good-enough alternative is found. (Simon, 1982, p. 3)

Second, the Brunswikian Lens Model is by no means restricted to quantitative modeling (e.g., when using regression analysis). This has already been conceptualized in Tolman's cognitive maps (see Gigerenzer & Goldstein, 1996; Tolman, 1948), which substitute the stimulus-response metaphor with a sign-significate theory. Approaches to bounded rationality (Selten, 1983, 1990) also refer strongly to the saticficing principle.

TYPES OF KNOWLEDGE INTEGRATION

Like the Brunswikian principle of vicarious functioning, casework requires different types of knowledge integration. This is particularly true for cases not artificially reduced by textbook-like writing.

We distinguish between the following four types of knowledge integration.

 1. *Disciplines:* A good method should provide the structure and procedures for systematically linking, or even fusing together, knowledge from different fields and branches of science. The method should organize a natural and social science interface and even allow for relating quantitative and qualitative research issues. Thus, a good method should establish genuine interdisciplinarity. The icon integrates the labeling common in some scientific communities, where α denotes "letters" (i.e., arts, literature, languages, history, and philosophy/theology), which were, for a long time, the main part of university studies. β stands for natural sciences—life sciences, particularly biology and medicine, as well as physics, chemistry, and geography. And γ is social sciences, such as psychology, sociology, anthropology, and economics, together with applied variants such as business studies. When referring to Figure 4.1, this type of knowledge integration links the bottom level of subprojects, usually performed in different disciplines, and brings it up to the synthesis level.

 2. *Systems:* A case is often divided into different subsystems. A physician, for example, traditionally distinguishes muscle from skeleton, and heart from blood, as well as gastroenterologic, dermal, and central nervous systems from one another. In an environmental study, one may separately study a given region's water, air, or soil systems (see icon). When studying an enterprise from a business perspective, one can consider the management, the financial and balance sheet numbers, and the equipment as individual systems. For the case study approach, these systems (which are regarded as constructs in an analytic understanding of medicine) need to be integrated and related to the soft factors (i.e., the case history, biography, and given circumstances). Syntheses of subsystems can often be considered as partial syntheses that are then subject to further knowledge integration and synthesis.

3. *Interests:* When considering a case from a research or a practical perspective, one certain interest usually is dominant. A practical neuropsychologist, for example, should primarily help the patient. However, systematic reflection on the various perspectives held by different interested parties is usually part of his or her casework. In order to find a suitable form of therapy or a place for housing the patient, the neuropsychologist has to consider the case from the perspective of the family, while taking into account the constraints of the intended hospital. Furthermore, the economic, societal perspective of health care regulations and institutions usually reveals limits and introduces different strategies that, although very robust, may be suboptimal. The diversity of interests is most obvious in planning or environmental studies. When a new industrial site or a national park for wetland conservation is planned, for example, the interests of the landowners, farmers, residents, and natural protection agencies are potentially conflicting. The icon is a metaphorical reference to a round table. Each party usually has different values, preferences, and issues in mind. In order to attain an appropriate, acceptable solution, these plans and perspectives should be integrated. Thus, one variant of knowledge integration is the mediation of different interests. Initially, the interests are inherent to the case. However, the study team may extract or classify certain interest groups. Then, the recording and mediation of interest groups can become the subject of one or more different subprojects.

 4. *Modes of Thought:* When approaching a case from a cognitive or epistemological perspective, there are different modes or qualities of thought involved in case analysis or case understanding. A helpful distinction is given by the complementarity between intuitive and analytic modes of thought (see Hammond, 1990; Hussy, 1984; Poincaré, 1948; Scholz, 1987). Because intuitive thinking is often attributed to the right brain and analytic thinking to the left, we have chosen the brain hemispheres as an icon (see Springer & Deutsch, 1985). There is no need to go into details about the different modes of thought in human thinking (see Box 12.3, p. 194). We will just mention that these modes are characterized by the way in which the case is mentally or externally represented. Thus, a case description may be shaped by a numeric-digital, conceptual-verbal, pictorial-analog, or episodic representation (see Hussy, 1984; Scholz, 1987; Tulving,

1972). These different types of representation allow for different inferences or, to express it in technical language, different cognitive operations. In general, we consider these two modes of thought to be different states of activation of one and the same cognitive system. In the intuitive mode that normally exists, an individual operates using directly accessible knowledge, often of a pictorial or episodic nature, and simple everyday heuristics, whereas in an analytic mode, he or she draws on knowledge that is more highly ordered, mostly of a numeric or conceptual nature, and usually acquired through formal education.

Generally, it is not possible to decide which type of inference is superior. Often, holistic intuitive judgment based on brief visual information is superior. This is what a trained expert draws upon. Many physicians know immediately upon facing a patient whether he or she has a serious disease, even if the laboratory values are all normal (for a discussion, see Shanteau, 1988). Within the framework of the Brunswikian Lens Model, the types of modes may be conceived as different cues that have to be integrated.

Referring to Figure 4.1, the type of knowledge integration describes two different ways to approach the case. Usually, case members have valid intuitive knowledge at their disposal. They can be considered case experts on their perspective. In contrast, scientists are trained in the analytic approach to case understanding. As mentioned earlier, this distinction also refers to the holistic and embedded case study design.

LESSONS TO BE LEARNED

▶ There are different types of knowledge integration, such as the integration of disciplines, systems, interests, and modes of thought. Other complementary knowledge systems to be integrated can be introduced, such as between different cultures or language codes.

▶ In order to understand the origin and to assess the validity of data, information, and knowledge, a specific architecture of knowledge integration is necessary. The architecture consists of the levels of understanding, conceptualizing, and explaining, which are linked to the case, the system models for synthesis, and the knowledge assessed by (mostly disciplinary) oriented subprojects.

▶ Depending on the design of the study and on the type of case, different synthesis strategies can be chosen. We distinguish between a synthesis by contemplation for the holistic design (Zabarella), a synthesis through a pure case model (Leibniz), a hypothesis-driven synthesis (Kant), and the integration of different aspects or complementary theses (Hegel). The latter is appropriate for complex, real-world problems.

▶ The Brunswikian Lens Model is a prototypical conceptionalization of synthesis work. Synthesis work has its own optimization criteria, including sufficiency, redundancy, vicarious mediation, and the satisficing principle, that hold for both analytical decomposition and knowledge integration. The Brunswikian Lens Model shows how a satisfactory synthesis can be achieved.

THE ETH-UNS CASE STUDY
ZURICH NORTH

W e will introduce, as an example, a case from our professional background at the Department of Environmental Sciences, Swiss Federal Institute of Technology (ETH Zurich). It is noteworthy that this new
department was founded in 1987 in response to environmental disasters
that occurred in the 1980s, such as the nuclear power plant accident at
Chernobyl, the dioxin contamination at Seveso, and the chemical industry's accidental contamination of the Rhine River.

These events provided the insight that neither the traditional natural
sciences nor the social sciences, with their sectorial, segregated, and abstract approach, were prepared or able to master this type of complex
problem. Note that the traditional sciences are theory oriented and oper-
ate on a sign level, whereas case studies start with the object level, which is
the main reference in case studies (Otte, 1994). Beginning in 1993, the
concept of the ETH-UNS case study approach was subsequently developed (see Scholz, Bösch, Koller, Mieg, & Stünzi, 1996; Scholz, Bösch,
Mieg, & Stünzi, 1997, 1998; Scholz, Koller, Mieg, & Schmidlin, 1995).
The main objective has been to attain an encompassing understanding of
the genesis, dynamics, and impacts of the complex relationships between
natural systems and social or technical systems.[1]

Cases are provided by real, complex, societally relevant problems that
are shaped by environmental issues. Typical examples of ETH-UNS case

studies are urban or regional development projects; planning projects, such as power plants or waste disposal facilities; companies; and technical inventions and products, such as food, clothes, and airplanes. Your computer, most recent holiday trip, or family car could also serve as a case. What is most decisive for a case study is that a specific object (e.g., your car and not cars in general) is considered. As mentioned earlier, the case limits the discourse of the universe, which is tied to cars in general. The case study permits only the relevant and salient features in response to a certain perspective or question of an individual, chosen item to be taken into consideration.

THE ZURICH NORTH CASE

We will now present the case dealt with in the 1996 ETH-UNS case study. The planning of the Zurich North site (*ZZN*, or *Zentrum Zürich Nord*) was difficult because it was a very complex case. We recommend that you read through this section carefully because we refer to this case in many of the methods in Part III.

In 1996, when the Zurich North case study was performed (see Scholz, Bösch, Mieg, & Stünzi, 1997), it was Switzerland's largest urban development project. The area planned had a dimension of 640,000 m² (about 4 square miles) (see Figure 5.1). The site became the object of urban development because of fundamental changes in the industrial sector in the 1980s. Because many mechanical technologies have been replaced by electronic ones, and industrial production has been outsourced to developing countries, more than half the former area was no longer used by site owners for industrial production. For the project, new buildings have been designed that would provide housing for 5,000 people and 12,000 working places.

This case was chosen for a number of reasons. First, the students and some professors of environmental sciences were interested in finding a complex, relevant, groundbreaking case that would allow for the advancement of a theory on sustainable development. Second, the case was judged in advance to be appropriate because of the presence of various salient environmental issues that are usually inherent in former industrial sites: how to maintain old buildings, what to do about the contaminated land, and so on. Many members of the study team were also interested in the site itself and its contribution to the sustainable urban development of

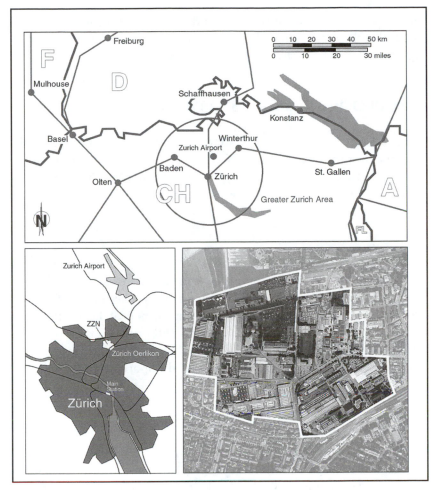

Figure 5.1. Maps and Overhead Photo of the Zurich North Site
NOTE: The Zurich North site is part of Zurich Oerlikon and lies between downtown Zurich and Zurich Airport.

Zurich and Switzerland. Third, the nine landowners and the city authorities who founded a planning cooperation were interested in the case study because they wanted to gain deeper insight into the deficiencies of their developmental project from an objective point of view. Common shared interests were understanding sustainable development and integrally assessing environmental issues and other topics from a holistic perspective.

Thus, the case agents and the case study team were intrinsically motivated. The vision of sustainable development may be regarded as the guiding light of the whole case study.

CASE PROSPECTS AND HISTORY

In any case study, we recommend that you begin with a solid anamnesis. The case history of the Zurich North site was derived from multiple sources, including archival records; planning documents; and open-ended interviews with current and former residents, owners, and planners (see Box 2.1).

Prospects

The document studies encompassed the analysis of papers and plans from the almost 10-year planning process, which began in 1988. The principal agents in the planning were the nine owners of the territory, city and county (i.e., from the Canton Zurich) authorities, several planning bureaus, and the architects (Roth, 1996) who worked together in a planning cooperative. This cooperative provided important documents and mission statements.

Targets

The vision of the owners (ABB, or Asea Brown and Boveri Company), who aspired to create a profitable eco-city, essentially formed the mission statement. This vision resulted from the electric company's experiences: "Eco-efficiency combines ecology and economy and translates the vision of sustainable development into a process of continually improving environmental performance and business performance" (ABB, 1996, p. 5). One can see from the plan (see Figure 5.3) that a temporarily shaped arrangement of buildings was designed that was typical of the early 1990s.

The architects formulated a far-reaching vision of urban design. The Zurich North site should become a new, vibrant, accessible, public downtown quarter with a mixture of uses that is free of car traffic and characterized by intense greenery, parks, and avenues (Roth, 1996, p. 24; Ruoss et al., 1994). As indicated by the label *Zentrum* (center), the architects also hoped to attain the function of a center.

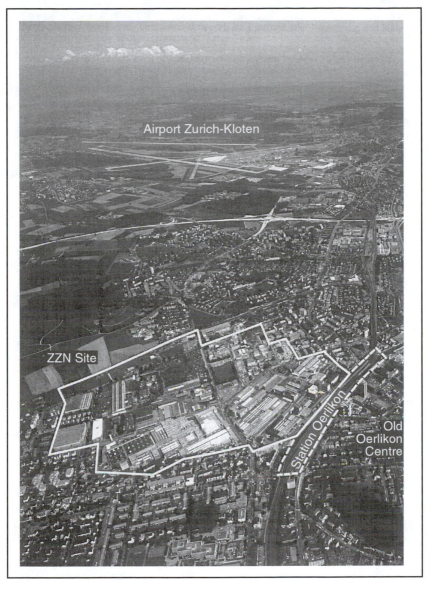

Figure 5.2. Aerial View of the Zurich North Site

NOTE: The Zurich North site was formerly a marshland. It is located next to the Zurich Oerlikon train station just between the center of Zurich and the industrial centers of Winterthur and Schaffhausen. The boundary of the case must be crisply defined.

History

According to the principle that cases are understood through the study of their system changes, the case study team is obliged to investigate the history of the case first. They must understand the limits, potential, and character of cities, suburbs, landscapes, and rivers by tracing the course of change and stability up to the present state.

The Zurich North site is part of Oerlikon ("kon" is a former suffix for small villages). Oerlikon was located on a plain, closely behind a wide saddle in a moraine chain east of Zurich and the Zurich Lake (see Figure 5.2). Hence, the site had and has some strategic and logistic potential.

Before 1800, the Zurich North site was a marshland surrounded by small, wooded green areas and fields. The logistic potential of the site became important through the railway battle, which, in Switzerland, began 25 years later than in other European countries. The Zurich North site was located just at the junction where Zurich meets the metal and machinery industrial centers of Winterthur and Schaffhausen. Zurich (including a couple of factories around Zurich Lake) not only was an industrial center with cotton and silk industries, but it also advanced early as a merchandising and financial center.

It is interesting that in 1855, the railroad tracks from the northern industrial centers ended in Oerlikon. The difficult connection through the moraine saddle to Zurich was finished almost 5 years later. The railway routes offered new potential. In 1863, the first iron and hammer smithy was founded, and it developed rapidly into a huge machinery factory. By 1891, 1,000 workers were employed at the Machinery Factory Oerlikon (MFO).

The former marshland lying in a plain was being used for various purposes. In the beginning, peat was cut for gas production. Later, up to six meters of pits and peat holes were filled with the waste products of industry: foundry sands, slags, oils and grease, metals, and isolation materials. Trucks were continuously bringing waste products from different branches of industry. This is why, today, there is an extraordinarily heterogeneous composition of contaminants that is many layers deep. After World War I, new factories were built on the waste disposal ground, including a battry factory.

Around 1910, the MFO split into two branches. One branch supplied the machine tool industry but specialized in high-quality weapons, and

Figure 5.3. Model of the Project

NOTE: The light blocks represent new buildings. The Zurich Oerlikon train station is just in front of the area. Most of the trains operating between Zurich Central Station and the airport stop there.

the other branch specialized in electric trains. This second branch was bought by the ABB (formerly BBC) company in 1967. Consequently, old buildings were destroyed and replaced by new offices and production halls. As may be seen by a comparison of Figures 5.2 and 5.3, some of these buildings will, presumably, be destroyed 30 years later.

The small village of Oerlikon grew rapidly. In 1950, 15,000 residents were already living in the small industrial town, which had joined Zurich in 1934. A shopping center with a marketplace developed just east of the train station. Currently, about 450 trains stop daily at the station. Housing cooperatives and apartment houses for workers, many of whom came from foreign countries, were built around the site. Oerlikon is a typical Swiss suburb with low-cost housing. In spite of this, however, there is an arena that hosts indoor sport events.

When analyzing a complex case, it is usually helpful to understand the case history. Pictures often reveal, in a holistic way (see Figure 5.4), values, aspirations, and factors that have an environmental impact.

UNDERSTANDING THE CASE

One of the arts of conducting a case study is understanding the system development, particularly ascertaining the right balance between change and stability. This one task of the study team is to attain a good and sensitive understanding, including which changes can be introduced at which time, and whether the system will be disturbed, fragmented, or even completely destroyed. For example, if the planning of the Zurich North site should not result in an isolated project, then it has to be linked to the old Oerlikon center and its neighboring residential areas. Therefore, documents and interviews are an indispensable step toward understanding a case, but they are by no means a substitute for direct and participant observation.

A direct case encounter immediately revealed some limits to the project's development. First, the long distance and the old, tiny footpath tunnels below the four railway tracks form a severe barrier. Therefore, the integration of the Zurich North site with the old center of Oerlikon seems to be exceptionally difficult.

Second, when planning new apartments, considering the type of neighborhood in which they will be located is essential. Oerlikon is a typical labor district. Most pubs and stores are oriented toward the labor class. Thus, it would be difficult to successfully promote expensive dwellings here. The noisiness of the airport is another drawback.

Experiential Case Encounters

In order to attain an insider's view of the site, experiential encounters should be organized. In the ETH-UNS case studies, every participant had to change sides for one day. This means that all participants of the study team became members of the case (see Box 5.1). Some years ago, at the beginning of the ETH-UNS case studies, the students and academics viewed these encounters with severe skepticism, but they are now accepted and considered worthwhile. Clearly, they broaden the view of a case, its qualities, deficiencies, potential, dynamics, and limits.

Figure 5.4. Pictures About the Zurich North Case History

NOTE: The upper engraving shows the location of the Machine Factory Oerlikon (ca. 1900). The somewhat lower area and two tiny ponds, which were later filled with industrial waste, can be seen. In those days, most of the farmers were so-called backpack peasants. They lived in the country and worked on their farms in the evening and on the weekends. The rapid change to an industrial area can be seen easily by comparing this engraving with Figure 5.3. Only the building in the front left, closest to the tracks, is maintained. In 1950, the traffic behavior of the workers had not yet fundamentally changed (lower left). The workers commuted from the new residential areas around the site (see Figure 5.2). Increased motor traffic in the 1950s (lower right) created new demands, altered lifestyles, and affected the case in new ways.

Box 5.1   Experiential Case Encounter

Experiential Case Encounter is an essential method of supporting knowledge integration in case studies. In order to supplement the academic, analytical perspective of case analysis, each member of the study team should experience such an encounter.

The best strategy is simply to arrange an entire change of sides. The study team has to live or work on the site or with the case for at least 1 day.

In order to gain real, direct experience in regional studies, one could simply look for a normal job on the case site and work for 1 day. In urban areas, one might work as a gardener in a park, a street sweeper, or a canal cleaner; in rural areas, one may work in the fields or in river construction.

Direct experience with the social systems may be attained easily by helping out in restaurants, pubs, schools, or homes for the elderly.

One might get a close look and acquire lots of information about the dynamics, potential, and limits of a company by working as a porter or receptionist or doing the mail delivery for a day.

For the Experiential Case Encounter to be successful, it is essential that the change of sides be complete, voluntary, and clandestine. There is usually no problem convincing case members of the necessity for direct experience as part of their case study work. Of course, the case study analyst may not be able to prevent case members from finding out about his or her identity and intentions. The case analyst has to make clear, however, that he or she will not behave as a spectator, and that the experience makes sense only if he or she behaves like a regular member of the case. Consequently, the case analyst should not ask for any special treatment during that day.

During the Experiential Case Encounter, the case analyst should concentrate only on his or her work and role. No formative data recording is allowed, because this will certainly interfere with a good performance as a case agent.

Note that similar experience gained previously (as a farmer, worker, etc.) may not replace but may support the Experiential Case Encounter. It is crucial to experience the case and gather unexpected situational information about the site and its dynamics from a holistic perspective, one that employs the whole sensory system and includes one's personal experience.

FACETING THE CASE FOR EMBEDDED CASE DESIGN

Complex cases like the sustainable development of the Zurich North site require an embedded case design. For the Zurich North case, the guiding questions concerned the conditions to be fulfilled in order to support sustainable development.

When looking for an embedded design, the following three-step procedure was applied.

First, after gathering some basic knowledge about the case, the study team constructed a preliminary list of the crucial aspects of the case and its development. Then, the principal players were identified, that is, the case experts and major agents of the case. Case experts are individuals or representatives of institutions who have in-depth knowledge about the case. A case agent has a direct relation to the case, such as a resident, an owner, or a stakeholder. Usually, these agents can be identified through a telephone chain, a method wherein the people contacted provide names of other people to contact. During the call, simply ask the person if he or she knows of someone who might be an expert on the case from the perspective of investigation. The conversation should also cover deficiencies and issues critical to future development. As each call leads to the next, the result is the unveiling of the first social network of people significantly related to the case. The interviews conducted for the Zurich North case were recorded carefully and provided valuable data.

Second, a questionnaire was sent to all known supposed experts. The questionnaire contained the simple question: "How do you judge the importance of the following aspects/issues for the development and/or quality of the Zurich North site?" The people asked simply had to rate the aspects/issues on a seven-point scale, and they were asked to add aspects that had not yet been included.

Third, the study team decided according to which facets the embedded design should be organized. This decision was a result of the study team's interests and values, the responses from the questionnaire, and the resources available. The larger a study team is, the more facets may be considered. Figure 5.5 presents the six facets relevant for sustainable development that were chosen for the Zurich North study.

Mobility and Transportation	Urban Development	Building and Construction
Parks and Green Areas	Soil Contamination	Water Management

Figure 5.5. The Six Facets (Synthesis Groups) of the Zurich North Site

CONSTRAINTS OF THE STUDY

The ETH-UNS case study approach has some specific constraints that should not confuse you. Note that the approach of knowledge integration presented in this volume is recommended for small teams of 4 to 12 people.

The ETH-UNS case study approach is part of the eighth semester of the 5-year master's program in environmental sciences (see Table 5.1). The study is a hybrid in that it combines training, research, and application.

- *Training.* One hundred twenty-six environmental science students and 29 members of the science staff composed the study team. The educational target was that students learn to define and overcome ill-defined problems shaped by environmental issues through knowledge integration. Defining and solving problems should be arranged within a process of mutual learning between science and society. This means that the case study team and the case agents have to initiate a process of cooperative learning. The case study should contribute to the development of an encompassing environmental problem-solving ability (Scholz, Flückiger et al., 1997; P. Frischknecht, 1998).

- *Research.* The elaboration of the methods presented in this book is part of the study. Concepts of case study research are being developed.

- *Applied problem solving.* The case study should support the problem-solving process and foster local, sustainable development at the Zurich North site.

Table 5.1 Constraints and Number of Participants in the ETH-UNS Case Study Approach

Constraints	Number of Participants
Obligatory course for all students in the 8th semester, duration 14 weeks, 18 hours per week	
Participants in the process of mutual learning	
Students of environmental sciences specializing in different fields (i.e., environmental hygiene, soil management, etc.)	126
Tutors (i.e., professors, assistants, and scientists from outside the university who are hired on a daily basis under a part-time contract)	26-29
Case Study Bureau (2½ positions with job sharing)	3
ETH Institutes (partially participating)	8-15
Others (ministries, owners, representatives, agents, etc.)	100-150
Total	250-300

ORGANIZING THE STUDY

The study course has three phases (see Figure 5.6). The first phase is organized by a commission and starts with the election of a suitable case. In the ETH-UNS case study approach, possible candidates from outside the university and the members of the department are invited to suggest potential cases for a groundbreaking case study. Then, a careful examination procedure is planned for checking a potential case as part of a feasibility study.

The first phase also entails faceting the case, which involves selecting both the case (defined as a physical system) and the organizational subunits of the study. The latter is important because the subunits (synthesis groups) of the study, presented in Figure 5.6, also serve in the course of vicarious mediation and knowledge integration.

The ETH-UNS case study was a cooperative endeavor, not only between the university and industry, but also between students, landowners, scientists, and the public (Mieg, 1996). In the 1996 ETH-UNS case study, the external partners were the "problem owner" (e.g. the landowners, represented by ABB); municipal authorities (the City of Zurich); professional organizations (particularly the Swiss Contractors' Association); and investors (banks). Within the ETH, cooperation was established with

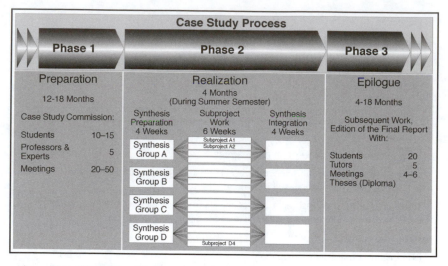

Figure 5.6. The Three Phases of an ETH-UNS Case Study
NOTE: The course may be modified easily for small study teams.

scientists from other departments (e.g., civil engineering and architecture).

Three main bodies of coordination and cooperation existed for the Zurich North case: The ETH-UNS Case Study Commission prepared and headed the case study (see Figure 5.7). The commission consisted of 10 to 15 students, as well as experts and the members of the Case Study Bureau. The Case Study Bureau (three permanent members, including one of the authors, holding 2½ job positions) provided professional project management. The steering board (one session monthly) consisted of representatives of the project partners involved. It discussed project strategies and commented on the actual work done during the case study.

The second phase is the realization. For 4 months, the whole study team worked on the case. The facets of the case (see Figure 5.5) determined the topics of the synthesis groups. The synthesis groups were organized according to the small group team model of instruction (see Scholz, 1979). Four to five tutors supervised a group of 15 to 20 students.

Phase 2 had three parts. First, the group had to understand the case, find the relevant issues, and find a project target. This was done in close cooperation with the stakeholders of the case. Thus, a process of mutual

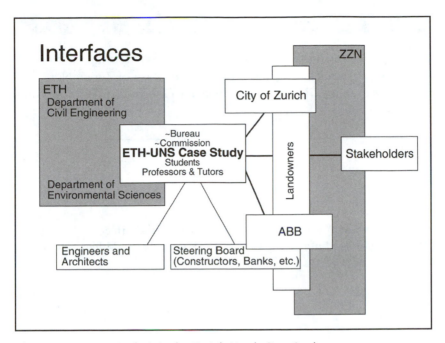

Figure 5.7. Agent Analysis in the Zurich North Case Study
NOTE: See Mieg (1996).

learning was initiated. Furthermore, the steering board provided a kind of external quality control. In addition to the target and the project plan, the methods of knowledge integration to be applied have to be selected.

Second, the subprojects had to organize the scientific knowledge and the data necessary for a sound scientific synthesis.

Third, in the final 4 weeks, the synthesis was performed and all data were composed. Furthermore, a first draft of the case report was written. The core of the third part of Phase 2 is the synthesis process organized with the methods of knowledge integration.

In Phase 3, the reports of the synthesis groups are elaborated further and completed. There is an extended review process, including in-depth feedback from scientists and from the case. The study finishes with an official event. All members of the case and the study team are invited for the presentation of the final results. Finally, the case report is submitted to the public.

LESSON TO BE LEARNED

▶ The design and theory of ETH-UNS case studies may be applied for real, complex, societally relevant problems. The case of Zurich North is a typical example. The proceeding with the case can be used as a model for other cases.

NOTE

1. The case study was developed with reference to the former use of case studies in geography (Buff-Keller, Gilgen, & Pfister, 1989; Müller- Herold & Neuenschwander, 1992).

Part

METHODS OF KNOWLEDGE INTEGRATION

6

OVERVIEW

In Part III, we will present 11 methods of knowledge integration, all of which have proven to be valuable in the synthesis process of the ETH-UNS case study approach for regional development and urban planning. The methods presented have been adopted from different branches of science or specially developed for the ETH-UNS case studies.

Most of the methods are general in that they allow for application in presumably any case study, as well as for particular companies, products, patients, legal cases, curricula, or inventions. Some methods are particularly suited for planning and decision making, but usually, they also help in the course of general case description, analysis, evaluation, or case-related decision making.

From Case Representation and
Case Evaluation to Case Transition

The methods may be classified into the following four categories:

- Case representation and modeling
- Case evaluation
- Case development and transition
- Case study teams

Some of the methods are more or less specific to the environmental sciences. For these methods, we will discuss analogue methods for business and the medical sciences using examples.

The Lens Concept of Knowledge Integration

With the presentation of each method, we will systematically refer to the Brunswikian Lens Model (see Figure 4.3). Each method contains both an analytic decomposition leading to cue representation in certain perceptors and a process of knowledge integration in the form of one or more of the methods. This latter part often involves both formal analytic and subjective intuitive processes. Finally, we end up with new knowledge, evaluations, insights, and epistemics on the case.

Types of Knowledge to Be Integrated

We will distinguish between four types of knowledge integration (see Chapter 4 or Box 7.1). According to the metaphor of the Brunswikian Lens Model, the information sampled in the different perceptors comes from different disciplines, environmental systems, interests, and modes of thought. Box 7.1 shows the primary focus of knowledge integration of the methods presented.

THE METHODS IN BRIEF

W e will present brief descriptions and key questions that are posed when applying a certain method (see Table 8.1).

Formative Scenario Analysis

Formative Scenario Analysis provides hypothetical future states of a system/case that are called scenarios, and they help to gain insight into a system and its dynamics. The scenarios are based on a sufficient set of system variables (impact factors). These variables are related to different disciplines and subsystems. Scenarios are judged according to possibility and consistency.

System Dynamics

System Dynamics refers to a family of mathematical models that provides insight into the dynamics of a system. The interactions of the system variables can be modeled by interactive computer programs, which are becoming progressively more user-friendly. The goal of the synthesis is not to create a system model in the Leibnizian sense (see Chapter 4) that "perfectly and sufficiently" models reality. Rather, the process of constructing a System Dynamics model implies a vicarious functioning, and the resulting model should be considered but one component of a more encompassing synthesis (i.e., the case analysis). System Dynamics modeling may follow a Formative Scenario Analysis.

Multi-Attribute Utility Theory

Multi-Attribute Utility Theory (MAUT) represents a family of methods that describes and models integral evaluations based on different attributes. The criteria may represent different interests, subsystems of the case, or disciplinary perspectives.

Integrated Risk Management

If there are different alternatives available or expected, the question is often which alternative poses the least risk or best meets one's own evaluations. Integrated Risk Management provides a framework for supporting decisions about case-specific actions.

Mediation: Area Development Negotiations

Area Development Negotiations are a unique mediation technique that has been specially developed for the ETH-UNS case studies. The method provides a nested Lens Model. First, the different interest groups are determined. Then, their interests are identified via a multicriteria utility evaluation procedure. The canon of data sampling techniques is supplemented by the *Exploration Parcours technique*, which provides a close-to-reality encounter between case agents and their environment.

Future Workshops

Future Workshops are a special family of creativity tools. When seeking new perspectives or solutions, the lens should be widened to reveal unconventional solutions. This technique elicits the analytic and intuitive knowledge available in the case agents.

Experiential Case Encounter

Experiential Case Encounter is a strategy used to attain an insider's view of the case by a change of sides. Case analysts act as case members. The technique was described briefly in Box 5.1.

Synthesis Moderation

Synthesis Moderation encompasses a set of techniques for group management, idea generation, case analysis, and project management. On the one hand, this method supports the study team's organization and communication and provides rules for creating a productive atmosphere. On the other hand, Synthesis Moderation supports the case study team in selecting and combining the different methods in embedded case studies.

Material Flux Analysis

The Material Flux Analysis handles the recording, description, and interpretation of critical fluxes of a system. Although, for the most part, we refer to material and energy fluxes within environmental systems, the methodology introduced can be transferred easily to other systems.

Life Cycle Assessment

Often, the state of a case is judged with respect to its impacts on other systems. This is one of the core intentions of a Life Cycle Assessment (LCA). The impacts of certain elements of the case, such as a building on the Zurich North site, are assessed throughout the element's whole life cycle (i.e., from resource extraction through waste treatment). Although this method has been specially developed for the natural sciences, the same principles could easily be true for other types of cases. It should be noted that within the LCA framework, an impact assessment stresses abiotic impacts on the global level.

Bio-Ecological Potential Analysis

Bio-Ecological Potential Analysis (BEPA) is complementary to LCA. BEPA uses an evaluation process that focuses the biotic quality of a site within its regional frame. It is a semiquantitative diagnostic method assessing the bio-ecological value of an area or landscape.

See Box 7.1 for a summary of the types of knowledge integration in these case study methods.

Specific Methods for Medical Cases

In the medical sciences, the patient is often considered to be a case. If a major intervention, such as brain surgery, organ transplantation, or plastic surgery, is planned, the outcomes can be assessed with respect to different domains (see below). We will not and cannot present a systematic overview of these methods in this book, but we want to present some

| **Box 7.1** | Types of Knowledge Integration in Case Study Methods |

Distinctions are made between four different types of knowledge integration. The methods of knowledge integration presented in this book differ with respect to their potential and appropriateness for integrating various types of knowledge. (Two crosses indicate the main type of knowledge integration.)

Case Study Methods Combine These Types of Knowledge Integration:

 Different *disciplines* of natural and social sciences. These methods are interdisciplinary.

Different *modes of thought.* These methods integrate different cognitive representations, such as the experience of a farmer and the expertise of a scientist.

Different *systems* such as water, soil, air, anthroposphere. These methods are holistic.

Different *interests* of stakeholders. These methods are socially integrating and mediating.

| Case Study Methods | The Four Types of Knowledge Integration | | | | Synthesis groups (1–6) from the ETH-UNS Case Study *Zurich North* that used this method |
	Disciplines	Systems	Modes of Thought	Interests	
Formative Scenario Analysis	XX	X	X		(1) Urban Development, (2) Traffic, (4) Contaminated Sites, (5) Water
System Dynamics	XX	X			(5) Water
Multi-Attribute Utility Theory	X	X		X	(2) Traffic, (3) Green Areas, (4) Contaminated Sites, (5) Water, (6) Buildings
Integrated Risk Management	X	X			(4) Contaminated Sites
Mediation: Area Development Negotiations		X	X	XX	(3) Green Areas
Future Workshops			XX	X	Not applied in the Case Study *Zurich North.*
Experiential Case Encounter			XX	X	All groups
Synthesis Moderation			X	X	All groups
Material Flux Analysis	X	XX			(6) Buildings
Life Cycle Assessment	X	XX			(1) Urban Development, (6) Buildings
Bio-Ecological Potential Analysis		XX	X		Not applied in the case study *Zurich North.*

examples in order to illustrate which methods can take the place of the Material Flux Analysis, the Life Cycle Assessment, or the Bio-Ecological Potential Analysis.

One common and well-accepted domain is the physical status and functional abilities of a patient. Different standard methods for assessment are available depending on the type of disease and intervention. These methods resemble the Material Flux Analysis and Life Cycle Assessment in that they look at physical performance.

If the patient has a severe metabolic disease, such as endogene diabetes, and has to take heavy pharmaceuticals, the state of the patient can be assessed by laboratory tests measuring blood sugar level and weight.

After a cardiovascular operation, such as a cardiac transplant, a valvular surgery, or angioplasty (see Raczynski & Oberman, 1990, p. 295), the physical performance of the patient can be assessed by ergometric tests. These tests assess physical abilities, such as walking endurance, and they also measure heart rate, blood pressure, and pulse.

Likewise, neuropsychologists have specific methods at their disposal for assessing the neurological functioning of the brain, spinal cord, or peripheral nervous system.

The morphological and physical status of a human, however, is a limited concept. Physical status and functional abilities belong to one domain, but they must be supplemented by assessments of the psychological status and well-being, social interactivity, economic status, and performance of the patient. We recommend the introductory book of Spilker (1990), which presents diverse quality-of-life assessment methods. In some respects, these methods correspond to the Bio-Ecological Potential Assessment.

Specific Methods for Business Cases

In business, Balance Sheet Analysis, with its accounting, finance, and production arithmetic (see Ronstadt, 1993), takes the place of Material Flux Analysis. Formative assessments rating management performance or organizational efficiency, such as those performed by banks to assess a credit rating, can take the role of the Bio-Ecological Potential Analysis.

8

HOW TO CHOOSE
THE RIGHT METHOD

One question is critical in case analysis: Which is the right method for attaining the goals of a case study? To find an answer, Table 8.1 is helpful because it contains key questions that may indicate the appropriateness of a specific method.

The first four methods listed in Table 8.1 (Formative Scenario Analysis, System Dynamics, Multi-Attribute Utility Theory, and Integrated Risk Management) are general methods that can be applied to most cases. System Dynamics requires a certain standard of data quality and often follows parts of a Formative Scenario Analysis.

Representing the Overall State
and Dynamics of the Case

Formative Scenario Analysis and System Dynamics are tools for describing the current state and dynamics of a case. These methods facilitate encompassing case representation and case modeling but do not include any type of case evaluations. The same holds true for Material Flux Analysis, a specific method from the environmental sciences that investigates the case metabolism by displaying the stocks and flows of the system.

71

Table 8.1   Key Questions for Methods of Knowledge Integration in
Embedded Case Studies

Chapter	Method	Key Questions
	Case Representation and Modeling Methods	
9	Formative Scenario Analysis	What are the variables crucial to the state of a system and its change? What can be? What ought to be? What can happen?
10	System Dynamics	Which variables are the most decisive in temporal dynamics? Which (counterintuitive) outcomes result from the dynamic interactions of the variables?
17	Material Flux Analysis[a]	What are critical fluxes in materials for the case? What are the sources and sinks of the system/case?
	Case Evaluation Methods	
11	Multi-Attribute Utility Theory	How can different evaluation criteria be integrated? Which misperceptions are inherent in an integral evaluation?
12	Integrated Risk Management	In a set of different alternatives, which are the least risky ones? Which alternative is the best according to my evaluation? How can/shall I cope with uncertainty?
18	Life Cycle Assessment[a]	How can the main environmental impacts (on a global level) be evaluated?
19	Bio-Ecological Potential Analysis[a]	How can the bio-ecological quality of a case site be evaluated?
	Case Development and Transition Methods	
13	Mediation: Area Development Negotiations	What causes the conflicts between the principal agents/key players of the case? What misperceptions do the case agents have? How can we attain Pareto-optimal solutions?
14	Future Workshops	Which ideas may guide the questions of What can be? and What ought to be?
	Case Study Team Methods	
15	Experiential Case Encounter	What does the case look like from the case member's perspective?
16	Synthesis Moderation	How can I optimize teamwork to improve the synthesis process? How can I find the right method of synthesis?

a. These methods are specific environmental science methods.

Case Evaluations

Case evaluations can be supported by Multi-Attribute Utility Theory and Integrated Risk Management. Both techniques are general and require both conceptual/qualitative and numerical/quantitative approaches. Life Cycle Assessment and Bio-Ecological Potential Analysis are specific methods for environmental evaluation, which may be generalized in part to other fields.

Developing Cases

Two methods support case development and transitions—Area Development Negotiations and Future Workshops.

Area Development Negotiations are a special type of mediation technique originally created for studies in urban planning. However, this technique can be modified easily to fit any case study in which different interest groups have to work together in a process of evaluating and negotiating certain future options. Area Development Negotiations promote transitions in cases by integrating the different interests.

Future Workshops should be arranged whenever study teams need access to new ideas for the qualitative transformation of the case. Usually, case agents' values and visions are involved in Future Workshops.

Supporting Team and Synthesis Work

Case Study Team Methods refer to means by which a study team can gain access to a case or ways in which the case can support and enhance teamwork. We will introduce Synthesis Moderation methods that specifically combine general group moderation techniques with knowledge integration techniques for case modeling, evaluation, and transition.

Specific Environmental Case Assessments

Finally, three environmental science methods (Material Flux Analysis, Life Cycle Assessment, and Bio-Ecological Potential Analysis) are introduced. These methods assist the study team in penetrating the case structure by revealing certain constituents and qualities. Note that similar methods exist in other branches of science.

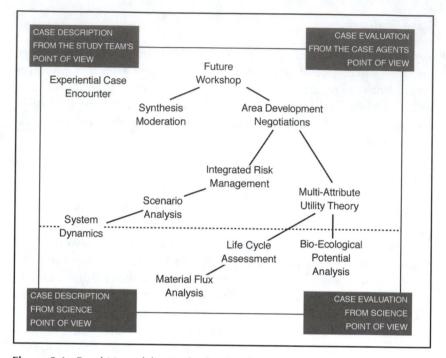

Figure 8.1. Road Map of the Methods of Embedded Case Studies

NOTE: Specific environmental science methods are situated below the dotted line. For further explanations, see text.

We finish the overview on the methods for embedded case studies by presenting a road map. Figure 8.1 has both a dimensional and a hierarchical structure: it is suggested as a heuristic to illustrate the neighborhood and the relationship between the different methods. The vertical axis provides an ordering according to the scientific foundation of the data and of their interrelations (below) versus individual, experience-based case description and evaluation (above). Material Flux Analysis requires quantitative data measured according to physical scales. On the other hand, Future Workshops rely mostly on qualitative judgments of the case members.

Horizontally, descriptive perspectives are on the left, and evaluative approaches are on the right. System Dynamics is placed on the left primarily because it targets case description. Experiential Case Encounter is also posed on the left side because it supports the study team's aptitude for case description and understanding. Multi-Attribute Utility Theory is on the right side because it is an evaluation method. Bio-Ecological Potential Analysis and Life Cycle Assessment should be put almost at the same place; however, Life Cycle Assessment usually entails an elaborate description of the material fluxes. The specific environmental science methods are situated below the dotted line. These methods are to be replaced by other methods depending on the nature of the case.

Area Development Negotiations are a pivotal element in the hierarchical structure because they entail Multi-Attribute Utility Theory as a component and the thinking in alternatives as required for the Integrated Risk Management. Bio-Ecological Potential Analysis and Life Cycle Assessment are special variants of Multi-Attribute Utility Theory. The subsequent descriptions of the methods entail more detailed explications of the other relationships of Figure 8.1.

LESSONS TO BE LEARNED

▶ The methods of knowledge integration in embedded case studies can be classified into four categories. We distinguish case representation/description methods, case evaluation methods, and case transition methods. The fourth category consists of case study team methods.

▶ The methods organize knowledge integration according to one or more of the subsequent dimensions: disciplines, systems, modes of thought, and interests. Further dimensions, such as the north-south dialogue, could be supplemented.

Part III

THE METHODS IN DETAIL

FORMATIVE
SCENARIO ANALYSIS

THE RATIONALE

Formative Scenario Analysis is a scientific technique to construct well-defined sets of assumptions to gain insight into a case and its potential development. Scenarios can be constructed for any kind of case. The term *scenario* originates from the Greek word σκενε, which was used to refer to an outline of a play or a stage script. Formative Scenario Analysis provides a script describing steps that a study team must take in response to the current state and possible future states of a case. Because the term *scenario analysis* is often overused and applied inaccurately in science and everyday language, the adjective *formative* is added to indicate that we are presenting a technique that is organized in a strictly systematic way.

The scenario technique was developed by Herman Kahn soon after World War II. At that time, Kahn was working for the RAND Corporation. RAND (an acronym for Research and Development) was one of 11,000 independent think tanks that advised the U.S. government in strategic planning (see Cooke, 1991). The scenario technique has been widely used in business, technology assessment, and environmental sciences (Batelle-Institute, 1976; Brauers & Weber, 1988; MacNulty, 1977; Minx and Mattrisch, 1996). However, it can be transferred easily to other fields.

Scenarios can answer two kinds of questions: "How might some hypothetical situation come about (step-by-step)?" and "What alternatives exist at each step to prevent, divert, or facilitate the process [of case development]?" (Kahn & Wiener, 1967, p. 6). Scenarios are constructed for the purpose of focusing attention on causal processes and decisive points.

A scenario describes a hypothetical future state of a system and provides information on its development up to this state. This is done by introducing so-called impact factors. An impact factor is simply a system variable that describes the current state and dynamics of the case. Impact factors are also called *impact variables*. The art of scenario analysis consists of creating a sufficient set of impact variables and linking the variables in such a way as to gain a valid case description.

A scenario may contain qualitative and/or quantitative statements. Techniques for judging the probability of scenarios have been developed (see Helmer, 1977), as we will see. Nevertheless, the focus in scenario analysis is clearly on *possibility*. It is noteworthy that Kahn, who understood the basis of decision making and probability theory quite well, considered both approaches inadequate because complex case analysis is usually performed in groups, and the result relies on the opinions, assumptions, hypotheses, and suppositions of the groups' collective reasoning (Mieg, 2000, p. 75). However, concepts such as subjective probability and subjective utility were constructed for an individual, and the classical theory of probability and utility does not offer any procedures for assessing joint group probability or utility function (Cooke, 1991, p. 10). Simple averaging of event probabilities is not allowed, as the example of conditional probability shows (Scholz, 1987, p. 29). Although these arguments may be disputed, probability statements do not play a significant role in the scenario-analytic approach. In general, scenario analysis provides consistent hypothetical future states of a case and should not be mixed with traditional methods of prognosis, such as time series. A specific method for analyzing continuous case dynamics will be presented in Chapter 10 on System Dynamics.

The starting point for a scenario analysis is the case in its existing state. The state of the case varies depending on the changes in and development of its internal and external system variables. The more time that has passed, the greater the change and deviation from the case's initial state. This is displayed in the scenario trumpet (Figure 9.1). Disturbances or interventions can affect the discourse and future state of a case.

The Formative Scenario Analysis procedure guides the study team toward a differentiated and structured understanding of a case's current state and its dynamics. It is usually performed by small groups with

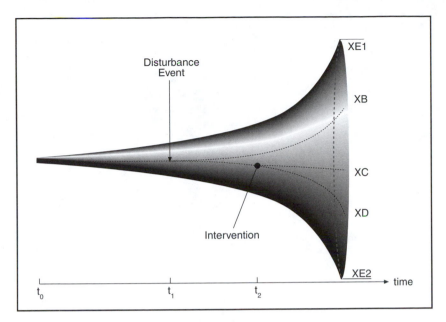

Figure 9.1. The Scenario Trumpet Metaphor

NOTE: The starting point of scenario analysis is t_0. All possible future states of the case are represented in the trumpet. The upper and lower margins represent the most optimistic and pessimistic states, respectively. Deviations from surprise-free development (i.e., the trumpet's midline) may be caused by disturbance events at t_1 or interventions at t_2. XB, XC, and XD represent different scenarios. XE1 and XE2 are also scenarios, but extreme ones.

specialized expertise about different aspects of the case, which they share with one another.

According to the concept of the Brunswikian Lens Model (see Figures 4.2 and 9.2), the procedure requires that the study team specifies the case clearly, identifies its problems, and poses relevant questions. In Brunswikian terminology, the case and its problems are called the *initial focal variable*, whereas the study team's construction of future states is labeled the *terminal focal variable*. It is crucial that the whole study team knows what the focal variables are and remains aware of them throughout the study. This holds particularly true for the terminal focal variable because a common fixed future date is required in all constructions.

In the analytic decomposition, the study team is required to construct a sufficient set of impact factors or impact variables (see Box 9.1). Impact variables are used to construct a simple system model of the case. When

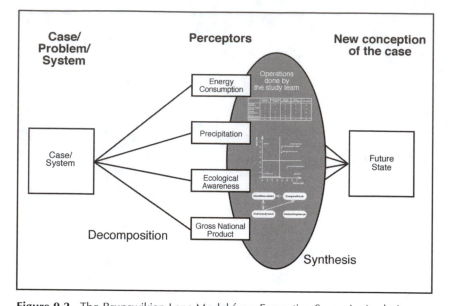

Figure 9.2. The Brunswikian Lens Model for a Formative Scenario Analysis

NOTE: The first step is the analytic modeling/decomposition of a case's initial state to identify impact variables that serve as perceptors. Then, in a step called formative synthesis, various operations are carried out on these impact variables, resulting in changes in representation. This is indicated by the table, grid, and chart in the oval lens. A number of different, internally consistent, and thus possible future states of the case are the end result. The procedure of Formative Scenario Analysis provides a better understanding of the case and its dynamics.

selecting impact variables, the study team should particularly strive for sufficiency. As Brunswik's label *stray causes* implies, complete reliability does not exist in the process of constructing and selecting impact variables. However, the process of vicarious mediation provides an opportunity to organize the synthesis in a robust way. As mentioned before, vicarious mediation can be achieved if the impact variables are constructed in such a way as to partially supplement each other. Thus, there will be some redundancy, which allows for mutual substitutability, or vicarious functioning. The process begins by creating networks of the impact variables. In order to attain an encompassing system model of the case and organize vicarious mediation, the impact variables must be interlinked by a network.

Box 9.1   Sufficiency in Case Modeling and Evaluation

In the course of a case study, the study team is required to construct a sufficient set of variables or factors for case modeling and/or evaluating the case.

The term *sufficient* is defined precisely in statistics (see Mood, Graybill, & Boes, 1974, p. 300). In general, a *statistic* denotes a function of observable random variables that does not contain any unknowns.

Let us consider a random variable, q, that provides the sample X_1, X_2, ..., X_n. If we find a function $f(q)$ that tells us as much about q as the sample itself, this function is called a *sufficient statistic.* Let $X_1, X_2, ..., X_{100}$ be a random sample provided by a normally distributed random variable. We know that a function, $f(q)$ that maps these measurements into the two-dimensional set of real numbers providing the mean, $\bar{x}$, and the standard deviation, s, is a sufficient statistic.

Although in complex, real-world problems, the term *sufficient* may not be used in its strictest sense, the case analyst looks for a construction (this means, in an abstract sense, a function) that yields a set of variables that allows for sufficient system description, modeling, or evaluation. During this process, the case analyst has to obey the *satisficing*, rather than the optimizing, principle. This means that he or she has to seek a sample that satisfies his or her aspirations for precision and completeness in a robust way.

The whole study team usually performs the selection of the impact factors. However, definition of the impact factors and elaboration of the relations between the variables should be investigated individually or in subprojects. Thus, Formative Scenario Analysis usually requires an embedded case design (see Figure 4.1).

One key issue in the synthesis is the change in representation. This means that the synthesis process starts by confronting the study team with alternate representations of what has been constructed in the process of analytic decomposition and variable networking.

The construction of a consistent set of scenarios to fill the scenario trumpet is the final stage. In Formative Scenario Analysis, a scenario is formally defined by a combination of levels of all impact factors. Thus, the case study team also portrays those possible future states of the case, which could result as stray effects of the impact factors.

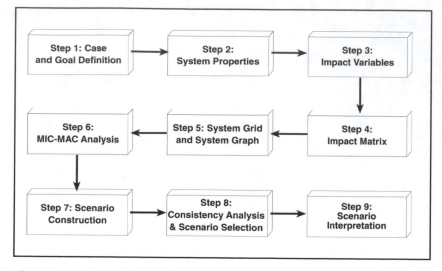

Figure 9.3. The Nine Steps of Formative Scenario Analysis

THE METHOD IN DETAIL

Formative Scenario Analysis is a nine-step procedure that should be worked through sequentially (see Figure 9.3). When describing the method, we will refer to the ETH-UNS case study on urban development, Zurich North, as an example (see Chapter 5).

Step 1: Case and Goal Definition

First, the study team must find a clear answer to the question "What is the case?" Sometimes, this question is not simple to answer. Many cases have fuzzy margins. In the case of the Zurich North site, for instance, the study team had to clarify whether or not Oerlikon Station was part of the case. Initially, the station owner, the Swiss Railway Company, was a member of the planning cooperation, and thus the station property was included in the case. However, before the beginning of the case study, the railway company withdrew, and so the case area became smaller.

Experience shows that it is best to specify the time and space limitations of a case. This is best done by providing a clear physical definition of the case. For the Zurich North site, we considered the case area to be the properties of those parties who, on April 1, 1996, were registered

	S_1	S_2	S_3
V_1	$set_{1,1}$	$set_{1,2}$	$set_{1,3}$
V_2	$set_{2,1}$	$set_{2,2}$	$set_{2,3}$
V_3	$set_{3,2}$	$set_{3,2}$	$set_{3,3}$
V_4	$set_{4,1}$	$set_{4,2}$	$set_{4,3}$

Figure 9.4. Construction of Scenarios on Different Scales

NOTE: Often, it is favorable to separate the construction of local scenarios (subsequently denoted as variants, or V_m) from global scenarios, S_k, which provide frames or shells for variants. The combination of a variant with a (shell) scenario is labeled $set_{m,k}$. The figure provides the schema for and example of four variants and three scenarios.

members of the planning cooperation. A crisp physical case definition is an essential component of the initial focal variable.

Second, a specific perspective on the outcome of the case analysis (i.e., the terminal focal variable) must be determined. The critical question for this step is "Why is the scenario analysis being performed?" The answer to this question will define the terminal focal variable in the Brunswikian Lens Model. Note that different terminal focal variables require completely different system variables. We will illustrate this by introducing different levels of consideration of the case.

In the ETH-UNS case study Zurich North, we wanted to determine which future realizations of the case might be judged sustainable. However, this required a two-level scenario analysis. Because two-level scenarios are typical constructions for many case studies, what follows is a brief introduction into multilevel scenario analysis.

It is important for the future of a case to reflect on both the larger context in which development takes place (i.e., its frame, or shell) and the inner case activities and developments. This requires separating the variables of the case into two groups, those that are global in scope and those that are local. Defined bundles of levels of global impact variables provide shell scenarios (see Figure 9.4). For example, in the case of the ETH-UNS case study Zurich North, the shell of the case was the evolution of the Greater Zurich area. An example of one of the variables in the shell scenarios was Switzerland's membership in the European Union.

The majority of the second group of variables often results from the decisions of the local case agents. Constructed sets of possible outcomes of these local variables are called *variants*.

Because many local decisions are dependent on the outcomes of global decisions, it is necessary to link the variants with the shell scenarios. The combination $V_m \times S_k$ of the variants, V_m, with the shell scenarios, S_k, is labeled $set_{m,k}$ (see Figure 9.4).

The distinction of case variants from global scenarios is also motivated by epistemological reasons, because the linkage of global variables (e.g., whether or not Switzerland will join the European Union) with microlevel issues (e.g., what level of architectural quality the buildings on the site should have) in one and the same model is not recommended.

Scenarios are often the objects of further evaluation. In order to have the appropriate information available for the evaluation procedure, the study team should already have thought about which evaluation criteria/variables are crucial at the very beginning of the study (see Box 9.2). In the ETH-UNS case study Zurich North, the specific perspective taken was provided by the guiding light of sustainable urban development. However, the reader may also think about more specific terminal focal variables, such as the lowering of the crime rate or the optimization of the water flux on a small site.

LESSONS TO BE LEARNED

▶ A concise case definition is indispensable. Even seemingly well-defined cases, such as companies, are often interpreted differently by different people. Often, physical characterization provides the best case definition. Each scenario of the case must be constructed for the same common fixed future date.

▶ Scenario construction must be functional. This implies that the question "What is the analysis for?" has to be answered at the very beginning of the study.

▶ It is often useful to construct local and global scenarios separately and then link them in a later step.

Box 9.2   Dependent and Independent Variables

The terms *dependent variable* and *independent variable* will be used throughout this book. Within Formative Scenario Analysis, for instance, scenarios act as independent variables, and the evaluations are considered dependent variables (see Hays, 1963, p. 39).

Scenarios are considered independent because the study team is free to construct a scenario in the domain of future possible states of the case. However, given a well-defined scenario, an evaluation of it is completely determined, making it a dependent variable.

Formally, the scenarios are denoted S_k and the evaluations $v(S_k)$.

Step 2: System Properties

The scenario analyst must mentally delve into the case in order to determine the factors that establish the current state of the case and its dynamics. There are two proven strategies for determining these crucial impact variables.

One strategy is to perform a plus-minus analysis. Table 9.1 presents a cutout of the plus-minus analysis done for the Zurich North shell scenario analysis. Note that there is ambivalence over some issues. For instance, for certain financial transactions, Zurich's nonmembership in the European Union is positive because the Swiss franc has traditionally guaranteed a stable currency; however, the nonmembership hinders liberal trade and employment. Similarly, from the long-term perspective, high environmental standards should be considered positive, even though they may yet harm quick, environmentally questionable, but profitable constructions.

Sometimes, it makes sense to perform separate plus-minus analyses, because what may be considered strengths from an economic perspective might be considered weaknesses from a social or environmental perspective. Thus, two or more plus-minus analyses should be performed. Table 9.1 was developed while studying the salient documents of the municipal authorities (City of Zurich, 1995; Hochbaudepartement der Stadt Zürich, 1996) and business organizations (Bignasca, Kruck, Maggi, Schellenbauer, & Schips, 1996; Bretschger et al., 1995) on the future urban development of the Zurich area. The more extended version of plus-minus analysis is the Strengths-Weaknesses-Options-Threats (SWOT)

Table 9.1   Cutout of the Zurich North Plus-Minus Analysis

Plus	Minus	Ambivalence Over
• International finance and trade center • High living standard • Excellent research and development units, universities, etc. • International airport • Attractive and safe downtown areas • High environmental awareness • . . .	• Not perfectly integrated into the European railway net • High cost of living • High wages in Europe • Outsourcing of industrial production • . . .	• Switzerland is not a member of the European Union • High environmental standards • . . .

analysis, which also can be conducted at this step of Formative Scenario Analysis.

Another strategy for grasping the case structure and its dynamics is to study formerly planned projects or interventions. Usually, several plans for improving the case already have been proposed. Each plan generally provides insight into the structure and dynamics of the case, highlighting the case's potential while revealing sensitive features and factors that could have an impact on case development.

For the ETH-UNS case study Zurich North, studying the booklet *Ziele der Stadtentwicklung* (Goals of Urban Development) (Hochbauamt der Stadt Zürich, 1996) was very helpful. It contained a list of more than 50 helpful plans and suggested actions, such as ensuring work permits for foreign specialists, securing the existing supply of apartments, and improving the quality of residential areas. Because the booklet was written about the specific region in which the case is located, reviewing the list helped to identify many local impact factors relevant to the case. Such sources can provide the scenario analyst with clues for describing and modeling the case that may not be found anywhere else.

LESSON TO BE LEARNED

▶ Studying a case's weaknesses, deficiencies, and any former interventions provides insight into its structure, dynamics, and history.

Box 9.3	Key Definitions in Formative Scenario Analysis

Impact variables: The impact variables, d_i, $i = 1, \ldots, N$, are also called system variables, impact factors, or case descriptors.

    Impacts: The mutual impacts between the variables d_i and d_j are $a_{i,j}$. In general, impacts are positive because only the absolute values of the impacts are rated.

    Impact matrix: The impact matrix $A = (a_{i,j})$, $i,j = 1, \ldots, N$, contains the direct impacts of d_i on d_j.

    Levels of impact variables: Each impact variable d_i has at least two levels ($N_i \geq 2$). The levels are discrete and denoted by $d_i^1, \ldots, d_i^{n_i}, \ldots, d_i^{N_i}$,

    Scenario: A scenario is formally a vector $S_k = (d_1^{n_1}, \ldots, d_i^{n_i}, \ldots, d_N^{n_N})$ with $k = 1, \ldots, k_0$; the number of scenarios is $k_0 = \prod_{i=1}^{N} N_i$

    Consistency matrix: The consistency matrix $C = \left[c\left(d_i^{n_i}, d_j^{n_j} \right) \right]$ contains the consistency ratings, $c(\cdot, \cdot)$ for all pairs of impact variables at all levels c, ($i,j = 1, \ldots, N$, $i \neq j$, $n_i = 1, \ldots, N_i$, $n_j = 1, \ldots, N_j$).

    Consistency value: For each scenario, the consistency value $c^*(S_k)$ is a conjoint measure of all of the different consistency ratings, such as

$$c^*(S_k) = \sum c\left(d_i^{n_i}, d_j^{n_j} \right),$$

$i, j = 1, \ldots, N$, $i \neq j$, $d_i^{n_i}, d_j^{n_j} \in S_t$

Step 3: Impact Variables

In general, the aim of this step is to develop a set of impact variables sufficient for valid description and modeling of the current state of the case and its dynamics. The selection and definition of impact variables or impact factors is the most crucial and time-consuming step of a scenario analysis. We formally define the impact variables as d_i ($i = 1, \ldots, N$). We use the letter d because impact variables also act as descriptors of future states of the case (see Box 9.3).

To answer the question "What are the most decisive factors for the Greater Zurich area regarding sustainable urban development?" the study team chose a top-down procedure. First, four different domains of

Table 9.2   Impact Variables From the Zurich North Case Study

Society	Economics	Policy	Environment
Social Classing	Job Market Supply	Switzerland's Membership in the European Union	Traffic
Populousness	Segmentation of the Job Market	Energy Price	Environmental Protection
Values	Innovation	Environmental Regulations	Impacts and Emissions
Living Standards	World Business Cycle	Equalization of Burdens	Parks and Greens
	Real Estate Pricing	Regional Planning	
	Centralization of Investments		

impact variables were determined: society, economics, policy, and environment. Then, a long list of potential impact factors were considered in a brainstorming session and condensed into a list of 19 items.

For each impact variable, the study team had to create a crisp definition. One good way of doing this is to provide a one-page description. The study team tried to relate these variables to key concepts that are used in different branches of science. In this step, reference to state-of-the-art knowledge is required.

What follows are short definitions, extracted from their one-page descriptions, along with the level classifications of each of the variables in the Society domain of Table 9.2.

- *Social classing:* Social classes, distribution of incomes/salaries (levels: polarization vs. normal distribution-like mixture)
- *Populousness:* Inhabitants per square kilometer in the Greater Zurich area (levels: increase of more than 10% in the next decade, decrease of more than 5% in the next decade, less than 10% increase and 5% decrease in the next decade)
- *Values:* Willingness to change perspectives, public participation, commitment toward urban living (levels: active vs. passive)

- *Living standards:* Extent to which individual needs will be fulfilled, such as emissions, safety, number and quality of job positions, availability and frequency of cultural events (levels: high vs. low)

The reader can easily see that different qualities of scaling are necessary for each variable. Some of the variables are rated on a nominal scale, and others on an interval scale.

The variable Centralization of Investments presumably is not understandable to readers who are not acquainted with the political constraints of Zurich. In Switzerland, taxes are assessed by the communities. Due to the extra costs of urban infrastructure, the City of Zurich must demand higher taxes than do small, rural communities. At the time of the ETH-UNS case study Zurich North, the trend was toward decentralization. Many companies preferred the lower taxes charged by the small communities in the vicinity of Zurich. The variable Equalization of Burdens is a reference to this issue with two levels—one where there is an equalization of burdens between the city and the surrounding communities, the second where there is not.

Usually, it is best if the study team ends up with no more than 20 variables. From these, according to the satisficing principle (see Box 9.1), not more than a dozen impact variables should be created. We will introduce a strategy for condensing impact factors when introducing the bottom-up approach to selecting impact factors.

A typical bottom-up procedure for the creation of impact variables is organized in the following way. After the study team has explicitly recalled the goal of the study, each team member is asked to think about potential impact variables and then write them down on cards. All of the cards are compiled and then grouped and regrouped sequentially on the floor or pinned on a wall. If the grouping yields (hierarchically) separable clusters, one may presumably end up with a list such as that in Table 9.2. Usually, this list is very large, presumably containing 40 or more variables. In order to reduce the list, the following strategy works well.

First, the study team cancels variables that are considered secondary.

Second, the study team decides whether some impact variables are already represented implicitly by others, and cancels them. In the Policy column of Table 9.2, for instance, one would consider whether Energy Price is already covered by Environmental Regulations. Similarly, one might cancel the variable Impacts and Emissions, considering it subordinate to Environmental Protection.

Third, new variables are created that encompass and replace a set of existing variables. For instance, Social Classing and Quality of Life could be fused into a new impact variable called Welfare.

Of course, selection and construction of impact variables is best done cooperatively with case experts by organizing a roundtable, questionnaire, or Delphi study (see Linstone & Turoff, 1975).

LESSONS TO BE LEARNED

▶ The construction of impact variables is the most important step in the whole process of Formative Scenario Analysis. It corresponds to the construction of perceptors in the Brunswikian Lens Model.

▶ Analytic decomposition has to be performed with the functionality of the specific goal of the analysis in mind. The study team has to construct a sufficient set of variables that depicts the current state of the case and its dynamics.

▶ There are top-down and bottom-up procedures for clustering, ordering, and eliminating impact variables. Which procedure is recommended depends on the knowledge of the study team.

Step 4: Impact Matrix

The formation of an impact matrix initiates the actual synthesis process (see Figure 9.5). The matrix is defined as $A = (a_{i,j})$, $i,j = 1, \ldots, N$. A cell, $a_{i,j}$, of the matrix assigns (the absolute value of) the direct impact strength of one variable, d_i, on another variable, d_j $(i \neq j)$.

In constructing the impact matrix, the study team has to determine the scale for the impacts. Because there is no natural scale for judging impact strength, the rating has to be assessed on a subjective scale. To formulate a scale for impact strength, the scenario analyst must link his or her case-specific knowledge with the available textbook or scientific knowledge about the variables under consideration. The scaling may have different degrees of refinement. Theoretically, any kind of scale between a simple, nominal 0,1 coding and an absolute scale using arbitrary rational numbers is possible. Figure 9.5 presents an excerpt from the impact

	Social Classing	Populousness	Values	Living Standards	Job Market Supply	Segmentation of the Job Market	...	Environmental Protection	Impacts and Emissions	Parks and Greens	Activity
Social Classing	0	1	1	2	0	1		0	1	0	10
Populousness	0	0	1	2	2	0		1	2	0	13
Values	0	0	0	2	0	0		2	2	0	14
Living Standards	2	2	2	0	0	0		1	1	0	10
Job Market Supply	0	0	0	2	0	1		0	1	0	9
Segmentation of the Job Market	2	0	1	1	1	0		0	0	0	9
...											...
Environmental Protection	0	0	0	2	0	0		0	2	0	10
Impacts and Emissions	2	1	2	2	0	0		1	0	0	15
Parks and Greens	0	0	1	1	0	0		0	0	0	3
Passivity	*13*	*8*	*16*	*25*	*11*	*12*	*...*	*14*	*18*	*2*	*207*

Figure 9.5. Excerpt From the Impact Matrix of the Synthesis Group "Urban Development of the Greater Zurich Area"

NOTE: The impacts, $a_{i,j}$, are rated on a 3-point scale (0, 1, 2). Activity refers to the sum of the impacts that one variable, d_i, has on every other variable, d_j ($i, j = 1, \ldots, N, i \neq j$). Likewise, denoted as a sum, Passivity reflects the impacts that all the other variables, d_j, have on d_i.

matrix of the ETH-UNS case study Zurich North. For this study, the following three-level scale was chosen: 0 = *no or very little impact*, 1 = *medium impact*, 2 = *high impact*.

In practice, the impacts should be rated on a 3- to 7-point scale, but within this range, no general rule exists that clarifies which scaling is the most appropriate. When rating the impacts between variables, the scenario analyst must be aware of several prerequisites and acknowledge potential biases. The following list outlines the six most important ones.

1. The analyst needs to assess the direct impact of one variable on another (e.g., Impact and Emissions on Job Market Supply), which is not a simple task. It is particularly important that the analyst exclude any indirect impacts that a variable has via any other variable that has been defined (see Figure 9.5). This requires that in the course of rating the mutual

impacts, the analysts always remain aware of any other variables that are involved. For instance, if, in a subsequent step, the number of impact variables would be reduced and a variable (such as Populousness) canceled, the ratings of some impacts could change, and, in principle, all ratings should be repeated! This is because the partial impact of a variable (Impact and Emissions) on another (Job Market Supply) via Populousness has to be subsumed in the rating after the elimination of the intermediate variable. Therefore, if the impact variable Populousness would have been deleted as a result, then the impact of the variable Impact and Emissions on Job Market Supply should be 1 instead of 0.

2. The analyst has to construct causalities instead of correlations. This issue refers partly to the previous argument in that the judgment switches from being one of causality to one of correlation if indirect impacts (the canceling of the variable Populousness) are included in the rating. This can also happen when confounding the impact of one variable on another with the opposite impact of the other variable on the former one.

3. The analyst needs to rate the current impacts, not those that were present previously.

4. The analyst should provide a judgment that includes as much information as possible. In other words, do not rate all impacts as medium (given a scale with more than two levels). The analyst should not forget that the informativeness of an impact matrix is zero if all of the ratings are on the same level.

5. The analyst should make sure that the impacts are rated with respect to the specific case being considered, rather than rating general relations. This task is often made easier by encountering the case visually.

6. The analyst needs to be aware of judgment shifts in the course of filling out the impact matrix, two of which should be corrected explicitly. One is the burnout phenomenon. If the impacts for 15 impact variables have to be rated, the analyst will need to consider 210 impacts. A good strategy for coping with the burnout phenomenon is to define blocks of 10 to 20 impacts, which will subsequently be rated. If there is a study team, the blocks to be rated should be presented in a random order by all members.

The other shift is the group choice shift (see Asch, 1956; Stoner, 1961; Zuber, Crott, & Werner, 1992), which has been investigated recently for judgments about impacts between system variables (see Crott, Grotzer, Hansmann, Mieg, & Scholz, 1999). This shift shows that, on the average, the longer the group spends discussing a certain impact relation, the higher its rating will be. Certainly, this is an artifact that has to be corrected in a suitable post hoc procedure.

Before the impact rating starts, the study team must make sure that it is well prepared for the rating procedure. As Reibnitz (1992) suggested, one should strive for each impact judgment being reasoned. In practice, this is both difficult to accomplish and time-consuming. From our experience with Formative Scenario Analysis, we recommend the following reference procedure for study teams of 3 to 10 analysts.

First, the group has to discuss all impact variables qualitatively. Reference should be made to state-of-the-art textbook knowledge if such knowledge is available (e.g., for the business cycle's impact on environmental attitudes, specific publications should be consulted). The rating for the impact should be specific to the case and not represent the relationships between the impact variables in general. If the group feels that it lacks solid knowledge, case or subject experts should be consulted.

Second, each member of the study team must fill out the impact matrix individually (see Box 9.4). Standard statistics (mean, variance, etc.) of all group members' ratings should be calculated, compared, and discussed. Furthermore, the study team should also be presented with the total distribution of ratings and should check whether it shows unwanted properties, such as too many medium-range ratings. Naturally, each analyst should check whether he or she was affected by one of the biases reported earlier. If necessary, the case members should review the ratings individually and make adjustments.

Finally, the study team has to visualize all distributions of impact ratings that exceed a certain degree of heterogeneity. The criteria for heterogeneity have to be assessed according to the scaling, the group size, and so on. Those ratings that are considered divergent or heterogeneous should be discussed by the group, and, subsequently, adjustments should be made for them. The group should correct for impact shifts (see Item 6 in the list above) by, for instance, adjusting post hoc the mean of the discussed impacts to be compatible with the overall mean of those not yet discussed.

Clearly, not all of the problems that could occur in the course of constructing an impact matrix will be discussed here. For instance, we do not address the self-referential dynamics that some variables show.

Box 9.4	Structuring the Case Through an Impact Matrix

The cells of an impact matrix $A = (a_{i,j})$, $i,j = 1, \ldots, N$, provide information on how different system variables of a case are interrelated. The numbers $a_{i,j}$ indicate how strongly the variable d_i affects d_j. If we calculate the sums of the rows and the columns, we gain insight into the relative influence of d_i and the dependence of the variable d_j. The following figure represents the formal notation of an impact matrix A and some indicators.

	1	..	N	$a_{i,\bullet}$	$a_{i,\bullet}/a_{\bullet,i}$
1	$a_{1,1}$	..	$a_{1,N}$	$\sum_{j=1}^{N} a_{1,j}$	$a_{1,\bullet}/a_{\bullet,1}$
..	..	..	..	..	..
N	$a_{N,1}$	..	$a_{N,N}$	$\sum_{j=1}^{N} a_{N,j}$	$a_{N,\bullet}/a_{\bullet,N}$
$a_{\bullet,j}$	$\sum_{i=1}^{N} a_{i,1}$	..	$\sum_{i=1}^{N} a_{i,N}$	$a_{\bullet,\bullet} = \sum_{i=1}^{N} \sum_{j=1}^{N} a_{i,j}$	
$a_{\bullet,j} * a_{j,\bullet}$	$a_{\bullet,1} * a_{1,\bullet}$	..	$a_{\bullet,N} * a_{N,\bullet}$		

We will now discuss the final impact ranking of the ETH-UNS case study Zurich North's study team. The ranking reveals the study team's perspective.

At first glance, it appears that World Business Cycle and Environmental Regulations are the two impact variables judged highest in importance, with both scoring 17. From a sustainable development perspective, however, Environmental Regulations, Impacts and Emissions, Values, and Populousness are also regarded as having a high impact (see Table 9.3).

But a closer look at the cells of the impact matrix reveals that most people rated global variables such as the World Business Cycle or Switzerland's Membership in the European Union to be of medium impact on a 3-point scale (0, 1, 2). If the medium ratings are downgraded and just a

The subsequent descriptions are helpful to better understanding the case model.

Activity: The activity of a variable (i.e., the extent to which a variable's impact on other variables is active), d_i, is the row sum of all of the impacts that this variable has on all other variables d_i, formally $a_{i \cdot} = \sum_{j=1}^{N} a_{i,j}$. Activity correlates to the medium impact of a variable on other variables.

Sensitivity/passivity: The sensitivity/passivity of a variable, d_i, is calculated by summing up the cells of the column i, that is, the impacts that all of the other variables have on it. Formally, $a_{\cdot j} = \sum_{i=1}^{N} a_{i,j}$. The sensitivity is correlated with the medium dependency of a variable on other variables.

The subsequent indexes provide some further information on the relative importance of variables according to the study team's ratings.

Impact strength: If we calculate the ratio between activity and sensitivity, $a_{i \cdot} / a_{\cdot i}\, (a_{\cdot i} > 0)$, we get a summary indicator of the medium impact strength of a variable on the case.

Involvement: The involvement of a variable, d_i, is the product of activity and sensitivity, $a_{\cdot j} \cdot a_{j \cdot}$, and indicates how strongly the variable d_j is interlinked with the system. It should be noted that some researchers consider the difference and sum to be more appropriate than the quotient or product. Regardless, these indexes shed light on certain aspects of the variables and their positions in the system model.

dichotomous 0-1 rating is considered when transforming the ones to zeros and the twos to ones, a more concise shell model appears. The activity of the general factors, World Business Cycle and Switzerland's Membership in the European Union, become tremendously downgraded. Conversely, the relative importance of Populousness and Energy Price rise.

LESSONS TO BE LEARNED

▶ The impact matrix initiates the synthesis process by rating the variables' current, direct, mutual impacts. The outcome is as good as the rating and depends on the study team's worldview, knowledge, and methodological awareness of potential biases and fallacies.

Table 9.3   Activity Ranking of All Variables in the Zurich North Case
                  Study

Rank 1-5	Rank 6-10	Rank 11-15	Rank 16-19
1. World Business Cycle	6. Populousness	11. Energy Price	16. Centralization of Investments
2. Environmental Regulations	7. Switzerland's Membership in the European Union	12. Environmental Protection	17. Traffic
3. Regional Planning	8. Social Classing	13. Job Market Supply	18. Equalization of Burdens
4. Impacts and Emissions	9. Living Standards	14. Segmentation of the Job Market	19. Parks and Greens
5. Values	10. Real Estate Pricing	15. Innovation	

NOTE: This ranking was taken from the Formative Scenario Analysis of the synthesis group
"Sustainable Urban Development of the Greater Zurich North Area."

▶ The assessment of mutual impacts requires being knowledgeable
  about the case and recognizing the system variables' dependencies.
  The study team should make sure that at least state-of-the-art textbook
  knowledge is applied in rating the mutual impact strengths.

▶ The assessment of impacts in groups has many advantages, but because of potential shifts and other effects within the groups, it can also
  contain some risks. The case study team should discuss and deal with
  these effects explicitly.

Step 5: Graphical Representations:
System Grid and System Graph

We all know that a switch from words to numbers may cause a crucial
change in communication even when the message that is sent is inten-

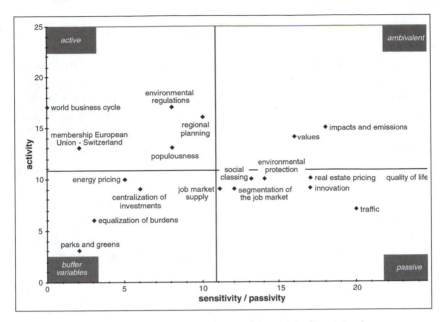

Figure 9.6. A System Grid of the Activity and Sensitivity/Passivity Scores

tionally the same. Step 5 simply provides a transformation of the information from an algebraic impact matrix to a geometrical system grid and system graph. The step is exploratory in nature and resembles strongly the procedures used in exploratory data analysis (Tukey, 1977).

Activity and sensitivity ratings are displayed in a system grid. A system grid is a conjoint display of the column and row sums. In Figure 9.6, the plane is divided by a vertical and a horizontal line through the mean activity and sensitivity/passivity scores. Hence, the impact variables are partitioned into four sets.

The variables Values and Impacts and Emissions are considered above average in both sensitivity and activity, which places them in the Ambivalent quadrant. Five variables in Figure 9.6 are both above average in activity and below average in passivity; they are located in the Active quadrant.

In contrast, eight variables are in the Passive quadrant because they are below average in activity but above average in passivity. Finally, four variables are called Buffer Variables because they are below average in both activity and sensitivity/passivity.

The system graph is a structured network that presents a structural view of the system model. It visualizes how the different variables are interlinked. If only a few impact variables are present, the different strengths of the impacts can be displayed by varying the boldness of the lines and arrows.

The impact matrix of the ETH-UNS case study Zurich North produced too many arrows when the medium impacts were also drawn. Thus, a new dichotomous scaling was established in which low and medium impacts were combined and labeled "0," and those that had formerly been rated "2" became "1." If we enter the data into a suitable software program for networking (e.g., Krackhardt, Blythe, & McGrath, 1994), we get a graph like that in Figure 9.7, which provides comprehensive insight into the study team's system model of the case.

Because a system grid with 19 variables is still rather confusing, we have supplemented the network slightly by inserting the activity and passivity values of the variables and displaying the impact variables in differently marked boxes. We now receive a clearer image of the frame of the Zurich North site shell model.

According to the study team, the variables found to play the most active role in sustainable development were Environmental Regulations, Values, and Impacts and Emissions. Of secondary importance were Populousness, Energy Price, and Regional Planning. Those variables that were clearly on the passive side were Living Standards, Traffic, Innovation, and Impacts and Emissions.

LESSONS TO BE LEARNED

▶ System grids and system graphs are visualizations of a "grainy" case model through impact variables. They provide insight into the study team's assessment of the relative importance and mutual relationships of all the variables.

▶ Graphical representations should be used in an exploratory manner. Changes in a variable's relative importance resulting from an overall coarsening of impact levels should be viewed as clues. The study team should reflect these in the overall process of synthesis.

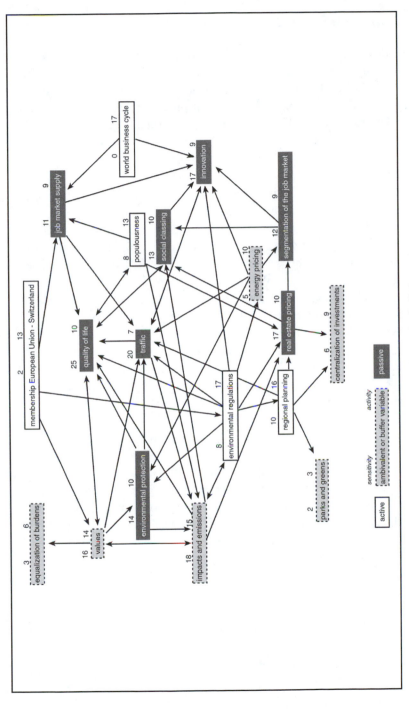

Figure 9.7. A System Graph of the Impact Matrix of the Zurich North Shell Scenario

NOTE: Only strong impacts are displayed to prevent information overload. In order to support the reader's conception of the system model, the sum of low, medium, and strong impacts that a variable has on other variables is noted on the top right. Conversely, the number of impacts that a variable receives from other variables is noted on its top left. The most active variables are framed, the most passive variables, shaded. Impacts and Emissions is considered to be the core variable for sustainable development in the Zurich North shell scenario.

101

Step 6: MIC-MAC Analysis

Until now, we have considered only the direct impacts between system variables. Furthermore, our considerations were static. The goal of the MIC-MAC (*Matrice d'Impact Croisés-Multiplication Appliqueé à un Classement,* or Cross Impact Matrix-Multiplication Applied to Classification) Analysis (Godet, 1986, 1987) is to take the indirect impacts into account in order to gain a more detailed insight into the impact variables' importance from a System Dynamics perspective.

The starting point of analysis is the impact matrix (see Box 9.4). For the MIC-MAC Analysis, this matrix needs to be coarsened, such that it contains information only on whether there is a (strong) direct impact or no impact. To take into account the indirect impacts, the impact matrix is multiplied with itself repeatedly, and after each multiplication, the column sums and row sums are calculated. If this has been done often enough, the rankings of the column and row sums mostly become stable. The row sum is generally considered to be indicative of a variable's activity, including indirect impacts. Similarly, the column sum is indicative of a variable's passivity, including indirect impacts.

The procedure can be described formally as follows. The impact matrix $A = (a_{i,j})$, $i,j = 1, \ldots, N$, is coarsened by setting the coefficients $a_{i,j}$ to 1 (*strong impact*) or 0 (*no impact*). For reasons of simplicity, we will label this matrix A as well. Matrix A is then multiplied with itself

$$A^2 = \left(a_{i,j}^2\right) = \left(\sum_{k=1}^{N} a_{i,k} \cdot a_{k,j}\right)$$

(where the 2 in $a_{i,j}^2$ denotes a superscript, not an exponent). The cells $a_{i,j}^2$ of the matrix A^2 are the number of direct impacts of second order, that is, the number of indirect impacts that a variable d_i has via any other variable d_k $(i \neq k)$ on d_j. The product $a_{i,k} \cdot a_{k,j} = 1$ if, and only if, the variable d_i has a strong impact on d_k and d_k has a strong impact on d_j. If we sum up along k, we attain all second-order impacts of d_i on d_j.

Similarly,

$$A^3 = \left(a_{i,j}^3\right)$$

denotes all third-order impacts that a variable d_i has along the variables d_j and d_k :

$$A^3 = \sum_{l=1}^{N} a_{i,l} \cdot a_{l,j}^2$$

$$A^3 = A \cdot A^2 = \sum_{l=1}^{N} a_{i,l} \cdot \sum_{k=1}^{N} a_{l,k} \cdot a_{k,j}$$

In general, the cells of A^n contain the number of indirect impacts of length n. If n is sufficiently large, the rankings of the column and row sums of A^n mostly become stable.

The scores of direct and indirect impact activity (or passivity) have to be compared. The greater the difference between an impact variable's direct and indirect activity ratings, the more attention should be paid to it in scenario construction (see Step 6). If a variable's scores for its indirect impacts are higher than those for its direct ones, one might conclude that this variable is of higher importance than the study team had supposed.

A MIC-MAC Analysis was performed for the ETH-UNS case study Zurich North. The impact variable World Business Cycle was judged to be more important than Environmental Regulations when their indirect impacts were considered, although they had had the same score when their direct impacts were assessed. Furthermore, the variables Impacts and Emissions, Values, and Environmental Protection showed lower rankings in the MIC-MAC Analysis than they had based on direct activity. At this point, we can conclude that ranking of the variables World Business Cycle and Regional Planning increased, but so did Segmentation of the Job Market and Job Market Supply. This latter increase alarmed the study team, which was composed mainly of environmental science students, into checking whether they had overstressed the environmental perspective in their direct ratings.

Clearly, the procedures in Steps 5 and 6 are rules of thumb. Their value should not be judged only according to classical criteria, such as validity or objectivity. Rather, the value of these representations has to be seen in terms of the aid they provide in understanding the case and reflecting on one's own opinions.

Most of the methods are semiquantitative, and variables, which do not have a rational scale, are sometimes multiplied. Thus, the study team should watch out for artifacts based on scaling. This can best be done by performing a sensitivity analysis on the ratings of the initial impact matrix A.

LESSONS TO BE LEARNED

▶ MIC-MAC Analysis can also be considered a simple model for case dynamics. This is best done by referring to automata theory (Hopcraft & Ullman, 1979), because the multiplication of matrices can be considered a spreading of impulses on a discrete time scale, assuming that there is a multiplicative amplification of impact strength over time. The MIC-MAC Analysis provides access to the indirect impacts of a case and a rough model for its dynamics.

▶ The rank in importance of a variable based on the assessment of its indirect impacts may differ from the rank based on its direct impacts. Special attention should be paid to those variables that score higher in the activity of their indirect impacts than they do in the activity of their direct impacts.

Step 7: Scenario Construction

In the ETH-UNS case study Zurich North, the variable Populousness has three levels. To construct one of the possible scenarios, the second level of Populousness was combined with the first level of the impact variable Social Classing, and so on. Hence, a scenario is simply a combination of levels of all impact variables.

If there are 10 impact variables and each of them has only two levels, we will have $2^{10} = 1,024$ different scenarios. If we have 15 impact variables with three levels each, there will be $3^{15} = 14,348,907$ formally constructed scenarios.

For each impact variable d_i, we have defined different levels $d_i^{n_i}$ ($n_i = 1$, ..., N_i), where N_i denotes the number of different levels that we have allowed for the impact variable d_i (see Step 3). For instance, the three levels of the variable Populousness are as follows:

d_i^1 = increase of more than 10% in the next decade

d_i^2 = decrease of more than 5% in the next decade

d_i^3 = less than 10% increase and 5% decrease in the next decade

Formally, a scenario, S, is simply a complete combination of levels of impact factors $(d_1^{n_1}, \ldots, d_i^{n_i}, \ldots, d_N^{n_N})$ for all factors d_i $(i = 1, \ldots, N)$. Thus, a scenario is a vector

$$S = (d_1^{n_1}, \ldots, d_i^{n_i}, \ldots, d_N^{n_N})$$

At this point in the analysis, it becomes apparent that scenario analysts should be parsimonious in defining impact factors and their levels from the very beginning. Even so, for Step 7, the number of variables should be reduced out of the differentiated insight gained from the MIC-MAC Analysis. This can best be done by referring to the system grid and system graph (see Figures 9.6 and 9.7). An impact variable's activity is the most decisive criterion of the selection procedure. In the ETH-UNS case study Zurich North, we retained the nine impact variables with the highest activity scores. The variable Centralization of Investments was kept as well because it was thought to be crucial to the future of the Zurich North site.

LESSONS TO BE LEARNED

▶ Scenario construction relies on parsimony in the number of impact variables and their levels.

▶ The insights provided by the MIC-MAC Analysis and the system graph may help in selecting the variables most important to the System Dynamics of the case.

Step 8: Consistency Analysis and Scenario Selection

Consistency analysis is an analytic procedure for cleaning up a set of scenarios. The rationale behind this cleaning procedure is logical consistency. For a given scenario, specific combinations of levels may be relatively inconsistent. If, for one scenario, all pairs of impact variables are rated, whether their levels are consistent or not, we get information about the scenario's logical consistency. In order to provide a better understanding of the objectives of consistency analysis, we want to remind the reader of the difference between possibility and probability. A scenario might be

considered logically consistent, and thus possible, without being probable. However, a prerequisite of probability is possibility.

Scenario selection is a two-step procedure for assessing possibility.
First, we produce consistency measures for each scenario. These allow us
to distinguish between consistent and inconsistent scenarios. For instance, on the Zurich North site, a doubling of Populousness was judged
to be inconsistent with a reduction of resource use. The remaining set of
consistent scenarios is what fills the funnel of the scenario trumpet. Second, we have to screen this set in order to select a small number of scenarios that represent the set of future states of our case. The following is a
brief outline of the technical procedure.

Let S_k be one scenario of the set of all possible scenarios $\{S_k\}$. For each
pair of impact variables, a consistency measure

$$c(d_i^{n_i}, d_j^{n_j})$$

is assessed. Abstractly formulated, the function $c(.,.)$ is a mapping from
the set of possible combinations of impact variables into the space of
(judged) logical inconsistencies.

As with impact rating, the question of which scaling is appropriate
arises again. No definite answer to this question exists. A scaling with few
(three to four) levels is generally recommended. It is advantageous to pe-
nalize strong inconsistencies by giving them drastically low ratings. In the
Zurich North case, for instance, the following ratings were applied:

$c(.,.) = 3$ Complete consistency, the levels of the impact
                factors are coherent and support each other

$c(.,.) = 1$ Partial or weak inconsistency

$c(.,.) = 0$ Inconsistent

$c(.,.) = -99$ Strong inconsistency, scenarios including
                combinations of logically contradictory levels of
                impact variables are not considered thinkable

Then, a consistency matrix (see Table 9.4), which includes all combinations of levels of impact factors, has to be filled out by the study team. This
task is time-consuming and should be done in a well-organized and structured group process (see Chapter 16).

To construct a value $c^*(S_k)$ that assigns a conjoint consistency measure
for each scenario, the consistency matrix is defined as

Table 9.4   Excerpt of the Consistency Matrix for the Zurich North Scenario Analysis

		d_1^1	d_1^2	d_2^1	d_2^2	...	$d_i^{n_i}$	...	$d_N^{n_N}$
d_1^1	Srong environmental regulations	—							
d_1^2	Weak environmental regulations	—	—						
d_2^1	Low impacts and emissions	0	-99	—					
d_2^2	High impacts and emissions	3	0	—	—				
...				—	—				
$d_i^{n_i}$	Populousness strongly increasing	0	1	3	0	—	—		
...							—		
$d_N^{n_N}$	High living standards	0	1	0	0		1		—

NOTE: The study team judged the combination of weak environmental regulations with low impacts and emissions to be strongly inconsistent ($c(d_2^1, d_1^2)$ = -99).

$$c = c(d_i^{n_i}, d_j^{n_j})$$

There are several different options for the calculation of $c^*(S_k)$. The above scaling is arranged for an additive value. Thus, we simply add up all the $\binom{n}{2}$ consistency values for pairs of a scenario S_k:

$$c^*(S_k) = \sum_{n_i, n_j \leftrightarrow S_k, i \neq j} c(d_i^{n_i}, d_j^{n_j}) = \sum_{i=1}^{N-1} \sum_{j=i+1}^{N} c(d_i^{n_i}, d_j^{n_j})$$

The sign "↔" is used for indicating that the level n_i of an impact variable d_i and the level n_j of an impact variable d_j are part of scenario S_k. Table 9.4 shows how the data may be organized.

There are also other consistency values offered in the scenario analysis literature (see Missler-Behr, 1993, p. 33). We will not deal with this problem in detail. However, a multiplicative structure might also be considered appropriate. The case study should deal with the consistency analysis in an exploratory manner. This means that if the study team is of two minds about the consistency of several pairs of variables, the application of different measures is recommended. There are several computer programs available that support consistency analysis (von Nitsch, 1989), but most of the operations are easily programmable with spreadsheet software.

Of course, no specific rules define when a scenario is consistent, but various techniques are commonly used. One technique is to define a threshold value below which a consistency measure should not drop. Another technique is to take the 10, 20, or 100 most consistent scenarios, or the upper 1%, 2%, or 5%. However, there are no general criteria for this threshold. Thus, we will introduce an inductive, exploratory approach that provides a small set of scenarios with high consistency filling the funnel of the scenario trumpet.

When selecting representatives for the scenario funnel, a distinction can be made between data-driven, bottom-up strategies and concept-driven, top-down strategies. For the bottom-up procedure, the study team should have a well-organized spreadsheet at its disposal (see Table 9.6). We suggest Table 9.6, which is partially derived from Table 9.5 by rotating the matrix. Furthermore, only the levels of the impact variables (being the upper indexes in Table 9.5) are listed in order to reduce the complexity of notation. In the first two columns of Table 9.6, both the labels and the levels of the impact variables are noted to provide semantic information for facilitating the interpretation and comparison of different scenarios. One option is that the study team starts with the most consistent scenario and compares it with the subsequent ones successively. Often, the study team will notice that the top scenario differs from the next highest in the levels of only one or two impact variables. The team has to decide whether this difference is semantically important (which means defining a new type of scenario), or whether it just represents gradual change and modification. In the example given in Table 9.6, the radical change occurs when switching from Scenario S_4 to S_5.

Data-Driven, Bottom-up Procedure. It is possible to successively classify scenarios by concentrating on their "sign level" for a long period of time. This means that the grouping of similar scenarios and the choice of a representative scenario for every group initially is done exclusively by comparing similarities in the consistency ratings on the number level. Once a coherent group has been identified, however, the essence of the class has to be identified semantically. In the end, the representative that allows for the best interpretability and best matches the label of a class should be chosen. Usually, between three and five scenarios will result.

Table 9.5 The Schema of a Consistency Spreadsheet After Consistency Assessment

Rank	Consistency Value	Scenarios (Sk)					
1	$c^*(S_1)$	d_1^2	d_2^2	...	$d_i^{n_i^1}$	...	d_N^3
...	...	...	...	...	...	...	...
k	$c^*(S_k)$	$d_1^{n_1^k}$	$d_2^{n_2^k}$	...	$d_i^{n_i^k}$	...	$d_N^{n_N^k}$
...	...	...	...	...	...	...	...
k_0	$c^*(S_{k_0})$	d_1^2	d_2^2		$d_i^{n_i^{k_0}}$		d_N^3

NOTE: The k_0 scenarios (see Box 9.3) are renumbered according to their consistency ranking $c^*(S_k)$. In order to avoid overly complicated notation, specific levels are chosen (e.g., two for d_1, two for d_2, and three for d_N in scenario S_1) for the scenarios S_1 and S_{k_0}. For row k and column i, the general notation is written in the upper indexes.

Table 9.6 Spreadsheet of Scenario Selection

		S_1	S_2	S_3	S_4	S_5			S_{k_0}
Environmental Regulations	strong (1), weak (2)	2	2	2	2	1			1
Impacts and Emissions	low (1), high (2)	2	2	2	2	1			2
Populousness (x)	x < 5% (1), 5% < x < 10% (2), x > 10% (3)	3	3	2	1	1			1
...	...								
...	...								
...	...								
Living Standards	low (1), high (2)	2	1	2	2	2			1
(Additive) consistency measure $c^*(S_k)$		24	23	23	19	19			-91

NOTE: Without any loss of generality, the scenarios are numbered according to their consistency ranking.

Clearly, there is the option of supporting the bottom-up procedure with multivariate statistical analysis. One such analysis, the cluster analysis method (see Aldenderfer & Blashfield, 1984), is a very flexible instrument that permits different measures of defining similarities between different scenarios. Actually, cluster analysis is nothing more than a procedure that establishes classes of items automatically.

Concept-Driven, Top-Down Procedure. Often, the study team has conceptual ideas about the future of the case. For example, in the Zurich North case, a long-standing economic depression and increase in the unemployment rate in Zurich's metropolitan area gave rise to a belief that there was, at the time, a trend toward polarization (see Box 9.5). Generally speaking, a study team should first reflect on the case and its dynamics, then identify a small set of scenarios that are characterized by certain ideas, knowledge, and designations. Scenario identification has deep roots in the understanding and conceptualizations of the case.

In both the bottom-up and top-down procedures, the study team has to identify which combinations of impact factor levels are compatible with the study team's (previously) formed ideas about the future state of the case. Thus, a notion (i.e., a conceptual, semantic idea) is transferred into the semiotic framework of Formative Scenario Analysis. Some notions will provide small sets of formally defined scenarios that are subsets of the set of consistent scenarios. Of course, certain techniques and criteria for defining the set of consistent scenarios have been provided (see above). These criteria, such as taking the top 1% most consistent scenarios, fall into the category of rules of thumb. Note that these rules of thumb depend on the number of impact variables, their numbers of levels, and the structure of the consistency ratings.

It should be noted that for any certain scenario idea, more than one formatively assessed scenario may be considered appropriate, because some impact variables within one scenario idea are ambiguous. In the ETH-UNS case study Zurich North, the variable Living Standards is ambiguous given the idea of a polarized society, in that polarization may be accompanied by a mean higher or mean lower standard of living.

Each of the two procedures, bottom-up and top-down, has strengths and weaknesses. On the surface, the top-down approach seems to be the more economic and sophisticated, although it has the obvious danger of overlooking crucial scenarios. Furthermore, even if levels of pairs of

Box 9.5	Novelistic Case Description of the Scenario *Polarization* of the Zurich North Shell Scenarios[1]

Switzerland has been integrated into the European Union (EU) (7).[2] Poorly paid jobs are covered by women and immigrants (8). However, the living conditions of immigrants have changed because of membership in the EU; they may now live together with their families.

There is liberal regional planning (3) in the Zurich area, and the municipal and cantonal authorities control the granting of construction permits for offices and housing in areas formerly declared as industrial zones. Environmental regulations are of about the same rigor as today. Environmental issues, however, have lost their importance. Because of high economic uncertainty, people are much more concerned with money and everyday problems (5).

The job market shows high polarization (4), and the service industry is booming. There is a lot of pressure on the middle class. In the service industry, extraordinarily well-paid positions for management contrast with many low-wage jobs for cleaning, security, and so on. Time-sharing is promoted to save on social security (14).

No commercial center can be localized. Many companies settle in peripheral or suburban areas. There are only a few offices, for representational purposes, in the old downtown area (16).

Environmental emissions are rather high (4). This is due to fairly liberal environmental regulations (2). Furthermore, industry has few investments motivated by environmental reasons (12). Companies do not care about resource efficiency or recycling (11).

Living standards (9) and job market supply (13) are low. Polarization especially is increasing because of sociocultural issues. There is little low-income housing in the vicinity of the companies. Compared to other regions, the job supply in the Greater Zurich area is still favorable (1). Thus, there is an increase in population (6).

impact variables are considered consistent in this approach, the combined consistency of levels of three or more impact variables may not hold true. This kind of problem arises at many places in scenario construction (see also Box 9.6).

Box 9.6   Cross-Impact Analysis: Can We Access the
Probability of Future Developments of a Case?

Cross-Impact Analysis refers to a group of methods by which one can determine the probability of the occurrence of a scenario (see Brauers & Weber, 1988; Götze, 1993). The aim is to go beyond consistency analysis, which yields assessments on the logical consistency $c^*(S_k)$ of a scenario S_k.

In order to assess overall probability $p(S_k)$, most cross-impact techniques try to assess inductively the conditional or conjoint probabilities of pairs of impact variables, that is, the probability of the impact variable d_i having level m, given that variable d_j has level k (i.e., $p\,(d_i^m \wedge d_j^l)$), and the conjoint probability of variable d_i having level m and d_j having level l (i.e., $p\,|\,[d_i^m \wedge d_j^l])$).

Papers on Cross-Impact Analysis recommend that these probabilities be rated by experts or with a Delphi procedure.

Most Cross-Impact Analysis procedures try to derive the overall probability for a scenario S_k from knowledge about pairwise probabilities.

However, according to the rules of probability, it is generally true that knowledge about all pairwise conditional and conjunctive probabilities is not sufficient for the calculation of conditional or conjuncture probabilities entailing more than three events.

This has important consequences for an assessment of the probability of a scenario S_k. There is only one way of getting the probability of the occurrences of the scenario; there must be access to the likelihood of all combinations of different impact variables and their levels (pairs, triples, etc. up to length $k - 1$). In practice, this is impossible.

Furthermore, it is well-known that human beings, including experts, are not good probability estimators. They are inconsistent and do poorly, particularly if they are rating the probability of nonobservable events or events with only slight probability. Nevertheless, various procedures have been developed to provide estimations. Generally speaking, we do not think that these procedures are suitable tools for case analysis.

The process of scenario selection is at the core of the synthesis in Formative Scenario Analysis. By the time the study team reaches this step, it will certainly be well prepared in trend extrapolation from the previous steps of analysis. The crucial issue in scenario construction is, without a doubt, the attribution of meaning. The selected scenarios should be regarded as representatives or prototypes of future states of the case. This is why an encompassing verbal scenario description is indispensable. The scenarios should also receive indicative labels.

In the ETH-UNS case study Zurich North, the shell scenarios were derived through a combination of top-down and bottom-up strategies. The study team formulated a set of intuitive ideas about what could be or what should be. Then, it split into two groups, one starting with the top-down approach, the other with the bottom-up approach. In this way, the previously formulated ideas were revisited, shaped, and modified. Finally, the study team ended up with four scenarios: economic uprising(S_1), crises —loss of orientation (S_2), polarization (S_3), and new societal values (S_4). A crucial step in scenario construction is creating a novelistic case description to assist in the interpretation of a scenario. Box 9.5 provides an excerpt from the polarization scenario description. The links between the descriptions and the levels of impact variables tied to the scenarios are documented in the text (see Box 9.5).

LESSONS TO BE LEARNED

▶ Consistency analysis yields possible, logical, coherent scenarios that represent future states that a case could have. Because possibility is a necessary, but not sufficient, prerequisite for probability, special techniques must be applied in rating the likelihood of a scenario (see Box 9.6).

▶ There are no definite normative rules for determining when a scenario is consistent or not. Likewise, there is no maxim to decide whether two scenarios should be considered the same. Thus, decisions on scenario selection have to rely not only on formal criteria, but also on rules of thumb, which must be appropriate to the crispness of information inherent in the whole procedure.

▶ The part of the synthesis process that occurs through consistency analysis is characterized by a permanent transformation from operations on numbers to operations on concepts, or to express it in epistemological terms, by a complementarity in the expression of information between the sign level and the object level (or meaning). The crucial issues in scenario selection are the assignment of meaning to formally assessed sequences of numbers and the interaction between the different aspects of semiotics (i.e., syntax, semantics, sigmatics, and pragmatics).

Step 9: Scenario Interpretation

We will describe briefly four ways of interpreting scenarios.

Conversation. The most natural way of interpreting scenarios is by simply discussing them—their differences, their genesis, and their quality with respect to certain criteria and perspectives. This seems trivial, but in our experience—gathered from about a half-dozen formative scenario analyses—this step is not sufficiently acknowledged by some study teams. A lot of time needs to be reserved for in-depth discussions about the scenarios. Scenario descriptions should provide concise patterns to facilitate a much more elaborate discussion of possible future states than had been possible before the analysis.

Evaluation. Evaluation can be thought of as a specific form of interpretation. Usually, evaluations are inherent parts of most case discussions, but there are both soft and hard methods of evaluation.

We call an evaluation soft if the criteria and procedure for evaluation are not explicitly revealed, but rather are implicitly involved in the inferences and conclusions. In contrast, we consider an evaluation procedure hard if the criteria and procedure are made explicit. This means that they are displayed in a way that allows at least enough objectivity for there to be a high probability that another evaluator who starts with the same premises would end up with the same conclusion. As an example of a hard method, in Chapter 11, we introduce the Multi-Attribute Utility Theory, a highly formative procedure of scenario evaluation.

Many scenarios are constructed intentionally for an evaluation procedure. As previously stated, the scenario should be constructed such that, at least implicitly, it conveys the information necessary to judge its favorability.

Best Reply Strategies. Another way of working with scenarios is to think about which intervention or strategy would be the best for the case in response to a certain scenario. A procedure for linking local interventions (also called variants or strategies) with global scenarios was already introduced earlier in Figure 9.4.

To optimize evaluations, a value function must exist that evaluates each set, or each combination of a local and a global scenario (see Figure 9.4). Then, for every global scenario, the best variant can be determined.

There are many ways to determine, and many criteria for defining, which of a set of strategies is the best. A well-known robust strategy is the max-min strategy. This strategy presumes that, for all the possible intervention options (i.e., variants), the worst global scenario will occur. Under this (pessimistic) assumption, the maximizing variant is chosen.

If every global scenario is considered to have some known likelihood, one option for determining the best strategy is to choose the variant that maximizes the average expected evaluation. We will not go into detail here; we want only to show that new questions arise at the end of a scenario analysis that had not been present before the study.

The formal representations of the best reply strategies are as follows.

If the value function is $v(.)$, then for each S_k, the optimum can be obtained as $\max_m \{v(set_{m,k})\}$.

The *max-min* strategy is formally: $\max_m \min_k \{v(set_{m,k})\}$.

If p_k is the probability of the global scenario S_k, then the maximum of the expected evaluation is $V_{k'} = \max_m \left\{ \sum_k p_k * v(set_{m,k}) \right\}$.

Scenario Manipulation. One way of understanding a scenario is through studying and interpreting it by manipulating the impact strengths. This manipulation provides information about the sensitivity of the case structure and, therefore, where the case can be affected. In Formative Scenario Analysis, because only the absolute values of the impacts are assessed (and not their higher functional relationships), this approach seems to be more promising when the System Dynamics are modeled in a more differentiated manner, as introduced in the next chapter.

LESSONS TO BE LEARNED

▶ Interpretation of scenarios is time-consuming. Through the process of Formative Scenario Analysis, the study team will have already penetrated the case. Interpretating the results of this analysis is a challenging task that leads to new questions and perspectives that provide a higher level of case understanding.

▶ Both the construction and the interpretation of scenarios should be functional. Thus, preferences are inherent in the interpretation of scenarios (i.e., in discussing the future states of a case).

▶ Scenario interpretation often employs explicit or implicit evaluation processes. This holds true for both the discussion of future states of the case and the development of strategies for coping with desirable or undesirable states of the case.

▶ Scenario interpretation and evaluation can be organized qualitatively and/or quantitatively.

NOTES

1. See Baumgartner, Kurath, Ranke, and Stauffacher (1997), p. 126.
2. The numbers refer to the enumeration of impact variables in Table 9.3.

10

SYSTEM DYNAMICS

THE RATIONALE

The main task of a System Dynamics model is to attain insight into future case development. This task is embedded within three goals. First, the representation of the system within a dynamic model is achieved using a specific language. This language serves as the communication within the study team and between the study team and external experts. Second, during the development of the model, the study team improves its knowledge, particularly about the relevant impact variables and their dynamic behavior, and thus develops a new conception of the system and the case. Third, the model can become a part of case management, which includes understanding the case, describing the system, understanding the case development, developing management strategies, and investigating the possible effects of those strategies.

The System Dynamics model has to provide evidence on salient aspects of the case and may answer the following questions:

- What type of dynamic behavior does the system exhibit, and which consequences for the case emerge?
- Which impact variables seem to be relevant for the system and possibly for the case? Also, because the modeling allows for creating different variants, which system structure seems most desirable?

- From a case management perspective, which development of the case may occur or is expected? Which management strategy is effective and efficient?

To successfully apply System Dynamics, several prerequisites for the case and the study team have to be fulfilled. Concerning the case, enough information about the possible development of the case has to be available. In particular, System Dynamics requires the quantification of the relevant impact variables. Moreover, the system model should represent an important and relevant part of the case. The study team should be well trained and experienced with System Dynamics modeling, and it is recommended that an expert support the modeling process. Because modeling is time-consuming, attention has to be paid to providing the results within the available time frame.

Historical Background

The roots of the dynamic systems view are the mathematical investigations of Newton, d'Alembert, Euler, and Lagrange on differential equations. These investigations followed the formulation of the axioms of mechanics by Newton and the increasing use of Cartesian coordinates (Dieudonné, 1985). Since the 17th and 18th centuries, many approaches to describing the trajectories (i.e., the path of a body in space) of dynamic systems and integrating the corresponding differential equations have been developed. The first models were applied to geometrical, mechanical, or astronomic problems. It became clear that a system of ordinary differential equations can describe each mechanical problem with multiple mass points (Dieudonné, 1985). The state variables were the coordinates (e.g., of celestial bodies). The considered effects were due to the internal forces (e.g., gravity) that change the body's position in time and space. The idea was to calculate the system state at any given time, depending on the initial system state and referring to the valid system laws, which are modeled by differential equations. In this way, the largest problem of astronomic mechanics—the stability of the sun system—was made plausible, but it was not proven (Dieudonné, 1985, p. 44). Although the simulations were close to the observations, they could not explain perfectly the long-term trajectories as postulated in the Leibnizian sense. Thus, there was no perfect "pure case model." This is due to the fact that the model does not include all system properties, which are relevant on a long-term scale (e.g., shift of the helix).

Forrester's (1961) book *Industrial Dynamics* can be considered the foundation of modern System Dynamics. He opened the field of scientific management by means of mathematical modeling. Two tasks of the industrial manager were to develop models and analyze the system. Special compilers—in this case, the famous DYNAMO compiler—facilitated this task. The proof of the mathematical and logical consistency of the models was delegated to mathematical experts. The objective of the work in Forrester's management laboratory was to design more effective industrial and economic systems. This was done by a series of controlled mathematical laboratory experiments. The state variables were information, orders, materials, personnel, money, and capital equipment. Please note that Forrester stresses the correct use of these experiments by giving the example of wind tunnel experiments for an aircraft: "The erroneous design of the model or mistaken interpretation of laboratory results can lead to a disaster in the final airplane" (Forrester, 1961, p. 43). Thus, System Dynamics was applied under a functional perspective. The objective was not mathematical sophistication, but rather to attain management success.

The use of differential equations in management science is only one example of the application of System Dynamics. Besides modeling in physics, chemical (thermodynamics, laws of reaction) (see Ingham, Dunn, Heinzle, & Prenosil, 1994; Rice & Do, 1995); biological (populations, growth processes) (see Brown, 1993); and social (Kemeny & Snell, 1962) models were developed. During this process, not only did the number of applications increase, but the mutual dependencies and kinds of state variables changed as well. Clearly, many different fields of mathematics contributed to scientific modeling. Because we introduce System Dynamics as a method of knowledge integration in case studies, we will concentrate on System Dynamics as a paradigm in scientific management.

One of the prototypes of System Dynamics is the World Model (Forrester, 1971; Meadows, Meadows, & Randers, 1992; Meadows et al., 1974), which describes socioeconomic and environmental dynamics on a global scale. This model contributed to a better understanding and awareness of the riskiness of our present economic behavior and use of environmental resources.

Fundamental for the use of System Dynamics is the distinction between open and closed systems. In open systems, external effects such as boundary conditions may result in internal changes, or, vice versa, the internal dynamics may influence the environment.

Hard and Soft Models

We will call a model "hard" if the model is constructed using hard facts, such as scientific laws (e.g., from Newton mechanics) or scientific measurements (e.g., see Richter, Diekkrüger, & Nörtersheuser; 1996; Richter & Söndgerath, 1990). In case the information on the structure or the data is missing, ideas, or assumptions about the structure of the system model, have been coded into the language of System Dynamics. Some of these models became very popular, like the World3 model (Bossel, 1994; Meadows et al., 1992).

We refer to models as "soft" if the assumptions about the system state and the relations of the state variables in a System Dynamics model rely merely on a mental model. The term *mental model* became very popular in the psychology of problem solving (Baron, 1994; Garnham & Oakhill, 1994; Johnson-Laird, 1983). It indicates that an individual has an elaborate cognitive representation of operations leading to a problem solution.

Note that, to a certain extent, soft models contain reasonable, personal, or subjective assumptions instead of scientific knowledge; hence, the predictive validity of a soft model cannot be shown. In contrast to the toxicokinetic models (see Box 10.1), where data for model tests are available, in some cases, even the behavior of the system to be modeled is not known (e.g., because salient measurements are not available). In one of the ETH-UNS case studies, the study team mapped its common understanding of the future development of the construction industry into a System Dynamics model. This model contained variables such as Applicable Environmental Knowledge, Environmental Awareness, and Environmental Regulations, which were conceived of as continuous variables without being defined in such a way that measurement became possible. In this example, even the trajectories were qualitatively judged by the model makers. It is very difficult to assess the rationale and the validity of such a proceeding. The soft modeling technique is reasonable insofar as the study team develops intrinsic interests into the case development and considers the System Dynamics approach to be an appropriate tool to communicate and to represent the case knowledge.

| Box 10.1 | The General and the Specific: System Dynamics in Case Analysis |

We will illustrate the benefit of System Dynamics in case analysis by an example from the medical sciences. System Dynamics serves for modeling the decay of substances injected into certain compartments, such as blood or tissues. Such toxicokinetic models are very important for the development of medical drugs.

When practical physicians give a diagnosis or decide on a drug therapy, they rely on this knowledge about the dynamic development of the substances' concentrations. This knowledge can be conveyed well by interactive computer programming, which visualizes the dynamics in a mathematical microlaboratory. Through the use of these programs, physicians will also learn how the medication, the weight of the patient, and the velocity of the metabolism dynamically interact, and how this interaction affects the dose-response relationship. The models underlying these computer simulations are based partly on knowledge of chemical reactions (system structure) and partly on a description of what has been observed in medical experiments (system behavior).

When, in an individual case, physicians have to decide on the amount, form, portioning, and duration of a certain drug to be prescribed, they refer to their experience with similar cases, the specific observations in this case, and the general knowledge on the dynamics. The two sources of general knowledge (system structure and system behavior) will be integrated with a third: case-specific knowledge. Obviously, the parameters of the model (e.g., the decay constants) may vary considerably between an adult woman and a young boy. Thus, physicians must consider age; sex; height; weight; vigilance; smoking, eating, and drinking behaviors; medical treatments; and other factors from the anamnesis. In general, physicians will know the impact of these parameters on the effects of the drug, but this knowledge will not be complete. Nevertheless, they will build an opinion or an estimate about the best therapy. We want to emphasize that in medical therapy, the System Dynamics model is part of the case analysis and is the transmitter of general, scientific knowledge.

Vicarious Functioning With Graphical Representation

The developments in both mathematics, such as the analytical and numerical solution of differential equations, and computer science caused a revolution in the practice of System Dynamics. The method became very easy to apply in recent decades. Crucial in this progress has been a shift in representation: Instead of describing the systems by mathematical formulas and codes, modern software tools provide an easy, graphical representation of systems. These new techniques enhance the application of System Dynamics as a constructive, synthesis-oriented approach rather than as a reductionistic, analytically oriented tool. In this context, the Brunswikian principle of vicarious functioning can be conceived of in different ways.

First, according to a conventional perspective, each state variable in the system model can be conceived of as a perceptor in the Brunswikian Lens Model. The art of modeling consists of creating a set of variables that provides a robust representation of the case dynamics, even if a single variable and its relations are not defined perfectly. Second, vicarious functioning can be interpreted as a mutual substitutability of parts of the model (modules) in a way similar to what has been done with the single variables. Third, from the perspective of the study team, each single model represents one facet of truth. Thus, the study team realizes multiple representations of the case through different models, repeatedly replacing parts of the model, playing with the model in order to optimize the model structure, and discussing and verifying the results. Hence, in the ETH-UNS case study, the System Dynamics approach represents a much more Hegelian research concept than Leibnizian, which is the concept traditionally associated with it (see Chapter 4).

Language Elements of System Dynamics

The specific vocabulary of the System Dynamics language consists of compartments, fluxes, parameters, and control variables (Figure 10.1). The study team, external experts, and case agents are forced to express their own knowledge quantitatively using these terms. But they are not obliged to use mathematical formulations because these remain hidden behind a graphical user interface. A model moderator should assist inexperienced study team members in translating their ideas into the graphical model language. Thus, the model moderator makes sure that the appropriate functional relations between the elements of the language are found. The model moderator also checks to see that inadmissible models —such as those resulting in stiff differential equations, which cannot be

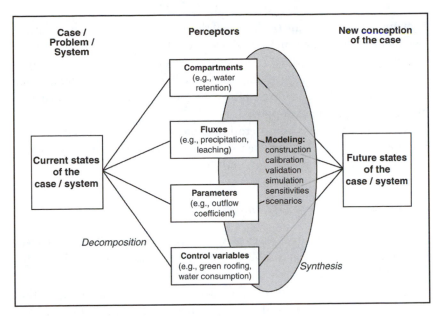

Figure 10.1. The Brunswikian Lens Model for System Dynamics

NOTE: A salient part of the case is represented by the model in terms of the System Dynamics language. The specific synthesis process of modeling comprises the construction, calibration, validation, simulation, and calculation of sensitivities and scenarios. The examples are from the synthesis group Water Budget of the ETH-UNS case study Zurich North (see Chapter 5).

treated by the too-simple numerics of the software—will not occur. The shift of representation from differential equations to icons and arrows also facilitates the mutual understanding of the study team members and external experts. This has been very helpful for contact with external experts and agents within the ETH-UNS case study.

In the course of forming the System Dynamics model, the study team clarifies its own perception of the system and explicitly expresses its developing knowledge about the case. The structure of the system is presented by means of the relevant variables. Within this process, the causalities become subject to communication in a way similar to the construction of impact variables of scenario analysis. As the reader may have noticed, the System Dynamics method may be linked directly to the construction of scenarios. In a Formative Scenario Analysis, the absolute values, irrespective of the direction, of the mutual impact strengths at a time t_0 are assessed and included in the impact matrix (see Table 10.2). In the System

Dynamics model, the rate of change of the impact variables is the information included in the system matrix (see Table 10.2). As we have noted (see Chapter 9), the MIC-MAC Analysis of the Formative Scenario Analysis can also be conceived of as a simple approach to a dynamic system, which uses models of finite automata. However, there is a discrete time structure and a special dynamics supposed.

A System Dynamics consideration usually includes the assessment of the effects of system changes (sensitivity). The discussion process leads to a new conception of the system and the case (Figure 10.1).

Advantages of System Dynamics

There are various advantages of System Dynamics in different fields of natural and social sciences. We will describe some important issues for case study research.

In ecology, there is a wide range of applications. Models for population dynamics and for water and substance dynamics in groundwater may serve as examples to illustrate which relations between the case and the modeling can be established. One crucial issue is the study team's motivation toward the case. In research, the predominant way of using cases is instrumental (see Table 2.1). In the extreme, the researcher formulates a model and then screens the universe for an appropriate case to demonstrate the coincidence of the theory and the case reality. In this approach, the predominant criterion of validation is how well the model fits the data. The opposite extreme is an intrinsic type of case study. In this approach, the case and the understanding of its dynamics are both the starting point and the target. The ETH-UNS case studies are intrinsic. The dominant criterion for validity is how much the study team's and the experts' case understanding is improved by the model and its application. In these studies, the development of new models is neither efficient nor manageable within the given time frame. However, it is possible to apply existing models and to use them, for example, for the calculation of scenarios and decision variants (see above).

In the social sciences, we will present only two typical ways of applying System Dynamics. First, in economics and game theory, the model case relations are similar to those identified in the natural sciences. Second, in the psychology of complex problem solving, we find another type of instrumental case study use. Highly structured cases (see Table 2.1) are designed in order to analyze the problem-solving ability for complex, dynamic problems (Dörner, Kreuzig, Reither, & Stäudel, 1994; Funke, 1999). Thus, in these psychological experiments, rather than real cases, highly structured virtual realities are investigated. The core message of this psychological research is that people are poor at assessing and understanding the nonlinear dynamics of a case. Although these results have been doubted because they are based on artificial models with the environmental settings removed, we consider these findings a motivation for the use of System Dynamics in the ETH-UNS case study. Because people are not good at both anticipating dynamics and predicting the effects of a single value within a system, System Dynamics helps to assess the temporal development of complex systems.

In ETH-UNS case studies, we repeatedly encountered unexpected low impacts of changes of a single variable. This mirrors the experience of simulation and gaming. Here, only a concerted change of several variables leads to success.

System Dynamics is used for the assessment of the future development of the case. It serves for a detailed, formal analysis of the possible case development. This may be necessary when the study team has only an intuitive, qualitative view into the future. System Dynamics can be conceived of as a means to prove one's own heuristics for doing prognoses. They may stem from all-day assessments and may not be able to assess correctly the complex interactions in a dynamic system.

Experience With System Dynamics in ETH-UNS Case Studies

The application of System Dynamics in the Zurich North case study was an important part of the synthesis conducted by the water management group. A water balance model was constructed to assess the water flows due to precipitation in the case of green roofing. This application is a typical example of a hard model. The soft model approach can be found in another ETH-UNS case study on construction and environment (Scholz et al., 1996).

In the Zurich North study, different hydrographs for the site were calculated. Each calculation was associated with an engineering project or variant. On one hand, each project included, for instance, a certain amount of green roofing in the area (control variable). On the other hand, each project was assumed to depend on certain boundary conditions, such as economic development, which has been assessed in a Formative Scenario Analysis (Chapter 9). The different engineering projects were then assessed using Multi-Attribute Utility Theory. Thus, the purpose of the model was not only to predict the dynamic behavior of the water flows in the case area, but also to develop and assess variants of hydraulic engineering measures under different realistic boundary conditions.

Like Formative Scenario Analysis, the System Dynamics model is descriptive (see Chapter 2) and requires that the cause-impact effects rely on known relationships. Note that the System Dynamics model can be based on results, such as the system graph, of Formative Scenario Analysis (see Chapter 9).

LESSONS TO BE LEARNED

▶ System Dynamics provides a case representation relying on a set of variables. In general, the variables describe different compartments and are defined under several disciplinary perspectives. This suggests a corresponding embedded design of case analysis.

▶ System Dynamics supports the assessment and the mental modeling of the dynamic behavior of complex systems. It corrects biased and fallacious anticipations of the temporal development of the case.

▶ In the ETH-UNS case studies, System Dynamics is intentionally used for synthesis. In particular, it integrates theoretical knowledge with empirical measurements and the various mental models of the case.

▶ System Dynamics goes far beyond applications in traditional natural sciences and includes industrial management and complex socioeconomic modeling of the real world.

▶ A valid model structure is crucial. One part of the structure of a System Dynamics model has to be derived from scientific principles. The other part must be determined by comparing the model behavior with measured data.

▶ System Dynamics modeling has to be supported by a model moderator. This model moderator should know the special language of System Dynamics and the limits of the System Dynamics tool.

THE METHOD IN DETAIL

System Dynamics modeling has been characterized by many authors (e.g., Bossel, 1994; Hannon & Ruth, 1994; Roberts, Andersen, Deal, Garet, & Shaffer, 1994; Ruth & Hannon, 1997), most of whom concentrate on the system analysis approach. We will explain the most important aspects of System Dynamics modeling within six levels (see Figure 10.2 and Table 10.1). Because System Dynamics is one of several possible conceptions of the case, our focus is on the relation between the system and the case and on the chances and constraints of System Dynamics modeling within the realization of the case study. The six levels introduced (see Figure 10.2 and Table 10.1) correspond to the steps given by Roberts et al. (1994):

1. *Problem Level:* Problem definition and modeling purposes

2. *Model Level:* System conceptualization using different languages

3. *Implementation Level:* Model representation

4. *Case Data Level:* Model behavior

5. *Application Level:* Model evaluation

6. *Management Level:* Policy analysis and model use

Each level has to provide a product that answers a specific question. These products and the corresponding questions are given in Table 10.1.

Problem Level: Problem Definition and Modeling Purposes

In the initial phase of the case study, the synthesis group has to determine the purpose of the synthesis, and, if System Dynamics is going to be applied, it has to check three questions:

1. What does modeling contribute to the synthesis?

2. Is System Dynamics the right method?

3. What can we do with the model?

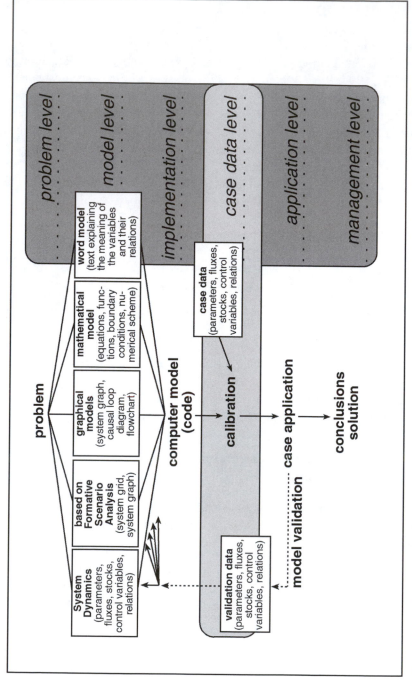

Figure 10.2. System Dynamics Levels

NOTE: See Table 10.1.

Table 10.1 Important Aspects of System Dynamics Modeling

Level	Starting Question	Hints	Product	Evaluation
Problem	What is the problem to be solved? What are the model purposes?	Quantities varying over time? Causal forces? Closed system of feedback loops?	Problem formulation, a list of questions to be answered	Is the expected solution of the problem interesting? Does it support the synthesis? In what way?
Model	Which are the important elements and influences?	Graphical models, mathematical model, word model, model expressed in System Dynamics language	Model concept, conception of the case	Is the model concept consistent? Does it describe a relevant aspect of the case?
Implementation	How can the important elements be put into the computer?	Software to solve ordinary differential equations (e.g., Stella®, Powersim®)	Computer program	Easy to apply? Comprehensible? Modules? Informative output? Manual?
Case data	Which case data can be used in which way to quantify the necessary parameters, initial conditions, and boundary conditions?	Calibration, parameter identification, model behavior, sensitivities	Calibrated program (model that works for the case)	Does the program give realistic output? Is the case realistically described? Is the output consistent with case development?
Application	What are the simulation results of the case? To what extent are the results justified?	Case application, simulations, model evaluation and validation	Validated program (model that works for all similar cases), a list of application cases	Is the model structure transferable to similar cases? Does it indicate a behavior due to general system structure?
Management	What is the solution to the problem? What recommendations have been investigated?	Definition and assessment of management alternatives	Policy analysis, application results, conclusions	General results? Applicable for case synthesis? Benefits for case agents?

NOTE: The column heads represent System Dynamics levels, their starting questions, hints for the corresponding answers, the desired product, and crucial questions for the evaluation of the intermediate products. The levels are explained in the subsections.

Contribution to the Synthesis

Modeling can be thought of as both a very specific type of synthesis and an embedded case design (see Chapter 4). Clearly, the philosophical strategy of contemplation (Zabarella; see Chapter 4) is not sufficient and usually results in inconsistencies, particularly if there is a quantitative access to the case, its structure, and its dynamics.

Sometimes, it is possible to apply generally accepted model structures (a pure case model in the Leibnizian sense) to the case. However, in real-world applications, the modeling has to be restricted to idealized systems, which deal with only a certain part of the case, such as the water compartment. As has been noted, this is done mostly on the subproject level and not on the level of synthesis (see Figure 4.1). This was the case for the water management group in the Zurich North study. Applying an existing model (Beins-Franke & Heeb, 1995), the hydrographs with and without the implementation of green roofs could be described. The results were that green roofs have very positive effects during stormflow events. Please note that such a model allows only for conditional inference. It allows thought experiments similar to those in Forrester's management laboratory. The model predicts the outcomes in the model world given hypothetical initial states and boundary conditions of the case. Clearly, the validity of the conclusions depends on how far the model represents the real case.

When synthesis is intended as a method for complex problem solving (Hegel), an additional integrating strategy is necessary. The water management group organized the synthesis in the following way. They calculated model results for four different scenarios, consisting of assumptions about the amount of future water use per inhabitant and day (130-170 liters per day per person), and four variants, consisting of different levels of control variables that describe hydraulic engineering measures such as the percentage of green roofs and the use of gray water. Subsequently, 16 calculations could be used for economic and multiattribute utility evaluations. The main conclusion was that the alternative use of gray water, rainwater, and green roofs is ecologically and economically positive, but it lacks application because wastewater costs are allocated to the use of drinking water, which results in misleading price signals.

The specific contribution to the synthesis may be shown in a Brunswikian Lens model (Figure 10.1). It is clear that knowledge integration, achieved by System Dynamics, is primarily the integration of disciplines (see Box 7.1). Often, this integration is organized according to "classical" systems such as water, air, soil, and anthroposphere and creates a new single system. For the most part, soft and hard components can be integrated into the model. Sometimes, mental models do have a significant relevance within the modeling process. Different interests may be included by the determination of control variables or goals (Roberts et al., 1994) that, for example, control the desired amount of water in a reservoir.

Selecting the Method

To answer the question "Is System Dynamics the right method?" the case has to provide the following:

- Quantitative variables, which vary over time
- Relations between the impact variables, which may be described by cause-and-effect relations
- A closed system of feedback loops

Operating With the Model

A System Dynamics model can be used for (a) the analysis of time series or trajectories, (b) sensitivity analysis, (c) scenario assessment, (d) assessment of management variants, (e) structure investigation, (f) model analysis, (g) risk assessment and evaluation, and (h) construction and assessment of possible future system states.

Time Series or Trajectories. The most frequent purpose is to calculate the trajectories of the variables in order to assess the dynamic behavior of the system.

Sensitivity Analysis. The sensitivity analysis consists of a systematic variation of impact variables in order to assess the resulting direction and magnitude of system change.

Assessment of Future System States. The target of this step is to investigate future system states, which are derived from consistent sets of assumptions (see Chapter 9). The consistency is determined according to Step 8 of the Formative Scenario Analysis (Chapter 9). Please note that in modeling, a scenario analysis is often applied as a special form of sensitivity analysis (see above).

Assessment of Management Variants. In general, case agents have different possibilities to influence the case development. The management variants can be arranged according to a simple nominal or continuous variation of a single variable, or they can rely on a complex variation of several variables controlled by one or more agents. If there is more than one agent involved, the study team may be confronted with a complex, dynamic situation. Then, the application of System Dynamics may become too complex, and a game theoretic framework is necessary (see Chapter 13).

Structure Investigation. The task of the structure investigation is to check whether all state variables or modules are necessary or whether additional variables or system modules have to be introduced. This should be organized as a test of hypotheses, such as "Do the attitudes toward ecology or the legal framework have a relevant influence on the system development and, hence, on the case management?" The procedure is somewhat similar to the calibration and validation procedure of the system model (see below). Therefore, any constraints due to the availability of test data apply here as well.

Model Analysis. One of the most prominent results of dynamic system modeling is the characterization of the case dynamics. This conveys whether the case reacts slowly or quickly, predictably or in a chaotic way. The reader is referred to the literature on stable or unstable equilibria, bifurcations, and chaos (Devaney, 1989; Verhulst, 1990).

Risk Assessment and Evaluation. The results of the model can be a salient part of Integrated Risk Management (see Chapter 12) or an application of Multi-Attribute Utility Theory (see Chapter 11). For this, the study team has to consider not only the uncertainty associated with the model results, but also the corresponding perception by the decision maker.

Construction and Assessment of Possible Future System States. In addition to the above-mentioned model purposes, System Dynamics can also be used to investigate qualitative future images that may result from

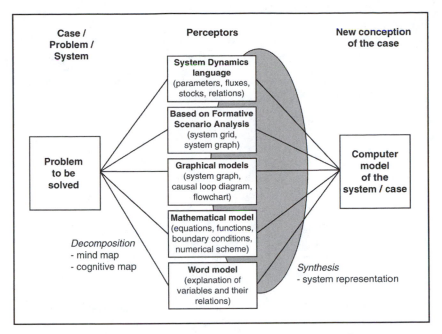

Figure 10.3. Techniques for Conceptualizing and Representing the System Model

Future Workshops (see Chapter 14). The objective is to explore whether a certain image can become reality or whether the assumptions underlying a certain vision are not realistic, or, even more, to discover constraints and rules for the construction of such images.

Model Level: System Model Representations

There are several techniques to conceptualizing and representing the system model (see Figure 10.3). In any case, the parameters, fluxes, stocks, and relations have to be represented by paper and pencil or in the computer. Steps 1 to 3 of Formative Scenario Analysis (Chapter 9) provide a proven procedure for an encompassing assessment of these variables. Note that Formative Scenario Analysis also presents certain aspects of the system structure by means of graphical representations, such as the system grid and the system graph. Other graphical representations, such as the causal loop diagram, are typical for System Dynamics. The traditional way to represent the system model is to specify the mathematical

---

Box 10.2   Key Definitions for System Dynamics and Its Relation to Formative Scenario Analysis

---

In the System Dynamics model, $\dot{y} = f(y) = f(y, p, c)$, hence, in this case, a system of first-order, ordinary differential equations.

$\dot{y}$ is the vector of derivatives $\dot{y} = \begin{pmatrix} \frac{dy_i}{dt} \\ \vdots \\ \frac{dy_n}{dt} \end{pmatrix}$, $f(y) = \begin{pmatrix} f_1(y) \\ \vdots \\ f_n(y) \end{pmatrix}$ is a vector

function that specifies for each compartment y_i, $i = 1 \ldots n$, the rate of change depending on the system state y, the parameter vector $p = (p_1, \ldots, p_m)$, and the vector of control parameters $c = (c_1, \ldots, c_k)$.

If the function f is required to be linear and homogeneous, then the model equation reduces to $\dot{y} = A \cdot y$ because $f(y) = Ay + B$ with $B = 0$. The $n \times n$-Matrix A substitutes for both the parameter vector p and the vector of control parameters c. The coefficients $a_{i,j}$ of A describe the rate of change of y_i that is due to the level of y_j.

The differences between this Matrix A and the impact matrix defined in Formative Scenario Analysis are summarized in Table 10.2. Hence, if an impact matrix is given, if the direction of the impacts and a self-impact is considered, if the unit changes from impact strength to a rate of change, and if the scale of the corresponding variables is extended, then a linear System Dynamics matrix emerges, which can be considered an extension of the impact matrix. Please note which kind of information is additionally necessary for System Dynamics relative to a Formative Scenario Analysis.

---

equations (see Box 10.2). In either case, the description of the variables and their interrelations with text—a *word model*—is a prerequisite for working with the model and communicating the results.

We aim only to roughly describe core elements of System Dynamics and how to proceed in its application (for a more detailed explanation, see Bossel, 1994; Roberts et al., 1994). As demonstrated in Box 10.3, the application often starts with qualitative knowledge like "the larger the number of births, the larger the population," and displays this graphically in causal loop diagrams that include the exact definition of the elements. In subsequent steps, these diagrams are then further refined by the quantification of each element and by a change into flow diagrams, which describe the model more formally and with more detail, and are therefore used for model implementation.

Table 10.2 Differences Between the Matrix of a Linear,
             Homogeneous Dynamic System and the
             Impact Matrix Defined in Chapter 9

	Impact matrix	System matrix
Direction of impact	Neglected (assumed positive)	Included (positive or negative)
Self-impact	Not included	Included
Unit	Impact strength	Rate of change
Linearity	Linear	Linear (simplification of nonlinear function, not necessarily homogeneous)
Scale	Ordinal scale Finite number of levels	Interval scale Infinite, unbounded

Implementation Level: Computer Model

Generally, in computer programs such as the famous DYNAMO compiler, Stella®, Powersim®, and RAMSES (Fischlin, 1991), the elements of
the System Dynamics language are coded graphically.[1] A window interface shows only the model concept, which consists of the model structure
with stocks, variables, fluxes, and control variables that all can be
changed and supplemented by using the mouse. Clicking on variables or
relations opens a new window to input the relations. For example, Stella®
provides tabular functions, stepwise linear functions, or nonlinear functions. The results are calculated numerically and presented simultaneously as time series on the screen.

Please note that not every program allows for the treatment of any differential equation. In general, such problems do not arise when applying
System Dynamics for management purposes.

Case Data Level: Model Behavior and Calibration

After the model has been implemented into the software, the parameters of the model have to be specified. Within System Dynamics, the parameters are the constants of the model, which do not vary during the time
of simulation. In contrast are state variables, which vary during the simulation and characterize the system state at each point in time. The procedure to identify the parameters of the model is called *calibration*.

Box 10.3   Causal Feedback Loops

The construction of causal feedback loops is characteristic for System Dynamics. Figure 10.4 shows a causal loop diagram for a population model and has been adopted from the world model (Meadows et al., 1974). A causal loop diagram consists of elements such as population, births, deaths, fertility, and life expectancy that are connected with signed arrows. An arrow signifies that a change in the element at its tail causes a change in the element at its head. A plus sign at the head of an arrow indicates that these changes are in the same direction (e.g., if the population increases, the number of births will increase as well). A minus sign indicates that the changes of the elements at the tail and the head of an arrow are in the opposite direction (e.g., if the number of deaths increases, the population will decrease). Please note that if a decrease of one element (e.g., the number of births) causes a decrease of another element (e.g., the population), the causal impact is represented by a positive signed arrow because the changes are in the same direction.

A causal feedback loop may consist of several (two or more) causal influences, each represented by a single arrow. The causal feedback loop is called positive when all of the arrows indicate changes in the same direction. The population and the births (see Figure 10.4) build such a positive causal feedback loop, indicated by ↺. In such positive feedback loops, the changes are mutually reinforced and hence may lead to a drastic increase or decrease (e.g., the exponential growth of a population). In a negative feedback loop, the changes in the elements counteract. In the negative feedback loop, indicated by ↻ in Figure 10.4, an increase in population leads to more deaths, but a larger number of deaths will decrease the population. This illustrates that to some extent, such loops stabilize the system.

A causal loop diagram specifies the substructure of the model. It may contain a small or large number of causal feedback loops. Experienced scientists can read such diagrams qualitatively and possibly can assess the dynamic behavior characterized by the positive or negative feedback loops. Figure 10.4 shows a causal loop diagram containing a positive and a negative causal loop, which depend on the fertility and the life expectancy, respectively. That biological, social, and economic factors also influence the system is, for simplicity, only indicated here. The population sector is only a submodel of the World3 model. The main part of this submodel is, of course, to describe *how* the indicated factors influence the population dynamic.

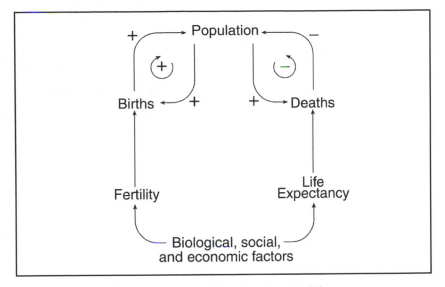

Figure 10.4. Causal Loop Diagram for a Population Model
NOTE: Adopted from the World Model (Meadows et al., 1974).

Calibration means measuring the parameters and checking the coincidence of (a) model predictions with corresponding measurements, and (b) the resulting trajectories with the trajectories that were expected. There are different kinds of data necessary for the model calibration.

• *Constants:* Generally, there is a surprisingly long list of constants, such as flow rates, size of reservoirs, and so on, that are necessary for the simulation. Some of these constants have a low influence on system behavior and therefore are allowed to be rather inaccurate. Other constants, or special combinations of constants, determine the trajectories and must be specified with great accuracy.

• *Initial conditions:* Dynamic simulation must have a well-defined starting point. For each of the state variables, an initial value has to become specified. These values can be subject to calculations in the sense that only conditions that define these values are given.

• *Boundary conditions:* The exchange of the system with its environment is defined as a set of boundary conditions. These may be constants, such as a constant leaching coefficient of the water model, or conditions that evaluate the exchange of the system depending on the system state, such as the overflow of a reservoir.

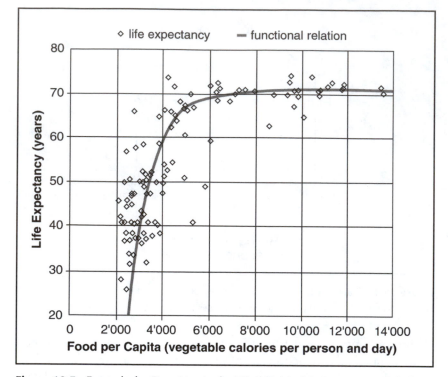

Figure 10.5. Example for Data Use in the World3 Model: Data From Global Statistics and Their Approximation

• *Functional relations:* The relations between the state variables are often given as functional relationships. Figure 10.5 shows an example of a functional relation between two state variables, nutrition energy and life expectancy, adopted from the world model (Meadows et al., 1974). It is essential for System Dynamics to have ideas to define such kinds of functional relations.

• *Test data:* The comparison of the first simulation results with test data shows whether or not the model gives the desired output with sufficient accuracy. As a consequence, it may be necessary to make changes to the model concept and recalculate new model results.

Application Level: Validation Checks

There are two modes of validity testing.

• *Construct validity* is shown if the elements of the System Dynamics model are valid. This is particularly true when the model structure corresponds to the system structure and when the driving forces of the case correspond to the driving forces included in the model. For example, the latter may be true for (a) a physical law, such as energy conservation; (b) a simple relationship for which the validity is evident; or (c) another element for which the validity was already shown scientifically.

• *Predictive validity* is shown if the model is able to predict independent observations. The validity can be calculated as a statistical measure, such as the root of the mean square error. This includes the calculation of confidence limits. The difference between upper and lower limits will grow increasingly larger the more the predictions proceed into the future.

For the ETH-UNS case studies, construct validity is the preferred concept because the investigation of predictive validity often lacks data to test the model performance using an independent data set. In rare cases, a model is available for which this case would be the independent data set. If enough data were available for the case, a predictive validation on a separate period would be possible.

The difference between calibration on the case data level and validation is the transferability to another case. Because there is no test of uniqueness, different model structures may adequately describe the calibration data, but "wrong" models will fail when they are transferred to other, similar cases. The idea of construct validity is that if the elements of the model are valid and validly combined, no "wrong" models can be created. The idea of predictive validity is that if a model can be applied to many cases, the model must be considered valid. Within the ETH-UNS case study, construct validity is decisive. We are interested in the model-case relation. Therefore, we are investigating whether a model, calibrated for a given time period, can be used to draw conclusions about the future.

Management Level: Policy Analysis and Model Use

Dynamic system modeling may be used to approach several different objectives, such as forecasting, prediction, and theory testing. Within the ETH-UNS case study approach, similar to what was proposed by Forrester (1961), the main focus is on case management. Within a System Dynamics management laboratory, the study team may conduct a single experiment or develop and evaluate complex decision alternatives.

Within the ETH-UNS case study Zurich North, the management alternatives were four different variants, V_1 to V_4, to control the water budget of the area. These variants were combined with four scenarios, S_1 to S_4, for the boundary conditions. Thus, we have the same situation as in Figure 9.4. The scenarios were as follows:

- S_1 *Economy:* People change their minds, sustainability and nature gain much interest, the booming economy supplies innovative water technologies, the administration supports its implementation, and the water use in the region decreases.

- S_2 *Crisis:* The economic situation is bad, and innovative water use-reducing technologies are not developed, supported, or implemented. Mainly, people have to obey their own economic interests, which leaves little space for ecological aspects.

- S_3 *New Concepts:* The economic situation is bad, but everyone has to pay for his or her own amount of water used. Therefore, water use declines mainly because of financial pressure rather than ecological reasons.

- S_4 *Experts:* Experts estimated that the price for drinking water would remain near the current level. Other water characteristics also exhibit little change. Economic growth declines a little.

Management variants were characterized by three control variables: the percentage of green roofs realized in the area, the amount of gray water use, and the renaturation of a small river. Four variants were developed that were possible measures to control the water budget of the area. They can be characterized as follows:

- V_1 *Maximum:* Maximum percentage of green roofs, maximum use of gray water, renaturation of a small river
- V_2 *Minimum:* Minimum percentage of green roofs, minimum use of gray water
- V_3 *Innovative:* Mean percentage of green roofs, large use of gray water
- V_4 *Mean:* Mean percentage of green roofs, low use of gray water

For each combination of a scenario and a variant, the water budget model calculated results to be used in the multi-attribute utility evaluation. It was possible to conclude that a high percentage of green roofs cuts the enormous water fluxes that are the consequence of strong precipitation; the model also showed—through the calculation of the net present value of the alternatives—that the green roofs are economically attractive as well.

Please note that there are two kinds of control information used in the model. The first kind is the boundary conditions. Within the Zurich North case study, and in many other cases as well, it was quite uncertain whether the current boundary conditions would hold for a longer period of time. Because of this, a Formative Scenario Analysis (see Chapter 9) was applied in order to specify reasonable boundary conditions for the model. The second kind of control information depends on local management decisions. The case agents are faced with a prospect of alternatives (e.g., the percentage of green roofs realized in the area) that have specific impacts on the model system.

It is necessary for the System Dynamics model to be capable of simulating both different boundary conditions and different decision variants. Note that for each scenario or set of boundary conditions of the model, if the model evaluates another optimal management strategy (set of control variables), the results can pose a difficult decision problem. In this case, the minimax principle (Savage, 1972) or another decision strategy (see von Neumann & Morgenstern, 1943; Yoon & Hwang, 1995) are required.

LESSONS TO BE LEARNED

▶ System Dynamics is a formative method that integrates six levels: problem level, model level, model implementation level, case data level, application level, and management level.

▶ If there is enough knowledge or data available, the method is a powerful tool for attaining improved case understanding. The value of the case understanding and the validity of System Dynamics depend on both an appropriate system structure and case data.

▶ Several representations support the development of the model: the System Dynamics language, tools from Formative Scenario Analysis, graphical representations, the mathematical model formulation, and the word model.

▶ The developed models are management oriented.

NOTE

1. Please note that the specified System Dynamics software packages are only a few examples, and many others are available. Additional information can be found for Stella® at www.hps-inc.com; for PowerSim® at www.powersim.com; and for RAMSES at www.ito.umnw.ethz.ch/SysEcol/SimSoftware/SimSoftware. html.

11

MULTI-ATTRIBUTE UTILITY THEORY

THE RATIONALE

Multi-Attribute Utility Theory (MAUT) is a label for a family of methods. These methods are a means to analyzing situations and creating an evaluation process. The objective of MAUT is to attain a conjoint measure of the attractiveness (utility) of each outcome of a set of alternatives. Thus, the method is recommended when prospective alternatives must be evaluated to determine which alternative performs best.

The evaluation process encompasses both analytic decomposition and synthesis. MAUT decomposes the overall attractiveness (von Winterfeldt & Edwards, 1986) of an alternative into a number of attributes. Attributes are preference-related dimensions of a system. System variables, such as CO_2 emission or the number of students finishing with a high grade, can become attributes in the evaluation process. But preference measures, such as quality, aesthetics, or cognitive salience, which are not necessarily considered system variables, can also become attributes. If all alternatives have been rated according to all the attributes, MAUT composes the ratings and organizes a synthesis resulting in a one-dimensional utility measure.

This makes it possible to adequately describe important properties of highly complex cases by means of the attributes and their utility for the decision maker. On the other hand, different importance weights (von

Winterfeldt & Edwards, 1986) are included to provide trade-offs between (the utilities of) the attributes. The functional relationship between the system variables, their utility, and the weighting of the attributes depends on individual representations and subjective values. The MAUT method may be used to characterize different stakeholders to support the negotiation of different interests (see Chapter 13) by means of making different stakeholders' evaluation processes explicit, transparent, and comprehensible.

The application of MAUT may answer several important questions:

- What is the specific structure of the case evaluation? How are the different evaluation criteria integrated?
- Which part of an evaluation should be substantiated by a scientific assessment, and which part should rely on individual preferences?
- What are the preferences of the most important stakeholders?
- Which misperceptions or pitfalls may be found in the evaluation and decisions of the case agents?

Historical Background

The development of the Multi-Attribute Utility Theory is associated with the work of von Neumann and Morgenstern (1943), Savage (1972), and Fishburn (1988). Keeney and Raiffa (1976), as well as von Winterfeldt and Edwards (1986), helped in the breakthrough for the general acceptance of MAUT, particularly when demonstrating the power of the methods in complex, real-world planning projects (von Winterfeldt, 1978). Furthermore, there were many applications, particularly in economics.

The use of MAUT was accompanied by different philosophies and conceptions about decision support, ranging from information sampling support through decision aid to expert systems. The constructors enthusiastically appreciated the models. Some of the modelers obviously believed that a one-to-one mapping exists between the model structure and the real evaluation. From this position, no entire breakthrough has been attained.

The implementation problem is an overall demanding affair. The history of MAUT applications has shown that five issues should be present in order to understand why and when an application of MAUT will have a high probability of success or why and when it fails. When applying MAUT, the study team should have the following:

1. Sufficient problem/system/case knowledge, in order to realize whether decisive attributes have been overlooked, are not well-defined (depend on each other), or overlap

2. A user model that describes what the user knows, which questions he or she is able to answer, and which interests may bias his or her evaluations

3. Knowledge about the appropriate level of graininess—in particular, preventing the application of an overly detailed or aggregated procedure

4. Good acceptance from the applicants, a relationship free of mistrust that allows the fear of being instrumentalized or of losing control of oneself when participating in a computer-controlled session to be overcome

5. Suitable technology, including a convenient, robust, user-friendly computer interface and an appropriate algorithm for modeling the evaluation

In our opinion, the missing breakthrough in the 1970s and 1980s lies in a too-narrow technological perspective from the proponents of MAUT. Or, to formulate it more pointedly, the model builders focused only on the MAUT computer technology and believed that their model would be accepted automatically if it was theoretically sound and plausible. This position was subject to controversial scientific discussions that disputed concurring theoretical approaches.

Two camps can be identified: The larger one is utility oriented and postulates a one-dimensional utility function that exists independent of any alternative. The main proponents are Fishburn (1988), Keeney and Raiffa (1976), and von Winterfeldt and Edwards (1986). The smaller, mostly francophone school's modeling relies on an inductive procedure. A utility function is not a priori postulated, but, for a given set of alternatives, a utility function (outranking degree) is established based on comparisons of the attributes of each pair of alternatives (outranking approach). Two of the main proponents of the second school are Roy (1991) and Vincke (1992). The problem with this approach is that the utility functions depend on the set of alternatives considered, and the preference between two alternatives can change if new alternatives are introduced.

A specific position has to be attributed to Saaty (1990), who developed the analytical hierarchy process as a closed theoretical framework, postulating that the attributes are ordered by decision tree-like structures.

It seems that today, there is a more relaxed handling of multicriteria decision-making tools (Yoon & Hwang, 1995), and that case-related and user-specific issues such as those listed earlier are taken into account, as has already been suggested by Humphreys and Wisudha (1989).

As the title of this chapter indicates, this book concentrates on the utility approach.

Attribute Rating and Attribute Weighting

Utility serves as a subjective measure for the attractiveness of the outcomes (consequences) of an alternative (von Winterfeldt & Edwards, 1986). The alternatives exhibit partial utilities with respect to each of the different attributes. The attributes are aspects that are considered relevant for the evaluation. They may be considered objectively measurable, such as costs or concentration of contaminants in the groundwater, or they may be assessed subjectively, by the people's perception (e.g., the aesthetic value of a landscape). In all instances, each attribute has two functions: It is part of the case description, and it is part of the perception of the agent who evaluates.

The construction of the multi-attribute utility evaluation is shown in Figure 11.1. State variables of the case are the origin. These variables constitute different attributes that are transformed to the utility (attractiveness value) scale and then aggregated to calculate the overall utility using a composition rule. Please note that the composition rule specified in Figure 11.1 is a very simple example. The application of MAUT is much more encompassing, because each step shown in Figure 11.1 establishes a process with several substeps.

The starting point for a decision analysis is defining the problem, the objectives, the system under consideration (Figure 11.1), and the people whose evaluations are going to be investigated, all of which influences the possible results of the application. The next important step is to define which alternatives are available in the decision situation or which states of a case shall be evaluated alternatively. Then, the alternatives have to be described by characteristic attributes (system variables describing the system state) (see Figure 11.2). Those variables that may be relevant for the evaluation and are different for the alternatives will be taken as attributes. To be realistic, the set of attributes has to be sufficient, relevant, and available with respect to the objectives. These attributes may be determined by a scientific assessment, such as the measurement of the concentration of a

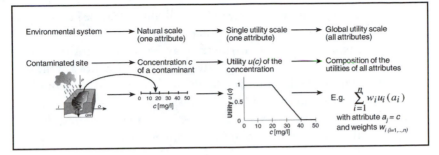

Figure 11.1. Construction of the Overall Utility of an Alternative

SOURCE: Adapted from von Winterfeldt and Edwards (1986).

NOTE: This process needs four steps. The starting point is the case, such as an environmental system. From its model, certain variables or issues relevant for evaluation are selected (von Winterfeldt & Edwards, 1986). Then, the utility (attractiveness value) of the selected variables is specified. Finally, the different utilities have to be aggregated.

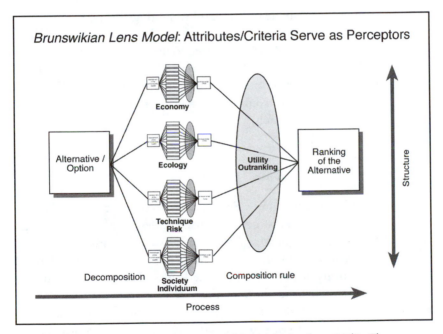

Figure 11.2. The Brunswikian Lens Model for Multi-Attribute Utility Theory

NOTE: The analytic decomposition of the environmental system describes the alternatives using the attributes as perceptors. The synthesis consists of the composition (aggregation) of the single utilities of the attributes into the overall utility of the alternatives. This process provides both a better understanding of the environmental system and a more detailed description of the alternatives and their evaluation.

contaminant in a groundwater extraction well. But it may be necessary to assess some attributes within the evaluation process. This is especially true when it is unclear which attributes may be relevant for the stakeholders, or when they represent subjectively perceived qualities of the system, such as the aesthetic value of a landscape. For the assessment of attributes, various techniques will be introduced below.

When the problem has been decomposed into the attributes, the following questions remain to obtain the overall evaluation:

1. How can the alternatives be rated validly and reliably with respect to the attributes?

2. How should the utilities of the attributes (single utilities) be assessed, and in what manner?

3. How should the weights be assessed?

4. How should the single utilities and weightings be aggregated?

For each of these questions, many possible solutions exist, some of which are going to be described in the following pages (see The Method in Detail section), including a description of some computational tools. The solutions are based on methods from empirical social research, cognitive psychology, and decision research.

Normative, Prescriptive, and Descriptive Approaches

MAUT can be used in either a descriptive or a normative way. Within the descriptive approach, the method is used to describe the actual structure and process of an evaluation performed by an individual, group, or organization. Within the normative approach, the evaluation is derived from general norms or prescribed by fixed rules. The target is to define how a decision should be made. Sometimes, a distinction between normative and prescriptive models is introduced. Normative models should be cohesive, rational, and free of contradictions, as in rational choice theory. On the other hand, prescriptive approaches have engineerlike rules of thumb. They may not be free of contradiction, nor may they have the status of a norm—an ethical and/or socially accepted regulatory rule.

We will illustrate the differences between the normative, prescriptive, and descriptive approaches by an example from the Zurich North case study. The overall target of the study was the sustainable development of the case. Sustainability can be considered a societal norm for which generally accepted verbal (but no quantitative) definitions exist. Hence, experts in sustainable development can and must define attributes for the evaluation. The attributes and their quantitative definitions cannot be derived directly from the overall principle of sustainability or from a set of axioms, but from normlike rules that apply for each attribute separately. Note that the definition of the attributes and their quantification are accompanied by a switch from the normative to the prescriptive proceeding. For example, from an environmental perspective, the form of energy (renewable or not renewable) is regarded as a crucial attribute for system maintenance (see Chapter 3). Hence, to use renewable resources rather than fossil energy may be a prescriptive rule of thumb. A descriptive approach would be used if the attributes and weights of laypeople or politicians were sampled.

Discourse Processing With MAUT

MAUT can be used as a kind of evaluation language. This may be helpful in dispute resolutions (see Chapter 13) because it allows comparisons among what people do, what people want to do, and what they should do. A special discourse is given if a study team tries to improve evaluations of case members. A common situation occurs when a case member wants to evaluate a planning alternative and has conveyed an attribute highly important from his or her point of view (e.g., the economic outcomes of a remediation alternative). However, the detailed knowledge of how to assess this alternative is not yet available. The study team discovers this and tries to substantiate, correct, or unbias the assessment by empirical data or scientific results.

LESSONS TO BE LEARNED

▶ MAUT is a suitable tool if an evaluation for alternatives (for case development) is desired and no salient, agreed-on evaluation criteria are available.

▶ Knowledge integration in MAUT is organized in multiple ways, such as by linking the system knowledge to the evaluation criteria and by integrating attributes from different compartments and disciplines.

▶ MAUT supports the analysis of decision situations, makes them transparent and comprehensible, and allows the comparison of judgments of different agents.

▶ There are normative, prescriptive, and descriptive approaches to applying MAUT.

THE METHOD IN DETAIL

The following steps have to be considered when applying MAUT:

- Analysis of the decision situation
- Conditions and goals of the MAUT application
- Inquiry of existing evaluative structures
- Hierarchy of attributes
- The alternatives vs. attributes matrix
- Utility functions
- Importance weights and preferences
- Composition rules
- Evaluation and discussion

The reader should note the formal definitions of the multi-attribute utility situation (Box 11.1) to which we refer throughout this chapter. By means of illustration, we refer to applications in the ETH-UNS case study Zurich North. See Table 11.1 for a summary of the characteristics of these applications with respect to the objectives and to the last five steps above.

Step 1: The Case as a Decision Situation

In the beginning, one of the keys to gaining information from the multi-attribute utility analysis is analyzing and characterizing the decision situation. This involves (a) the definition of the system to be

---

| **Box 11.1** | Formal Definition of the Multi-Attribute Utility Situation |

The situation of multi-attribute utility decomposition may be formally characterized by the following:

- The set of (decision) alternatives $A = (A_1, \ldots, A_i, \ldots, A_n)$
- The set of attributes (criteria) $c = (c_1, \ldots, c_j, \ldots, c_m)$, which may be sorted hierarchically (the attributes are the leaves of a tree, with the overall goal as the stem and subgoals as branches)
- The alternatives vs. attributes matrix $M_{i,j}$ $(i = 1, \ldots, n; j = 1, \ldots, m)$, $M_{i,j} = c_j(A_i)$
- The set of utility functions $U = (u_1, \ldots, u_j, \ldots, u_m)$, $u_j = f[c_j(A_i)]$ that enters one not necessarily linear and continuous function for each attribute
- The set of importance weights $W = (w_1, \ldots, w_j, \ldots, w_m)$
- The composition rule, which is a function F of the vectors W and U:

$$U(A_i) = F(W, U(c(A_i))) = F(W, U(M_{i, \bullet}))$$

The composition may, as in many cases, be simple and linear, such as the weighted sum of the utilities (so called additive utility):

$$U(A_i) = \sum_{j=1}^{m} w_j u_j (c_j(A_i)) = \sum_{j=1}^{m} w_j u_j (M_{i,j})$$

---

evaluated and the problem to be solved with respect to the boundary conditions (system constraints), (b) the personal decision framework, and (c) possible alternatives and their consequences.

The most critical point is the personal decision framework. This framework encompasses most of what has been called the user model. The personal decision framework is characterized by the following questions:

- Who evaluates?
- Why does he or she evaluate?
- What is the overall task that builds the framework of the evaluation?
- What are the problem constraints?
- What is the knowledge basis of his or her evaluation? What additional means can he or she use to obtain a good evaluation?
- What are the personal consequences of the evaluation?

Table 11.1 Characteristics of the Multi-Attribute Utility Applications in Different Study Teams in the Zurich North Case Study

Topic	Synthesis Group			
	Parks and Green Areas	Soil Contamination	Water Management	Mobility and Transportation
Objectives	Describing differences between five stakeholder groups and their evaluation of the planning	Valuation of four remediation alternatives	Valuation of future system states depending on four scenarios and four sets of control variables	Evaluation of the sustainability of traffic models (i.e., estimated future states of the traffic system)
Hierarchy of attributes	Eight attributes on one level	Ten attributes on two levels	Ten attributes on three levels	Thirteen attributes on two levels
Data acquisition, alternatives vs. attributes matrix	Attributes generated by the repertory grid method, assessment of attributes of three alternatives and elaborated by the synthesis group on a scale from 1 to 9	Quantitative criteria calculated by life cycle assessment, qualitative criteria estimated by the synthesis group on a scale from −1 to 3	Two assumptions given by the synthesis group and eight variables of a dynamic system model	Qualitative estimations by the synthesis group and quantitative calculations, based partly on standard traffic evaluation indicators
Utility functions	Automatically generated by the program MAUD (Humphreys & Wisudha, 1989), generally linear	Linear utility functions, convex and concave utility functions representing different future boundary conditions	(Piecewise) Linear utility functions constructed by the synthesis group in strong cooperation with three experts	Linear utility functions, calculated by critical loads (levels) for sustainability, a standard quantitative scale, or direct definition through the synthesis group
Importance weights and preferences	Assessment using the hypothetical alternatives method of MAUD, weights given by several representatives of stakeholder groups	Computer-aided data sampling using LOGICAL DECISIONS®, weights given by the synthesis group	Computer-aided data sampling using LOGICAL DECISIONS®, weights given by the experts and by the study team	Weights between 1 and 5 have been supplied by the synthesis group for both hierarchy levels
Composition rule, calculation, and presentation	Simple weighted sum of utilities, mean weights calculated for each stakeholder group, cluster analysis and comparison with parallel investigation methods	Simple weighted sum of utilities, calculation of mean weights for each of the assumed future boundary conditions	Simple weighted sum of utilities; mean weights calculated for the experts, the tutors, and the synthesis group; comparison with a net present value calculation	Simple weighted sum of utilities applied to both hierarchy levels

If there are no clear answers to these questions, fundamental misunderstandings will probably arise, particularly in the communication within the study team, between the study team and the applicants, and between the study team and those who want to use the results. These misunderstandings will make it impossible to conduct the evaluation and to interpret and present the results.

Within the ETH-UNS case study Zurich North, possible remediation techniques for contaminated sites have been evaluated using MAUT. The system was a plot of land, the *Stierenried,* a former swamp, which was subsequently filled with waste material that resulted from industrial production, demolition, and gardening activities. There was a health risk to people intending to live or work there, as well as a risk of groundwater contamination (especially because of the short distance to the aquifer). The personal decision framework was defined as follows.

- *Who:* As the owner of the area, the Asea Brown and Boveri Company (ABB) (see Chapter 5) had to decide on the best remediation technology, which had to be accepted by the responsible officials.

- *Why:* ABB wanted to actualize an engineering building and a production facility, and it had to comply with the regulations of the water protection and maintenance administration of the Canton Zurich.

- *Problem constraints:* ABB had to obey the *Gestaltungsplan* (i.e., municipal construction obligations) for this area and incorporate financial and environmental interests. Furthermore, the standards set by the cantonal authorities had to be fulfilled.

- *Knowledge:* The decision is based on the site report provided by an environmental consulting bureau. It investigated the contamination of both the soil and the groundwater. Further consulting was provided by the cantonal authorities (administrative guidelines for the treatment of contaminated sites).

- *Consequences:* Financial and political consequences were expected. The inhabitants and the administration showed high sensitivity, especially because the area is part of a large, ambitious, and prominent project of city development in Zurich.

The possible alternatives have been identified as capping (i.e., installing a waterproof coverage), soil washing, or water leaching with subsequent treatment. Very different consequences were expected for these alternatives, at least with respect to sustainability, costs, and time for the remediation. Initially, a qualitative assessment was performed by ABB. On the basis of this example, the synthesis group Soil Contamination of the Zurich North case study decided to investigate whether a sustainable treatment of contaminated sites is possible. The group took the role of the owner and used a multi-attribute utility approach to evaluate ABB's problem in order to optimize the process to making such decisions.

LESSONS TO BE LEARNED

▶ The first step—the analysis of the decision situation—includes system and problem definition, the personal decision framework, and possible alternatives.

▶ The personal decision framework should be examined carefully and described explicitly, because it is a prerequisite for a successful application of MAUT and an appropriate interpretation of the evaluation.

Step 2: Objectives of the MAUT Application

There are two main questions that have to be answered based on the analysis of the decision situation:

1. Is there a visible benefit to applying MAUT?

2. What are the goals of MAUT application?

The analysis of the decision situation (Step 1) may show that the decision is simple and that the best alternative can be obtained easily. In this case, a formal preference modeling with a multi-attribute utility approach is not necessary. In all instances, there must be legitimization for a MAUT procedure.

There is an essential distinction between the goals associated with the evaluation (What do the stakeholder want to achieve? See Step 1) and the goals of the study team (What is the reason for formal decision support using MAUT?). The goals of the study team can be the following:

- The investigation of the stakeholders' evaluative structure, their pitfalls, peculiarities, grouping, and so on (see synthesis group Parks and Green Areas).
- The communication of the decision situation as well as the most important attributes and their assessment (see synthesis group Soil Contamination)
- The introduction of a normative evaluation as a reference point for decisions or for a comparison with actual evaluations
- The combination of MAUT with a Formative Scenario Analysis and System Dynamics to look for possibly acceptable scenarios, as in the synthesis group Water Management

This list of possible objectives is far from being complete. These objectives approximate the scientific reasons for the investigation and define the product, which is intended at the end of the case study.

LESSONS TO BE LEARNED

▶ A normative evaluation, introduced and calculated by the study team, may serve as a reference point for decisions or for correcting and improving actual evaluations.

▶ MAUT should be applied only if a benefit is evident.

▶ The goals of the study team have to be defined explicitly and must be separated from the goals of the stakeholders (even if they largely coincide).

Step 3: Inquiry of Existing Evaluative Structures

Within the case studies, the evaluative structures underlying the individual or organizational decision making can be investigated by means of the following four techniques: questionnaire, interview, computer-aided data sampling, and focus groups (Greenbaum, 1998). These techniques may be used to sample all of the necessary information for the application of MAUT. The questions that can be investigated are as follows:

- What are the alternatives under consideration, and which properties do they exhibit with respect to the associated attributes? (Step 5)
- By which attributes can the evaluation be structured or modeled? (Step 4)
- Which scale best measures an attribute, and which utility function is associated with this scale? (Step 6)
- What significance (weights) do the clients allocate to the attributes? (Step 7)
- How are the alternatives and their properties, the attributes and their utility function, and the weights integrated into an overall evaluation? (Step 8)

In practice, not all of these questions are investigated empirically. For the most part, some of the questions can be answered by the study team. There is no general answer for which question has to be investigated in which detail. The depth of empirical analysis depends largely on how important the knowledge about the case agents' real evaluative structure is for the study team. If the emphasis is more on prescription, then this step is of more marginal importance.

Different information may be obtained by different techniques (see Figure 11.3 and Box 11.2). The structure of the attributes can be obtained with a focus group, whereas the preference of the case agents is best assessed using computer-aided data sampling.

LESSONS TO BE LEARNED

▶ If the study team is interested in analyzing conflicts between the case agents or suspects misperception, an empirical inquiry of existing evaluative structures is recommended.

▶ The study team has to decide which information it can supply, which information has to be investigated empirically, and which technique will be best for doing so.

▶ An inquiry into the evaluative structure of case agents can be made in accordance with the formal arrangements of MAUT.

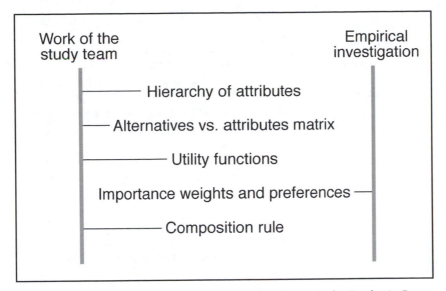

Figure 11.3. Application of Multi-Attribute Utility Theory in the Synthesis Group Parks and Green Areas

NOTE: Before the start of the multicriteria evaluation, the study team has to determine which parts it will predefine and which parts are subject to empirical investigation (e.g., within an *Exploration Parcour*. In the ETH-UNS case study Zurich North, within the group Parks and Green Areas, only the importance weights and preferences have been investigated empirically.

Step 4: Hierarchy of Attributes

Once the study team decides which parts it must predefine and which are subject to empirical investigation, it must then define the attributes. The study team has to decide whether a hierarchical organization of attributes is advantageous, appropriate, or necessary. If there are too many attributes, a hierarchical order is recommended. In this order, we find the attributes on the lowest level. Several attributes are subsumed under one (sub)goal if there is more than one level, and in this way, a hierarchical tree arises with the general or overall goal of the evaluation on top. Thus, an overall goal typically exists that can also serve as a starting point (in a top-down procedure).

On one level of the goal hierarchy, there should be three to seven different (sub)goals. In general, the study team must derive a sufficient set of

Box 11.2   Techniques of Inquiry

For assessing the evaluation empirically, we present the following techniques as an example (see also Box 2.1) and make reference to the investigation of evaluations.

Questionnaire: The questionnaire is often seen as an easy method of investigation, but the following issues have to be mastered:

1. The topic has to be decomposed into a clear, commonly acceptable structure. Unfortunately, such a structure or the knowledge of it sometimes does not exist.

2. Respondents should give their answers from a common perspective on the topic to allow for comparison between different evaluations. This requires an introduction that is capable of reminding people of the relevant aspects of the topic and that induces a common framing of the questionnaire session. Note that many people react very sensitively to certain formulations. Therefore, the introductory text, including its layout, has to be created very carefully and with considerable knowledge about the situation and the people who build the sample.

3. The questions have to be understood easily because some of them are answered in a quick and intuitive way. On the other hand, the questions have to withstand tough analysis because they may be objects of detailed investigation. At all times, the respondent has to know exactly what to do and how to proceed.

4. The questionnaire must be worded in such a way that the respondents' comments will truly provide answers to what the study team wants to know. The questions have to be related to each other such that all the desired inferences can be made. This is true for both qualitative conclusions and statistical analysis.

5. The researchers must give forethought to how the questionnaire will be conducted—the distribution of the questionnaire (face-to-face or via mail, e-mail, or the Internet); the time of distribution (probably not during popular events like the Olympics); the time of day when questions will be answered (during or after work); and length of time needed to complete the questionnaire. All of these items have to be optimized in order to get as many questionnaires returned as possible and to get reliable results.

6. The possible consequences for respondents of filling out the questionnaire have to be considered. If respondents fear publication of their answers, they probably will not fill out the questionnaire or may not be honest in their responses.

To overcome as many difficulties as possible when creating a questionnaire, it is necessary to have time and to find people for a pretest.

Interview: Interviews can take many different forms, such as structured, focused, and open-ended (see Box 2.1). An interview may be a personal, unscripted talk, guided solely by the intuition of the interviewer, or it could be structured in such a way that only prescribed information is given and the questions are formulated in advance, like a questionnaire. The advantage of an interview is that the respondent may ask questions when he or she does not understand something. In the middle of the spectrum, there is a *Leitfaden* (guideline) interview, in which the contents of the interview are prescribed so that all interviews ask the same questions. In general, interviews are too long for a quantitative (statistical) analysis. Most of the interviews have to be analyzed qualitatively. Perhaps it is possible to make an analysis of their contents, but because the comparability of the interviews is questionable, making data analysis difficult, interviews generally are not recommended.

There are only a few scientifically convincing applications of interviews. The reason is that interviews must be interpreted on a case-by-case basis; the time demands for transcription, its control, content analysis, interpretation, and so on are so large that they prohibit the application in most case studies. On the other hand, interviews are an excellent tool to make the study team knowledgeable about the case. Thus, interviews should be used mostly at the beginning of the study, for hypothesis generation, or at the end of the study, to complement findings of quantitative studies.

Computer-Aided Data Sampling: A multicriteria decision analysis sometimes leads to a formal multi-attribute utility decomposition (MAUD) (Humphreys & Wisudha, 1989). The computer can support several steps of the multicriteria decision analysis. Generally, MAUT models can be programmed easily for the computer. This also holds true for the techniques for (a) finding the attributes (repertory grid) (Kelly, 1955), including their hierarchy levels; (b) assessing the trade-offs of the attributes (graphic methods, direct weighting, swing weights, analytical hierarchy process); (c) calculating the composed utility value; (d) ranking the alternatives; and (e) calculating and presenting graphically the contribution of the different attributes to the overall utility, sensitivity analysis. LOGICAL DECISIONS®, MAUD, and Electre® are prominent examples (see Box 11.4 on p. 167).

Focus Groups: Focus groups were created as a marketing tool for getting access to customers' preferences. However, the technique can also be generalized and used to determine the attributes, weights, and so on of an evaluation. For more information on focus groups, see Box 16.3 on p. 263.

goals on each hierarchy level. The definition of attributes can refer to given standards or common knowledge (e.g., to divide sustainability into ecological, economical, social, and technical aspects). There are special methods from the social sciences that can be applied for generating the attributes (e.g., the repertory grid method, Kelly, 1955; Fromm, 1995) or for ordering the goal structure or hierarchy. This is a deductive procedure.

If an inductive approach is chosen, the starting point is either the available information or the answers to two questions: What do we know about the problem? What can we realistically find out? Then, it is possible to group the attributes into more general subgoals. In this way, a hierarchy of attributes may be constructed in a bottom-up way. If the empirical investigation suggests having only one hierarchical level (such as within the Parks and Green Areas synthesis group; see Table 11.1), a small number of attributes are allowed.

The attributes to be included in the investigation have to exhibit certain properties. They should be relevant for the topic, information on them should be available, and they should be relevant for the decision. For example, if price is an attribute, then the alternatives should have different prices.

Attributes work best when their levels (e.g., their measurements) are independent, at least on the natural scale or on the (single) utility scale (see Figure 11.1). For instance, the criteria concentration of a contaminant in soil and the maximum allowed amount of discharge mass of the contaminant are usually highly correlated with each other on the natural scale. But on the utility scale, the weighting of these attributes may be different. Someone who uses the drinking water would like to have a low mass of discharge, whereas someone who is concerned with soil protection wants the soil concentration to be low. If attributes are highly correlated on both scales, they should be redefined. Clearly, the results of the multi-attribute utility application depend on the design of the goal hierarchy. Different meaningful evaluation structures should be tested, and a kind of sensitivity analysis should be performed.

The set of attributes (evaluation criteria) $c = (c_1, \ldots c_j, \ldots, c_m)$ may be ordered within a tree (see Figure 11.4). The overall objective can encompass several criteria and subgoals, which again can include subgoals and criteria corresponding to their place within the hierarchy.

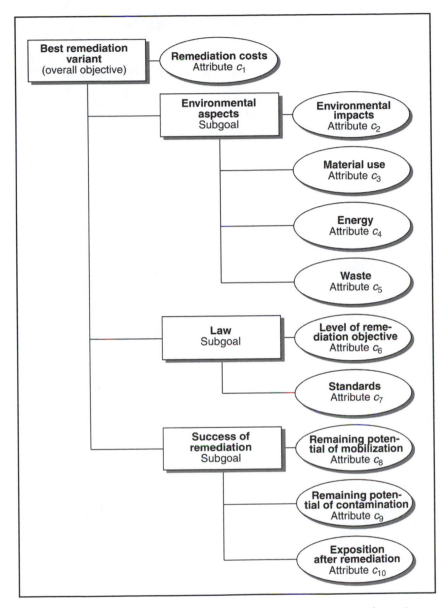

Figure 11.4. Overall Objective, Subgoals, and Attributes in the Synthesis Group Contaminated Soil

LESSONS TO BE LEARNED

▶ There are bottom-up and top-down strategies for identifying the subgoals and attributes. A good method for the construction of attributes is the repertory grid method.

▶ Goals can be ordered hierarchically in a tree. More than one goal level is recommended if more than seven attributes are considered.

▶ The selection of the attributes and the design of the attribute hierarchy can have a big effect on the results. A sensitivity analysis is necessary if the robustness of the hierarchy has to be checked.

Step 5: The Alternatives vs. Attributes Matrix

The alternatives vs. attributes matrix is the basis for further calculations in any kind of multicriteria evaluation, even if a hierarchical structure of the goals is used. For each alternative, all attributes must be rated. If the goal hierarchy is considered a tree, all of the leaves (attributes) must be specified. Within the four steps of multicriteria evaluation (Figure 11.1), the attributes represent the natural scale. If attributes such as costs or contaminant concentration are considered, then values have to be determined for each of the alternatives (see Table 11.2 and Figure 11.5). This seems somewhat trivial, but in practice, attributes are sometimes proposed that may be rated for only one alternative.

The construction of the alternatives vs. attributes matrix is important, but it is also a difficult and time-consuming task. Sometimes, not all attributes can be measured directly for all alternatives. Thus, the study team must provide estimates and must cope with the problem of different kinds of ratings (measured/estimated). When there are possibly different views and the stakeholders may reasonably specify different values, parts of the alternatives vs. attributes matrix may be subject to empirical investigation (see Step 3).

LESSONS TO BE LEARNED

▶ The alternatives vs. attributes matrix is the basis for any kind of MAUT.

Table 11.2   A Portion of the Alternatives vs. Attributes Matrix

		...	Attribute c_4	Attribute c_5	...
	Alternatives		Energy $(10^7 MJ)$	Waste (Three-Step Scale[a])	
A_0	No treatment		0	++	
A_1	Capping		19.5	0	
A_2	Soil washing		1.64	++	
A_3	Water leaching		2.34	++	

NOTE: The waste of no treatment (A_0) consists of contaminated water flowing out of the contaminated zone. Most of the waste is produced by soil washing (A_2), part of which can be compensated for by recycling.
a. 0 = no waste, ++ = much waste.

▶   If the attributes are not directly measurable for all alternatives, parts of the alternatives vs. attributes matrix have to be estimated by the study team or measured by stakeholder inquiry (see Step 3).

Step 6: Utility Functions

The attractiveness of an alternative with respect to an attribute is measured by means of a utility function, which makes utility the quantitative operationalization of the evaluators' preferences with respect to the attribute(s). The axiomatic foundations by von Neumann and Morgenstern (1943) focused attention on the fact that utility functions are order preserving (see Fishburn, 1988). In other words, if one value of an attribute, x, is preferred over another value, y, of the same attribute, then the utilities $u(x)$ and $u(y)$ should exhibit the same order [$u(x) > u(y)$]. This does not imply that the utility function is linear.

Figure 11.6 shows different utility functions. In the case of stringent law enforcement, even small environmental impacts (attribute c_2) exhibit a small utility for the landowner (ABB). In the case of lenient law enforce-

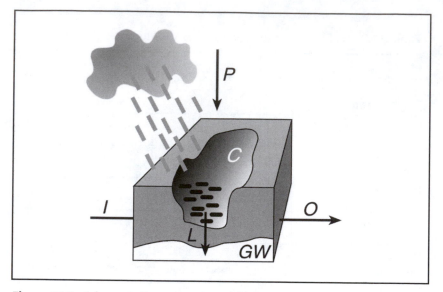

Figure 11.5. Schematic Representation of the Contaminated Zone (C) With Precipitation (P), Leaching (L) to the Groundwater (GW), and Inflow (I) and Outflow (O)

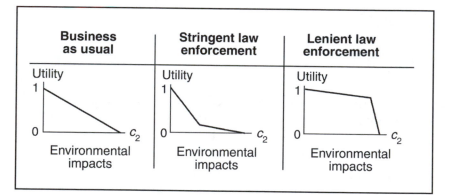

Figure 11.6. Example of Utility Functions as Used in the Evaluation of the Synthesis Group Contaminated Soil

NOTE: Because of different administrative strategies (business as usual, and stringent and lenient law enforcement), linear, concave, and convex utility functions were implemented.

ment, the same environmental impacts lead to a larger utility because less punishment is expected. Remember that the utility functions have been specified by the synthesis group, which acted from the perspective of the landowner. If the utility function has to be investigated empirically, a simple linear function is recommended in most cases. (For a discussion of the relation between evaluation and utility, see Box 11.3.)

The available software (see Box 11.4) offers different methods for users' specifications. In MAUD, the utility functions are automatically calculated after the user has specified that point on the natural scale x_0, which has the highest utility $u(x_0) = 1$. The utility values of other realizations on the natural scale are obtained by linear interpolation. Both the minimum value, x_{min}, and the maximum value, x_{max}, on the natural scale have a zero utility if they do not coincide with x_0. LOGICAL DECISIONS® offers the most flexible method, where the (stepwise) linear or nonlinear utility functions can be approached by using numerical input or a graphical user interface.

LESSONS TO BE LEARNED

▶ Utility functions are order preserving and express the attractiveness of an alternative with respect to attributes or goals.

▶ Formally, utility functions are normalized to have a maximum value of one and a minimum value of zero.

▶ It is difficult to determine the utility functions in such a way that they correspond to the stakeholders' preferences, even when they are subject to empirical investigation.

Step 7: Importance Weights and Preferences

Importance weights are used to trade-off the importance of the attributes. Ideally, the numerical weights should correspond to the evaluators' values; therefore, in most applications, the weights are assessed empirically. We will introduce four methods (see also Step 3):

Box 11.3   The Relation Between Evaluation and Utility

Utility—as defined and used by MAUT—is a construct that has three objectives: First, utility serves as a measure of attractiveness (of an alternative with respect to attributes or goals). Second, utility is a measure that makes the scales of different attributes comparable. And third, utility functions are constructed for individuals, groups, or organizations and thus reflect personal values and intentions.

In the example of Figure 11.6, the magnitude of an attribute is related to utility as follows: the smaller the environmental impact of a remediation alternative, the larger the utility of this alternative with respect to this attribute. Of course, for other attributes, utility may be defined completely differently. For instance, the maximum or minimum sales value of a product will have a utility of 1 or zero. In principle, the most positive (attractive) level of an attribute will have a utility of 1, and the most negative (least attractive) level will have a utility of zero. This implies that the most attractive level of an attribute may well be in the middle, such as the availability of water for a plant; the options of too much or too little water are not attractive.

It is not important how small or large the minimum or maximum utility of an attribute may be. It is only important which magnitude of an attribute is related to which (relative) magnitude of utility (see Figure 11.6, where a stringent and a lenient law enforcement exhibit a convex and a concave utility function). Therefore, the maximum utility is generally set to 1 and the minimum utility is set to zero. In principle, however, the utility could be given in percentages or any other relative measure.

Utility represents an evaluation that takes place in our head: The intended meaning (Tietje, Scholz, Heitzer, & Weber, 1998) is very important because the utility of the attributes is the basis for the trade-off between the advantages and disadvantages of alternatives. If, for instance, the cost of a car is compared to various other attributes (like size, power, image, etc.), it is necessary to define the intended use or properties of the available alternatives. Then, the intended meaning of utility can be the degree of agreement with an ideal (target) alternative. Thus, utility can serve for the comparison of alternatives and their attributes.

Clarifying the intended meaning reveals that utility, as perceived by several individuals, may be very different: the sales value of a product for the producer is related to a cost factor for the client. Similarly, this holds true if utility of environmental properties (such as biodiversity or soil contamination) is going to be assessed.

Box 11.4   Special Features of Multi-Attribute Software

The philosophy of MAUD (Humphreys & Wisudha, 1989) is to support the empirical investigation of all steps of the multicriteria evaluation. It is a kind of computational interview rather than a supplier of computational aid. The repertory grid method (Kelly, 1995; Fromm, 1995) is used to find out the users' criteria. The user of MAUD has to undergo a special procedure. Therefore, it is a good idea for the study team to first use MAUD to define briefly the goals of the application, the criteria, and the alternatives, and to make a preliminary assessment. Generally, different people will find different criteria. Therefore, if MAUD was applied in ETH-UNS case studies for empirical investigation, several steps were left out in order to obtain comparable results from each interview. Because MAUD is not yet using modern window techniques, other programs may be more appropriate, especially if a graphical user interface is required.

LOGICAL DECISIONS® supplies graphical, functional, and computational features for the multicriteria evaluation process. The study team has to design the process of multicriteria evaluation completely outside the program. The program helps in visualizing, analyzing, calculating, and presenting the hierarchical evaluation structure and supplies a graphical user interface for the input of the utility functions and the weights.

ELECTRE is an outranking multicriteria evaluation method (see Vincke, 1992), the several variants of which require the corresponding programs for the necessary calculations, graphical representation, and sensitivity analysis. As with LOGICAL DECISIONS®, the process of the evaluation has to be designed outside of the program (as opposed to MAUD), because the program gives little conceptual or computational help for the input of the necessary criteria and the required parameters. For instance, a graphical user interface is missing in this program.

---

1. Direct weighting

2. Swing weights

3. Hypothetical alternatives

4. Analytical hierarchy process

Direct weighting means that the evaluator is asked to simply specify the weights numerically. This is, of course, possible for only a small number of attributes. If many (more than 10) attributes have to be assessed, a hierarchical ordering is required, and each of the hierarchical levels has to be weighted separately. The weight can be specified in percentages (with all weights summing to 100%) or in parts of one (with all weights summing to 1). These weights can also be derived using other weighting methods, such as swing weights, hypothetical alternatives, or the analytical hierarchy process.

Swing weights are numbers between zero and 100 that are associated with each attribute. The swing weight of $w^{s,max} = 100$ is assigned to the most preferred attribute(s). All of the other attributes get a smaller swing weight w_i^s ($i = 1, \ldots, n$). For each attribute, the direct weight w_i is calculated by division of the swing weight w_i^s by the total sum of all swing weights ($w_i = w^s/S$. If there are two swing weights ($w_1^s = 50$ and $w_2^s = 100 = w^{s,max}$), the corresponding weights are $w_1 = \frac{1}{3}$ and $w_2 = \frac{2}{3}$.

Hypothetical alternatives may be presented to the evaluator as in the example of Figure 11.7. The user is asked which of the two alternatives he or she prefers. Then, the preferred alternative is replaced by one, which is only slightly worse on the positive attribute. The user is again asked for his or her preference. This procedure is iterated until the preference switches to the other alternative. The switching point is used to calculate the ratio of the weights of the two attributes. If enough such ratios between the attributes have been determined, they are used to calculate the direct weights of all the attributes. Note that it is not necessary to specify these ratios for each pair of attributes. This is an engineerlike procedure. A closer look reveals that there are some problems involved. First, there are mathematical problems; for example, if all pairs of the attributes have been rated, this can result in a contradictory system of equations. Second, details of the procedure can bias the ratings. For instance, the selection and the sequence of the pairs of attributes is crucial. Furthermore, the overall preference of two hypothetical alternatives also depends on the levels of nonspecified attributes (see Figure 11.7). This paragraph shows the difficulties of an empirical assessment of values, which appear in a similar way when measuring utilities.

The *analytical hierarchy process* has been proposed by Saaty (1990). The first step is to have a hierarchy of attributes. The elements of one level of this hierarchy are compared pairwise to each other "in their strength of the influence" (Saaty, 1990, p. 17) on the element of the next higher hierarchy level. Table 11.3 shows the ratios of influence of each pair of criteria on the subgoal of Environmental Aspects. Saaty (1990) specifies four

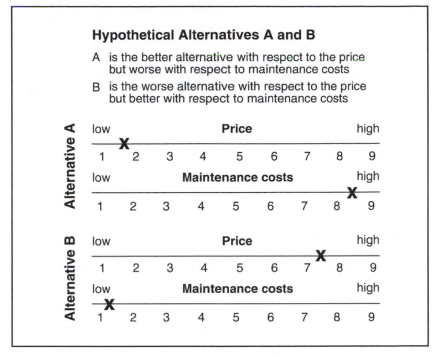

Figure 11.7. Hypothetical Alternatives for Hypothetical Cars as Presented by the MAUD Program

NOTE: The crosses mark the size of the attributes (normalized on a 1 to 9 scale). If the user prefers Car A over Car B, a new pair of hypothetical alternatives (cars) is constructed by increasing the price of Alternative A, which is then slightly worse than before.

crude methods to calculate the direct weights from this matrix, but the correct method that he proposes needs a computer to calculate the so-called eigenvalues of this matrix.

LESSONS TO BE LEARNED

▶ There are several methods used to assess the weights of the attributes.

▶ All methods have strengths and weaknesses. No method can provide crisp and definite values. The most preferred method is the one that seems most adequate for the evaluators.

Table 11.3   Example of a Pairwise Comparison Matrix According
to the Analytical Hierarchy Process for the Evaluation
of Contaminated Sites

Environmental Aspects	Environmental Impacts	Material Use	Energy	Waste
Environmental impacts	1	5	6	7
Material use	1/5	1	4	6
Energy	1/6	1/4	1	4
Waste	1/7	1/6	1/4	1

Step 8: Composition Rules

After assessing the utilities of the alternatives and the weights of the attributes, the results must be composed. In most cases, a weighted sum is built as

$$U(A_i) = \sum_{j=1}^{m} w_j u_i \left[c_j(A_i) \right] = \sum_{j=1}^{m} w_j u_i \left(M_{i,j} \right)$$

(see Box 11.1 for the explanation of the symbols).

This approach is *compensatory,* which means that a low utility of one alternative with respect to one of the attributes may be compensated by a high utility with respect to another attribute (see Figure 11.7). Because an alternative may exhibit an attribute value that is sometimes not acceptable, a so-called cutoff level may be specified that defines the limit beyond which an alternative is disqualified, no matter what overall utility it may have. Thus, some unwanted effects of compensation may be suppressed.

The ETH-UNS case studies always used this composition rule. It proved appropriate especially because the empirical investigations require a simple method. An overview about simple compensatory and noncompensatory approaches such as dominance, lexicographic, and satisficing, as well as outranking methods, can be found in Yoon and Wang (1995). The outranking methods (e.g., PROMETHEE, ELECTRE, and others) compare each pair of alternatives with respect to each attribute using a nonsymmetric outranking function. The result may be that in certain cases, a comparison is not possible. Therefore, not all of the alternatives are directly comparable with each other. But the results of all of the existing outranking evaluations finally lead to a hierarchy of the alternatives, from which the most attractive alternative can be mostly identified.

It is clear that the composition rule cannot describe completely how people make evaluations because the cognitive process of evaluation is far more complex, includes different kinds of knowledge, and is highly dependent on the current decision situation (Meehl, 1966). But corresponding to the Brunswikian principle of vicarious functioning, in order to communicate, rethink, discuss evaluations, and initialize a process of finding consent, such a simple and robust model is very useful.

The power of the introduced linear composition rule has already been proven in the 1960s and 1970s. Various investigations on real decision making showed that real evaluations, judgments, and decisions can be well described if measured weights and assessments are put in the linear composition rule. Furthermore, some studies showed that these modeled evaluations even outperformed intuitive expert evaluations. This phenomenon has been called *bootstrapping* (Dawes, 1971).

LESSONS TO BE LEARNED

▶ Within the ETH-UNS case studies, the simple composition rule is preferred because the simple approach can describe in a robust way what people think and how they evaluate.

▶ There are many more methods available (including the corresponding software) than were presented here.

Step 9: Evaluation and Discussion

Figure 11.8 shows the results of the multi-attribute utility evaluation of different treatments of the contaminated sites. For each alternative, the overall utility has been calculated using the previously mentioned composition rule and the attributes in Figure 11.4. In Figure 11.8, the sensitivity to the different utility functions (see Figure 11.6) can be seen.

Within the scenarios "business as usual" and "lenient law enforcement," capping received the highest overall utility. In the scenario of "stringent law enforcement," soil washing is preferred where the better remediation had to be traded-off against the larger costs.

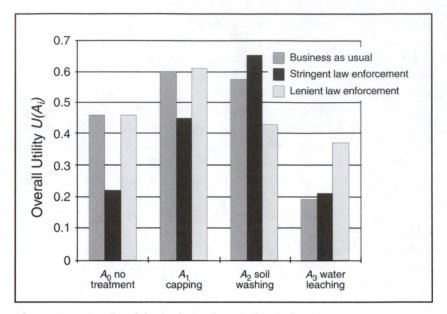

Figure 11.8. Results of the Multi-Attribute Utility Evaluation

The example shows that MAUT may normatively give hints for the trade-off between the alternatives. The simplified evaluation process is no description of the cognitive evaluation process. This may be reflected in the aversion of a number of people to quantifying the utility and the weights of the criteria. In general, however, the application of MAUT is appreciated because it presents the evaluation and decision process in a transparent way. In the example of the synthesis group Contaminated Sites, MAUT succeeded in supporting the optimization of the decision process.

LESSONS TO BE LEARNED

▶ MAUT facilitates communication about the evaluation and, hence, the finding of consent evaluations. It makes a subsequent decision more reliable because the relevant information may be included in the evaluation. MAUT is capable of integrating different disciplines, knowledge, systems, and people.

▶ MAUT helps the stakeholders reflect their own attitudes. In the evaluation, the differences between groups of stakeholders may emerge. MAUT supports the stakeholders' decisions because it investigates how other agents would evaluate.

▶ By an application of MAUT, the study team learns about the different evaluations of the stakeholders.

12

INTEGRATED RISK
MANAGEMENT

THE RATIONALE

Integrated Risk Management is a decision-making framework (see Chapter 13) for situations in which the case agents face uncertainty about the outcomes resulting from their decisions and refer to the notion of risk. The Integrated Risk Management model is introduced as a tool that will support analysis and description of risk situations and/or improve the process of decision making under risk.

In general, we recommend that the study team use the Integrated Risk Management model if the case agents' or the study team's focus of prospect essentially shifts toward uncertainty. The latter is expressed more precisely with the help of the definition of an elementary risk situation (see Box 12.1). A case agent is facing an elementary risk situation if he or she has two or more different action alternatives, and uncertainty is inherent to the choice of at least one alternative in the sense that different outcomes can result with certain likelihoods (probabilities).

The Integrated Risk Management model is a tool that provides the following:

- Structural analysis of a risk situation, thus reducing the complexity of case analysis
- Access to the situational and semantic context of the agents' risk perception and behavior

Box 12.1   Formal Definition of Risk Situations

An elementary risk situation is given by the following:
- An agent must have a choice between at least two alternatives, A_1 and A_2.
- With the choice of one of the two alternatives, uncertainty arises. Which event of two events, E^+ or E^-, will be the outcome of the chosen alternative?
- The agent[1] considers the value, $v(E^-)$, of at least one uncertain event as a loss, relative to the other event(s).

This is a minimal definition of a risk situation. It is well reflected by the example that you have the choice between doing nothing or participating in a lottery with either winning or losing.

We can easily generalize the definition for the elementary risk situation. A general risk situation is defined as the following:
- An agent has the choice between different alternatives from a set $A = (A_1, \ldots, A_i, \ldots, A_n)$.
- For each alternative A_i, there is a set of possible events $E_i = (E_{i,1}, \ldots, E_{i,n_i})$.
- For each alternative A_i, there is a probability vector $p_i = (p_{i,1}, \ldots, p_{i,ni})$. The probability $p_{i,j}$ denotes the probability of $E_{i,j}$ if A_i is chosen, there is $0 < p_{i,j} < 1$ for at least one i and j.

This definition is for discrete events and a finite set of alternatives. It can be extended easily to infinite or continuous sets of events and alternatives (see the following figure).

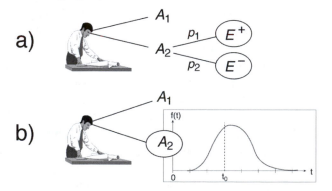

Figure Note. This figure represents an elementary risk situation (a) and a more general situation (b) with a continuous set of events. In both cases, the agent has two choices. In the discrete case, (a), two events, E^+ and E^- can result with probabilities p_1 and $(1 - p_1)$. In example (b), we consider a continuous set of events, such as the time duration until a certain reward will be given. If A_1 is chosen, a known fixed time t_1 will result. In the case of A_2, the probabilities of different times are described by a probability density $f(t)$. The value t_0 denotes a threshold between wins and losses (e.g., in terms of money). Note that this definition considers payoffs $v(E)$ on the natural scale and does not rely on the agent-dependent utilities $u(E)$. $v(E)$ is objective, whereas $u(E)$ is subjective.

- Integration of different perspectives—economic, sociological, environmental, and cultural approaches (see Renn, 1992)—which also integrates concepts from different disciplines

Currently, the risk concept is used and applied widely. However, it is still a disputed and multifaceted concept. This is highlighted by the statement that experts more often discuss the meaning of risk than how big a risk is. In order to understand the different meanings of risk, risk situation, risk function, and the Integrated Risk Management model, we will introduce these concepts and their genesis.

Uncertainty

One origin of the scientific risk dispute is the question of how uncertainty should be conceptualized. In general, two sources of uncertainty (see Wallsten & Whitfield, 1986; Jungermann, 1997)—data and knowledge—can be distinguished.

If the case dynamics are complex, such as in regional development, national markets, or in many neuropsychological cases, the study team may consider the uncertainty to be a property of the case. If possible, one will refer to case data or empirical evidence (e.g., statistical data on the effectiveness of a certain therapy), which may help in order to model and assess uncertainty.

But uncertainty may also be conceived of as a property of the case agent or the study team. A situation may be considered completely deterministic, but because of the lack of knowledge, the case agent may feel uncertain about the outcomes. One possible strategy in this case is to conceptualize the situations by the means of subjective probability, perhaps according to the de Finetti (1974) approach. De Finetti considered subjective probability to be the degree of belief an agent has regarding the occurrence of an event.

For an understanding of different variants and of the power of the risk concept, we will provide a historical view on the genesis of risk (see Fine, 1973; Hacking, 1975). Readers who are not familiar with standard definitions of risk, however, should first study Box 12.1.

Genesis of the Risk Concept

Historically, preconcepts of risk were already known by the Mesopotamians about 3,000 years before Christ. As Mumpower, Menkes, and

Covello (1986, p. 520) report, when relying on archaeological-historical research (see also Oppenheim, 1977), a group of wise men, called *Ashipu,* was responsible for the risk management of the Mesopotamians. The Ashipu were elected because they could read the signs of the gods and thus could provide an excellent decision aid service to their clients. In order to assess the likelihood of positive and negative outcomes of different alternatives (e.g., war), they simply noted advantageous or disadvantageous signs associated with each alternative on clay disks. After this data recording, they simply recommended the alternative that had the more positive signs.

The term *risk* became common in the 15th century in northern Italian merchandising. Etymologically, risk refers to the Latin *ricare,* which originates from the Greek concept ρι ζα, which in turn means "root" but also "cliff." A Hellenistic sailor took ρι ζα if he chose a route close to the cliffs that increased the peril of wrecking his ship but also abbreviated the travel.

In his *Théorie Analytique des Probabilités* Pierre-Simon Laplace (1816/ 1921) gave a scientific definition of risk. In his philosophical discussion of probabilities he emphasized "the probability of events may be useful in determining the hope. . . or fear of people affected by their occurrence" (Laplace, 1995, p. 5). In this context, hope is defined as the expectation of an uncertain but likely benefit. Note that Laplace already defined risk as the product of all harms and benefits with the probability of their occurrence.

The notion of risk got another accent with the rise of the industrial age. At that time, harm was considered to be the opportunity cost for getting access to the pleasure tied to new technologies. Simple and naive definitions of risk, such as "risk is the probability of loss," have dominated literature for a long time. In Europe, for example, the discussions about technological risks in the 1970s were almost exclusively characterized by definitions of risk in which only the losses are considered. These conceptions are also denoted as pure risk. The historical context also reveals why the risk concept has been narrowed to the probability of losses.

The risk concept has become a very popular scientific object in recent decades. Risk is believed to be universal in the sense that all sciences, from the natural sciences through technical, medical, and social sciences to the humanities, deal with this concept. There are various reasons for this extraordinary prominence of the risk concept. Some researchers (Krohn & Weingart, 1986) consider phylogenetic reasons to be responsible for the genesis of risk management; for example, risk management developed because the human species became able to cause worldwide endangerment from microcosmic systems, such as when it mastered nuclear fission. Others argue more fundamentally and substantiate the presumed ubiquity of the risk concept epistemologically, such as when referring to stochastic properties of material as they have been described in quantum mechanics (see the Heisenberg Indeterminacy Relation).

Broader definitions of risk and the incorporation of the chances/wins linked with risky alternatives were introduced later (see Brachinger & Weber, 1997; Fishburn, 1982; Scholz, Heitzer, et al., 1997). We present a general definition of risk functions in Box 12.2.

Constructing the Risk Function: An Illustration

The construction of the risk function in this book (see Box 12.2) goes beyond the traditional approaches of defining risk as a function of damage and probability. We illustrate by example what this function is about.

When testing students on risk, we often offer a simple lottery, L_1, in order to determine whether the risk concept has been understood. We usually put a 1 Swiss Frank coin on the table and ask the student to do the same. We tell the student that he or she has the choice between participating (A_2) in a coin flip lottery or not (A_1). By this, the alternatives of an elementary risk situation are defined (see Box 12.1). The student is told that if the coin lands heads up (E^+), he or she will win one Frank [$v(E^+)$], otherwise (E^-), he or she has to pay 1 Swiss Frank [$v(E^-)$]. Thus, all components of an elementary risk situation can be defined.

We will now describe the constituents of the student's risk function. From the student's behavior and interviews, we can infer that he or she becomes aware that there is both potential loss and uncertainty. Most of the students take the coin-flipping option (A_2). As we ask them to take one Frank [i.e., $v(E^-)$] out of their pocket and put it on the table, we make it clear that they are participating in a lottery with real wins or losses. Uncertainty about the outcome was generated by the coin flipping. Because this is the standard procedure for generating uncertainty in games, we assume that the lottery is linked to the student's space of risk cognition, and that he or she also believes that there is a 50-50 chance of winning or losing (i.e., he or she considers $\tilde{p}_{i,j} = p_{i,j}$; see Box 12.2). There are no extra costs, $v(A_2)$, in neither money nor time, for entering the lottery.

Box 12.2   Risk Functions

Even within an elementary risk situation (cf. Box 12.1, see Fishburn, 1984; Vlek & Stallen, 1981; Yates & Stone, 1992), different definitions of risk can be worked out. Depending on the focus, the interests, and the constraints of the agent, risk may be one of the following:

- The probability of loss
- The size of the maximal possible loss
- A function, mostly the product of probability and size of loss
- The variance of the consequences of a risky action
- The semivariance of all possible losses
- Other functions of the entities (mean, variance, maximum, etc. of outcomes) of the risk situation

These definitions are variants of pure risk because they rely only on losses.

Constituents of the general risk function, $r(A,p,E)$, are a

- Value function $v(A_i)$, which represents the costs of getting access to the alternatives, $A = (A_1, \ldots, A_n)$.
- Value function $v(E_{i,j})$, which constitutes the preference structure of an agent with respect to all events $E = (E_1, \ldots, E_i, \ldots, E_n)$; $E_i = (E_{i,1} \ldots, E_{i,n_i})$
- Subjective conceptualization $\tilde{p}_{i,j}$ of all probabilities $p_{i,j}$, with $p = (p_1, \ldots, p_i, \ldots, p_n)$; $p_i = (p_{i,1}, \ldots, p_{i,n_i})$

As a constituent of a risk function, we assume a value function v on the natural scale, which permits the preference building and thus the distinction between wins and losses. Therefore, the development of a utility function, u, is not necessary (see the first bullet point above). In a similar way, with the subjective conceptualization, we assume that the agent must understand uncertainty but need not necessarily have probability assessments developed.

We do not know the risk function of the student, but from the reactions, we infer that the lottery is considered a very low risk. This is appropriately reflected by the second or third risk functions in Box 12.2 as the maximal loss ($r_{(b)} = -1$ Swiss Frank) and the expected value of the loss, $r_{(c)} = 0.5$ (this is the traditional definition of risk as probability times damage), are clearly small on the student's subjective valuation function. Of course, the actual risk function $r(A,p,E)$ is not known. However, it could be explored by a psychological inquiry, for instance, with the help of the thinking-aloud technique.

According to interviews, we assume that many students understand the expectancy value to be zero for both alternatives. Note that the expec-

Note that we consider risk (and the risk function) as a construct and thus as highly subjective (whereas the general risk situation may be conceived of as a mostly objective instance[2]). The introduced risk definition considers not only losses, but also the potential benefits that may result from one alternative. This type of risk is also called *speculative risk* (see Brachinger & Weber, 1997; Fishburn, 1982).

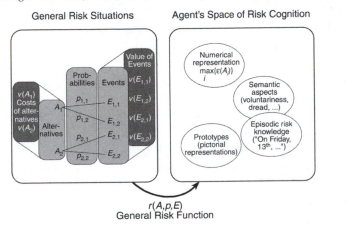

$$r(A, p, E)$$
General Risk Function

Figure Note. The general risk function, $r(A,p,E)$, is a special valuation function that represents the risk evaluation of an agent for general risk situations. In abstract terms, the risk function $r(A,p,E)$ maps general risk situations into the space of risk cognition. The latter entails the constituents of the risk evaluations of an agent. We will provide no general definition for the space of risk cognition here. As indicated by the different domains, risk cognition entails a variety of different aspects ranging from numerical calculations to arousal and feeling. Access to a precise formal definition of the risk function is given in the section on constructing the risk function. In general, the space of risk cognition is considered as the part of knowledge that is saliently associated with the semantics of risk.

tancy value also establishes a risk function. Let us assume that this function is the student's risk function. Then, we have to question why most of the students prefer to take part in the lottery (A_2) and do not refuse (A_1). A plausible explanation is that there are some incentives (negative costs) linked to A_2 that are not found in A_1. These (negative) costs, $v(A_2)$, can be understood as extra time for thinking or the time of the coin-flipping game that can be subtracted from the examination time.

But other issues can also be involved in the risk function. Imagine that a student joins a party, and someone offers another coin-flipping lottery and proudly presents a 1000 Swiss Franks bill. For some reason, the student is challenged to participate. Clearly, this situation differs from the above example, particularly in the costs of acceptance $v(A_2)$ and refusal $v(A_1)$. Let us just consider the position of the student if he or she had accepted. Certainly, there is an involvement of emotions close to the joy of winning 1000 Swiss Franks, but also to the fear of losing money or being laughed at as a loser. Furthermore, the uncertainty of the coin flipping may cause high arousal and trembling. Thus, the risk situation elicits much more than numerical cognition in the agent (see the figure in Box 12.2).[3] The feelings associated with risk can also be labeled, such as lack of control, dread, or catastrophic potential.

Structural Analysis: Risk Situations and Risk Definitions

If a case requires uncertainty management, a precise structural analysis should come first. By structural analysis, we mean a formal description of the case. This description has to represent the agent, decision alternatives, possible outcomes and their values (see the definition of the natural scale in Figure 11.1), valuation (utility), and likelihoods (probabilities) using mathematical terms (i.e., sets, variables, functions, etc.). The basic concepts for this description are provided in Box 12.1. The target of the structural analysis is to describe the case in terms of a general risk situation.

Although we have postulated that the general risk situation is foremost independent of an individual, we have to acknowledge that risk is a construct. This is already important in the structural analysis and in the definition of the general risk situation. The study team can create its own model of the risk situation, for instance, by defining alternatives, probabilities, events, and so on. Usually, this model will be more of a normative type. Of course, attaining a representation that is close to the reality of the case is ideal. However, in most cases, there are some degrees of freedom, and, in general, there is not just one single model that is considered appropriate.

It is, however, also possible to model the case in terms of a general risk situation (i.e., alternatives, probabilities, events, outcomes of events) as perceived by the agents. This provides a descriptive approach to the construction of the risk situation. The study team should formulate both models because one's own model is a helpful reference point.

In the descriptive approach, the case agent is asked to face different alternatives and to consider uncertainty with respect to the outcomes that result with the choice of at least one alternative. However, the approach neither implies that the agent himself or herself has generated or even calculated probabilities and/or utility valuations for all events, nor that there are (interval-scaled) utilities or probabilities guiding the agent's behavior. These entities may appear only in the study team's (descriptive) model on how the agent is facing the case.

Context and Behavioral Analysis

A structural analysis is only the basis of the case analysis. In order to understand the real process of uncertainty management, the study team has to investigate the psychological factors of risk and risk cognition because they are included in the space of risk cognition. For a behavioral or psychological analysis, a contextualization and thus an understanding of the subject-task relation (i.e., the agent's situation) is necessary (see Fischhoff, 1996; Scholz & Zimmer, 1997). Thus, the study team particularly has to explore the qualitative characteristics of the perceived risk. According to the seminal work of Slovic, Fischhoff, and Lichtenstein (1985), risk has a kind of personality. Obviously, decision makers are not only taking the actuarial (statistical) data into account, but they are also influenced strongly by their own interpretation of the situation characteristics. Judgments of riskiness rely on many aspects other than statistical frequencies (see the figure in Box 12.2). For instance, air travel is judged more risky than travel by car, although it is much safer on a per-mile basis. This is presumably due to the uncontrollability of air travel by passengers and the cognitive salience of spectacular accidents (see Nisbett & Ross, 1980).

According to Slovic et al. (1985), the most influential factors in risk judgments are the perception of dread and voluntariness with respect to the outcomes/events, the conviction of having personal control over the likelihood or the magnitude of the outcomes, and whether the risk is known or unknown, that is, the familiarity with the risk (sometimes split into novelty and knowledge). Naturally, the situational characteristics, such as the expected number of fatalities or losses (i.e., the catastrophic potential), are decisive factors (see Renn, 1992). However, although the perceived average number of fatalities correlates to the judged riskiness of a situation, the relationship is weak and generally explains less than 20% of the declared variance (Jungermann & Slovic, 1993; Renn, 1983). Finally, risk is rated greater if it violates common equity principles (see Figure 12.1).

Meanwhile, there is a solid body of knowledge about peculiarities and consistent patterns of a subject's risk perception. Thus, decision makers

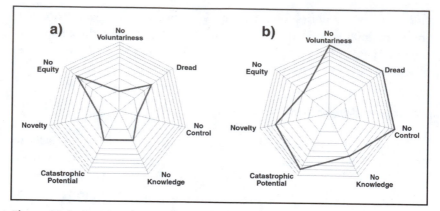

Figure 12.1. Egg Graphic of Risks as Investigated by Slovic.

NOTE: The aspects of risk are rated on a 10-point scale (the outer circle means highest rating). Risk situations show certain profiles and are thus also judged to have a kind of personality. We present two profiles of risk perception of an individual: (a) the risk of car travel, and (b) the risk of a nuclear power plant.

are risk averse if the stakes of losses are high, and they are risk seeking if the stakes for gains are high (Kahneman & Tversky, 1979, 1992). A puzzling aspect of risk is that an outcome may be framed differently by an agent if he or she refers to different reference points. So, an outcome may be considered as either a loss or a win. Thus, an agent may exhibit either risk-averse or risk-seeking behavior in a situation depending on his or her framing (Kahneman & Tversky, 1981). The bounded rationality of individual behavior was also demonstrated nicely by Svenson's (1981) investigation. Driving a car can be considered complex system management, and individuals systematically overestimate their own control over this system. In Svenson's study, the mean individual judges himself or herself to be superior to the average individual. Case analysis on risk management has to incorporate these findings from psychological decision research and to answer the question of what impact the context of the agent has on his or her risk perception. The reader is referred to the papers of Slovic (1987, 2000), Fischhoff (1987), or Jungermann, Rohrmann, and Wiedemann (1991).

INCORPORATING DIFFERENT PERSPECTIVES

As we have seen, risk is a multifaceted and multidimensional construct. There are different basic definitions, personality dimensions, framings, and so on. Risk has normative and descriptive aspects, and, similar to multi-attribute decision making (see Figure 11.2), the agent may also consider different attributes or even dimensions. These attributes or dimensions may not differ only with respect to the utility dimension (e.g., economic vs. ecological utilities). Even within one attribute, different risk perspectives may be distinguished. For instance, if a new pesticide is applied, the case agent may consider the risk of health effects on farmers and consumers. For assessing these uncertainties, we usually have some information from toxicological studies, which allow for a more or less reasoned probability distribution. But applying a new chemical to the environment also includes the potential of harm to the environment of which we are unaware. This idea underlies risk prevention, and there are already some techniques developed in the field of environmental sciences for the measurement of the unknown (see Hofstetter, 1998).

According to the multi-attribute utility approach, one could simply define different attributes—one for the human intoxication and another for the unknown environmental harm. The crucial issue, however, is that the assessment of the uncertainties is usually based on completely different notions and procedures with a qualitatively different epistemological status. Within the Integrated Risk Management model, these sources and conceptions of risk must and can be integrated. In this context, we want to mention that risk is not only a construct but also a means to reduce complexity.

Organizing Risk Management

The first step in Risk Management is the modeling of the risk situation. According to the conceptualization in Box 12.1, the study team has to construct an encompassing model of the decision situation provided by the case (i.e., to conduct a structural analysis). This model has to encompass at least all alternatives that are considered by the case agents. According to the definition of the general risk situation, one of the alternatives has to be followed by uncertain events. According to the Brunswikian Lens Model, the agent understands this situation by different perceptors. The perceptors of the Brunswikian Lens Model can be conceived of as different cognitions (including calculations) and physical arousals (including emotions) represented in the agent (see the figure in Box 12.2). These cognitions may refer to the cost of getting access to an alternative or the likelihood of certain events, but they can also refer to the outcomes and the psychological "personality" (e.g., the dread) associated with the alternatives.

LESSONS TO BE LEARNED

▶ The Integrated Risk Management model should be applied if the study team's or the case agents' focus of attention shifts toward coping with uncertainty and risk evaluation.

▶ Risk is a means to reduce the complexity of a case; thus, simplifications are wanted and not a burden.

▶ Risk is also a means for uncertainty management; thus, different conceptualizations of probability (such as frequentistic or Laplace) may be applied in risk assessment.

▶ Risk is multifaceted. It has different notions, dimensions, and a personality in the sense that certain features of the risk situation influence the risk judgment.

▶ The case agents' and the study team's risk judgments are often systematically biased. This can be due to the illusory belief of control (Langer, 1975; Langer & Roth, 1975) or to an overrating of the probability of events with a high cognitive salience, which distorts the subjective risk estimation.

THE METHOD IN DETAIL

We will introduce the Integrated Risk Management model and describe the single steps in detail. Reference will be made to contaminated site management of the Zurich North case (see also Chapter 5). Because no explicit risk management was performed in the Zurich North case study, we will illustrate by a fictitious example how risk situation and risk function can be modeled.

Defining the Situation

Most important is the study team's modeling of the decision situations. Starting from a case understanding, the case agents' goals, their perspectives, and their relationship to the situation should be depicted. The left box of Figure 12.2 represents this initial step of analysis.

The study team and/or the case agents have to define the following:

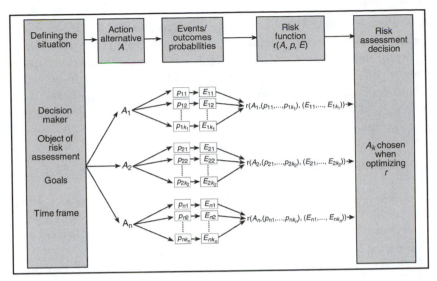

Figure 12.2. The Brunswikian Lens Model of Integrated Risk Management

- Which case agent(s) is (are) the decision maker(s)?
- What are the objects (i.e., the system considered) and goals of the decision?
- Which time frame is considered?

And, at least vaguely and qualitatively, the following question must be answered:

- Which criteria (in the space of risk cognition) are the most decisive with respect to evaluation and uncertainty?

For instance, in the ETH-UNS case study Zurich North, we may consider a potential investor who wants to build a big housing construct. The investor (i.e., the case agent) is a 40-year-old, dynamic, well-considered deputy of a big company who got his master's in business science. His company decided to invest a certain amount of money in real estate. This investment should show high interest rates over the next 10 years. According to the management plan, the houses should be sold at that time because the money will be needed for another investment (time frame). He has already made up his mind which lot is the most appropriate (i.e., the object). The main criterion for decision making is clearly a good but not-too-risky yield (as the company takes the option of real estate investments for safety reasons). The seller of the property has already lowered the price because of soil contamination, so no further bargain is expected.

According to the soil experts' opinion, the ground of the desired property is considerably contaminated. However, the experts felt uncertain about the exact area and degree of contamination. Additionally, they suspect that there were some peat holes excavated and later filled with industrial wastes.

Constructing Action Alternatives

According to the Integrated Risk Management model, decision alternatives have to be defined. If there are no alternatives and only uncertainty with respect to a peril, we speak about danger (*Gefahr*) (see Luhmann, 1996), and other models are appropriate.

The set of decision alternatives $A = (A_1, \ldots, A_n)$ is a model of the agent's action space. This space should be elaborated on according to the satisficing principle (see Box 9.1). If new alternatives are generated in the course of the case study, they may be supplemented. Note that the action space may be continuous, too.

In the Zurich North case study, the investor faces the situation of what to do once he acquires the property. Three different alternatives were on the short list.

A_1 was the status quo, that is, doing nothing and ignoring the soil contamination until the authorities explicitly intervene.

A_2 was safeguarding, or covering the ground with a water-resistant layer (capping). This measure would eliminate, or at least reduce, groundwater contamination and human exposure. No basements are allowed with this variant.

A_3 was soil washing. This procedure was promoted by the cantonal authorities. All contaminated soil would be excavated and treated by an approved environmental engineering company.

A fourth alternative, which will not be presented here, was hydraulic remediation, or pumping off the groundwater, cleaning it, and reinfusing it to the site (water leaching; see Table 11.2). This introduces a continuous set of alternatives because the time of the application may be varied.

Possible Events/Outcomes

For each action alternative A_i ($i = 1, \ldots, n$), a sufficient set of possible events $E_{i,j}$ ($j = 1, \ldots, n_i$) has to be defined. Furthermore, for at least one alternative, A_i, more than one possible event must exist. At least one of them must be regarded as a loss.

Let us consider briefly the construction of possible events tied to A_1 to A_3.

Because the focus of the case agent is on profitable yield, for each alternative, we have to consider events that compel investments (a detailed graphical representation is provided in Figure 12.4).

With A_1 (status quo), it is theoretically possible that the authorities do not intervene because of a more relaxed environmental policy until the property is sold again (E_{11}). However, if the environmental board does not accept the proceeding, one must additionally install a mandatory safeguarding (E_{12}) or soil washing (E_{13}). Extra costs have to be expected, presumably due to a time delay, because the construction will be stopped for some time until the required remediation plan becomes accepted.

With A_2 (safeguarding), one possible event is that the intended safeguarding will be expected by the authorities (E_{21}). However, one also has to be afraid of the request of soil washing within the next 10 years (E_{22}) if the environmental regulations become stricter.

With A_3 (soil washing), there is only uncertainty as to the amount of soil to be excavated (E_{31}) and thus to the actual cost. No complications or further investments are to be expected.

Note that the definition of the events is not sufficient for the final risk assessment. Because the agent will consider only the net costs of the remediation, for each event $E_{i,j}$, the possible costs $v(E_{i,j})$ have to be specified.

Assessing the Probabilities

For each action alternative A_i, each event $E_{i,j}$ has a certain probability $p_{i,j}$ of occurrence. Although the formal definition may be easy, the modeling and assessment of probabilities is the most difficult issue of the risk assessment.

First, the study team has to decide which concept of probability (objective, subjective, or other) is the most appropriate for conceptualizing the decision situation. There are two basic variants of objective probability, classical or Laplace, which refer to arguments of symmetry and the frequentistic probabilities that rely on replicated observations under stable constraints. In many cases, there will be no appropriate data available to assess the probability by objective means.

In case of missing data, one has to refer to facets of subjective probability, such as the de Finetti/Savage approach of subjective probabilities, which conceives strength of belief as a constituent of probability.

However, there are also conceptions of possibility at the fringes of the concept field of probability, such as the fuzzy set theory of Zadeh (1978), the Shafer-Dempster approach of belief functions (Shafer, 1976), or the Baconian probabilities (Cohen, 1977). An excellent overview on these approaches is provided by Walley (1991). We will not go into detail here, but we recommend the subjective probability conception as the appropriate method for most cases.

Second, after the appropriate conception of probability is elected, the task is to assess the probabilities. If a frequency count can be attributed to an assessment of events, there are standard statistical procedures for estimating the probabilities and distributions (Hartung, Elpelt, & Klösener, 1993; Mood et al., 1974). The main difficulty in this approach is finding the appropriate data for the case. Even if seemingly appropriate frequentistic data (e.g., for dose-response curves) are available, the study team has to reflect carefully on how the situation of the case may be linked to the data.

The measurement of subjective probabilities is a difficult task. A number of techniques were developed (see Nothbaum, Scholz, & May, 1996; Wallsten, 1990). For the ETH-UNS case study Zurich North remediation problem, a two-step procedure seems appropriate (see Figures 12.3 and 12.4). In a first step, the task is to assess the probabilities of the occurrence of discrete events. For instance, the one-wheel fortune wheel measurement technique (see Box 12.3) is useful. Then, in a second step, the probability distribution of the costs should be determined. This can be done by direct or indirect methods (see Nothbaum, 1997; Yates, 1990). Because the case agent had a master's in business science and was used to the graphical presentation of probability distributions, a semiformative direct graphical method seems agreeable. This method first asks for the range of expected costs, then qualitatively assesses the presumed type or shape of the probability function (Gaussian, log normal, beta, etc.) and finally calibrates some percentiles (particularly the quartiles and the 95, 99, and 99.9 percentiles). The proposed procedure was already practically

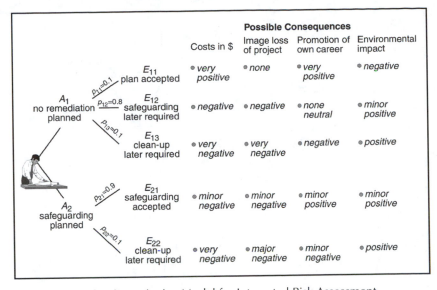

	Costs in $	Possible Consequences		
		Image loss of project	Promotion of own career	Environmental impact
E_{11} plan accepted	• very positive	• none	• very positive	• negative
E_{12} safeguarding later required	• negative	• negative	• none neutral	• minor positive
E_{13} clean-up later required	• very negative	• very negative	• negative	• positive
E_{21} safeguarding accepted	• minor negative	• minor negative	• minor positive	• minor positive
E_{22} clean-up later required	• very negative	• major negative	• minor negative	• positive

Figure 12.3. A Semiquantitative Model for Integrated Risk Assessment
NOTE: See Fischhoff, Bostrom, and Quadrel (1993). The model requires a quantitative assessment of probabilities and a qualitative assessment of the evaluation of aspects. The example refers to the ETH-UNS case study Zurich North.

approved (see Scholz, Popp, May, & Nothbaum, 1994), and practitioners considered the graphical presentation a useful decision aid. We presume that the procedure requires only minimal statistical literacy.

Constructing the Risk Function

As has been mentioned, the risk function is a conjoint function that incorporates the cost of having access to the alternatives and the valuation of outcomes/events, as well as the cost of the probability. In the example of the ETH-UNS case study (see Figure 12.4), the mathematical expectation has been taken. But there are also different ways to evaluate. One possibility is an evaluation based on visualizing the distribution, as displayed at the right side of Figure 12.4.

Note that these three functions may, but do not necessarily have to, be assessed separately. A risk evaluation is a conjoint evaluation of the situation that incorporates these three aspects. Yet the agent must have known only these constituents. Note that it is not necessary to assess utility

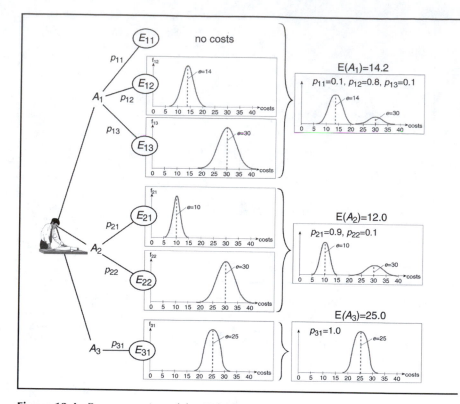

Figure 12.4. Representation of the Risk Management Model for the Zurich North Soil Remediation Case

functions, because in this case, the costs indicate the value of the events sufficiently.

Risk Assessment

After passing through the procedure of the Integrated Risk Management model, an analytic model of the risk perception of the agents is at the study team's disposal. Often, this model is oriented toward numerical outcomes and utilities, but the context and qualitative aspects of the decision alternatives and their consequences can also be integrated. Nevertheless, the model will always remain incomplete and mostly of a static nature. On the contrary, risk assessment is an integral, dynamic, and almost holistic activity. Thus, the results of the analytical framework are a starting point for improved understanding of the case.

NOTE: There are three remediation alternatives A_i (see text). If A_3 (soil washing) is chosen, the soil is cleaned up and no additional activities have to be considered ($p_{31} = 1$). Uncertainty is with the amount of soil to be cleaned up. (High) costs will result from the soil excavation and treatment. The uncertainties of costs are presented as probability density f_{31}.

If A_2 (safeguarding) is chosen, lower costs (described by f_{21}) are expected with a large probability p_{21}. However, there is a small probability, p_{22}, that soil excavation will become necessary because of more rigid environmental laws that are implemented within the time frame of 10 years. This will cause costs (described by f_{22}) with probability p_{22} to increase as compared to the costs of A_3.

If A_1 is chosen, there is a small probability, p_{11}, of no costs. With probability p_{12}, an uncertain amount has to be spent for safeguarding. These costs are a little higher than those of E_{21} (see text). Finally, there is a small probability p_{13} that the authorities require a soil cleanup procedure (as if A_2 is chosen, but with a larger probability).

If the probability functions $p_i = (p_{i,1}, \ldots, p_{i,n_i})$ and the densities $f_i = (f_{i,1}, \ldots, f_{i,n_i})$ are folded by multiplication, distributions for the costs may be derived. For this folding, the probabilities $p_{i,j}$ have to be assessed. In the example, we see that the expectancy value, ε, holds: $\varepsilon(A_2) < \varepsilon(A_1) < \varepsilon(A_3)$.

Which alternative is chosen depends on the agent's risk function. Note that this risk function usually differs from the expectancy value and, for instance, also incorporates the costs, $v(A_i)$, for an alternative A_i. These costs can include the trouble valuation that the agent may have when presenting an alternative to his or her company or to the public authorities (see Figure 12.3).

LESSONS TO BE LEARNED

▶ When decision making under uncertainty is essential for case analysis, risk and the Integrated Risk Management model are appropriate concepts for obtaining a better understanding.

▶ The Integrated Risk Management model relies on the basic definitions of the general risk situation and the risk function.

▶ Risk incorporates probability. Probability has different conceptions. In general, subjective probability is an appropriate concept to model the agent's uncertainty perception.

▶ The general risk situation is a tool supporting the thorough structural analysis of the case, including the assessment of the risk function of the agents.

Box 12.3 How to Measure Risk and Subjective Probabilities

Risk was introduced by defining risk situations and the risk function. The risk function $r(A,p,E)$ is a conjoint measure for the agents' evaluation of events $(E_{i,j})$, their probabilities $(p_{i,j})$, and of the costs/profits, $v(A_j)$, for choosing an alternative (A_j). Risk is a cognition related to uncertainty. There are many methods for normative risk assessment (Covello & Merkhofer, 1993), axiomatic modeling of risk (Weber & Bottom, 1989), and psychometric assessment of risk (Fischhoff, Slovic, & Lichtenstein, 1981), but there are comparably few methods that allow a descriptive assessment of $r(A,p,E)$ in a practical way that is applicable in case studies. We will present some exemplary methods.

• In some cases, the outcomes are well-defined and evaluated, and the risk evaluation narrows down to an assessment of probability distributions, p_j. For this, there are various techniques available (see Nothbaum, 1997; Yates, 1990, p. 15). We have to distinguish direct methods, such as verbal protocols, rankings, ratings, fortune wheels, odds judgments, and so on, from indirect methods, such as the cumulative probability method, indifference method, and so on (see Yates, 1990, p. 23).

• In what is called the fortune-wheel approach, someone (e.g., the study team) is asked to choose one out of two different bets: one bet is the choice of a color or a sector on a fortune wheel. This color or sector repre-

---

NOTES

1. This part of the definition includes a subjective valuation of events. If a purely objective definition is required (i.e., free of the case agents' values), one can request different alternatives that objectively have a different impact on the agent.

2. If there are fictitious alternatives and/or events assumed by the agent, they are subsumed in the model. However, they will have an objective probability of zero. Thus, the Risk Management model is in line with the Brunswikian approach and differentiates environmental aspects from organismic or psychological aspects (see Westenberg & Koele, 1994, p. 68).

3. The simplified example allows the following formal definition of the risk function. The space of risk cognition S_{RC}—in mathematical terms, the range—of the risk function also encompasses mental stimulation or physical excitation. In this fictitious case, it can be approximated by a two-dimensional vector $S_{RC} = (M,$

sents favorable event(s) (i.e., the win sector or a set of wedges with the win color). The study team has to imagine that this is used in a roulettelike spinner experiment. It would win if the spinner stops at the favorable sector. The second bet is with the decision situation of the case. The study team would win if the event $E_{i,j}$ occurs, given that A_i was chosen. By varying the size of the sectors of the fortune wheel and asking the study team which of the two bets it would prefer, the probability of the event $E_{i,j}$ is estimated as the ratio of favorable/nonfavorable events in the first bet when the study team exhibits indifference.

• One way of measuring risk is the generation of a joint function of outcomes/utilities [$v(E_i)$ or $u(E_i)$] and probabilities (p_i). An example is presented in Figure 12.4. This approach requires that the evaluation of outcomes and the (subjective) probability of their occurrence have to be assessed. If there is no quantitative one-dimensional utility function available, a Multi-Attribute Utility Theory procedure has to be linked to the Risk Management model.

The study team should note that the measurement procedure is affecting the agents' mental model of the risk situation. Thus, in a descriptive approach, the study team first has to find out which method is closest to the agents' natural model. The team then may stepwise introduce more formal models, ending up with highly formal technical models that may lead to better decisions.

T) consisting of the expectancy value M and the trembling T, both estimated by components of the vectorial risk function $r(A,p,E) = (r_M, r_T)$, namely, $M = r_M(A,p,E)$ and $T = r_T(A,p,E)$. Both the expectancy value and the corresponding risk function can be assessed traditionally, whereas the trembling and the corresponding risk function r_T have to be investigated empirically (including the influence of T on the real behavior of the agent).

13

MEDIATION

Area Development Negotiations

THE RATIONALE

Case studies often include the analysis of divergent interests and aspirations formulated by different agents, stakeholders, or interest groups (see Chapter 4) with respect to the current state or the future development of a case. In the course of case analysis, however, the study team can also become involved in the process of conflicting interests that determine case dynamics. This is especially true for land use development as a prototype for ecosystem-based management. Area development often includes mixed ownership and/or the consideration of the residents' or other pressure groups' interests. Although many sections of this chapter cover mediation in general, Area Development Negotiations is a special procedure that was developed during the case studies we ran on urban and regional planning.

Area Development Negotiations (ADN) hypothesizes that groups of case agents or stakeholders have divergent interests and different powers with respect to the case dynamics (see Figure 13.1). ADN provides an assessment of the case agents' interests (benefits) and utility function in an *Exploration Parcours*. An Exploration Parcours is a sequence of stimuli, interviews, experimental settings, and encounters for an individual or a group in order to provide a framing for measures on judgment and

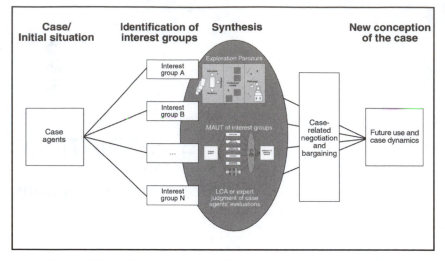

Figure 13.1. ADN Within the Display of the Brunswikian Lens Model

NOTE: The initial focal variable (see Figures 4.2 and 4.3) is the case agents' conflict. The perceptors are representatives of the interest groups. The synthesis is an organized procedure of identifying common and divergent evaluations/interests by means of an Exploration Parcours. The Multi-Attribute Utility Theory (see Chapter 11) is a means of assessing the interest groups' evaluation. A Life Cycle Assessment (LCA) is a specific aspect of evaluation. The terminal focal variable (see Figures 4.2 and 4.3) is an improved case dynamic.

decisions that are close to reality. The Exploration Parcours entails decision alternatives that are evaluated by the study team or experts.

Thus, ADN allows not only for the identification of domains of consensus and conflict between the different interest groups, but also for the examination of case agents' misperceptions. ADN should allow for a more reasonable conflict solution, particularly for the establishment of Pareto-optimal solutions (see below). The synthesis process should end up with a joint strategy of the agents toward the future of the case.

The procedure of ADN is summarized in Figure 13.1. The case agents and their interactions are the focus of the analysis. The study team determines the different interest groups. The synthesis is prepared by a set of procedures, particularly by the Exploration Parcours. ADN organizes negotiation and bargaining processes between the case agents, at least within a setting that is close to reality. The process should end with an improved understanding and new conception of the case and its dynamics for both the study team and the case agents.

ADN is a hybrid. It is a method not only for analyzing case dynamics, but also for promoting them. Furthermore, it integrates different research areas and integrates other methods of knowledge integration, particularly Multi-Attribute Utility Theory (see Chapter 11) or Life Cycle Assessment (see Chapter 18). The latter is used to develop reference evaluations that allow for an identification of misperceptions.

ADN is also a mediation procedure because it not only encompasses a comprehensive recording and analysis of the case by the study team, but it also provides a tool to intentionally promote case development. The concept was advanced in the course of the ETH-UNS case studies on regional and urban development. However, it can also be applied to many other cases in which different conflicting parties are involved.

Mediation itself has a rather long tradition. The mediator has a well-known role in policy science, particularly in international conflicts and labor management disputes. Usually, mediators are consulted if the conflict resolution process is blocked and the parties involved become aware that breaking off the discussion is a very unfavorable solution. We should mention that mediation is sometimes differentiated from arbitration (see Bacow & Wheeler, 1987, p. 156). The latter is a more formally and often legally prescribed procedure (e.g., in family court adjudication or neighborhood conflicts) performed by established institutions.

In general, mediation procedures provide mechanisms for facilitating agreements in conflicts (Susskind, McKearnen, & Thomas-Larmer, 1999). Mediation procedures are a subset of alternative dispute resolution methods. Within these methods, Susskind and Madigan (1984) differentiate between unassisted negotiation, facilitated policy dialogue, collaborative problem solving, passive (or traditional) mediation, active mediation or mediated negotiation, nonbinding arbitration, binding arbitration, and adjudication. As we will see, ADN is a kind of hybrid method combining knowledge and techniques from adjudication/arbitration, mediation, and negotiation/bargaining.

In order to gain a better understanding for what is special and new with ADN, we want to provide a kind of topology of approaches (see Figure 13.2).

Mediation as a Policy Process

As a policy process, mediation has a long history and is a feature of democratic conflict resolution (see the top box in Figure 13.2). Knoepfel

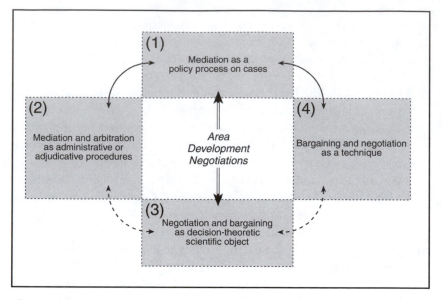

Figure 13.2. The Relationships Between Four Types of Activities and Research in Mediation, Arbitration, Negotiation, and Bargaining Related to Case Analysis

NOTE: The arrows indicate which relations are more established (broken lines indicate weak relations). The ADN particularly integrates (1), experience-based mediation as a policy process, and (3), the empirical decision-theoretic research on negotiation and bargaining.

(1995b) pointed out that mediation processes may be traced back to the foundation of the Federal Union of Switzerland. Thus, in 1481 at Stans, in an overall twisted bargaining on the rights and duties of the members of the Federal Union, the parson Heinrich Imgrund became a mediator and succeeded in promoting a contract in an almost hopeless situation. Furthermore, in 1803, Napoleon Bonaparte, who was the first Ambassador of the French Republic, mediated litigation between the different cantons of Switzerland. The compromise he established resulted in a new constitution and was explicitly denoted as the *Helvetische Mediationsakte* (Helvetic Mediation Document). Two lessons can be learned from the Napoleon style of mediation. First, mediators (and also case analysts) have their own interests. And second, mediation processes (like case studies) are by no means gratuitous. Thus, Napoleon's way of mediation service was honored with permission to hire 16,000 Swiss soldiers, who provided the soil for his empire. In the United States, mediation practice was established at the end of the 19th century. The state of Massachusetts allowed mediation in 1898, and in 1913, the Board of Mediation and Conciliation was founded.

Mediations have been performed in many fields, particularly in education (Cohen, 1995), labor disputes, and family conflicts, but the field of environmental conflicts is also typical (Oppermann & Langer, 2000). Since 1970, there has been an abrupt increase in case studies on environmental conflicts. Because of their impacts, environmental problems could no longer be ignored, and unwanted strategies such as Not in My Backyard (NIMBY) became matters of public concern. Thus, case studies on Locally Unwanted Land Use (LULU) became a scientific object, and the Yes in My/Many Backyards (YIMBY) principle was developed in response to the NIMBY strategy (Mazmanian & Stanley-Jones, 1995). YIMBY provides procedures on how unwanted land uses, such as waste disposals, can become acceptable when a discourse of mediation is initiated that allows compensation of interests.

The case study approach was present overall in research on environmental dispute resolution (see Bingham, 1986; Susskind, 1975; Susskind, Bacow, & Wheeler, 1984). However, when referring to the Harvard Law School tradition, it "soon became clear that the case studies . . . had a powerful teaching potential" (Bacow & Wheeler, 1987, p. vii). It is remarkable that most salient books and reports reflecting national and international experiences dedicate most of their text to exemplary case description (see Bacow & Wheeler, 1987; Claus & Wiedemann, 1994; Gassner, Lahl, & Holznagel, 1992; Knoepfel, 1995a; Moore, 1996; Renn, Webler, & Wiedemann, 1995; Zillessen, 1998).

Mediation and Arbitration as Adjudicative Tools

From its beginning, mediation was a supplementary tool of the legal system. Whether and how far it is accepted as a genuine part of the legal system differs from country to country. In 1992, more than 2,000 statutes and prescriptions regulated mediation practice in the United States. Legal practice in Europe is much less advanced. In environmental conflict resolution, for example, mediation is mostly considered an informal, precourt process. The reserved reception of mediation, particularly in German-speaking countries, is due to the less case-oriented origin of the law systems and the fear of loss of administrative power (see Breuer, 1990; Hoffmann-Riem & Schmidt-Assmann, 1990a, 1990b). On the other hand, in Germany, the *Güteprinzip* (benign principle), which inevitably required, for certain juridical cases, a precourt arbitration procedure, was canceled in 1944 by the Declaration of the Total War (Breidenbach, 1995) and has not been renewed.

Negotiation and Bargaining

Negotiation and bargaining is a field of decision sciences that is a rising discipline on individual, organizational, and societal decision processes. Decision sciences are descriptive, normative, and prescriptive (the distinction between these three approaches is explained in Chapter 11). A comprehensive summary book that may help study teams with a more detailed understanding of the decision-theoretic concepts is provided by Kleindorfer, Kunreuther, and Schoemaker (1993).

For case studies, the knowledge acquired about negotiation and bargaining in decision sciences is a means to do the following:

- For the structure analysis of social conflicts, to understand whether the case agents are interacting in a dilemma such as a malignant situation, or whether the situation is benign in the sense that a smooth conflict resolution is to be expected (see Box 13.1)
- To record, analyze, and understand factual case dynamics, such as the psychological mechanisms or social rules at work

One issue of the art of mediation is a profound situational analysis. The mediator should help to attain a minimum rationality. Although we know that rationality may be defined in various ways, we consider Pareto-optimality (see Box 13.2) as an undisputed target of nondefective interactions. The mediator should support the situational analysis and coping with interactional deficiencies.

In many books on mediation as a policy process, at least the core concepts of decision structure analysis are taken into account. The concept of ADN, however, also aspires to record the diverging perceptions, preferences, and valuations through solid empirical processes. This is why we introduce the concept of the Exploration Parcours, which promises a valid survey of the case agent's interrelation.

In order to gain insight into which types of knowledge are incorporated into case analysis by decision research, we now provide some historic information.

Box 13.1   Malignant and Benign Conflict Structures

According to the social psychologist Lewin (1939), the individual's (conflict) behavior B is a function of the person(ality) P and his or her environment (i.e., the given situation) S. Thus, $B = f(P,S)$.

Heider (1958), another psychologist, found that people tend to overestimate the impact of the personality, P, on the behavior and to fundamentally underestimate the situational impact. For instance, whether a person behaves cooperatively or competitively depends heavily on the given conflict structure.

For a better understanding of the social dynamics, we introduce the distinction between malignant and benign conflict structures. A malignant structure yields severe intra- and interpersonal conflicts and is a dilemma-like situation. The intrapersonal conflict is caused by opposing motives and evaluations that are tied to all preferred decision alternatives. The interpersonal conflict is due to unsatisfied aspirations that sustain at least one party after conflict resolution.

The Prisoner's Dilemma (see Axelrod, 1984) is a well-known malignant conflict structure. In order to give an example that may require ADN, we will introduce 3-Person Quota Games.

Here is the situation (see Tack, 1983). You are an owner—Adams, Brown, or Clark—of one of three park meadows in downtown Berlin. The properties are highly attractive for buildings. According to a new law, which becomes operative tomorrow, the meadows will remain as public parks for the next 99 years if you do not mail a definite construction contract to the municipal authorities today. There are four proposals by real estate companies that fulfill the requirements of the new law. These proposals are only on combinations of properties. All owners know that there is definitely no proposal or chance to submit a proposal for a single real property.

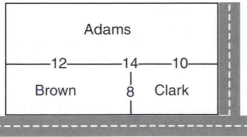

Figure Note. This is a schematic representation of the estates. The numbers display the payoffs for pair coalitions and the coalition between all three players in millions of dollars.

(continued)

Box 13.1   Continued

You are obliged to contract today. If you end up without an agreement with one of the other owners, your situation does not change. The payoff (utility u) of each single property is zero:

$$u(A) = u(B) = u(C) = 0.$$

The value of the proposals to each of the three pairs (AB), (BC), and (AC) of estates are as follows (in million of dollars): $u(AB) = 12$, $u(BC) = 8$, $u(AC) = 10$. Furthermore, $u(ABC) = 14$.

Rules of the game: We want to encourage the reader to experience the conflicts with two other people according to the following rules.

The positions (ownership) should be attributed to the lexicographic order of your name. One of the players should place the offers of each round into a spreadsheet with the columns Number of Offer, Coalition Wanted, $u(A)$, $u(B)$, and $u(C)$ in order to trace and discuss the dynamics later.

The players should analyze the situation for 5 minutes. Then, the bargaining should start with a formal welcoming.

* The player who (then) argues toward a solution should end up with an offer. This offer has to entail a proposal on the coalition and on the payoff distribution among the members of the coalition.

The other players should then respond whether they agree or disagree. If at least one of the players does not accept the offer, the next round starts (see "*"). The parties who disagreed have the chance for a new offer.

The bargaining is definitely finished with Round 9. Furthermore, a time limit of 20 minutes is helpful.

If the bargaining is not finished before Round 9, the players have to discuss who provides the last offer. This offer can be rejected only by members of the proposed coalition.

The reader should play the Quota Game and then discuss the outcome after reading Box 13.3 at the end of this chapter.

The cradle of negotiation and bargaining is clearly the seminal work of von Neumann and Morgenstern (1943) on *Game Theory and Economic Behaviour*. This book combined concepts from mathematics and the behavioral sciences and used concepts such as strategy or equilibrium point (see Box 13.2) for an in-depth structural analysis. This type of analysis is

Box 13.2	Key Definitions for Decision-Theoretic Situation Analysis

Decision and game theory provides an excellent language and tools for describing social conflicts inherent in case analysis. We present a vocabulary of the most important concepts (see Kleindorfer et al., 1993).

Players: The people or parties involved are called players, P_i ($i \in N = \{1, 2, \ldots, n_0\}$).

Strategy: In a decision situation, the players have to choose between different decision alternatives. An individual player's strategy, $s_i \in S^i$, is a complete behavioral plan that determines what the player, P_i, will do in each possible situation of a given decision situation. $S = \Pi S^i = \{s = (s_1, \ldots, s_i, \ldots, s_{n_0}) \mid s_i \in S^i\}$ denotes the set of all possible game tracks.

Payoff Functions: The payoff function u_i^s provides the outcomes in monetary, utility, or other units for a player, P_i, depending on the strategies $s \in S$ chosen by the players.

Bargaining Situation: In a bargaining situation, at least two players, P_i, who have partly opposing interests have the opportunity to provide offers. If the offers are not compatible, this does not (always) necessarily imply breakdown.

Bargaining Set: A bargaining set D is specified by three parameters—X, x_0, and U, where X is the set of available outcome alternatives. x_0 denotes the status quo, or the outcome that will result without bargaining. U describes the set of utility functions for all players: $U = \{u_i(x) \mid i \in N, x \in X\}$.

Pareto-Optimality: An outcome alternative $x_p \in X$ is called Pareto-optimal if no other outcome alternative x exists at which every player can be at least as well-off as at x_p, and at least one player can be strictly better.

Equilibrium Strategy: A strategy $s^* = (s_1^*, \ldots, s_k^*, \ldots, s_{n_0}^*)$ is called equilibrium strategy if any player P_k who singularly deviates from the strategy s_k^* ends up with a utility worse than with s_k^*.

Formally: Let $s^* = (s_1^*, \ldots, s_k^*, \ldots, s_{n_0}^*)$ provide the outcome alternative x^*, and let $s^{*k} = (s_1^*, \ldots, s_k^*, \ldots, s_{n_0}^*)$ with $s_k \neq s_k^*$, $k \in N$ provide x^{*k}. The outcome alternative x^* is an equilibrium point if and only if $u_k(x^*) = u_k(x^{*k})$ for all strategies $s_k \in S^k$ and each player P_k, $k \in N$.

normative and tied to the conception of man as an economic, rational being. Case analysts, however, should know this body of knowledge, because a crisp analysis of the situation should always precede a behavioral analysis. The books of Nash (1950), Raiffa (1968), Fishburn (1970), and

Shubik (1983) present the framework for the structural analysis along the lines of the von Neumann and Morgenstern approach.

However, case agents are not rational beings. Conflict resolution is based on subjective interpretations of the human actors. Psychological processes such as motivations (Berkowitz, 1962; Deutsch, 1949, 1973); bargaining behavior (Siegel & Fouraker, 1960; see also Neale & Bazerman, 1991; Pruitt & Carnevale, 1993; Bazerman & Neale, 1993; Bazerman, 1998); group dynamics; or cognitive decision biases and fallacies (Kahneman, Slovic, & Tversky, 1982; Scholz, 1983a) are the object of social psychological research. This research is substantiated by solid, experimental-empirical research that allows for a clear validation of the theories and assumptions. It is noteworthy that mediation as an aid for conflict resolution was already investigated systematically in the late 1960s (see Pruitt & Johnson, 1970) but was not continued intensively (see Steiner, 1983). Through the concept of the Exploration Parcours, we will tie this valuable body of research to the embedded case study design.

Bargaining and Negotiation as a Technique

The fourth field in Figure 13.2 encompasses social techniques on how to perform well in negotiations, how to avoid breaking off discussions, and unwanted positional combats. With respect to its objects, this type of knowledge is in between the decision-theoretic and policy process knowledge and relies highly on reflections of practical experience attained in consulting. Best known is the Harvard Project. A whole series of books provides heuristics and rules of thumb that assist successful negotiation. The titles of the books, such as *International Mediation: A Practitioner's Guide* (Fisher, 1981); *Getting to Yes: Negotiating Agreement Without Giving In* (Fisher & Ury, 1981); *Getting Together* (Fisher & Brown, 1988); or *Getting Past No* (Ury, 1993), best illuminate the range and philosophy of this type of work. These books are "bargaining handbooks" (see also Fuller, 1991) that were written primarily for a lay audience. For case study teams, however, the books may become valuable if practical help is necessary in inefficient discourse dynamics of a case.

Normally, ADN supports, rather than substitutes for, the real decision process. If the study team becomes involved in the bargaining and negotiation and all key players are participating in the discourse, one may assume that ADN is substituting for the real bargaining process. However, this assumption does not hold true for various reasons.

LESSONS TO BE LEARNED

▶ Mediation is conceived of as a synthesis method that integrates the different interests of the participants. ADN creates a close-to-reality assessment of interests and conflicts related to planning variants by means of the Exploration Parcours.

▶ Different approaches to mediation have to be delineated—mediation as a policy process on cases, mediation and arbitration as administrative or adjudicative procedures, negotiation and bargaining as a decision-theoretic paradigm, and bargaining and negotiation as behavioral techniques. ADN links case-related policy processes with decision theory. The latter encompasses both a game-theoretic description of the situation and a cognitive and behavioral psychological analysis.

▶ The game-theoretic description of the situation should precede the cognitive and behavioral psychological analysis.

THE METHOD IN DETAIL

ADN is a seven-step procedure:

Step 0: Case Analysis, Method Selection, Hypotheses

Step 0 is not part of the actual ADN process. It entails the case analysis and the faceting of the case, including the study teams' election of ADN as the appropriate method.

For illustration, we will refer to the SEW site, another study on the reintegration of industrial areas (see Scholz, Bösch, et al., 1997) that is highly similar to the Zurich North case study. For the historical background of the case, see Chapter 5.

The principle differences between the Zurich North site and the SEW site are the closer proximity of the latter to Zurich downtown and the smaller size of the SEW site. The SEW site encompasses only one sixth of the area of the Zurich North site. The most decisive difference, however, lies in the relations between the owners and the municipalities. These were much more strained in the SEW site than in the Zurich North site.

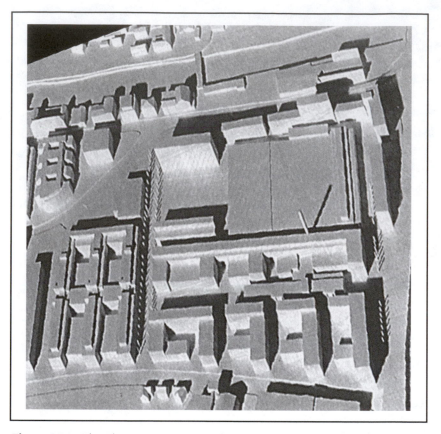

Figure 13.3. The Planning Project Developed by the Owners
NOTE: This project was the object of ADN. The planning variant (PV_1) was guided by the vision of a close-to-industry quarter. Only 10% of the area was for apartments, with the remaining area broken down into 35% offices, 20% laboratories, 10% infrastructure, and 1% leisure/culture.

The strained relation between the owners and the municipalities was one reason that the study team introduced an ADN synthesis group. We formulated a series of specific hypotheses and a general guiding thesis. We conjectured that the projects desired by the owners (see Figure 13.3) will yield no Pareto-optimal solution (see Box 13.2) if an environmental perspective is introduced. Furthermore, we assumed that not only do case agents show different evaluations, but also that their perception is at least partly biased, and that there was a typical win-win situation. In general, we hoped to improve the case through ADN.

When the study was performed, the final contract had to be drawn up between the city government and the owners. The *Gestaltungsplan,* which is a contract according to the canton construction regularity, entailed the maximum number of floors and the maximum share allowed for apartments, service industry, or industrial production at different lots. The contract also entailed a minimum area left for parks and squares. Because these numbers were the outcomes of a 10-year bargaining between municipalities and owners, the study team and the owners agreed to consider them as constraints and for the ADN. In addition to the *Gestaltungsplan,* the owners had developed a planning variant to support the bargaining and the promotion (see Figure 13.3).

Incidentally, the ETH Department of Architecture also became interested in the creation of planning variants for the SEW site. Based on the constraints of the *Gestaltungsplan,* student groups had designed different models. Like the owner's projections, these planning variants (PVs) entailed extensive descriptions of future use; traffic concepts; the share of old buildings sustained; and infrastructure, including energy supply. Assisted by the professor of the class (Henz, 1995), the study team selected three different variants that filled the funnel of potential developments in a comprehensive manner. These variants were called PV_2: Green Network, which was characterized by a large green belt park crossing the area; PV_3: Working and Living, which referred to a social project called *KraftWerk1* (Blum & Hofer, 1993); and PV_4: Art, in which a main issue is a projected art academy. These planning variants and the owner's project PV_1 were regarded as suitable objects for the ADN discourse.

LESSONS TO BE LEARNED

▶ The formulation of hypotheses is an important part of case study work in ADN. The hypotheses organize the decomposition of the case, data acquisition, and synthesis.

▶ The participants of ADN or the bargaining set may be restricted for various reasons. The study team should explore and reflect these constraints carefully before the ADN begins.

Step 1: The Authorities' Will for Cooperation

ADN should be performed only if the parties who are authorized by law or democratic rules accept bargaining on the property and want to improve the case through a discourse like ADN.

The legalized people at the SEW site were the owners. In the beginning of the case study, they did not fully accept ADN. However, because of the difficult bargaining situation with the municipal authorities, the owners became open-minded and agreed on ADN.

LESSON TO BE LEARNED

▶ The willingness of the key players to participate is a necessary prerequisite for ADN.

Step 2: The Mediation Mandate

No one likes to join a game with unknown rules. This is why the mediator should receive a mandate. This mandate should detail the role of the mediator as well as the concerns and expected output of the mediation. The mediation mandate best describes the object and target of ADN, especially which and how many sessions should take place and which form of bill, mission, or recommendation is to be expected. The mediation mandate also has to fix the degrees of freedom, particularly in selecting participants and experts.

It is often also helpful to have an accompanying expert team or project that assists the participants in information acquisition. For instance, if a planning project is altered by a proposal, the participants in ADN should have the chance to provide a new financial calculation or environmental impact assessment. This expertise is particularly necessary if the misperceptions and biases of the participants are the object of ADN.

There was no full mediation mandate with the ETH-UNS case study. The main owner formally agreed on the case study and a synthesis group on ADN. However, the mediation task for the study team was not specified. The municipalities from the Department of Construction were also key players because any deviation from the construction permission has to be accepted by the Department of Construction. Actually, this department was exceptionally skeptical about ADN because the head of the department was afraid of a loss of power through a group decision process like ADN, which is a substitute for dyadic (two-person) bargaining.

LESSONS TO BE LEARNED

▶ The study team should receive a formal mediation mandate for ADN.

▶ If the misperceptions and biases of the participants are the object of ADN, the study team must have access to expert knowledge that generates generally accepted reference information if necessary.

Step 3: Selection of Interest Groups and Key Players

The mediator has to determine which parties or interest groups and key players should participate in the ADN. As shown in Figure 13.1, the number of groups and representatives determines the focal length of the decomposition and synthesis in ADN.

There is no push-button method for this step. In principle, there are two approaches. In the inductive approach, the study team should ask, in sequence, all known case agents whom they consider to be a key player, who is extraordinarily affected by the case, and who should participate (Laws, 1999). Furthermore, it is helpful to ask case experts who were involved for professional reasons, not only because the experts usually have detailed knowledge about the people and institutions interested, but also because experts may be necessary for a reference judgment (see Step 2). In the normative deductive approach, the mediator may determine interest groups according to a sociological or legal model that differentiates between certain groups or interests.

Both approaches were interlinked in the ETH-UNS case study. From a top-down perspective, four different groups were identified:

G_1: Economists, consisting of two subgroups, the estate owners and the investors

G_2: Residents

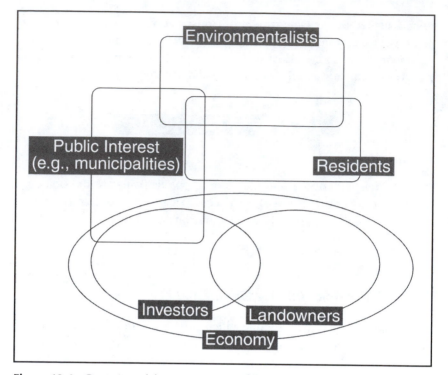

Figure 13.4. Grouping of the Participants in the Area Development
Negotiations on the SEW Site

NOTE: The groups are partly overlapping, as in many ADN.

G_3: Environmentalists

G_4: Governmental administration and municipal authorities

Several problems were encountered in this step. For example, the
groups were partly overlapping (see Figure 13.4). Thus, the financial
manager of the Zurich Theater is a potential investor but also a municipal
employee. Therefore, certain groups could have no representatives. This
is the case if future generations are represented in ADN (see Seiler, 1995).
At the SEW site, it was hard to find members of environmental interest
groups who were attracted by the downtown site. Furthermore, one has
to decide who should be elected. Because we wanted to have a maximum
input of opinions, we took a twofold strategy. We looked to have at least
one typical participant representing the modal opinion in each group and

at least one so-called criticizer. In the end, 18 people were determined to be the key players and were assigned to the four groups (see Figure 13.4) by the study team. The participants were informed about their group membership(s).

LESSONS TO BE LEARNED

▶ The selection of groups and participants is a crucial step of ADN. There is no push-button method for this step. Normative top-down and factual bottom-up strategies have to be combined.

▶ Often, some groups or critical voices are not wanted by some parties. Although there are different strategies in selecting the participants, a balance should exist between opinion leaders, typical representatives, and criticizers.

Step 4: Exploration Parcours: Recording Interests and Evaluations

The Exploration Parcours is crucial for ADN and yields an assessment of the participants' interests and evaluations.

Clearly, qualitative interviews are an indispensable part of this step and help the mediator to understand the specific perspective and relation of the key players to the case. However, we strongly recommend supplementary interviews with a more formative procedure. This procedure should confront the key players with the case and apply best practice and methods for measuring interests and evaluations of the participants in a close-to-reality encounter. This encounter has to entail salient segments or variants of the case and its future formation. Hence, the Exploration Parcours is best created by physical models or computer animation. We want to stress that the ideas of traditional sociopsychological research, such as experimental design, hypotheses, and independent and dependent variables, are helpful for an efficient survey of interests and evaluations (see Aronson, Ellsworth, Carlsmith, & Gonzoles, 1990). The study team should have sufficient skills in experimental design, inquiry, and statistical analysis available, if necessary, through the assistance of method experts.

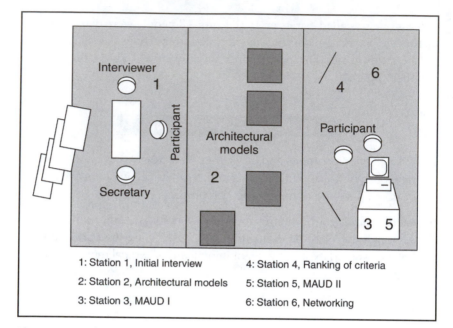

1: Station 1, Initial interview   4: Station 4, Ranking of criteria

2: Station 2, Architectural models   5: Station 5, MAUD II

3: Station 3, MAUD I   6: Station 6, Networking

Figure 13.5. The Six Stations of the SEW Exploration Parcours

Next, we will introduce the setting of the Exploration Parcours by example.

The 18 key players were called and asked to participate in an ADN that included an Exploration Parcours. The target and conception of the study was introduced. Then, the candidates received a formal invitation, a booklet with the description of different planning variants, and the assertion that all information would be confidential. With respect to interviews and data recorded in the Exploration Parcours, the participants were again promised that their data would be confidential. With quantitative data, this can be accomplished if only the mean values of the interest groups are published. Remarkably, none of the key players selected refused to participate. Upon attending to the Exploration Parcours, the targets of ADN and the Exploration Parcours, as well as the confidentiality agreement, were explained again.

As can be seen from Figure 13.5, we staged three rooms for this parcours. The parcours started at Station 1 with an introductory interview. During the interview, the participants were sitting in front of a large, bird's-eye view of the site. Furthermore, we posted maps from Zurich,

Switzerland, and Europe to indicate that a more general perspective is also permitted. The core target of this stage was to record the criteria used in case evaluation. Thus, we dealt carefully with the question, Which aspects or criteria do you consider important for a future creation of the site? From the answers, a secretary extracted a list of criteria.

Then, at Station 2, the close-to-reality encounter was organized. The participants were confronted with four planning variants of the future formation of the case that consisted of wooden models of scale 1:500 (see Figure 13.3). Detailed information was provided on each planning variant. Actually, each participant received a 24-page booklet several days before the parcours and was asked to read it carefully. To make sure that all information was present, the participants had to listen to a tape-recording of the text while watching the wooden models of the planning variants. After each variant, the participants were asked two questions: What is good or bad about the planning variant? With respect to which criteria does this variant perform well or poorly? After all of the models were shown, the participants were asked for a quick (intuitive) rank ordering of the four variants (evaluation v_1).

Note that the order of display of the four models was randomized. This was done because we know from cognitive psychology that the order of presentations causes primacy and recency effects that may affect the attractiveness and the recording of the variant.

Then, the evaluation criteria, which had been recorded by the study team at Stations 1 and 2, were displayed at Station 3 on a pin board for the participants. They were allowed to cancel, merge, or add criteria. A multicriteria analysis of utility judgment (see Chapter 11) was performed using the participants' own criteria. This procedure provided another, decomposed rank ordering of the variants (evaluation v_2), including weights and ratings of the variants with respect to the attributes.

Station 4 was also shown on a pin board. The study team introduced six attributes that they considered sufficient for an evaluation of the case, two each from the domains of ecology (c_1, c_2); economy (c_3, c_4); and of sociology of living (c_5, c_6). Note that some of these criteria are operationalized by methods that have to be considered themselves as methods of knowledge integration. The criteria were as follows:

c_1: Life Cycle Assessment (see Chapter 18)

c_2: Bio-Ecological Potential Analysis (see Chapter 19)

c_3: Interest rates

c_4: Risk of not renting

c_5: Integration to given social structures

c_6: Mixture of different uses (living, production, offices)

The definitions of these attributes were explained, and the participants had to rank these criteria according to their subjective rating.

At Station 5, a second, MAUD TWO session was conducted. In this session, only the criteria c_1 to c_6 were used. Furthermore, the study team, assisted by experts, had previously assessed each variant according to each criterion! For instance, an estate expert calculated the interest rates, and a subproject (see Figure 4.1) had performed an LCA. Using these data, the planning variants were rated by expert teams. The task of the participants was only to attribute the weights to the different criteria. MAUD TWO combines the knowledge available in experts' specific, criteria-bound assessments with the key agents' evaluations of the relative importance of the criteria.

Finally, at Station 6, in order to get insight into the mutual personal relationship between the participants, the people had to select the two key players they personally would like and dislike most in a mutual bargaining deal.

As can be seen from Table 13.1, there is a huge data set that allows for some statistical analysis. We will present, as an example, some results with the statistical method applied in order to provide insight into the value of statistical analysis as part of ADN.

With a simple frequency analysis, the number of criteria used were analyzed. We had a 4×3 table because we distinguished four groups, G_i, and three types of criteria, c_k. The mean frequency of the latter decreased from social criteria ($M = 6.6$) via ecological ($M = 4.1$) through economic ($M = 2.0$) criteria. It is noteworthy that the economists ($n = 8$) used the least economic criteria ($M = 1.6$); these criteria were more crisp and were dominated by the return of investment criteria (i.e., interest rates).

With statistical testing, we have the problem of not only small groups, but also overlapping groups. Fortunately, there is a simple, conservative strategy. When considering one group (e.g., the economists), this group may be tested versus its complement. Clearly, this does not allow for multivariate analysis of variance. But we think that statistical testing

Table 13.1   Stations, Objects Encountered, and Data of the
                   Exploration Parcours

Station	Encountered Objects	Data
1—Initial interview	Bird's-eye photo on SEW site, maps of Zurich, Switzerland, and Europe	• Criteria of evaluation of area quality • Impact factors for a successful promotion of an area (useful for a Formative Scenario Analysis)
2—Variant interview	Four planning variants of scale 1:500, plans and description of future use	• Criteria of evaluation of area quality • Intuitive preference order of variants (evaluation 1)
3—MAUD ONE	Four planning variants	• Criteria of evaluation of area quality • Variant rating on the criteria • Weights on criteria • Calculated preference of variants (MAUD ONE)
4—Pin board	Nine criteria	• Order of evaluation criteria
5—MAUD TWO	Four planning variants	• Weights on the six criteria considered sufficient by the study team
6—Network	List of actors	• Ratings on most liked/disliked bargaining partner

provides helpful additional information about the size of the difference between the groups, even if the α level in repeated testing is not corrected by a Bonferroni adjustment or a similar procedure, as recommended in statistical textbooks. Usually, nonparametric methods (see Siegel & Fouraker, 1960) are appropriate because no normal distribution can be expected. When using the nonparametric Mann-Whitney test, we detected that the group of governmental administration and municipal authorities, G_4, showed no difference from the other groups when testing the numbers of criteria, preferences, weights, or variant ratings according to criteria. However, the economists clearly differed from the other groups because they definitely rated the economic criteria as most important.

Table 13.2   Mean Ranks of Intuitive Ranking (v_1) and of Variant
Preferences According to MAUD ONE (v_2) and
MAUD TWO (v_3)

Evaluation Procedure	PV_1: Close to Industry	PV_2: Green Network	PV_3: Working and Living	PV_4: Art
Intuitive ranking (v_1)	3.3	1.7	1.9	2.5
MAUD ONE (v_2)	3.3	1.9	1.9	2.9
MAUD TWO (v_3)	3.9	1.0	2.1	3.0

NOTE: A "1" is the best rank, and a "4" is the worst. PV is an abbreviation for planning variant.

The homogeneity of the economist group, G_1, could also be illustrated by a cluster analysis on the weights attributed to the criteria c_1 to c_6. Further methods of multivariate statistics were applied. For instance, by correlation analysis, we could find that the interest rates (c_3) and integration to given social structures (c_4) were highly negatively correlated ($r = -0.72$, $p < .001$) (also see the note to Figure 13.7). This means that the conflict is created by controversial priorities toward these two criteria. Those who gave high ratings to the interest rates gave low ratings to the integration to given social structures, and vice versa. An improvement of the integration to given social structures would ask for planning and construction, which reduces the density and profitability.

Further insight into the conflict structure provided the analysis of the evaluations v_1 to v_3. As may be seen from Table 13.2, the planning variant PV_1, Close to Industry, scored the worst and the variant PV_2, Green Network, scored the best with all participants. The variant PV_1 does worse if a multi-attributive utility procedure (MAUD TWO) is applied. This is primarily because of the economist group's, especially the owners', rating. When they recognized their own project, they immediately scored it best. Yet this was much more difficult in a decomposed and indirect rating.

Through the work of various subprojects accompanied by experts, misperceptions could be detected. Thus, the interest rate of the owners' variant PV_1 was much smaller than the other variants'. The owners fallaciously supposed that the Close to Industry variant (PV_1), which was designed by them, would show the highest revenue of investments.

Finally, the sociogram derived from Station 6 of the Exploration Parcours shed light into the mutual personal affinities among and

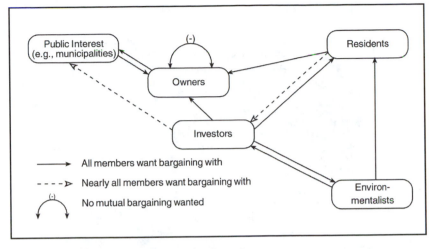

Figure 13.6. Sociogram Between the Four Groups

NOTE: The economists are split into the subgroups of owners and investors.

between the groups (see Figure 13.6). During the case study, there was a clear mutual desire for bargaining between the public administration and the owners. Owners and public administration (but not the investors, who naturally may not ignore the future renters' interest) were very reserved and were not interested in bargaining with the residents and the environmentalists.

In the eyes of the study team, all the statistical information finally ended up in a picture that conveys the essence of the conflict at the SEW site (see Figure 13.7). This picture condensed the conflict structure and displayed the mediator's knowledge before Step 5.

Figure 13.7 shows the economists and their main ties, the interest rates. This is just a reflection of their professional task and their specific relation to the case, but they can switch easily from dollar to eco-dollar, that is, from the financial balance to the eco-balance represented by a Life Cycle Assessment (LCA; see Chapter 18). However, an LCA is also of value for the environmentalists, who are traditionally oriented toward the green. Green is a part of quality of living, and this is important for the residents group. However, the public citizens want space for living, parks, and playgrounds, which causes some conflict with interest rates, at least in an area that is close to downtown.

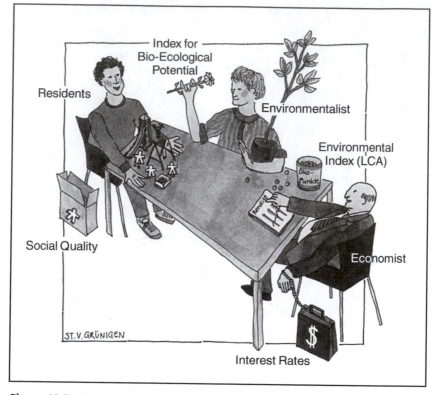

Figure 13.7. A Main Orientation of the Interest Groups at the SEW Site and the Essence of the Conflict Structure

NOTE: The main conflict is established by different priorities for interest rates and social quality, that is, the integration into the given social structure. Note that social quality and integration into the given social structure demand parks and playgrounds, which reduce the interest rates.

LESSONS TO BE LEARNED

▶ The case agents' values, criteria, weights, and so on are assessed in an Exploration Parcours. Data are sampled on similarities and differences between the interest groups and on the preference for planning variants.

▶ The identification of the case agents' misperceptions becomes possible when, first of all, the judgment of the agents can be assessed validly by a MAUD, and second, if the planning variants (alternatives) can be assessed validly according to these criteria by the study team.

▶ Statistical analysis, particularly a visualization of ratings, is a powerful tool for analyzing complex structures. It is most crucial for interpreting the data and obtaining a result on the essence of the conflict.

Step 5: Dedicated Bargaining and Negotiation

The target of ADN is threefold: gain a better understanding of the conflict structure, obtain better judgments and better interactions between the key players, and enable Pareto-optimal solutions.

Before arranging a negotiation, the results of the Exploration Parcours should be submitted to the participants. The study team introduced the main results as presented above. We started with presenting the diverging ratings between the interest groups. Then, the participants' ratings were compared with the experts' assessments. Note that the latter were calculated in subprojects based on disciplinary knowledge (see Figure 4.1). Finally, because some of the key players were still skeptical with respect to real bargaining as part of an ADN discourse, we presented some provoking propositions, for instance, that the owners and the municipal authorities did not really want bargaining in an ADN discourse. The results of the Exploration Parcours were discussed intensively in one 4-hour workshop with a long break.

We want to present only the most salient outcomes. It soon became clear that the planning by the owners was suboptimal and had to be revised. When analyzing the fallacious judgments, we revealed the following issues: An increase in the mixture of different uses (c_6), particularly a higher percentage of housing, and an incorporation of environmental aspects when improving the Bio-Ecological Potential (c_2) would increase the overall quality and evaluation of the planning. In particular, the owners and their architects were ignoring these advantageous issues. Also, the investors were not committed to this failure, presumably because they have better access to the market and know the needs and preferences of renters and future residents (for more details, see Scholz et al., 1996).

The representatives of the public administration agreed that they were afraid of a loss of power and hence did not want ADN. They presumed themselves superior in bilateral negotiations where they usually have a more powerful position than the other party. However, when they would be just one of a larger set of interest groups, they felt worried about losing their advantages.

The ETH-UNS case study on the SEW site was finished with this workshop. A mediation or direct participation in bargaining was not planned, especially because of the skepticism of the public administration. After the workshop, we got positive feedback from owners and investors; in addition, the public administration changed its mind in the course of the ADN.

After the case study, a brief conflict between the city and the federal administration arose. While enlarging a university campus from 5,000 to 7,500 places for students and university employees, the city wanted to decrease the number of parking places from 1,200 to 700. Apparently motivated by the positive experience with ADN, the city obliged the federal construction department by entering into an ADN procedure.

We will not go into the details of this project, but we want to provide information about the bargaining experience. There were only three, partly overlapping interest groups: three representatives from the city; two representatives from the federal authorities; and a group of six experts, including the mediator. The expert group also had to perform the subproject work and generate the data and technical knowledge. The proceeding was strictly organized along the steps of the ADN. In the final step, contracting negotiations were also planned.

According to the project plan, the study team intended to link the definite, final bargaining and the contracting on the number of parking places directly to the results of the Exploration Parcours. However, because of several issues, this plan was changed. First, the high-ranking people who initiated the ADN were not available for the time-demanding project sessions. The project sessions were necessary because the bargainers had to acquire data on the history, legal prerequisites, and the potentials of public transportation. However, the representatives were not authorized in the sense that they were allowed to do the final contracting. This presumably holds true for many mediation procedures (see Figure 13.8).

Second, the Exploration Parcours, which entailed the evaluation of four different traffic concepts for the new campus, had a broader range than the bargaining. Thus, we arranged two roundtables in which the final contracting took place. The Exploration Parcours, however, helped to find a common language, identify misperceptions, and understand the differences between the parties. It is noteworthy that, similar to the ETH-UNS case study Zurich North, the Exploration Parcours revealed that one variant, which was made taboo in the course of previous interaction, had a high rank in the Exploration Parcours.

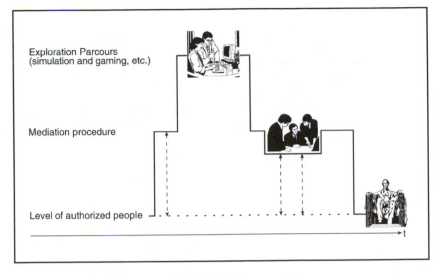

Figure 13.8. The Discourse of ADN With Representatives

NOTE: The initiators and the authorized people or groups send representatives, who have to coordinate with them. The Exploration Parcours, which also may entail gaming and simulation, is often a tool to support, but is not a substitute for, the final negotiation.

LESSONS TO BE LEARNED

▶ Even if the real negotiation process is not part of ADN, the study team may affect the bargaining.

▶ If representatives are participating in ADN, special attention must be paid to the relationship between representatives and representees.

▶ In general, the Exploration Parcours and ADN support the real bargaining; they are not a substitute for it.

Step 6: Submission of Results

If representatives are involved, the results of the ADN have to be submitted to the decision makers. Often, the public is interested as well.

In the case of the parking place negotiation, the roundtable did not end up with an agreed-upon solution. One party did not accept the mediator's proposal, presumably because of unfortunate group dynamics. The

---

Box 13.3 Solutions for Malignant Conflicts

What makes the situation in a Quota Game malignant or benign? The conflict is clearly shaped by the payoff $u(ABC)$ of the grand coalition (ABC). If the joint utility for the grand coalition is smaller than 15, there is the tendency to form a two-party coalition and to skip one player. If the payoff for the coalition $u(ABC)$ is greater than 15, the situation becomes (more) benign. The number 15 is the sum of the quota $q(A)$, $q(B)$, and $q(C)$. The quota results if the equation system

$$q(A) + q(B) = 12, \quad q(B) + q(C) = 8, \quad q(A) + q(C) = 10$$

is solved. There are various suggestions for what to do if the payoff of the coalition (ABC) does not equal 15 (see Crott, Scholz, Ksiensik, & Popp, 1983). For example, the parties may split the positive or negative difference between 15 and the payoff of the coalition (ABC) according to their quotas or according to other rules. Quota games induce an extraordinary behavioral dynamic and often yield irrational or inappropriate outcomes, particularly non-Pareto-optimal solutions. Note that with $12 < u(ABC) <$ 15, each pair coalition is not Pareto-optimal. With the payoffs given, for instance, only the coalition (ABC) allows for Pareto-optimal solutions (see Box 13.2).

---

results of the roundtable negotiation and a comment from the mediator were sent to the responsible decision makers. This comment entailed a differentiated assessment of the bargaining situation, the conflict structure, and game-theoretic analysis about aspiration adjustments and fair compromises derived from the Exploration Parcours. It was interesting to see that the decision maker ignored the refusal of the representatives and was completely satisfied with the mediated result.

LESSONS TO BE LEARNED

▶ Submitting the results of the study is a separate step of ADN.

▶ If representatives are involved in ADN, the responsible decision maker may deviate from the mediation proposal.

FUTURE WORKSHOPS

THE RATIONALE

Future Workshops is a label for a technique for creating unconventional goals, plans, designs, concepts, and prospects for the development or a future state of a case. Often, what is chosen for a case study is something that is in an unsatisfactory condition for which a case agent or study team desires a fundamental change. The study team might not consider Formative Scenario Analysis an appropriate method for constructing future developments because this method is believed to be too prone to common, linear extrapolations. Similarly, System Dynamics might be also doubted because, for instance, too little data are available. In such a situation, one potentially appropriate method is a Future Workshop. For case study purposes, the Future Workshops method should not stand alone, but rather should be planned as part of an exploratory embedded case study (see Table 2.1). Future Workshops have to be supplemented with the application of other methods or with a case data analysis that focuses particularly on the case's history and current structure (see Box 2.1).

Future Workshops were invented in the 1960s by the Austrian humanist and futurist Jungk (1973). Some researchers became very enthusiastic about Future Workshops, considering them a cure-all. Future Workshops are integrative, holistic, creative, basically democratic, and provocative; their participants should be communicative, encourage one another, and appreciate deliberation (see Jungk & Müllert, 1994; Weinbrenner & Häcker, 1991, p. 116). Jungk's concept of Future Workshops was that they would be a tool for participatory planning and conflict resolution as well as a means of eliciting new ideas through divergent thinking about the future state of a case. This chapter concentrates exclusively on the latter function, because participatory processes were already covered in some detail in Chapter 5 on Area Development Negotiations.

Future Workshops are a creativity tool. They help to answer questions such as, If the case agents were to break through their normal, linear, sequential way of thinking and acting, in what way might the case develop?

The Future Workshop technique provides scripts for group processes and thinking. Because of this, Jungk himself called his technique Future Creating Workshops, and the basic principle is to establish an organized process for switching between the intuitive and the analytic modes of thought at each of the three core stages of the workshops. This process is conceived of as having a double helix architecture (see Figure 14.2, p. 230). The basic principle of switching between intuition and analysis is one of the strengths of this method. In spite of the fact that we consider Future Workshops a fruitful tool for case study work, they should be handled with some skepticism. The outcomes of Future Workshops are often highly overestimated.

In order to optimize creative casework with Future Workshops, the study team should concentrate on six major foci, five Ps and one T. They are as follows:

- *Problems* dealt with
- *People* participating
- *Processes* being evoked and enhanced
- *Products*
- *Places* at which the workshops occur
- *Time management*

Problems. Future Workshops have been applied mostly in urban or regional planning, technology, and organizational development. However, they are also used at times for other purposes, like the search for a suitable clinical therapy, a marketing strategy, or an innovative conflict resolution technique. Thus, the problems (i.e., the types of cases dealt with by this method) may vary widely. Their common prerequisite, however, is that the case needs radical reconsideration and that (many) case agents feel dissatisfied with its current state and the proposals for its future development.

People. The optimal size for a workshop is about 20 people, although what these people are like makes a crucial difference. In Europe, particularly in Germany, many of the past Future Workshops were advertised openly, and a random sample of people participated. However, thorough evaluations of such workshops have indicated that with such a sampling, the ideas developed are neither innovative nor realizable in practice (Memmert, 1993). As cognitive science research reveals, creative, novel ideas are achievements of subjects who are highly competent in their field and have the desire for creativity. The necessity of the latter is illustrated nicely by a quote from creativity research in music: "I (and probably you) do not wake up in the morning with a new idea for a string quartet. . . . What is crucial is the personal goal of doing something creative" (Baron, 1994, p. 130). Thus, the participants must have some capabilities and the will for the creation of the future.

Processes. Future Workshops rely on creativity and divergent thinking performed by groups. To better portray the possibilities and limits (due to procedural constraints) of Future Workshops, we will review briefly some findings from cognitive science. Cognitive scientists, particularly psychologists, have taken many approaches in their study of creativity, and readers who are interested in this subject should consult Guilford (1967), Boden (1990), Johnson-Laird and Byrne (1993), or Sternberg (1988). Future Workshops target qualitative innovation and are rooted in the creative thinking methods developed in the 1930s and 1940s. Different techniques were developed, such as Crawford's (1954) attribute listing or Osborn's (1963) brainstorming. Idea checklists, another example of such tools, involved idea-spurring questions like, "What can be added?" or "How about a blend?" or "What are new ways to use it as is?" (see Mayer, 1992, p. 366). The techniques mentioned aimed at increasing the creativity of engineers, product designers, managers, and other professionals.

According to Osborn (1963), successful brainstorming groups have to obey the following rules (see Mayer, 1992, p. 366):

1. *No criticism.* The participants are instructed to follow the principle of deferred judgment. All critical comments have to be postponed until after the initial brainstorming session.

2. *Quantity is wanted.* Participants are encouraged to suggest as many ideas as they can without thinking about the quality.

3. *Originality is wanted.* Wild and unusual ideas are more valuable than practical recommendations.

4. *Combinations are wanted.* Participants are encouraged to use the suggestions generated previously in the session.

Products. According to the findings of cognitive science research, the goals and products of Future Workshops have to be considered carefully. Although it is important that the process be open to new and unexpected outcomes, the study team should define in detail which products they want to have as a result.

Places/Accommodation. The location and the spatial arrangement of the room are important (see Figure 14.1). For a workshop to be successful, there should be enough space to allow for flexible groupings and activities. Group activities should not be subject to outside disruptions, nor should any room changes take place. A special decoration should convey that something exceptional is happening, and that cooperation and new ideas are expected. Posters or photos of the case and its problems may be another element of the room equipment. In any case, the accommodations and the room service should be organized carefully, and their importance should not be underestimated. If the place is not appropriate for the needs of the Future Workshop, there is a low probability for a good process and good products.

Time. The core phase of a Future Workshop should take less than 2 full days so that it does not lose efficiency. The script for the Future Workshop should include a detailed schedule of all phases.

The case study team should always maintain a basic level of skepticism about Future Workshops and their products. Many people who consider themselves unrecognized geniuses have not sufficiently determined whether their ideas work. Furthermore, "unfortunately the grand claims concerning the effectiveness of industrial creativity courses have not always been substantiated by controlled research" (Mayer, 1992, p. 367). Thus, not only the novelty, but also the success of an idea or invention must be judged critically.

Skepticism about the performance of the group is also endorsed. As we know from social psychology, groups perform better only for certain types of problems. We have already discussed some limits of group work

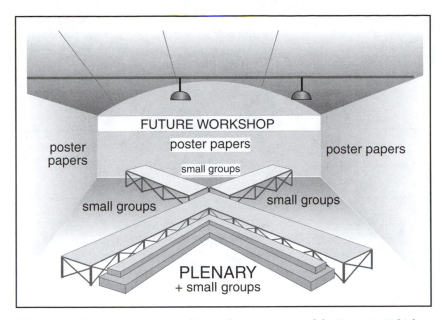

Figure 14.1 Sample Location and Spatial Arrangement of the Room in Which a Future Workshop Takes Place

in Chapter 9 on Formative Scenario Analysis. The study team should ensure that the workshop participants are well prepared and sufficiently competent with respect to the case and its constraints. The Future Workshops should, in particular, entail periods of individual reflection. Suitably long phases of individual work should antecede brainstorming and the collection of ideas. A more extensive review about recommendations for arranging effective and efficient group meetings are given in Chapter 16 on Synthesis Moderation.

Figure 14.2 presents the Future Workshops within the framework of the Brunswikian Lens Model. The perceptors are the different participants. Usually, a wide lens is necessary, that is, the group should be heterogeneous in terms of knowledge, age, sex, status, and so on. Future Workshops are structured such that they alternate between analytic and intuitive thinking. How this has to be organized is represented by a double helix (see Figures 14.2 and 14.3).

The concept of Future Workshops bears some resemblance to think tanks, as well as to the Delphi Method, Formative Scenario Analysis, and some other methods presented in this book. Think tanks are groups of

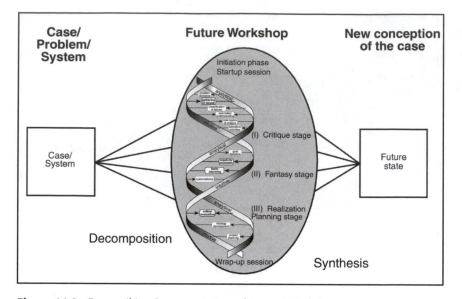

Figure 14.2. Brunswikian Representation of Future Workshops

NOTE: The lens entails three stages. Each stage includes a switching between the analytic and intuitive modes of thought. This overall process organizes a decomposition of the case, mostly in the analytic steps of the critique stage. The synthesis is done primarily in the intuitive steps, at the latest in the fantasy stage.

experts, often found in foundations or private companies, that do consulting in strategic management. The RAND Corporation is often considered the cradle of the movement of scientific planning after World War II (see Abelson, 1996; Smith, 1991). Western society obviously became aware of the necessity for long-term future planning. Questions such as how to protect and promote American national security interests during the nuclear age, and how to further welfare, education, and social security, became the subjects of planning projects. For instance, in the late 1960s, more than 10,000 independent professional think tanks were advising the U.S. government. Future Workshops are a kind of countermovement in that they try to incorporate randomly selected laypeople and use the energy and fantasy of the citizens to design and govern their own future (Jungk & Müllert, 1994). These ambitious goals naturally have to be curtailed. However, learning from this history, we derived a promising technique that is useful in case study work.

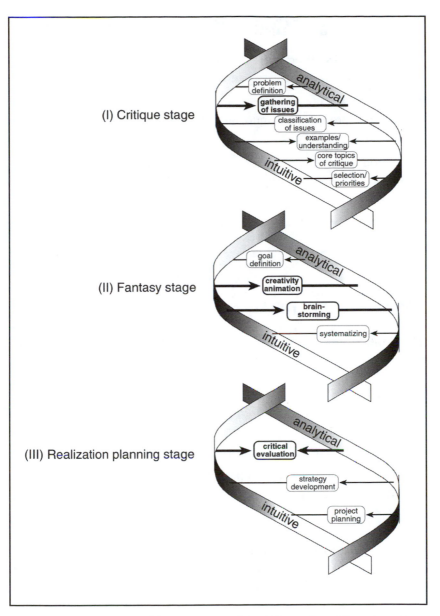

Figure 14.3. Integration of the Intuitive and Analytic Modes of Thought at Any Stage of the Project

NOTE: Also see Figure 14.2.

▬▬▬▬▬ **LESSONS TO BE LEARNED** ▬▬▬▬▬

▶ Future Workshops may be applied if no conventional solution meets the aspirations of the case agents.

▶ Random selection of participants does not guarantee that ideas, plans, or other products are innovative or have the chance of becoming realized.

▶ In order to get innovative ideas, competent knowledge about the case has to be combined with techniques that enhance the production of new ideas.

▶ Skepticism and critical evaluation are indispensable means to creativity.

THE METHOD IN DETAIL

The whole course of a Future Workshop can be broken down into seven parts:

- Initiation phase
- Start-up session
- Critique stage
- Fantasy and utopia creation stage
- Operation and realization planning
- Wrap-up session
- Follow-up stage/phase

The method focuses particularly on the integration between intuitive and analytic modes of thought at any stage of the project (see Box 14.1). Jungk and Müllert (1994) use the representation of a two-spiral double helix for describing when each mode should be applied (see Figure 14.3). The ETH-UNS case study Zurich North did not have a Future Workshop. We will thus adopt the Workshop on Housing and Living Areas for Children, Adolescents and Seniors in a district of Zurich (Koch & Trüb, 1993) because this workshop could be considered a part of the Urban Development synthesis group (see Chapter 5).

Box 14.1 Intuitive and Analytic Modes of Thought

Analysis versus intuition is a well-defined complementarity in cognitive science (Hadamard, 1945; Fishbein, 1975; Gigerenzer & Murray, 1987; Hammond, Hamm, Grassia, & Pearson, 1983; Scholz, 1987; Springer & Deutsch, 1993). Analysis and intuition are modes of thought that are based on qualitatively different cognitive processes and mental representations. Both can be defined operationally by a list of attributes. Experienced raters may assign these attributes based on thinking aloud or written protocols that report the individual's information processing (Scholz, 1986, p. 76; Scholz, 1987, p. 60).

Analytical thinking features (a) conscious information acquisition, selection, and processing; (b) pure intellect or logical reasoning, independent of temporary moods; (c) sequential, linear, step-by-step, ordered cognitive activity; and (d) separation of the details of information. Analytic thinking is (a) mostly independent of personal experience, (b) based on conceptual or numerical patterns, (c) of high cognitive control, (d) free of emotions, and (e) accompanied by high uncertainty toward the product of thinking.

On the other hand, intuitive thinking is characterized by (a) preconscious information acquisition; (b) understanding through feeling and empathy; (c) sudden, synthetical, parallel processing of a global field of knowledge; (d) treatment of the problem structure as a whole (i.e., Gestalt cognizing). The processing is shaped by (a) personal experience; (b) pictorial metaphors; and (c) low cognitive control, all of which are accompanied by emotional involvement. In the end, there is a feeling of certainty toward the product of thinking, but skepticism with respect to the process.

Initiation Phase

Definition of Case and Core Topic. When the study team has decided to conduct a Future Workshop, the object and goal of the workshop have to be defined. The study team has to reconsider the case. Will the whole case be part of the workshop, or just some subareas? Attention has to be paid to naming the Future Workshop, and the study team should communicate its specific expectations. Is the goal of the workshop primarily the production of ideas, or are some implementations expected? Already, in the very beginning, the team should consider what kind of support and resources might be necessary for the follow-up phase and any implementation processes in order to prevent unrealistic expectations and subsequent frustration. Core information about the Future Workshop and its goals should be printed on a leaflet, which may also be used as an invitation.

Note that the naming and the announcement of the Future Workshop predetermine the participants' habits, thinking, and motivation, and thus are very crucial.

Participants. The participants should cover a broad range of knowledge and case experience. Social competence and a willingness to enter an open process are required.

If the prospective realization is targeted, the study team should incorporate key agents and decision makers (e.g., politicians). If more than 20 participants are expected, there should be at least two moderators who are responsible for the organization, scheduling, and so on.

Invitation/Schedule. Usually, workshops last 1½ to 2 days, and the study team has to prepare a detailed schedule. The invitation has to include not only information about time and location, but also a brief description about the core problems and topics to be treated and the goals of the workshop.

Places/Accommodation. A suitable environment is a very important issue. The ideal room has no permanent interior fixtures. It should have soft lighting, moderate acoustics, light tables, chairs with rollers, and about 10 noteboards on which posters and other papers can be pinned. The environment has to allow for a flexible plenum and small group work. The study team should plan the structuring of the room carefully, because well-planned accommodations are a necessary prerequisite for good participant motivation and habits. All preparations should be finished at least 1 hour before the workshop starts.

Equipment. The equipment should be kept as simple and nontechnical as possible. Important are poster-sized paper of about 4 × 6 feet, colored paper, broad-tipped markers (at least one for each participant), adhesive tape, and a camera for photographing the noteboards.

Start-up

Start-up. The start-up session (30 minutes) should introduce the core topic and provide background information and the motives for the workshop. Furthermore, the procedure, the modes of group work, and the request for visualization are introduced. The three core phases and the plan to switch between analysis and intuition are presented. The schedule is introduced, but considered as a time frame.

Personal Introduction. An important step of the workshop is the introduction of the participants. Large nametags are indispensable if at least two of the participants do not know the majority of the others. Each person should introduce him- or herself, reveal his or her personal and professional background, and formulate his or her expectations for the workshop in one sentence. If the participants do not know each other and are not practiced in presenting themselves, the personal introduction can be arranged in small groups. One person will then present the members of his or her group.

The participants can also be asked to bring and show something from their professional or private world and to explain the significance of it for them and/or for the future of the case. After the start-up, the arrangement of the chairs should be changed to signal the beginning of an open, flexible, and active process in the workshop.

Critique Stage

This part is the real beginning of the Future Workshop, and it is organized along the Osborn brainstorming rules (see above).

Problem Definition/Gathering of Issues (30 to 45 Minutes, Plenary). The members are asked to think about the major problems of the case and to write labels for them on a red sheet. Each member is challenged to radically formulate what is wrong with the case, and what about it frightens, embarrasses, or irritates him or her. Group members are questioned sequentially and, for each subject, have a maximum of 30 seconds. This phase requires spontaneous, intuitive contributions. Any discussion, responses, or comments on the critiques of other group members are strictly prohibited at this stage. Note that the participants first have to think individually about critiquing the case with respect to the core topic(s) and then list their issues on paper. Once this is done, the public collection of issues and the group discussion finally begin.

Preliminary Prioritizing and Classification of Issues (10 Minutes, Plenary). The topics are grouped and displayed on a noteboard. Then, the issues have to be rated with respect to their relevance. This can be done in a group process if all participants allocate priority points to the issues.

Illustrating Issues by Examples (15 Minutes, Small Groups or Plenary). For participants to get a broad understanding, each issue has to be illustrated by a brief example. For instance, if the lack of "green" is criticized, the member has to name a place, street, or block that he or she considers negative. Some experts (see Memmert, 1993) also recommend that the critique be framed in positive terms at the first stage.

Construction of Core Topics of Critique/Improvement (20 Minutes, Two Problems for Each Small Group or Plenary). A short list of core topics is composed based on the previous two steps. The core topics are defined and characterized by attributes, and examples for improving are sampled.

Selection and Final Prioritizing of Topics (10 to 20 Minutes, Plenary). This phase ends up with an analytical discussion of the priority and the interrelationship of the core topics. The subjects of fantasy and utopia creation are defined.

Fantasy and Utopia Creation Stage

Goal Definition. This stage has to turn critiques into positive ideas, plans, wishes, longings, and visions. The participants are encouraged to provide ideas for a renewing or (re)creation of the case independent of political, financial, social, legal, or other constraints.

Creativity Animation. The moderator should arrange a relaxed, deliberate, enthusiastic, ardent fantasy atmosphere. The study team should also encourage "enactive" performances (like role-playing or imitation of animal encounters with the case) and visionary descriptions of the renewed case.

Brainstorming (30 to 60 Minutes, Small Groups). The participants have to formulate suggestions for the development of the case and its potential future state. In particular, peculiar, unconventional, strange, unrealistic, utopian ideas are wanted. This part is the most difficult but decisive phase of the whole workshop. Often, the participants make well-known conventional suggestions. An approved tool is role-playing within a science fiction framework. Ingenious ideas are often found in small groups. The groups should not invest too much time in the preparation of their plenary presentation; rather, they should focus on the generation and formulation of their ideas.

Systematizing (40 Minutes, Plenary). The ideas are presented in a plenary session. The study team should group, classify, and order the suggestions. The most fascinating and promising ideas should be listed.

Operation and Realization Planning

Critical Evaluations of Ideas and Utopias (20 Minutes, Plenary). At this stage, everyone's suggestions will be evaluated. Usually, most of the utopian ideas will be so realistic that they may be accomplished easily. As expected, some proposals will be beyond reality and will require some adaptation. For the most part, the case agents and the study team are interested in the development of the case, so specific strategies have to be elaborated. This will be the object of small group work again.

Strategy Development (45 Minutes, Small Groups). Plans for realizing and implementing the proposals will be developed in small groups. For utopias, it is necessary to achieve specific strategies on how these can be used for case progress. Bridges to reality have to be constructed.

Listing requests and demands is part of this step. At this stage, the study team may also plan a Formative Scenario Analysis in order to gain better access to the impact variables of the case.

Project Planning (30 Minutes, Small Groups). Some of the plans and projects developed should be accomplishable. Thus, many Future Workshops end with the foundation of initiatives and projects. A first project draft should be worked out in outline form using the poster format (few words, graphically structured information, on a large paper, readable by the group).

Wrap-up Session

Wrap-up Session (40 Minutes, Plenary). This segment has two targets. On one hand, the participants should show commitments for the future projects. Many new ideas and initiatives were born in the Future Workshop. The case study team (and not just the other participants) will have to incorporate these ideas into their plans. Usually, groups for the follow-up phase will also be created.

On the other hand, the process has to be examined critically and acknowledged. This is the formal end of the core phase.

Follow-up Phase

Each Future Workshop deserves a protocol. The study team has to provide a booklet entailing the most important documents (i.e., preparation material and invitation letter, list of participants, schedule, documents from each stage, project outlines, some photos, etc.).

Based on the documents, the case study team has to reflect upon and evaluate the Future Workshop. In particular, the study team has to think about whether its conception of the case has changed. Proposals should be made on how the results have to be integrated in the whole case study plan, and how the projects, which were presumably initiated, might be implemented and possibly supported by the study team.

LESSONS TO BE LEARNED

▶ Future Workshops are a potential tool for case transition if nonlinear case prospects are wanted.

▶ Creativity and innovative ideas are the exception to the rule. Creativity has to be prepared. Usually, innovative products (e.g., case prospects) result if the right people are put to the right problems/questions and stimulated for the appropriate processes at proper places within a suitable time frame.

▶ The key technique for appropriate processes consists of a sequential interplay between the analytic and intuitive modes of thought in the critique, fantasy, and operation/realization stages.

▶ The Future Workshop should *not* be regarded as a stand-alone method. Carefully prepared Future Workshops provide insight into the potential of the case.

▶ The study team has to consider carefully, in advance, what expectations may arise from a Future Workshop.

EXPERIENTIAL CASE ENCOUNTER

THE RATIONALE

Experiential Case Encounter is a method of enhancing the study team's case understanding. It consists of organizing activities, such as cleaning a sewage canal, working in a kindergarten, or selling a characteristic product, and thus realizing personal experiences with the case. The method complements the abstract scientific approach that mostly dominates the thinking of the academic study team.

Foundations of Experiential Case Encounter

There are two basic principles behind the Experiential Case Encounter process:

- *Enactive* learning, which is learning through direct physical interaction with the case and sensation
- A *side change* (i.e., a change of sides) by means of a specific type of participatory observation

A brief description of Experiential Case Encounter was given in Box 5.1. In this chapter, we will outline the theoretical foundations of this method and reveal how enactive learning and a side change are means of supporting case analysis and other types of case interaction.

Enactive learning (Bruner, Goodnow & Austin, 1956), knowledge acquisition by doing (Dewey, 1966), and sensomotory training and experiences are well-known fundamental principles of learning. These types of learning affect and refer to all sensory systems.

Enactive learning supplements alphanumerical or conceptual case representation with visual impressions and supplements higher-ordered declarative case knowledge with episodic case knowledge (Scholz, 1987, p. 172). The study team's concept of the case and its relation to the case change fundamentally when the case is encountered directly. Dealing with the case enactively opens the door to intuitive thinking and understanding.

The idea of side change is linked primarily to two theoretical psychological concepts: perspective-taking and empathy (see Steins, 1998; Steins & Wicklund, 1996).

Historically, perspective-taking has already been addressed in developmental contexts. According to Piaget's (1924, 1960) illustrations of visual-spatial perspective-taking, one example of perspective-taking occurs when children, sitting directly across from an experimenter, acknowledge that their own right is the experimenter's left. A modified notion of perspective-taking was developed by Flavell, Botkin, Fry, Wright, and Jarvis (1968). According to these authors, a perspective-taking response is a response in which one person, on the basis of the information to which another person has been exposed, infers his or her state of knowledge. A non-perspective-taking orientation is defined as one in which one judges another person's state of knowledge on the basis of his or her own privileged knowledge; this perspective thus implies egocentrism (Piaget & Inhelder, 1956).

Empathy is an understanding of the thoughts, feelings, and actions of another. Thus, as a result, the world becomes structured as it is for the other (Cottrell & Dymond, 1949). At times, empathy also requires that one have the ability to view another person in terms of morality (Hogan, 1969), or that he or she "feels into" the consciousness of another person.

Both perspective-taking and empathy are defined scientifically in terms of other people. However, we occasionally use these terms in reference to other systems, such as animals, villages, or other complex systems, such as landscapes. Here, perspective-taking means the ability to understand how a system functions. Although it seems somewhat peculiar to speak about empathy in reference to a landscape, some experts develop the ability to evaluate the integrity and stress of ecosystems intuitively (Baeriswyl, Nufer, Scholz, & Ewald, 1999).

A major difference between perspective-taking and empathy is that perspective-taking requires a certain (optional) distance from the person or case so that a switch in perspective can occur. Empathy occurs only within a certain emotional proximity.

The most radical Experiential Case Encounter and side change was carried out by the German writer Günter Wallraff (see von Linder, 1986). Wallraff began his work in the 1960s reporting on industrial workers' job conditions, occupational health, views on society, and so on. Each report was based on personal, on-the-job experience over the course of several months. His objective was to transmit these experiences to the public. Several of his case encounters, such as pretending to be an opponent of the former Greek junta or a foreign worker cleaning chemical industrial equipment (Wallraff, 1991), caused existential endangerment through torture or other perils. Obviously, Wallraff referred to strategies of participatory observation in anthropology, ethnology, and sociology in a radical manner.

Today, a professionalization of side changes is in the program of many management training institutes (see Hauser, 2000). For this, case encounters are used instrumentally. Their main focus is on creating experiences in which the participants are in a difficult or borderline life situation. Often, the intent of the experience is to increase understanding of common people's everyday problems. In this way, the managers develop a fundamental understanding of social work and obtain an early warning system that alerts them to potential changes in attitude, habit, and vulnerability in social systems. A ground rule in this type of side change is the acquisition of empathy through experience.

However, as mentioned earlier, Experiential Case Encounter does not claim to uphold the same standards in participatory research as some variants do, where the researcher simultaneously acts as a disguised case agent and a case data recorder.[1] During the Experiential Case Encounter, study team members are not disguised. They ask the case for cooperation and explain their principles and intentions frankly. The target of an Experiential Case Encounter is to open up the case, thereby getting views from angles that otherwise might remain hidden.

Experiential Case Encounter induces *press;* that is, participants feel compelled to deal with the case (see Murray, 1938). According to Wicklund and Steins (1996), press and conflict are the most important (independent) psychological variables that motivate one to leave an egocentric view and put together constructs about others. Note that, presumably, every Experiential Case Encounter causes (cognitive) conflicts, because new issues are detected that violate the study team's previously held expectations about the case.

In this chapter, no Brunswikian Lens Model representation is introduced because there is no compelling reference to the basic principles of probabilistic functionalism. Yet the new experience gained from an Experiential Case Encounter can be viewed as a perceptor in the lens concept.

LESSONS TO BE LEARNED

▶ Experiential Case Encounter is a means of broadening the study team's concept of the case. Its basic components are enactive learning and side changes. The applications of these principles induce perspective-taking and empathy, which cognitively and emotionally expand the concept of the case.

▶ An Experiential Case Encounter brings the study team into the case. According to social psychology theory, press—understood as a summons or demand to deal with an issue more intensively—and cognitive conflict are important for understanding and thus support the Experiential Case Encounter.

THE METHOD IN DETAIL

Option Selection

In the first step, a list of appropriate case activities has to be created. In most cases, there is a broad range of options. In the ETH-UNS case studies on regional or urban development, we could distinguish three different kinds of options.

First, there are jobs and activities whose physical encounters contribute to the enactive case experience. Spending one full day as a worker on a farm or in sewage canal cleaning (e.g., at the Zurich North site) provides a lot of insight into soil characteristics or material fluxes, and the experience reveals case views that usually remain hidden.

Second, certain activities provide intense access to the case agents, such as working in a kindergarten, a home for the elderly, or a nursing home. These activities stress the genesis of empathy and a side change with certain interest groups.

Third, if no direct access to the case exists, one has the option of looking at transactions with the case. For instance, if it is a case study on sustainable production in Costa Rica, one option might be selling a characteristic product such as fair-trade coffee or bananas.

Entering the Case

We recommend that the idea of a side change be communicated openly
to the case agents. In many studies, we have found that case agents easily
understand experiential learning and appreciate it. In general, they even
value this activity as a matter of mutual learning. Occasionally, if no appropriate activity can be offered at the time of the study, case agents try to
construct rather spectacular artificial activities. These options should be
avoided; looking back, a study team member might sometimes feel frus-
trated about having invested a lot of work in senseless activities. Furthermore, these artificial activities also entail the danger of mutual voyeurism
and case distortion.

Behavioral Rules

The most decisive principle is that the study team members should try
to do their job in the best manner, that is, as if case agents were doing the
work. Thus, the study team member should work in the usual way from
beginning to end and not mistreat his or her special position.

Discussions about the case study or about what the case researcher
considers significant should be postponed until the end of the Experiential
Case Encounter.

In an Experiential Case Encounter, the study team members should allow the immediate. It is best if they avoid continuously formulating hypotheses about the case and the case agents. Participants' primary focus
should be on their current task and on any obstacles to this work. Likewise, reflections on oneself and hypotheses about how the study team
members are thought of by the case members should be suppressed as long
as possible and postponed until after the Encounter.

Sometimes, the study team is not pleased at the idea of spending an extra day in seemingly unproductive activities. The range of arguments that
members raise is broad, from lack of cost efficiency to doubt that any-
thing new will be experienced. The latter is a particularly common argument when a person has performed a similar job in the past. As we found
out, this is typical before Environmental Case Encounter arguments. Post

hoc, the overwhelming majority of participants are satisfied and report that the experience they gained as study team members is processed in a completely different way now and seriously affects the understanding of the case and its representation. This holds true if the behavioral rules are obeyed.

Transmission of Results

The experience gained has to be discussed with the study team or, better still, disseminated in the form of a brief report. This allows the study team to share its experiences. Often, hypotheses about the case and about system models are changed after an Experiential Case Encounter. However, when making such changes, the study team has to pay attention to what information it takes, because members' experiences are individual and are not necessarily representative. Furthermore, the study team has to cope with the recency effect (Jarvik, 1951) and has to be sure that the new information will be judged appropriately and not overrated.

LESSONS TO BE LEARNED

▶ Experiential Case Encounter is a formative method involving several steps and rules that must be followed.

▶ Experiential Case Encounter is viewed with skepticism by most members of the study team prior to participation, but it is rated positively by the overwhelming majority of the case study researchers after the method is applied. Arguments against the encounter, such as it being an inefficient use of time, disappear, and the relationship between the study team and the case becomes intimate.

NOTE

1. Note that the researcher acts as a recorder. Tape-recording a conversation is illegal unless all participants have given permission for the recording.

16

SYNTHESIS MODERATION AND GROUP TECHNIQUES

THE RATIONALE

Moderation comprises techniques to support interaction, communication, information exchange, opinion creation, goal formation, and cooperation in and between individuals and/or groups by at least one moderator.

Synthesis Moderation in case analysis incorporates the following (see Figure 16.1):

- Group techniques and group management
- Idea and case analysis moderation
- Project management

Synthesis Moderation encompasses means and methods that support the synthesis work as it is described in general by the Brunswikian Lens Model (see Figure 4.3). Moderation aids a successful application of the methods presented in this book and furthers the incorporation of case agents into the study.

The moderator is a coach who masters idea and case analysis moderation, project management, and/or group techniques and thus promotes the efficiency of the group process. The role of the moderator is explicit in

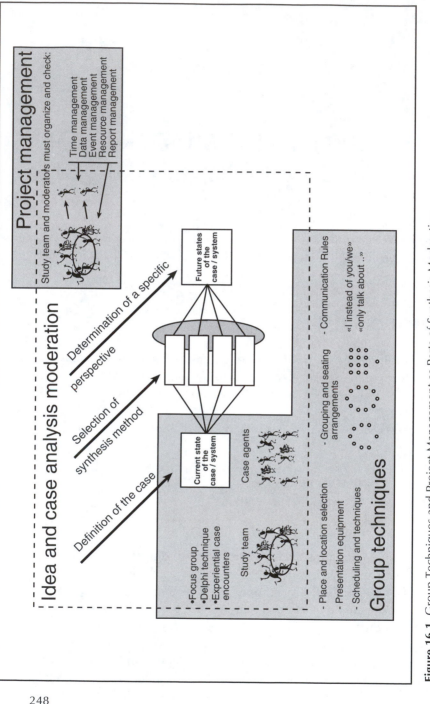

Figure 16.1 Group Techniques and Project Management as Parts of Synthesis Moderation

NOTE: The moderator also has to take care of the idea and case analysis moderation (i.e., definition of the case, goal formation, selection of the synthesis method, and goal formation). Synthesis Moderation can be structured according to the Brunswikian Lens Model.

the sense that the study team determines one or more people who temporarily or permanently take on the role and the tasks of the moderator.

The label *moderation* was developed as a technical term and became
very popular in German-speaking countries in the late 1960s. The reason
for this development is a reaction against the dominance of (militaristic)
hierarchical communication and the lack of teamwork experiences
(Decker, 1988, p. 19; Freimuth & Straub, 1996, p. 31). Thus, the traditional concept of a group leader or teacher was substituted with the concept of a coach, promoter, or tutor who is not necessarily a master in the
subject but a master in the methods of promoting group performances.

Moderation is different from mediation (see Chapter 13) in that overt
conflicts are not considered the primary object of moderation. Synthesis
Moderation starts from the assumption that the members of the study
team and the case agents involved share a common interest in a better understanding and promotion of the case. Conflict resolution may be part of
Synthesis Moderation, but the focus on it is temporary, and it is not the
principal topic.

Etymologically, moderation originates from the Latin *moderari* or
moderare, which means "temperate" but also "to set standards."
Moderare comes from the Greek *medomai,* which signifies deliberation or
reflection (Ziegler, 1993, p. 20). We can take from this that the moderator
should act with some reservation and circumspection.

Foundations of Synthesis Moderation

Synthesis Moderation refers to three major bodies of knowledge. First,
there is research in social psychology on small groups (for an overview, see
Blumberg, Hare, Kent, & Davies, 1983; Kerr, MacCoun, & Kramer,
1996a, 1996b; McGrath, 1984); group processes (Berkowitz, 1975;
Hastie & Park, 1986; Steiner, 1983); interpersonal behavior and communication (Bales, 1950); and social exchange theory (Piaget, 1960;
Thibault & Kelley, 1959). On the more sociological side, contributions on
interpersonal communication and symbolic interaction theory (Goffman,
1959; Schutz, 1971) or sociometry (Moreno, 1960) provided valuable inputs. As the reader may realize from the publication dates, the research
goes back to the heyday of theory formation in social psychology in the
1950s. The message of this research is that groups have their own dynamics, and their efficiency depends on their constraints (e.g., preparation,

time, size, communication tools); their motives and motivation; and their subject-task relationship (see Hackman & Morris, 1975). We reviewed these issues briefly in Chapter 14 on Future Workshops.

Second, we may refer to applied psychology, including group therapy (Kaplan & Sadock, 1971). Several psychological group techniques have been developed to improve group performance (Moore, 1987; Remocker & Storch, 1987) or interactions between groups (Hare, 1996; Krueger, 1988). Many of these techniques, such as the Delphi Method, Nominal Group Technique, or Communication Strategy Training Technique, were tested for planning, creativity, intellectual, or decision-making tasks (see McGrath, 1984, p. 60) and thus are of great importance for case study work. A well-known book that motivates the need for reflective group interaction and group techniques is Janis's (1982) book on disastrous policy decisions and fiascoes caused by groupthink.

Third, we will relate to the many handbooks on moderation. In German-speaking countries, moderation techniques were developed primarily after the pioneering work of Schnelle (1979). Schnelle was a management trainer who initiated the Metaplan® Method, which targets emancipatory teamwork, as it was desired following the year 1968. This can be seen from the title of the core book of Schnelle's group: *Methods of Moderation: The Shaping of Opinion and Decision Processes in Groups That Share Learning, Living, Working and Playing* (Klebert, Schrader, & Straub, 1991). According to these conceptions of group techniques, the moderator has to organize discussion groups, seating arrangements, breakdown into subgroups, role-taking, and so on. He or she has to order the discussion by types of communication, such as group discussions, dialogues, nonverbal communication, and so on, to increase awareness of crucial issues. All in all, the moderator has to be a jack-of-all-trades in a sociotechnical laboratory and has to accompany the group through the course of teamwork from the very beginning to its end.

Domains of Synthesis Moderation in Case Studies

Subsequently, we refer to the Brunswikian Lens Model of case analysis as it has been presented in Figures 4.2 and 4.3. Furthermore, we are considering a medium-sized study team of 5 to 20 members, or a synthesis group in an ETH-UNS case study (see Figure 5.6). Team selection and case study preparation, including case definition and the introductory report on the thematic perspective of case analysis, are not necessarily considered part of Synthesis Moderation. The case definition and goal formation are often done in cooperation with the case agents before Synthesis Moderation is organized. If case definition is part of Synthesis Moderation, the case agents should be included and procedures such as focus groups (see Box 16.3, p. 263) or Delphi Method can be applied.

A basic tool of Synthesis Moderation is group management by group techniques. If the study team is considered the engine of case analysis and knowledge integration, the moderator, group management, and group techniques are the gear oil. Group management includes the following (see Figure 16.1):

- Place and location selection
- Presentation techniques
- Scheduling and time management
- Grouping and seating arrangements
- Communication rules

When using the language of the Brunswikian Lens Model, the current state of the case and its conception is the initial focal variable, the goal of the study is the terminal focal variable, and the synthesis methods are the link between these two. The idea and case analysis moderation also encompass planning the synthesis process, especially finding the right method of knowledge integration, arranging experiential case encounters (see Chapter 15), and acquiring expert knowledge on demand. During the course of the study, Synthesis Moderation ensures that the study team holds on to the definition of the case, the determination of the system boundaries, and the goal of case analysis.

We want to note that our perspective differs somewhat from the strict qualitative, narrative case study approach. For instance, Becker (1992) states that case researchers should always question what the case is about and thus deal with a tentative case definition. In our experience, this is extraordinarily difficult for group processes and transdisciplinary case studies in which case agents are involved.

A very important aspect of moderation is goal formation, which continues as goal maintenance and goal change. We have observed hardworking study teams that did not have an explicit goal and ended up in dissent or confusion (see Box 16.1). Thus, experienced moderators have a

| Box 16.1 | Moderator Responsibilities in Embedded Case Studies |

The moderator is a catalyst and quality manager. In embedded studies, the moderator should, in particular, know about the methods of knowledge integration. Thus, the moderator needs to be able to recommend the appropriate methods for dealing with problems discussed or goals to be attained. Because this is a specialized area, a methods specialist should be partnered with the moderator. In general, the moderator is a member of the study team. However, when moderating, his or her tasks are restricted to process management, and he or she should not contribute to content matter.

The moderator is a master of the group process. He or she should be able to

- Define the do's and don'ts
- Remain in a neutral position without appraising or criticizing arguments and behavior of the members
- Promote the goal formation (see Box 16.2)
- Offer communication rules that stimulate discussion, consensus building, and collective goal formation
- Provoke discussion in order to reveal conflicting ideas and valuations
- Smooth defective interaction, uncover the scapegoat mechanism within the team, and reveal it as being destructive
- Observe the mood of the members and stimulate the group process
- Integrate all participants, even outsiders
- Refrain from competing with group members if sufficient knowledge is not available
- Abstain from the hierarchical role as a group dominator
- Suggest the right tools (such as the methods presented in this book) for interaction, knowledge integration, and problem solving (see Dauscher, 1998; McGrath, 1984; Schnelle 1979; Schultz, 1989)

brief summary of the goal or terminal focal variable (see Figure 4.2) written on a poster in a prominent place. Groups often develop a creative dynamic that leads to shifts in the objectives and even in the subject of investigation. Another phenomenon is that the group locks on to highly specialized or sophisticated questions.

Box 16.2   On the Role of Goal Formation

"Where are you going?" asks the eagle.

"I am off to seek fame and fortune," said the field mouse.

"Well," said the eagle, "for two coins I will sell you this feather that will speed you through the forest."

"Great," said the field mouse as he gave the coins to the eagle.

Soon the field mouse came across a squirrel.

"Where are you headed?" inquired the squirrel.

"I plan to see the world and make my fortune," replied the little field mouse.

"Well, in that case you will want to get there as soon as possible. I have these special acorns that will give you extra energy and help you get there faster. Ya got any coins?" asked the squirrel.

"Sure," said the little field mouse and he swapped two coins for two acorns and hurried on his way, until he was stopped by a wolf.

"You seem to be in a big rush," said the wolf. "Where ya going?"

"I am off to seek my fortune and I am going as fast as I can," replied the field mouse.

"There is a shortcut that will get you there immediately," said the wolf with a toothy grin. "Just go right through that hole over there," and the little field mouse dashed into the wolf's den, never to be seen again (Krueger, 1988, p. 51).

So, one important task of the moderator is to feed back the group process with respect to the overall goal of the study team and to correct the group process in case of shifting or deadlocks. The larger the group, the more important this issue becomes.

Within the framework of this book, project management will also be considered as part of the synthesis moderation. Hence, the moderators temporarily (e.g., for a meeting or a series of workshops) have to secure the management of time, personnel, budget, data, events, and reports.

THE METHOD IN DETAIL

The aim of this section is to sensitize the reader to the social dynamics and the organizational effects in case study teamwork. The reader should not expect a simple set of rules that allows frictionless synthesis work. This is impossible for two reasons. On one hand, the interactions during synthesis work are often both too complex and too specific. Therefore, no complete rule system can be provided. On the other hand, there are hundreds of books written on the relevant aspects listed above. The aim of this section is to stimulate awareness of trip wires that may hinder a successful case study.

Group Techniques and Management

Place and Location Selection

The environment matters (see Figure 16.2). This also holds true for case study teamwork. When choosing a location for case study work, the study team (and the moderator) has to answer the question, Is the location appropriate for the tasks that need to be completed? We will list some important issues to be checked. The first is the size and the flexibility of the location. One may distinguish between fixed feature, semi-fixed feature, and informal space. The logic of the space has to mirror the conception of the Brunswikian Lens Model (see Figures 4.2, 4.3, and 16.1). Space arrangements should allow meetings of the whole study team in the beginning and at the end, and of small groups during the middle of the case study.

Case study teamwork requires maximum flexibility for grouping and much space for displaying data, maps, pictures, posters, drafts, and so on. Thus, the place should look more like a laboratory than an office. Note that when synthesizing the data of the subprojects, (physical) space is necessary for synthesizing the knowledge and the data available in different people. Although there is considerable progress in computer technology (GroupWare) (de Tombe, 1999), and many issues can be represented and exchanged by the computer, the direct verbal and personal exchange is most important.

Case study teams are often temporary, ad hoc groups that are composed only for that study. Thus, the placing of the case study center and the meeting places have to be optimized with respect to the travel time of the study team members and the case agents. Despite the growing virtual world, the study team does need a home, that is, a permanent base that strengthens the team members' identification. Thus, make this home as attractive as possible.

Figure 16.2 Prerequisites to Moderation

NOTE: Prerequisites are necessary with respect to location, arrangement, equipment, and preparation. This is already illustrated by the upper left figure. It presents Catherine Vivonne de Rambouillet (1588-1665) in the middle of the picture. In this picture, although Pierre Corneille is reciting, the seating arrangement is essential for the art of conversation. Note that the color of the *chambre blue* and the whole house was intentionally designed for conversation purposes.

The upper right picture shows a moderation scene from the 1970s conducted by Metaplan. It has a similar arrangement as in the older picture, and the reader can ascertain the control power of the moderator. The lower left picture shows a small group that is clustering impact factors in Formative Scenario Analysis in one of the ETH-UNS case studies. Although the moderator is not visible, he prepared the interaction of the group carefully, including arrangements of tables and the mode of presentation (i.e., writing potential impact factors on slips of paper).

Grouping and Seating Arrangements

If you observe people in different situations, you will recognize that they tend to choose different seating arrangements. Thus, when placing the table(s) and chairs for a structured group activity in case analysis, it is important to consider the type of interaction that is wanted. The moderator has to ask which type of interaction is most appropriate. Note that

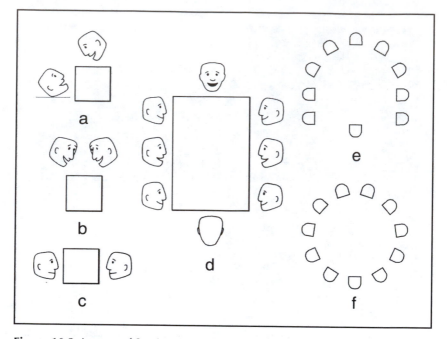

Figure 16.3 Impact of Seating Arrangements on Conversation

NOTE: For conversation, it is best to sit at the corner (16.3a). For intense cooperation, side-by-side placement (16.3b) is best, and for controversial interaction, face-to-face seating (16.3c) is superior. The impact of prominent positioning on conversation is illustrated in 16.3d. Depending on the need for moderator control, for instance depending on the type of the problem to be dealt with, the horseshoe (16.3e) or the circle (16.3f) is recommended. Note that there is also a clear difference if a table is inserted in the circle. Although it represents a barrier, it also supports the use of resource material (adapted from Remocker & Storch, 1987).

seating arrangements have sociopetal and sociofugal forces (see Figure 16.3; Remocker & Storch, 1987). For comfortable conversation, people like to sit at the corner of the table. When working together, they sit side by side, whereas in disputes and competitive tasks, they sit across from each other (see Harrison, 1974, p. 154).

Many group exercises request an open seating arrangement. Figure 16.3 (e and f) presents two arrangements that put the moderator into different positions. In the circle, he or she is primus inter pares, whereas in the horseshoe, the moderator's position of control is enhanced. Note that there is no general recommendation because different cultures and social levels prefer and interpret arrangements differently (Bernhart, 1976). The significance of the seating arrangement is often underestimated. Moderators tend to accept the given arrangements. We want to emphasize that the moderator should first have an idea of the ideal arrangement and then rearrange the given facilities accordingly.

Group Size

From the perspective of the moderator, groups are the instruments through which much work gets done. A crucial task of the moderator is to arrange the right group size for the tasks to be solved. For example, consider the first four weeks in an ETH-UNS case study. The general task is to define a project plan. This task includes a consensus process about a crisp case definition (i.e., the initial focal variable), the definition of a project goal (i.e., the terminal focal variable), the acquisition and communication of case knowledge, and so on. Clearly, some of these activities require plenum work. But working as a whole group should be the exception rather than the rule (see Figure 16.4).

In general, the following rules must be followed by the study team:

- Teamwork needs preparation. Often, it is beneficial to start a plenum session with a question that has to be worked on individually for 2 minutes.
- The more well-defined the task (i.e., if a task has a correct answer), the more profitable is small group work. The more difficult a well-defined problem, the less advantageous are large groups.
- The generation of conceptual frameworks and the formation of plans should be well prepared by the moderator and consented to by the whole study team.

Communication Rules and Regulations

"I" versus "you." The major task of moderation is to integrate knowledge from the study group or from different interest groups, for instance, if moderation takes place in Area Development Negotiations. Clearly, things or arguments are most easy to integrate if they have the same reference. Thus, all participants, including the moderator, have to be compelled to speak in the I-form. This commitment allows the moderator to

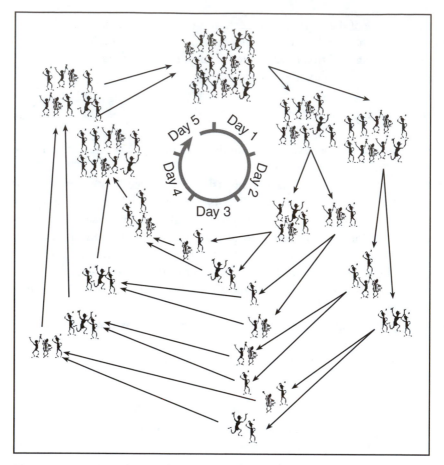

Figure 16.4 A Typical Procedure for a Synthesis Group in an ETH-UNS Case Study

NOTE: There is a sequence of alternation between plenary sessions (up to 20 people), part-plenums (6-10 people), small group work (3-5 people), mini-group work (2 people), and individual work in the course of case study analysis. The moderator should best plan for each realization phase (see Figure 5.6) a detailed sequence beginning and ending with plenary sessions.

identify the individual votes and to prepare reliable knowledge integration. If possible, the moderatees should even qualify their statements. This can be done in different ways, such as when making reference to the Types of Knowledge (see Chapter 4). Thus, the moderatees should use formulations such as, "I would say that . . ." or "If I reflect seriously . . ." or "As a representative of my company . . ." versus "Being a mother of . . ."

Start-up Communication and Goal Formation. The start-up session is crucial, particularly if a new group has to be built up. Before the introductory session, the moderator should make clear that all grouping and seating arrangements were completed before the first member arrived. The moderator should individually welcome all arriving team members. All materials should be placed on the table, and if the moderator or the moderatees do not know all other participants, big name tags should be worn so that at least the moderator can always read them. The moderator should always call the participants by name. We recommend a three-step procedure.

1. *Formal introduction:* The moderator has to introduce the goals, status, scheduling, and relevance of the session for the overall case study. In this step, only the information that is already known (e.g., by the invitation letter) should be repeated.

2. *Personal introduction:* Each participant has to introduce him- or herself briefly (if more than one member is not known to the others). The moderator should prepare a flip chart or overhead slide for this introduction and ask for the following information from each participant: full name, his or her professional background and any other reasons that qualify his or her participation, and his or her personal expectation with respect to the session and case study. Particularly in larger groups, the moderatees should be asked to formulate just one sentence and should not comment or react to other statements. The personal statements oblige each moderatee to put his or her attention toward the meeting and to speak in the group.

3. *Elaborated and consented goal formation:* From each member's personal expectation, the moderator will receive valuable information about the motivation, skepticism, barriers, or misperceptions of the goals of the session. It is his or her task to summarize and cluster the expectations, and to counter them with the formal goals. If necessary, the moderator should initiate a discussion that ends with an agreed-upon goal.

Making evaluations. Often, it is helpful to have explicit feedback, both for the group process and for the results accomplished. We will recommend so-called flashlights—each study team member expresses his or her feeling/opinion/evaluation in one sentence. Another technique is the explicit response to questions posed or alternatives presented by the moderator.

Ending up. Each session and the whole project should end with a clear summary by the moderator. The moderator should review and list all important results. Furthermore, a plan for subsequent work has to be defined in detail.

Arrangements for Knowledge Integration

Depending on the topic to be dealt with, and on the size and competence of the group, different techniques and instruments are apt to promote synthesis work. We will describe only the most important instruments and techniques (see Table 16.1).

If the moderator notices that the group lacks information on the case, the thematic perspective, or the methods of knowledge integration, he or she needs to arrange additional information acquisition, perhaps through brief lectures, a poster, or a video presentation. Also, expert panels may help to obtain specialized knowledge. If knowledge is missing about opinions, needs, or the evaluation of case members, telephone or mailed questionnaires are helpful. If these measures are still insufficient, focus groups (see Box 16.3) or a Delphi Technique (see Moore, 1987; Linstone & Turoff, 1975) can be used. However, the moderator should examine whether there is sufficient case knowledge in the group and, if necessary, organize a site visit or an Experiential Case Encounter (see Box 5.1 or Chapter 15). Finally, one flip chart should be reserved for noting all problems that may not be dealt with immediately.

A case understanding may also be promoted by conducting a plus-minus analysis (see Chapter 9) or a store in which all potential problems of the case are gathered. Note that a problem store on the case dynamics strengthens the study team's comprehension of the case.

Most important for the study team's knowledge integration are group sessions and brainstorming. However, the brainstorming method has to be used with some reservation. There is no overall superiority of group to individual performance. In order to optimize brainstorming, the moderator should always allow a few minutes for individual preparation before brainstorming. Anonymous card inquiry procedures are often advantageous to round-robin recording because all inputs have equal chances, and there is less filtering with respect to hierarchy or prejudices. One version of round-robin recording is idea writing (see Moore, 1987, p. 45), which provides an in-depth survey on the participants' views and knowledge.

Table 16.1   Instruments For Exchanging Information and Knowledge
Integration in Groups

Communication Goal and Format	Instrument/Technique	Main Purpose
Information acquisition	Brief lecture or video presentation	Eliminate basic information deficits
	Poster presentation	Equalize the knowledge in the study team
	Expert panel	Acquire specialist and master knowledge
	Telephone or mail questionnaire, Delphi study	Gain information from people not present in the group
	Focus group meeting	See Box 16.3
	Experiential Case Encounter	See Box 5.1 or Chapter 15
	Problem store	Record topics that may not be treated immediately
Case understanding	Plus-minus analysis	Promote insight into the case and its dynamics (see Table 9.1)
	Case problem store	Promote insight into the case and its dynamics
Idea sampling/ brainstorming	(Anonymous) card inquiry	Criteria, aspect, idea, impact, and system variable sampling
	(Overt) round-robin recording	Criteria, aspect, idea, impact, and system variable sampling
	Idea writing	In-depth assessment of opinions
Clustering	Ranking/voting	Structuring group discourse
	Grouping at the bulletin boards	Structuring group discourse
	Tables	Hierarchical structuring
	Mind mapping	Structuring group discourse
Questioning format	One-scope questions (mostly assessed graphically)	Opinion, attitude, estimation, expectation, and mood assessment
	Open questions	Problem, idea, topic, and solution sampling
	Card writing	Anonymous sampling of problems, ideas, topics, solutions
	Multiscope questions	Joint sampling of questions and their impacts, relevance, priorities, etc.

(continued)

Table 16.1   Continued

Communication Goal and Format	Instrument/Technique	Main Purpose
Response format	Verbal	Discussion of open questions
	Numerical (e.g., points)	Given for one-scope questions
	Behavioral	Discussion of feelings, attitudes
	Graphical	Used for dynamics and complex interrelationships
	Serial discussion	Used for developing evaluations
Grouping	Individual work	Preparation for group work; writing texts, facts, and results to be presented in the plenum
	Pair-wise discussions/ explanations	Mutual explanation of new and difficult problems, dealing with half-formed thoughts by thinking aloud
	Small group discussion/work	Used for ill-defined problems
	Plenum	Goal definition, collection of ideas, consent for project plan and valuations
Performances	Pro-and-con dispute	Treatment of latent conflicts
	Role-playing	Need for creativity

One of the central tasks of the moderator is the clustering and prioritizing of the sampled information. For doing this, the moderator needs solid knowledge about the case and about the synthesis methods applied for case analysis. Particularly in this session, couple moderation is needed so that one person can concentrate on the process while the other concentrates on the clustering.

Crucial for a successful moderation is the right response format and the right group size. The more complex and difficult the topic, the smaller the size of the group that deals with that problem. The more complex the task, the fewer responses should be exchanged quantitatively.

Box 16.3   Focus Groups

Focus groups are a qualitative method of inquiry. The method was originally developed in marketing to expose a new product concept, prototype, or packaging to a group of consumers, or to obtain information and new ideas about attitudes toward the image, strengths, and weaknesses of a product or company. Greenbaum (1998, p. 2) distinguishes two principal types of focus groups: groups of 8 to 10 (full group) or 4 to 5 (minigroup) people sampled to common demographics, attitudes, or case experience to participate in a session of about 90 to 120 minutes. Both sessions should be headed by an experienced moderator. The main difference between the two types of meeting is that in group meetings, the moderator has to stimulate the participants to make statements and offer information with respect to interesting issues from a well-prepared guide. If the moderator had had to ask for the information over the telephone, the interaction would be more along the lines of a questionnaire.

Focus groups may be used in the preparation of a case study as a first check on alternatives developed or suggested in the course of a case study, or for the evaluation of the results of the study. Focus groups are also popular in a nonbusiness context. When conducting focus groups, the study team should be aware of the limits of this technique. Focus groups are no substitute for quantitative research and should not be used as a substitute for decision making.

Finally, we note that methods such as pro-and-con disputes, role-playing, and sketches also can be appropriate means for information exchange.

Presentation Techniques

We consider two issues to be essential for effective presentation: visualization and structuring of the content. Visualization is a highly efficient communication tool in synthesis work. Discussions and information exchange may become enhanced by appropriate visualization techniques. The moderator has to make available enough bulletin boards for the current discussion and for the results already accomplished.

The visualization of arguments, results, and project plans

- Makes the major topics ubiquitously available
- Avoids the study team going in circles
- Intensifies the information processing, particularly in knowledge integration, because the eye is a more efficient sensory system than the ear

A good visualization technique must also fulfill various requirements:

- All members must have easy access to the presentation board for both reading and writing.
- Every participant should be trained to handle visual communication techniques as effectively as he or she uses speech and other communication tools.
- Presentations and interactions are to remain flexible (see Schnelle, 1979, p. 18).

Although there is tremendous progress in computerized communication technologies, and despite special GroupWare, the bulletin board is still a favored technology.

There is a set of presentation tools (e.g., ovals, rectangles, circles, or clouds) that may be used for representation. Each of them should have different colors, which supports classification and clustering. Furthermore, the moderator should be well trained in the use of different formats, such as one-dimensional scales, two-dimensional scales, tables, matrices, lists, mind maps, and scatter diagrams. Content organization should best be done with respect to the methods presented in this book.

Project Management

Project management is an area of management that focuses on accomplishing specific objectives and goals under conditions of complexity and risk-taking (see Dean, 1985). Project management entails human resource management, particularly group techniques and management that were discussed earlier. Thus, we will focus only on planning and scheduling technologies that are also helpful for case studies.

Although the moderator is usually not the project leader, he or she should check and control the case study team and whether the core elements of the planning are well arranged. According to the Four Corners Planning Principle, the moderator has to make sure that

1. The project goal outcomes and performance are well assessed and shared (common milestone).

2. The resources (personnel, budget, cost) are adjusted to the goal.

3. The duration of the project and its time schedule have been planned realistically.

4. The risk level of the project is appropriate.

Step 1 has to obey the backward planning principle (see Figure 16.5). In particular, the specific perspective taken in the case study and the expected new understanding of the case or the case transformation should be made as clear as possible. The moderator has to control the pitfalls of planning. Thus, he or she has to prevent the proliferation of an excessive number of "to do" plans so as to ensure that there is a number-one priority each week, and that small problems are solved before they become big problems.

Step 2 is obvious. The artistry of case study planning entails quality control through feedback and reviews. Thus, the realism of the resource-goal relationship can be judged much better from an outsider's perspective, such as a moderator or an independent reviewer. However, the moderator has to caution that reviews and critiques should not be too frequent or too drastic (Blair, 1993).

Step 3 is an important step in project management. A schedule is a conversion of a project action plan into an operating timetable. The schedule serves as a fundamental basis for monitoring and controlling. The landmarks of the project are the prerequisites of scheduling. As shown in Figure 16.5, these landmarks may be displayed and marked in the project scheme as arranged in the Brunswikian Lens Model. The landmarks also have to be linked to a time axis. Clearly, project activities are not only sequential, but also often parallel and interwoven. Well-known techniques exist for scheduling, such as arrow diagrams, node diagrams, and sophisticated network techniques like Gantt charts (Meredith & Mantel, 1995; Tavares, 1999). These techniques should be consulted in large-scale case studies.

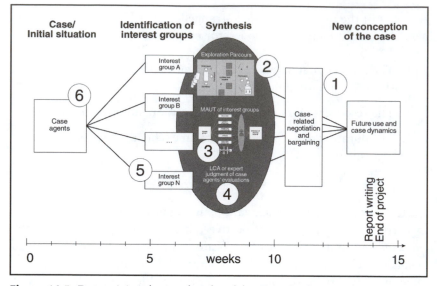

Figure 16.5 Determining the Landmarks of the Case Study

NOTE: Sometimes, this can be done in accordance with the Brunswikian Lens Model representation of knowledge integration. Case study planning should obey the backward planning principle as presented by the numbers. Step 1, the goal, should be formulated first but is best attained in the 13th week. Likewise, the case agents who will participate are determined after the project plan is completed and should be involved in the study by the end of the second week at the latest. The other planning steps are explained in Chapter 13, from where the figure is replicated (see Figure 13.1).

Another important task in project management, noted in Step 4, is to calibrate the risk level of the goals, processes, and outcomes. Thus, the moderator has to make sure that there is always a mixture of low- and high-gain goals and activities that can be attained with an appropriate mixture of probabilities. In particular, there must always be a fallback position in the event that the worst case comes to pass.

Idea and Case Analysis Moderation

Synthesis Moderation has to go beyond the form. The crucial task of the moderator of the study team is to guide the team in the selection and the use of the Methods of Knowledge Integration. To do this, the moderator has to be an expert in the methods for embedded case studies and has to know the following:

- Which case issue can be dealt with which method
- Which statements or results can be provided by which method
- Which knowledge must be at the disposal of the study team for a successful application
- How to select and combine different case study methods
- How much time is needed for the application of a method and a solid (scientifically acceptable) solution

Clearly, these points are demanding tasks. Thus the "standard rule" of moderation, that two moderators should be present, has to be fulfilled, in particular for idea and case analysis moderation.

Selecting and Combining Case Study Methods

The reader will have noticed that area development negotiations (Figure 16.6) already combine different methods such as MAUT and LCA. Figure 16.6 provides the general basic schema for linking different methods in synthesis. To help the case study researcher in organizing, selecting, and linking different methods, we present some basic principles and a prototypical schema. According to our experience, the following principles hold:

- Use the power of *lens model* when organizing a synthesis and combining methods
- Use *backward planning* by starting from the intended results and restricting the case study work only to the indispensable part
- Think in *variants*, both for action variants and for shell scenarios
- Organize the construction and evaluation of variants by means of *case study methods*.

When constructing the following prototypical schema the authors refer to case study work in regional and organizational development and planning. We present a 6-step procedure, which can be modified and certainly also applied in other cases. Note that synthesis planning requires that a *first level of case understanding must have been acquired*, as described in Chapter 5.

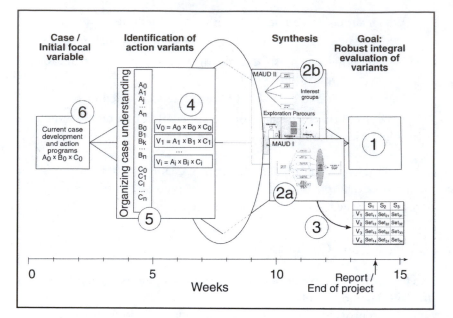

Figure 16.6. Prototypical Schema for the Architecture of a Synthesis

1. Start with a concise definition of the *terminal focal variable,* which represents the *goal* of the study. This has to be discussed and consented to within the study team, and also with selected case agents. In the example presented in Figure 16.6, the goal is a robust evaluation of the action variants V_i.

2. The presented goal asks for a selection of an appropriate evaluation procedure. The study team has to decide whether this evaluation is best done by scientists or by the study team itself (e.g., when arranging a MAUT; see Chapter 11) or whether different perspectives of various interest groups must be included. Further, a multicriteria evaluation usually requires the assessment of utilities for certain criteria that also may be assessed by means of formative case study methods such as LCA (see Chapter 18) or BEPA (see Chapter 19), as well as methods not presented in this book. Note that the Integrated Risk Management (see Chapter 12) offers a powerful tool if uncertainties are essential.

3. Many evaluations refer to action *variants V_i,* which will be considered in different contexts, environments, or future developments.

Sustainable regional planning, for instance, requires robust solutions for different global developments, including changes in societal needs and values, resources, or technologies. In Figure 16.6, this is illustrated by the matrix linked to Step 3 in which the *variants* are connected with different *frame* or *shell scenarios* S_i.

4. *Variants* can be intuitively built or constructed by means of the Formative Scenario Analysis (FSA) method (see Step 5). In the planning of a prospective regional ETH-UNS Case Study, a variant encompasses action programs in different sectors or facets (see Figure 16.1), such as tourism, landscape ecology, and so forth. In Figure 16.6, this is indicated by the variables A_i, B_i, and C_i, which represent action programs in different sectors. Often, programs in these sectors can be developed rather independently. If a case study develops and evaluates action programs in each facet (see Figure 16.1), the combination of these action programs can be considered an *overall synthesis*.

5. As already noted, the *construction of variants* or of action programs for various facets can be organized by means of Formative Scenario Analysis (FSA). In this case, an inventory of the salient system features and relevant measures has to be created. In an FSA for variant creation, the features and measures take the role of *impact variables* in scenario construction.

6. The planning continues with a kind of *second-level case encounter*. Steps 4 and 5 suggest which type of variants will be constructed by which methods, for which facet or facets, and for which part of the case—in particular, which specific case data, information, knowledge, or understanding is missing for a mature and adequate construction and evaluation of action variants. The study team becomes aware of the necessary graininess of case analysis. In the case of regional tourism, the graininess determines whether regional financial or marketing programs, individual projects, single hotels or commodities, or even smaller units are the focus of interest.

17

MATERIAL FLUX ANALYSIS

THE RATIONALE

In some cases, the understanding and knowledge about the material fluxes within the system or between the system and its environment are crucial for case analysis and management. In the ETH-UNS case studies, material fluxes of energy, substances, goods, products, waste, and emissions within the case region and between the case region and other compartments often create a simplified basic quantitative model. It describes the physical components, resources, and outputs that are important to the case. Thus, the first step is to identify those materials that are indicative of the qualities, vulnerabilities, sensitivities, and potentials of the case. The quantitative analysis of the material fluxes gives important information and guidelines on how to optimize the case, for example, by designing decision alternatives in order to reduce the impacts of the anthroposphere on the environment. Currently, many Material Flux Analyses are run under the perspective of sustainability.

The overall objectives of the Material Flux Analysis (MFA) are to understand the system, identify ecologically and economically relevant energy and material flows, and account for the material fluxes of the investigated system. The intended meaning of MFA is often described using the metaphor that the material fluxes represent the metabolism of the system (metabolism of the anthroposphere, Baccini & Brunner, 1991; industrial metabolism, Tukker, Jasser, & Kleijn, 1997). MFA, like System Dynamics, is a system description tool and gives no formal evaluation of the results (see Table 8.1), but a qualitative evaluation is often evident.

MFA investigates an open system. The fluxes are represented quantitatively in units of mass, volume, or energy. At the end, the balances of certain materials or elements are presented. In many cases, the results of an MFA cannot be used directly as a quantitative evaluation of decision options. But the presentation of the balances aims to draw general conclusions. If a material flux is relevant because it is large, then it is important to note whether an alternative results in a growing need for material treatment or whether the material is avoided.

MFA is a precautionary instrument. Just as the extended consumption of illegal drugs may damage the health of a person and produce drug addiction, an extended material flux may prove inappropriate for the metabolism of a region. For instance, the analysis of nitrogen fluxes in a region may reveal that high nitrate concentrations in groundwater may be influenced by agricultural practice (Baccini & Oswald, 1998).

The following overall questions are typically addressed by a Material Flux Analysis:

- Which material fluxes are relevant and substantial for a case?
- Which fluxes and stocks can be used as indicators of sustainability?
- What are the requirements for sustainability, and are they fulfilled?

Udo de Haes, van der Voet, and Kleijn (1997) emphasize that MFA is a tool for integrated chain management because it investigates a chain or a network of (economic, ecological) processes rather than a single component or process. Other such analytical tools are Life Cycle Assessment (see Chapter 18), Integrated Risk Management (see Chapter 12), or Substance Flow Analysis (SFA). SFA is similar to MFA, but it focuses on single elements (such as nitrogen or cadmium) or on groups of related substances (such as nitrogen compounds or chlorinated hydrocarbons), whereas MFA investigates total mass of material (e.g., waste) or bulk material like plastics or concrete. For Baccini and Brunner (1991), MFA includes the definition of so-called indicator elements. The mass, volume, or energy of these elements is calculated by means of their concentration within the materials. Therefore, it is clear that both methods are new and partly overlap in their formal methodological background.

Historical Background

Prior to SFA or MFA, input-output models have been designed with engineering or economic objectives (activity analysis, Gay, Proops, & Speck, 1999; input-output analysis, Moll, Hinterberger, Femia, & Bringezu, 1999; Leontief, 1966). Therefore, at the time of early approaches of MFA or SFA, the formal procedure (see Method section) was not completely new.

For both methods, the report by Ayres, Norberg-Bohm, Prince, Stigliani, and Yanowitz (1989) has been specified as a starting point reference where the metabolism metaphor has been given (industrial metabolism). The investigated system is viewed as an organism that exhibits a metabolism similar to that of organs or other subunits. The metabolism of organisms is a very complex system that we do not completely understand. In order to understand the metabolism of the anthroposphere, Baccini and Brunner (1991) investigated salient and corresponding material and energy fluxes. Within this philosophy, the main interest is on the total amount of fluxes.

An Enquete Commission of the German Bundestag (1994) took the MFA as a basis for the design of the industrial society in order to reach sustainable development. They explicitly refer to the reports of the Club of Rome (Meadows et al., 1992; Meadows et al., 1974) and try to relate political decisions, such as tax assessment and waste management, to the MFA.

Within the ConAccount project (Bringezu, Fischer-Kowalski, Kleijn, & Viveka, 1997; Kleijn, Bringezu, Fischer-Kowalski, & Palm, 1999), the aim is to intensify the exchange of methodological and data-related information about material flux accounting. The focus is on regional applications and on supernational levels. In order to create a benchmark, multiple materials are involved in the derivation of decision-relevant accounting schemes.

Currently, the pros and cons of substance flow analysis, material flux analysis, and life cycle assessment have been investigated thoroughly, including their specific area of application. These methods focus on goods and products that are organized in chains or networks of processes. Therefore, the next step toward sustainable management seems to be the development of an integrated chain management for which SFA, MFA, or LCA serves as a tool (Udo de Haes et al., 1997).

Recently, van der Voet, van Oers, Guinee, and Udo de Haes (1999) noted that available substance flow and material flux analyses have not found their way into political decisions. This is due because currently, the modeling and results of MFA are not presented to the stakeholders in a sufficiently comprehensive way. Van der Voet et al. (1999) propose a set of environmental and economic indicators that characterizes the results of a substance flow analysis and therefore can be used more easily in environmental policy.

From a case study perspective, the deficient reception of results from MFA into practice is due to several reasons. We think that an MFA has to be linked strongly to specific cases and action alternatives. This can be done in two ways. On one hand, MFA can be used for the construction of action alternatives. On the other hand, if different decision alternatives are available, a comparative MFA often can be conducted. In both cases, the case agents should be incorporated in order to guarantee that the results can be used for case evaluation or case improvement. The latter is best done in a transdisciplinary process. The MFA model can play the role of a communication and consensus-building instrument that provides a common language and case representation. Engineers and practitioners have to agree on the system and the characteristics of the stocks, flows, inputs, and outputs. The material flux system can be used to calculate the consequences of the alternatives.

Characteristics of Material Flux Analysis

The study team has to be aware that MFA has certain prerequisites and characteristics that must be taken into account. First, there is an anthropospheric perspective in the system definition. As with any case study, the system boundaries have to be well-defined. The study team has to determine the material or substance flows within the anthroposphere and between the anthroposphere and the environment. This is called the *metabolism of the anthroposphere* (Baccini & Brunner, 1991). Mostly, the subject of investigation is a case that consists of a geographical area (cf. the examples given by Bringezu, 2000) as opposed to a product life cycle, which is the subject of LCA. Many examples exist of enterprises that are investigated by an MFA (see Henseler, Bader, Oehler, Scheidegger, & Baccini, 1995).

When the materials and substances have been defined, the next step is defining the activities, such as to nourish or clean, in terms of processes

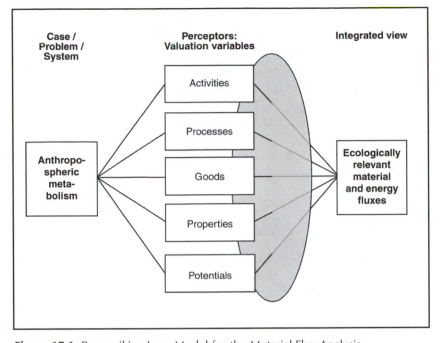

Case /
Problem /
System

Perceptors:
Valuation variables

Integrated view

Activities

Processes

Anthropo-
spheric
meta-
bolism

Goods

Ecologically
relevant
material
and energy
fluxes

Properties

Potentials

Figure 17.1 Brunswikian Lens Model for the Material Flux Analysis

NOTE: The perceptors are anthropospheric activities; the processes (material transformation, transport); the economic goods; the properties of the materials; and the resource and
pollution potential of indicator elements that are relevant to the material fluxes.

and goods. Note that at this stage, industrial, production, and economic
processes are considered and determine the definition of the elements of
MFA. The material fluxes are quantified in units of mass, volume, or
energy.

When calculating the flows, special attention has to be paid to the
properties of the materials and pollution potential (see Figure 17.1). This
is generally done when looking at the fluxes of indicator elements that are
relevant for the material fluxes in terms of mass and/or toxicity.

The result of the MFA is a system model of material fluxes and stocks.
In general, MFA is interested in a static representation, although recent investigations show the development of corresponding dynamic models
(van der Kleijn, Huele, & Voet, 2000). Because of the rapid changes in society and in the material fluxes in environment-anthrosphere systems,
the role of the MFA is to condense actual, possibly available information

from the bottom up. In a next step, the dynamics of substance flows can be analyzed and represented by a dynamic system (see Chapter 10; see also Udo de Haes et al., 1997).

In many cases, the variables of the MFA, such as processes and goods, are valid only on the average. Individual personal behavior is not considered (Baccini & Brunner, 1991).

The main problems of MFA are as follows:

- The definition of the system boundaries, which are constituted by the applied technology, time, and space

- The definition of the activities, processes, goods, and products

- The selection of indicator elements

- The assessment of output fluxes (pollution potential)

- The aggregation of fluxes over time and space, which cannot adequately represent local conditions

- No explicit valuation of the material fluxes

LESSONS TO BE LEARNED

▶ MFA is a method to investigate the complex metabolism of anthropospheric systems by means of accounting for the material fluxes.

▶ MFA concentrates on human activities. In general, the activities represent no single cases, but are valid on the average.

▶ MFA is suitable if the case is a geographical system, an enterprise, or another physical system.

▶ If practical impacts are desired, MFA should be linked to the generation or assessment of alternatives. This should be done in a transdisciplinary process in cooperation with the case agents.

▶ MFA is a precautionary method but does not formally include a valuation.

THE METHOD IN DETAIL

The MFA consists of five steps that may be more or less complicated, depending on the subject (Baccini & Brunner, 1991):

1. System analysis, which includes the selection of indicator elements

2. Measurement of mass fluxes of inputs and outputs of processes, which are the products or educts, such as emissions

3. Determination of concentrations of elements in inputs and outputs

4. Calculation of elemental mass fluxes as a product of mass fluxes and corresponding concentrations

5. Interpretation and presentation of the results

Udo de Haes et al. (1997) combine Steps 2 through 4 and characterize MFA by the three steps of goal and system definition, measurement and calculation, and derivation of conclusions. We will sketch only the five-step procedure. Additional information can be found in Baccini and Bader (1996) and Baccini and Brunner (1991).

MFA is predominantly applied to complex cases. An example is an MFA of a regional nitrogen cycle, where several chemical compounds and possibly their metabolites and a large geographic area have to be investigated. Within the ETH-UNS case study Zurich North, an MFA was conducted for a single building, an old four-story production facility. There were two alternatives. The total demolition of the *Ententeich* building, followed by the construction of a new building, was compared to an extensive renewal (Figure 17.2). We use this simple example for the illustration of the method.

System Analysis

The first step of the MFA must be to define the goal of the investigation. As stated earlier, the general objective mostly associated with MFA is the investigation of the material flows between the anthroposphere and the (natural) environment. The comprehensive representation of the substance flow system (Figure 17.2) allows for answering the following questions:

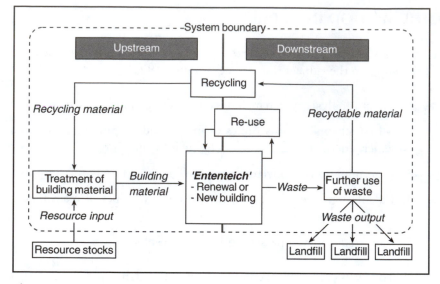

Figure 17.2 Overview of Material Fluxes Induced by the Renewal of the *Ententeich* Building vs. Its Total Demolition and New Construction

NOTE: The processes on the left side of the figure are known as upstream processes because they are linked with the production of the new building. The downstream processes are the material fluxes that are due to the demolition of the existing *Ententeich* building.

• Which are the most relevant processes? Do natural processes dominate the flux system, or do anthropogenic fluxes change and endanger the natural system?

• Where will the materials be stored or disposed? Is the environment in danger of depletion or contamination? Does anthropogenic storage possibly pose a problem in the future?

• Which are the most critical material fluxes caused by the alternatives? Please note that case activities, industrial and production processes, or goods and products can be relevant in the MFA because of the mass of the material, its environmental impacts, or its toxicological effects.

Another important objective of MFA is to determine trends, such as the accumulation of certain materials or substances, and causes for the current material distribution within the investigated system.

Figure 17.2 makes evident how measures to control the flux system can be developed. Starting with the material fluxes induced by the total demolition and new construction of the building, it is clear that decreasing waste and increasing recycling and reuse will reduce the material intensity of the *Ententeich* building. Unfortunately, the technical implication of a large story height will result in a low utility, which in this case is proportional to the gross floor area. Hence, the material fluxes relative to the gross floor area in the *Ententeich* example can be calculated. This shows that MFA can be used to identify and predict the effectiveness of measures.

The second step of this kind of system analysis is the system definition. This includes the definition of the processes and goods that are going to be investigated, and the definition of the boundary of the system (see Figure 17.2). In most cases, the spatial extension of the study will be on a regional scale, as is the prototypical example METALAND (Baccini & Brunner, 1991). But the scale may be much larger, up to a worldwide material flux analysis, or smaller, as in the *Ententeich* example. Figure 17.2 shows the involved processes, such as recycling or renewal, and goods, such as building material or waste. The material fluxes are divided conceptually into upstream processes, which are necessary for the construction of the new *Ententeich* building, and downstream processes, which occur because of the demolition of the existing *Ententeich* building. As can be seen from Figure 17.3, the expected material fluxes are lower for the renewal variant. But the renewal based on the old skeleton implies a large story height and therefore results in fewer apartments (46 vs. 64) and a smaller gross floor area (9,400 vs. 12,400 m^2). Therefore, the objective is to investigate the material fluxes relative to the available gross floor area. The time span of the investigation is the possible lifetime of the building.

Measuring the Fluxes of Goods and the Material Concentrations

The flux diagram presented in Figure 17.2 can be translated into a matrix presentation (Table 17.1). The processes T_1 to T_5—renewal, reuse, use of waste, recycling, and treatment of building material—are related to each other by the material fluxes indicated in the matrix $T = (t_{i,j})_{i,j = 1, \ldots, 5}$ in Table 17.1. For each arrow in Figure 17.1, a matrix coefficient has to be determined. Below that, the input matrix $R = (r_{i,j})_{i = 1, j = 1, \ldots, 5}$ specifies the input for each of the processes T_i. On the right-hand side, the output matrix $E = (e_{i,j})_{i = 1, \ldots, 5; j = 1, \ldots, 3}$ contains the outputs for each of the processes

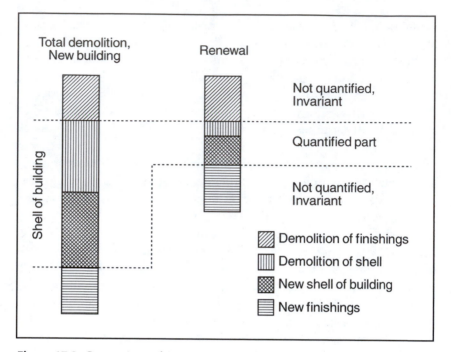

Figure 17.3 Comparison of Fictitious Material Fluxes for the Two Variants
Renewal and Total Demolition and New Construction

NOTE: The length of the bars indicates the presupposed material fluxes induced by the
variants, for instance, on a kilogram scale.

T_i. The notation was chosen to avoid confounding with other chapters. E
refers to emissions, such as wastes; R to inputs from resources; and T to
transmissions between processes.

Each of the fluxes given in Table 17.1 and Table 17.2 has to be specified
in terms of mass, volume (for gases), or energy. Baccini and Brunner
(1991) present three different ways to measure the necessary material
fluxes:

- Measurement of all input and outputs
- Measurement of easily accessible data only; the rest has to be calcu-
  lated applying the law of mass or energy conservation
- Use of existing measurements only

Table 17.1 Matrix Representation of the Material Fluxes for the Variant Renewal of the *Ententeich*

Ententeich	Renewal	Reuse	Use of Waste	Recycling	Treatment	Landfill	Landfill	Landfill
Renewal	0	Material for reuse	Waste^R	–	–	–	–	–
Reuse	Reuse material	0	–	–	–	–	–	–
Use of Waste	–	–	0	Recyclable material	–	Waste1	Waste2	Waste3
Recycling	–	–	–	0	Recycled material	–	–	–
Treatment	Building material	–	–	–	0	–	–	–
Resources	–	–	–	–	Resource input			

NOTE: The cell in the center, a_{ij}, presents the fluxes from row i to column j. The right part of the matrix shows the outputs to the storage sites, such as different landfills. The bottom row presents the input fluxes. A formal definition of this matrix is given in Table 17.2. See text for further explanation.

Table 17.2 Matrix Elements $t_{i,j}$, $r_{j,k}$, and $e_{k,l}$ Quantifying the
Material Fluxes Between the Processes, the Inputs
Into the System, and the Output From the System

	T_1	$\cdots$	T_n	E_1	$\cdots$	E_k
T_1	$t_{1,1}$	$\cdots$	$t_{1,n}$	$e_{1,1}$	$\cdots$	$e_{1,k}$
$\vdots$	$\vdots$		$\vdots$	$\vdots$		$\vdots$
T_n	$t_{n,1}$	$\cdots$	$t_{n,n}$	$e_{n,1}$	$\cdots$	$e_{n,k}$
R_1	$r_{1,1}$	$\cdots$	$r_{1,n}$			
$\vdots$	$\vdots$		$\vdots$			
R_m	$r_{m,1}$	$\cdots$	$r_{m,n}$			

SOURCES: Baccini and Bader (1996); Weisz, Schandl, and Fischer-Kowalski (1999).

For the *Ententeich* study, only the existing plans and investigations could be used to determine the material fluxes because direct measurements were not feasible.

Calculation of Material Fluxes

Not all of the internal, input, and output fluxes can be measured in complicated material flux systems, or even in some simple examples. But if enough data are available, a part of the fluxes can be calculated by means of the laws of mass and energy conservation.

In static simulations, the diagonal coefficients of the matrix T are zero, and for each process, the sum of all (internal or external) input fluxes must equal the sum of all (internal or external) output fluxes. Therefore, for each process T_i, the following equation holds

$$\sum_{\ell=1,\ldots,n;\ell\neq i} t_{\ell,i} + \sum_{\ell=1}^{m} r_{\ell,i} = \sum_{\ell=1,\ldots,n;\ell\neq i} t_{i,\ell} + \sum_{\ell=1}^{k} e_{i,\ell}$$

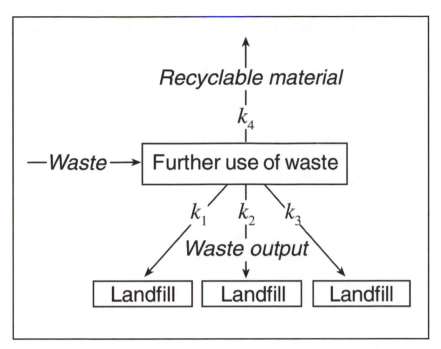

Figure 17.4 Transfer Coefficients k_1 to k_4 Partition the Educt (Input) of a Process Into Different Products

NOTE: In Table 17.1, the material flux Waste[1] to Landfill A equals the Waste[R] produced by Renewal times the transfer coefficient k_1.

where the variable names specified in Table 17.2 apply.

Transfer coefficients partition the input of a process into different outputs (see Figure 17.4). Generally, linear transfer coefficients are assumed (which, in dynamic MFA, may vary in time):

$$k_i = output_i/\text{input}$$

In some cases, the transfer coefficients are known. In the *Ententeich* example, the composition of the waste is known, and different substances are appropriate for recycling or for different kind of landfills. The partition coefficients sum to 1:

$$\sum_{i=1}^{4} k_i = 1$$

The equations above can be combined for calculating or assessing the range of missing data. Also, the uncertainties within the material flux system become accessible. This is very useful for some complex materials, such as the sewage of municipal solid waste, which are unknown in their composition. For further details, see Baccini and Bader (1996) and Baccini and Brunner (1991).

LESSONS TO BE LEARNED

▶ There are different representations that support the conceptualization of material fluxes. The study team usually starts with a graphical representation and then switches to a matrix representation (i.e., a mathematical representation).

▶ The matrix representation allows the assessment of missing data or data uncertainty using mass or energy balances.

▶ By the formal system, the composition of critical internal and external fluxes becomes transparent and thus becomes the object of case management.

18

LIFE CYCLE ASSESSMENT

THE RATIONALE

A Life Cycle Assessment (LCA) determines and evaluates relevant environmental impacts, such as ozone layer depletion or eutrophication, from beginning to end. The method integrates time and space and thus all former, current, and future impacts of the life cycle on the whole world. An LCA evaluates under a functional perspective. Thus, the functional unit is crucial because it defines all of the functions that the object under consideration will fulfill throughout its life cycle. For example, if a cottage has to be painted, the functional unit is a square meter painted wall, which fulfills the functions of "wall protection" and "aesthetic." In this evaluation, an LCA covers all important processes, such as resource extraction, production, transportation, distribution, usage, and waste treatment.

Within the ETH-UNS case studies, there are many decision situations where the case agents and the study team are interested in the assessment of the environmental impacts resulting from different alternatives. An LCA may contribute to the ecological part of an assessment of sustainability if additional information is supplied, such as how many emissions per functional unit are sustainable.

Two general questions are addressed by an LCA:

- Given several alternatives that are assumed to fulfill the same functions, which one should be preferred with respect to its environmental impacts?

- Within the life cycle, how and where is it possible to improve a decision alternative or product environmentally?

According to Barnthouse et al. (1997), the reasons to conduct an LCA
include environmental labeling, environmental product improvement,
ecodesign, and policy evaluation. They add that the aspect of general education is generally underappreciated.

Historical Background

Historically, environmental discussions in the 1960s and 1970s were
parallel to the first life cycle-oriented investigations. One of the first approaches was to evaluate the cumulative energy demand (see Boustead &
Hancock, 1979). It was expected that the direct and indirect energy demand, including "gray" energy, could serve as an approximation of the
environmental assessment. The material intensity per service unit (MIPS)
(Schmidt-Bleek, 1993) was developed later as another proxy indicator
(Hofstetter, 1998).

The method of LCA is relatively new and thus still experiences ongoing
changes and improvements. However, several elementary concepts, rules,
and assumptions are generally accepted in the scientific community. The
International Organization for Standardization (ISO) started a process to
find an international standard for life cycle assessment (ISO 14040 ff),
which was intended as a frame within which different LCA methods
should fit. According to the ISO standard 14040 "Life Cycle Assessment"
(ISO, 1997), the first step is the *goal and scope definition,* which includes
the definition of the functional unit. In the second step, *inventory,* the alternatives are decomposed into all of the processes that take part in their
life cycle. Processes are industrial, production, and economic activities.
All flows of energy, materials, and emissions are summarized in the inventory table. The *impact assessment* is the third step and compiles
the environmental impacts of all of these processes. This includes (a) the
classification of elementary flows into impact categories, and (b) their
characterization and quantitative evaluation. Optional considerations
are (c) the normalization relative to the global importance, and (d) the
weighting across different impact categories subject to individual or societal values. Parallel to these three steps, the *interpretation* of the material
is going on with respect to the quality of the assessment, the sensitivities,

the hidden valuations, and the resulting recommendations (see Figure 18.2).

LCA as a more formalized scientific management method developed in the 1980s. The Swiss Agency for the Environment, Forests and Landscape published an early study on packing material (Bundesamt für Umwelt, Wald und Landschaft, 1984) based on the "critical volume" approach, which had been developed in the 1970s. This Swiss ecoscarcity approach is presented in Ahbe, Braunschweig, and Müller-Wenk (1990; updated in Bundesamt für Umwelt, Wald und Landschaft, 1998). Meanwhile, important improvements within the field of LCA are related to specific aspects, such as the allocation (R. Frischknecht, 1998), assessment (Hofstetter, 1998), or valuation of impacts (Tietje et al., 1998).

In the 1990s, the methodology of LCA was discussed intensively. The Society of Environmental Toxicology and Chemistry (SETAC) emerged as the scientific organization for LCA. In 1996, the first scientific *International Journal of Life Cycle Assessment* was founded and now builds a forum for the LCA community. Within the same time frame, large databases (Frischknecht, Hofstetter, Knoepfel, Dones, & Zollinger, 1995) and many software products like Ecoinvent (Frischknecht & Kolm, 1995), Umberto (Schmidt, Möller, Hedemann, & Müller-Beischmidt, 1997), and EMIS (Dinkel & Ros, 1996) were developed. Meanwhile, many other programs are described on the Internet. In general, the software systems supply a user-friendly interface, a connection to existing databases, and a variety of impact assessment methods.

The SETAC workgroups from North America and Europe on Life Cycle Impact Assessment presented state-of-the-art reports (Barnthouse et al., 1997; Udo de Haes, 1996; Udo de Haes & Owens, 1998). The methodological improvements both established LCA as an accepted methodology and drew attention to still-critical issues such as the definition of system boundaries, allocation of impacts, data quality and uncertainty, impact assessment method, and value setting.

Characteristics of LCA

The life cycle approach tries to solve the problem that the relevant environmental impacts of a product, or, more generally, of a decision alternative, do not stem only directly from the alternative. Indirect impacts, such as those due to the necessary transport of goods, may make a considerable

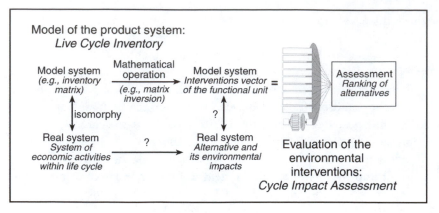

Figure 18.1 The Formal Model of the LCA

NOTE: The model consists of the life cycle inventory (LCI), which models the product system, and the life cycle impact assessment (LCIA), which evaluates the environmental interventions.

contribution. In order to answer the overall questions mentioned earlier, the method of life cycle assessment has to reveal how indirect impacts are going to be modeled and evaluated:

- Which environmental impacts have to be considered?
- Which environmental impacts are due to the product alternative at hand?
- How can different impacts be made comparable?
- How can the impacts of the pre- or postprocessing of the product in the life cycle be included in the method?

A life cycle assessment can be characterized as a management tool, which includes evaluation and modeling (Figure 18.1).

The model of the product system represents the industrial, production, and economic processes involved in the life cycle and accounts for the flows between these processes and the environment ("environmental interventions") (Heijungs & Hofstetter, 1996). Generally, this modeling step is called the life cycle inventory (LCI). But it goes beyond a mere inventory because it includes the choice of the life cycle model, the choice of the relevant impacts accounted for, and several assumptions to which the results of life cycle assessments are sensitive (see the Method section).

The evaluation of the environmental interventions resembles an application of the Multi-Attribute Utility Theory and is called a life cycle impact assessment (LCIA). It includes specific environmental information, a set of assumptions, and value settings that organize this scientific information.

The advantage of an LCA is that all environmental impacts and the whole life cycle are included. Several methods are available, ranging from a very detailed inventory analysis (Frischknecht et al., 1995) to streamlined LCAs, which can be applied rather quickly for an a priori assessment (Bundesamt für Umwelt, Wald und Landschaft, 1998). LCA, as an environmental evaluation method, is relatively well developed. Many parts of the assessment can be done routinely. Thus, the user of LCA programs has to acknowledge that assumptions and evaluations are inherent in the results provided by these programs. The procedure of LCA is largely standardized and simple to apply. This is due to several available inventories that cover a wide range of applications. A common data input format has been created that facilitates the exchange of data (Bretz, 1998).

The main problems of life cycle assessment are as follows:

- The definition of the system boundaries and the functional unit, the selection of impact categories, and the impact assessment can be biased by personal valuation.
- The inventory depends on the inherent assumptions and the availability and quality of the data.
- The allocation of the impacts to different by-products may influence the results.
- The impacts are aggregated over time and space and therefore may not adequately represent local conditions.
- The impact assessment methods currently available may provide significantly different results because they differ with respect to impact categories, classification, characterization, damage assessment, normalization, and valuation.
- Subjective weighting is necessary to fully aggregate the impact categories into a single score; otherwise, the results may be inconsistent and will not lead to a unique ranking of the alternatives.

Hofstetter (1998) argues that an LCA should be conducted from the top down rather than from the bottom up, as suggested in the ISO standard. In the top-down approach, the following questions have to be addressed subsequently (Hofstetter, 1998): What are the objectives of LCA? What kind of environment is going to be protected? Which impacts on the environment have to be considered, and what are their causes? The answers are guiding the whole LCA process. The answers also open the possibility of clarifying the intended meaning (Tietje et al., 1998) of the various variables (which describe the processes of the product system and their environmental interventions), the impact categories, and the calculation rules. The LCA, as a consequence, begins with the definition of safeguard subjects and proceeds with the assessment of damages to them. This top-down approach may reveal the important definitions, assumptions, and value settings more explicitly than the bottom-up approach. We consider the explication of definitions, assumptions, and value settings to be an important part of LCA application. The users should be aware that an interpretation of an LCA must include this step. The presentation of results should reveal the underlying principles, environmental goals, and interests in the LCA and possibly present different results that are due to other settings. This goes beyond the uncertainty and the variability in the models and the data inherent with the method.

Application in the ETH-UNS Case Study

Within the ETH-UNS case study, the life cycle assessment is a special environmental science evaluation method (see Table 8.1). It can be applied in a relatively wide range of cases and assesses products, materials, decision alternatives, or actions, such as the remediation of soils or even planning variants (Scholz et al., 1996). Within the ETH-UNS case study, an LCA is generally embedded within a practical decision problem. Usually, the ecological dimension is only one part and has to be integrated with the economic, societal, and technical assessments of the alternatives. Therefore, LCA can be applied if the following conditions are met:

- An ecological assessment of alternatives is desired by case agents, experts, politicians, the study team, or other people concerned.
- The indirect impacts due to the whole life cycle of the alternatives are considered to be of importance.
- Enough data are present for the LCA to be sufficiently accurate and reliably assessed.

- The value choices within the LCA are transparent to and accepted by the stakeholders.

LESSONS TO BE LEARNED

▶ Life Cycle Assessment (LCA) is an environmental management method and organizes a scientific evaluation of a functional unit using a beginning-to-end perspective.

▶ The definition of the functional unit is crucial for the validity of an LCA.

▶ Uncertainties and sensitivities in the data, the process model, and the impact assessment may influence the results greatly.

▶ The method must be interpreted carefully because of the inherent assumptions and value settings.

▶ LCA comprises a synthesis of environmental impacts and may contribute to an integral evaluation and a sustainability audit.

THE METHOD IN DETAIL

The four parts of the description correspond to the steps given in the ISO norm (see above). As indicated in Figure 18.2, the method is iterative in the sense that parts may have to be reconsidered after other parts have been conducted.

Goal and Scope Definition

The goal and scope definition largely determines the outcomes of the LCA study. Because of the standards defined by the International Organization for Standardization (ISO 14040/41) (ISO, 1997, 1998a), the goal statement should include answers to the following questions:

- Why is the study carried out? Which application is intended? Which information is necessary for a better case understanding or evaluation?

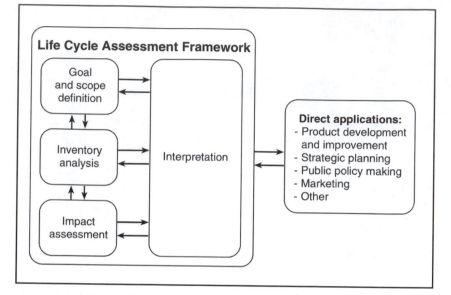

Figure 18.2 Phases of an LCA Due to ISO 14040
SOURCE: International Organization of Standardization (1997).

- To whom are the results presented? Which agents are supported with information given through the LCA study?

The scope of the study encompasses the following:

- The definition of the function of the system and the functional unit
- The definition of the system boundaries
- The data categories in which the inputs and outputs are collected for each unit process within the system
- The required data quality
- Orientations on how the validity of the LCA will be assessed in a critical review

The system that is going to be investigated may have several functions. For example, packing material may serve transport, conservation, and marketing purposes. The functional unit describes which functions of a product will be considered, such as conservation during a certain period. If some alternatives fulfill additional functions, then the study has to account for this by including these alternatives in the functional unit (ISO 14041). Furthermore, a reference flow must be determined. The reference flow of an alternative, such as a square meter painted wall, is the measurement unit for the comparison of the products.

The system boundaries define which processes, which inputs and outputs, and which releases to the environment are considered in the life cycle model. Criteria for establishing the system boundaries shall be identified and justified in the scope phase. For example, inputs may be considered only if the mass, the energy, or the environmental relevance reaches a relevant proportion of the total input (ISO, 1998a). The same criteria apply to the selection of the impact categories investigated in the study.

The detail of the processes and the corresponding data has to be defined. This means that the time frame and the geographical frame need to be covered in the LCA. Furthermore, the technological frame must be determined, and it can be specified either by the best available or by the current production practice. Additional data quality requirements must be considered, such as precision, completeness, representativeness, consistency, and reproducibility. Of course, the variability and uncertainty of data and methods have to be considered. Data collection is most efficient when the data quality is on the same level as and consistent with the goal throughout the study.

For an LCA, no predictive validity can be assessed. However, a construct validation is feasible. For this, a variety of critical reviews by internal or external experts, or by interested parties (see Chapter 20), can be provided. The type of review and the type and format of the report have to be specified within the scope definition (ISO 14041).

Marginal vs. Average Technology

Generally, the main focus of an LCA study is the analysis of a product system as a whole. But a different view for the LCI may be appropriate when changes in a large product system, such as the implementation of a new energy technology, are investigated. Changes from fossil energy to nuclear energy may serve as an example. Such changes in a product system imply comparison between different environmental impacts in contrast to a comparison between combustion processes for oil. We guess that for long-term decisions, the differences or residuals with respect to the dominant current technology should be assessed. This technique reveals more sharply the gains and losses on a quantitative or qualitative level and poses the focus of analysis to the comparison of real alternatives. Thus, LCA may become a strategic decision support tool.

Modeling: The Life Cycle Inventory

The LCI describes the activities that are part of the life cycle of all decision alternatives or products. This life cycle is called the product system (ISO 14041). The life cycle of each alternative is represented by a number of so-called unit processes, which are the smallest measurement elements (see Box 18.1). In the LCI for each of these unit processes, the following data are collected:

- The output of the unit process, that is, the resulting product
- The products needed as input, which are themselves output of other unit processes
- The elementary flows into and out of the unit process, such as energy and raw material inputs or emissions to air, water, and land

The LCI creates a system model that combines two parts. One part is a system model of the industrial, production, or economic activities within the life cycle. This is the product system represented by the involved unit processes, or commercial commodities. The other part consists of the environmentally relevant data collected for each unit process, which are known as elementary flows, ecological commodities, or environmental interventions. Because of ISO 14041, the links between the unit processes consist of physical flows. Hence, a mass and energy balance is a possible check of the unit process data.

The distinction between commercial commodities and ecological commodities in LCI was suggested by Rolf Frischknecht (1998). He considered at least commercial commodities to be connected to the unit process by a financial flow. He also emphasized that the product system should be modeled "according to the financial flows connecting the economic [unit] processes" (p. 21). In this way, "the 'real' economic system and its causalities [are] more adequately and more completely" represented (p. 5). Ecological commodities are flows without an economic value.

After the data for both parts, the commercial and the ecological commodities, have been supplied, the contributions of the unit processes needed for the functional unit have to be calculated. Hereafter, these

Box 18.1   Life Cycle Inventory Calculation

We will present the mathematical formula for the LCI to allow the study team to comprehend how the environmental interventions can be determined for general cases. The essence of the formula is easy to grasp. Using linear algebra, the environmental interventions of a functional unit are calculated as the sum of the environmental interventions of the unit processes.

The following table contains the matrix representation of a simplified LCI for sandwich packages. Columns 2 through 4 represent four simplified unit processes. Their inputs and outputs, which are the commercial commodities, are specified in Matrix A, above the dotted line. Matrix B, below the dotted line, contains the environmentally relevant elementary flows, which are the ecological commodities. The process Production of Electricity, for example, yields 1 MJ electricity as output, requires 0.01 kg aluminum and 0.5 kg crude oil as input, and induces the emission of 3 kg CO_2 and 2 kg solid waste. Above the dotted line, the last column is used to quantify the functional unit. In the example, the functional unit is defined as 10 sandwich packages, which can be seen in the last component, f_4, of the functional unit vector. Below the dotted line, the cells of the last column show the environmental interventions, x_i, induced by the functional unit. The contributions, y_i, of each unit process to the functional unit can be calculated when solving $Ay = f$. The environmental interventions, x, of 10 sandwich packages then can be calculated as $x = By$.

Table   Matrix Representation of the Simplified LCI for Sandwich Packages

	Production of Electricity	Production of Aluminum	Production of Aluminum Foil	Usage of Aluminum Foil	Functional Unit Vector f
Electricity, MJ	1	−50	−1	0	0
Aluminum, kg	−0.01	1	−1	0	0
Aluminum foil, kg	0	0	1	−1	0
100 sandwich packages	0	0	0	1	0.1
					Environmental Interventions
Bauxite, kg	0	−5	0	0	x_1
Crude oil, kg	−0.5	0	0	0	x_2
CO_2, kg	3	0	0	0	x_3
Solid waste, kg	2	10	0	1	x_4

NOTE: Adapted from Heijungs (1994).

intensities can be used to calculate the elementary flows due to the functional unit. An example for this modeling and calculation is given in Box 16.2. This procedure is called matrix approach, as opposed to the Petri Net approach (Schmidt et al., 1997).

There are other ways of formal representation as well. For small product systems, the life cycle can be represented in simple lists. Heijungs (1994) proposed a matrix model using an inventory matrix, which led to conceptually easy calculations by matrix inversion. These calculations are presented in Box 16.2. Möller and Rolf (1995) explained how a Petri Net approach can be used. These mathematical structures are important features of LCA software, but the underlying (mathematical) model is based simply on mass and energy balances. The life cycle inventory is linear because the elementary flows are calculated relative to the functional unit. In each case, the inventory model tries to describe the real product system of industrial, production, and economic activities within the life cycle and calculates the ecological impacts (see Box 16.2).

The predictive validity of the LCI model cannot be assessed because the ecological impacts of an alternative cannot be measured directly. However, there are some guidelines for attaining a good practice of LCI. Because the inventory model comprises very simple balance equations, the most critical points are due to qualitative model aspects that should already be addressed in the goal and scope definition (see above). This includes prerequisites and assumptions to which the results of life cycle assessments are sensitive:

- The intended completeness of the product system model and the definition of the system boundaries; the question is, which unit processes have to be considered?
- The consistent assessment of data availability and quality, including accuracy and uncertainty
- The choice of the environmental impacts accounted for

Furthermore, the following questions have to be answered:

- Which are relevant inputs and outputs to the system and must not be neglected?
- Which allocation rules are applied?
- How has the recycling of material and energy been accounted for?

We strongly recommend creating a graphical overview of the process network and checking for all of these aspects against the goal and scope definition.

Allocation

In a product system, if joint production occurs, it is necessary to allocate the environmental impacts to the different products. For example, if waste treatment is combined with energy production, joint production is assumed here to require a fixed ratio of the products. The distribution of the environmental impacts may be straightforward when physical relations can be found, such as mass or volume fractions (Azapagic, 1996). ISO 14041 says that wherever possible, allocation should be avoided by dividing the unit process into subprocesses or by expanding the product system in order to include additional functions of the co-products. Lower priority should be given to finding physical or other relations, such as those based on economic values of the products (for more details, see R. Frischknecht, 1998).

Evaluation: Life Cycle Impact Assessment

Conceptual Structure

The life cycle impact assessment (LCIA) assesses the environmental impacts of the life cycle, which have been calculated in the inventory. The conceptual structure of life cycle impact assessment consists of the following:

- *Classification:* Define which environmental interventions contribute to the selected impact categories (see the section on Formal Structure)
- *Characterization:* Quantify the contribution of the interventions to the impact categories, and select the calculation rule for the category indicator (see the section on Formal Structure, p. 297)
- *Normalization:* Analyze the calculated category indicators relative to the total contribution of the impact category within a region during a certain time period
- *Weighting:* Assess the relative importance of the impact categories against each other

Within the ISO/DIS 14042 (ISO, 1998b), the latter two steps are considered optional. The term *valuation* is perceived as an assessment of weights, uncertainties, and sensitivities. The last two topics are considered part of the interpretation (see below; also see Finnveden & Lindfors, 1996).

There are very different methods, and they range from adding up the material mass used in the life cycle of products or services (e.g., MIPS, which does not conform to ISO) (Schmidt-Bleek, 1993); to sophisticated indicators, which include emission, fate, exposure, and effect of many substances; resource depletion; and land use, such as the Eco-Indicator 98 (Goedkoop, 1998).

LCIA as an Application of Multi-Attribute Utility Theory

The LCIA includes a special application of Multi-Attribute Utility Theory (MAUT) (see Figures 18.1 and 18.3). There are some differences to common applications of MAUT. Usually, the choice of the attributes, their weighting, and their aggregation often relies on individual or subjective settings and values. MAUT applications are designed as simply as possible and are often performed to support a single decision. In contrast, the LCIA should be generally applicable and, ideally, relies on a generally accepted value setting. This setting guides the use of scientific information, environmental models, and technical data, all of which relate the life cycle of the product system to one or more indicators to evaluate the environmental burden of the functional unit. Of course, within this procedure, many environmental models are used, and many subjective choices are necessary, including the weighting of impact categories, damage categories, or endpoints. As generally assumed in MAUT, LCIA is linear, uses weighting factors and utility or damage functions, and is structured in a hierarchy.

Formal Structure of LCIA

Using the notation of Heijungs and Hofstetter (1996) the formal description of the life cycle impact assessment can be given as follows:

$$S_j = \sum_i Q_{ji} \times M_i$$

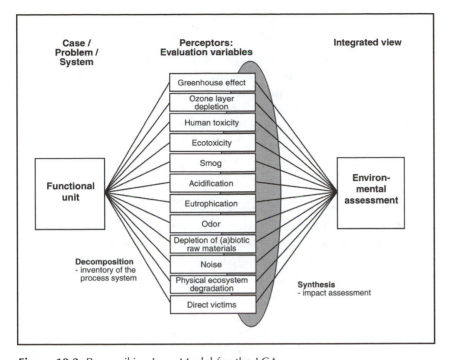

Figure 18.3 Brunswikian Lens Model for the LCA

NOTE: The impact categories used within the CML method (Heijungs, 1992) can be considered the perceptors.

In this formula, S_j is the impact score, or category indicator (ISO/DIS 14042), of an impact category j. An impact category is the formalization of an environmental problem that is going to be accounted for in the LCIA. M_i is the environmental intervention, such as the mass of the emission of a substance i that is calculated in the inventory. Q_{ji} is the characterization factor and a cell of Matrix Q, which contains the results of the classification and characterization steps in LCIA. The classification step specifies which environmental intervention i contributes to which impact category j. In the characterization step, the characterization factors are quantified. The discussion of how to determine the characterization factors is still ongoing. As an example, we give the formula of Heijungs and Wegener Sleeswijk (1999), who consider environmental fate F, intake I, and effect E as independent dimensions and arrive at the following equation:

$$S_j = \sum_n \sum_m \sum_i E_i^j \cdot I_i^{mj} \cdot F_i^{nm} \cdot M_i^n$$

Here, M_i^n denotes the emission of substance i to compartment n, such as air. F_i^{nm} denotes the fate of substance i in compartment n and reflects whether it is degraded or transported to a compartment m, where it is exposed to a target organism. I_i^{mj} denotes the intake of substance i from compartment m by target organism j, and E_i^j denotes the effect of substance i in the target organism j.

Modeling in LCIA

From a modeling perspective, the evaluation formula is a model that simplifies the real processes in order to arrive at an acceptable evaluation. Please note that the predictive validity of the evaluation cannot be assessed because S_j cannot be measured directly. To test the hypothesis that the evaluation formula describes the "real" processes adequately is difficult for a number of reasons:

- The real processes may not be understood completely or are still under discussion, such as the genesis of global warming and ozone depletion.
- What is really known about some processes is that they are not as simple as the presented formula.
- The evaluation has to aggregate over time and space and thus cannot represent what really happens locally.

Therefore, to create a rule to calculate the environmental impacts requires a sensitive modeling process where the necessary definitions and assumptions are very much influenced by individual perception of the environment and the intended value settings. Which variable is considered relevant for the evaluation depends largely on the researcher. Therefore, another reason is the following:

- The evaluation model depends, often more than is desirable, on the subjective value settings and on the individual perception considered relevant for the environment.

Interpretation

Because of ISO/DIS 14043 (ISO, 1998c), the interpretation step consists of the following:

1. Identification of significant issues based on the results of the LCI and LCIA phases of LCA

2. An evaluation that considers completeness, sensitivity, and consistency checks

3. Conclusions, recommendations, and reporting of the significant issues

The identification of significant issues will be based on the results of the preceding steps of the LCA. If the methodological choices, value choices, and interested parties coincide with the goal and scope definition of the study, then the significant issues are (a) inventory parameters, such as energy use; (b) impact categories, such as the acidification potential; or (c) parts of the life cycle, such as transportation, if they significantly contribute to the environmental impacts. The significance of the issues can be shown in a straightforward manner using tables or bar charts that compare the environmental interventions, the percentage of their contributions, or a ranking of their significance. An issue can be significant only if it contributes a greater percentage to the corresponding total than does the overall uncertainty.

The evaluation tries to measure the reliability of the results. To this end, the completeness, consistency, and quality of the data have to be assessed. The sensitivity analysis reveals whether the uncertainty of the significant issues influences the conclusions. The objectives may be to assess uncertainties due to the allocation rules, the definition of the system boundary, the assumptions, the method of impact assessment, the normalization and weighting, the data quality, and so on.

The last part of the interpretation phase of LCA is to draw conclusions and give recommendations, which should be done with great care. But the material compiled within this phase should generally help in doing so. Note that recommendations cannot be specified in all cases. Even clear conclusions may not be possible because the uncertainty of the results may be large or barely accessible.

Remember that subjective value choices are not included only in the weighting. Hofstetter (1998) argued that some figures that depend on individual value settings can be specified using cultural theory (Thompson, Ellis, & Wildavsky, 1990). Instead of many different attitudes leading to many different impact assessments, only five cultural types are regarded. These types are fatalism, hierarchy, autonomy, individualism, and egalitarianism. Hofstetter concludes that a very limited number of different evaluations are sufficient to represent the whole scale of individually different life cycle impact assessments. Methodologically, the different evaluations can be included in the LCA study with a sensitivity analysis of the cultural types.

Available Methods and Resources

When conducting an LCA study, many resources can be used that have already been compiled. Although the goal and scope definition and the interpretation have to be specified for each study, the work necessary for the LCA can be reduced primarily by using software that simultaneously includes existing databases, compiles the inventory, and presents several LCIA methods.

Several methods have been proposed, but we want to mention only the method of critical flows (Bundesamt für Umwelt, Wald und Landschaft, 1998), the CML method of environmental classification (Heijungs, 1992, 1994), and the Eco-Indicator95 (Goedkoop, 1995) and its current update (Goedkoop, 1998) in order to present the general structure related to the guidelines given by the ISO. The range of different impact assessment methods makes clear that the choice of a method may have a large influence, and results may be different. Modifications and improvements of the presented methods are likely and may lead to considerably different results.

LESSONS TO BE LEARNED

▶ LCA as an instrument for environmental evaluation is still developing.

▶ LCA is a formalized method with its own terminology. The core ideas are simple and based on linear models. If the study team is afraid of mathematical formulas, an expert can translate the LCA language easily and link it to the study team's worldview.

▶ LCA is a formative method that depends on both quantitative research results and, to a certain extent, subjective value settings. Therefore, the case agents should know and accept these values.

▶ A standardized procedure is very important. Results from commercial applications should be interpreted with great care. A critical review and reflection on whether the results are suitable for the case is necessary.

▶ A careful conduction, a comprehensive presentation, and a careful interpretation of an LCA study may yield very valuable insights into the relevant environmental impacts of a product, a service, or specific decision alternatives linked to the case.

19

BIO-ECOLOGICAL POTENTIAL ANALYSIS

THE RATIONALE

The Bio-Ecological Potential Analysis (BEPA) is a means of assessing the performance and vitality of an ecological or organismic system relative to its present possibilities and boundaries with respect to certain functions in a sustainable evolutionary dynamic. BEPA is a semiquantitative diagnostic and prognostic method. The method was originally developed as a specific ecological method to answer the question: How are the current and maximal bio-ecological performances of an area or a landscape to be evaluated? This question often arose in some of the ETH-UNS case studies on rural regions in which a certain landscape was considered as a case (see Scholz, Mieg, et al., 1998; Scholz, Bösch, Carlucci, & Oswald, 1999).

We want to begin by providing insight into the foundations of BEPA, which can be found in landscape ecology, and then discuss why we consider BEPA to be a method that also allows for an analysis of other organismic systems such as cities, organizations, or individuals.

Landscape ecology evolved in Europe in order to bridge the gap between ecological systems and agricultural, human, and urban systems that were increasingly interfering in the previous century. Thus, landscape ecology is a research domain focusing on the interaction between natural systems with social systems (Leser & Mosimann, 1997; Troll, 1971; Zonneveld, 1972). This makes clear that *Kulturlandschaften* (cultural landscapes), rather than natural landscapes, are the object of landscape ecology. Similar to what was outlined in Chapter 4, contemporary approaches consider landscape ecology both as a formal biological, geological, and human science and as a holistic approach and state of mind (Zonneveld, 1982). The latter simply refers to the holistic axiom that the whole is more than the sum of its parts (Smuts, 1926). From an epistemological point of view, landscape ecology acknowledges that meaning ultimately is a matter of intuitive cognition (see Box 14.1). Thus, the understanding, which is the topmost level of the architecture of case studies (see Figure 4.1), and Experiential Case Encounter (see Box 5.1) are indispensable parts of BEPA. According to Miller (1978), there are three different types of systems: concrete, conceptual, and abstracted systems. In modern approaches, the landscape as a whole is conceived as a real, concrete system that becomes comprehensible through linking conceptual and abstracted systems. This is done when referring to general systems theory (von Bertalanffy, 1968), theories of self-organization (Jantsch, 1980; Piaget, 1953), biocybernetics (Vester, 1978), and theories of control and regulation (Pontrjagin, 1964), resulting in a new theoretical approach called "ecosystemology" (see Naveh & Liebermann, 1994).

Presumably, the question now arises of why we chose the prefix "bio." There are a couple of reasons for this. First, BEPA is considered to be a method complementary to Material Flux Analysis and Life Cycle Analysis (see Chapters 17 and 18), which deal primarily with abiotic energy and material fluxes and the assessment of them in a global perspective. Like the Environmental Impact Assessment (EIA) (see Wood, 1995), the BEPA focuses on a local or regional scale. However, whereas in an EIA, the potential environmental impact of various forthcoming human activities or projects are assessed, a BEPA can be carried out regardless of whether a project is planned. Second, the prefix *bio* was chosen because the focus is the intercourse and dynamics of the organism in its environment, rather than its physical texture. This becomes even clearer upon closer examination of the etymology of the phrase Bio-Ecological Potential Analysis.

Bio-Ecological Potentials: From Landscape to Organizational Dynamics

The word *bios* (βι oζ) was used in ancient Greek as a reference to life. Note that the term *biology* (*Biologie*) is relatively new and presumably first appeared in an 1800 manuscript written by C. F. Burdach, *Preparatory Instruction on the Whole Art of Curing* (*Propaedeutikum zum Studium der gesamten Heilkunst*), in which morphology, physiology, and psychology are summarized under the label "biology" (Ballauf, 1971). Later, biology was used to describe that part of science that copes with the fundamental principles of life—principles derived from taking the design of the cell model as a core concept and basic reference for organic reproduction.

The term *ecology* is a composite, combining the term *oikos* (οι χοζ), which means house, home, or habitation, and the suffix -*logy,* derived from the Greek *logos* (λογοζ), which refers to one who is a scholar in a certain field. Haeckel (1866/1988) established ecology as the "science of the requirements in the struggle for existence" (*Lehre von den Bedingungen des Kampfes um das Dasein*).

The concept of potential goes back to the Latin *potentia,* which refers to both power and possibility. In physics, the potential, such as the potential energy, describes a system's possibility to do work. This has been generalized in other domains, such as potential denoting something that "exists in a state of potency and possibility for changing or developing into a state of actuality" (Merriam-Webster, 1993, p. 1775).

We will not refer to the etymology of analysis, but only remark that we will go beyond its notion of decomposing (see Chapter 4). Analysis includes a specific perspective and is a product of both the item to be analyzed and the capability, motives, intentions, and values of the person, institution, or other analyzing unit.

In this chapter, we are in line with another aspect of the Brunswikian functionalism that system (e.g., human-environment) relationships are investigated from a functional or performance perspective. This means that for a certain system, having potential/power is completely irrelevant if there is no opportunity for it to be applied. In other words, a general property of an ecosystem, such as the inherent energy, is irrelevant if it has no function.

These fundamental ideas are reflected in Figure 19.1. We will organize the BEPA of an ecosystem along the analysis of the structure, context, and function. According to Tansley (1935), the term *ecosystem* incorporates a community of interdependent organisms with the physical environment they inhabit. According to this concept, ecosystems are dynamic systems that, given constant constraints, show cyclical or progressive changes. These changes are due to population dynamics and evolutionary

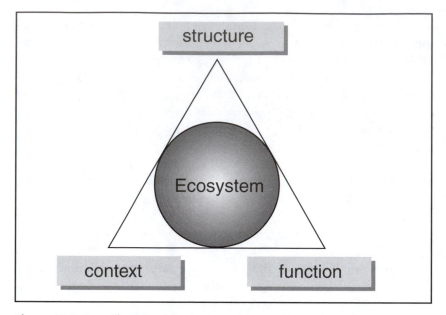

Figure 19.1 Core Elements Constituting an Ecosystem in Bio-Ecological
Potential Analysis

processes inherent in the structure of the ecosystem, that is, the current
distribution, relatedness, and organization of the system's units.

By "structure of the ecosystem," we mean the spatial and temporal relationship, connectedness, partitioning, and modularization of the system
units as well as its physical units. If the case is an enterprise, the structure
is given by the buildings, machines, and other physical properties belong-
ing to the company; the products; the company's owners; personnel;
knowledge; goals; habits; and, last but not least, the organization and
constitution of the firm.

The context (i.e., boundary conditions) of an ecosystem consists of external entities, such as the regional climate, and includes nutrients, food
chains, and water fed in from the environment. Landscape ecologists consider geomorphology or "bedrock" (e.g., lithology), hydrology, soil tex-
tures, vegetation, and wildlife (Steiner, 1991). Relevant contextual constraints of environmental ecosystems are droughts, pest viruses, floods,
fires, or climate changes. However, the type of administrational zoning is
also considered to be a constraint because the ecological standards in nature preservation, agriculture, and urban territories differ from one zone
to another. The context includes all environmental constraints that are

permanently relevant system or impact factors. If an enterprise is considered, the constraints are the regional market, business activities, labor market, distribution of incomes, and culture, but also the labor climate and education.

What is most crucial is having an understanding of and appropriate definition for ecosystem functions. Among ecologists, it has been widely accepted that ecosystem functions today can be defined only by considering the functional interrelations between the natural processes and components and the human needs and activities (see de Groot, 1992; Schulze & Mooney, 1994). Distinctions are made between production functions, carrier functions, information functions, and internal and external regulation functions, all of which are essential for defining the performance and vitality of a system. These functions can be used to define and measure a performance model. Ecosystem functions have also been dealt with occasionally under the heading of landscape potentials (see Haase, 1978; Leser & Mosimann, 1997; Neef, 1966) or biophysical and social land use needs and functions. The functional key variables encompass the biotic yield potential, water potential, biotic regulation potential, resource potential, construction potential, or recreation potential. In an enterprise, typical (eco)system functions are the annual profit, tonnage or number of products, number of employees, technological and business innovations, the impact of a company on a market, and so on.

We consider these criteria, presented in Figure 19.2, to be an incomplete but sufficient set of perceptors for rating the bio-ecological potential.

LESSONS TO BE LEARNED

▶ Bio-Ecological Potential Analysis was originally developed for local or regional landscape analysis and evaluation. It is a general method that, in principle, can be applied to organizations, individuals, and other systems whose structures are organismic.

▶ In BEPA structure, context and system are distinguished. The analysis of these units relies, on one hand, on conceptual and formal analysis, such as general system theory or biocybernetics, and on the other hand, on understanding as a type of cognition.

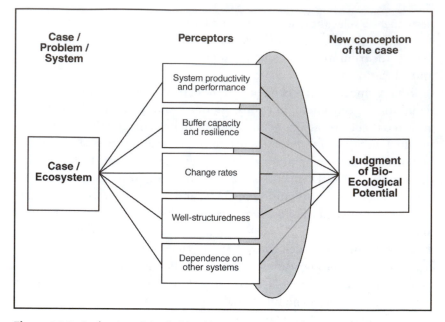

Figure 19.2 Evaluation Criteria Used in a Bio-Ecological Potential Analysis

Fundamentals

The BEPA method of case analysis is the most complex method presented in this volume. In order to illustrate how the proposed principles are related to the history of sciences and how they may be accomplished, we will briefly present some of the most important historical milestones: Darwin's theory of evolution, Piaget's structural theory of organismic development, Holling's theory of resilience, and Wiener's (bio)cybernetical approaches.

Darwin's evolutionary theory relied on ideas from philosophers and scientists, such as Leibniz, Harvey, Bonnet, and Herder. In his famous book *On the Origin of Species*, Darwin (1859) provided the theoretical framework for the development of the organism. According to his theory, two complementarities (change and stability, and similarity and diversity) are essential for development.

The Swiss psychologist, biologist, and epistemologist Jean Piaget ran many case studies on the genesis of human intelligence. He investigated cases on the origin, genesis, and development of such items as language

(1923), judgment and reasoning (1924), moral judgment (1932), intelligence (1936), numbers (with Szeminska, 1941), conception of space (with Inhelder, 1956), time (1946), and equilibration of the cognitive structure (1975). His theory was founded on three fundamental principles. The first, *accommodation,* is understood as the potential of an individual to adjust existing cognitive structures to new problems. The second, *assimilation,* is the capability to develop new cognitive schema and abilities. Through these two principles, Piaget was able to understand the dynamics of adaptation (adaption). He noted, "In short, intellectual adaption, like every other kind, consists of putting an assimilatory mechanism and a complementary accommodation into progressive equilibrium. ... But ... adaption only exists if there is coherence, hence assimilation" (Piaget, 1953, p. 7). Piaget formulated the third principle, *equilibration,* almost 50 years later (Piaget, 1975). According to his theory, he did not consider equilibration as a static concept (as many others did), but as a self-regulatory process that permits an organism to attain higher and better adjusted schemata and achievements. We can learn from Piaget that stability is relative and that the system must have the ability to make qualitative structural changes in order to assimilate. An organism must develop anew if accommodation is insufficient. Thus, these concepts show connotations to the criteria of change rates, and buffer capacity and resilience.

Clearly, conservation biology is a highly relevant discipline providing concepts and models for defining and understanding ecological structure and functions. Modern nature conservation theories are far beyond the static equilibrium "nature constant" model. Holling (1987), for instance, introduces "multiple equilibria state models" and "organizational change" concepts. The first models postulate the existence of more than one stable state and emphasize the "qualitative properties of key ecological processes (e.g., water supply) that determine the existence or not of stable regions and of boundaries separating those regions" (Holling, 1987, p. 140). Ecosystem development is supposed to show some Resilience within a certain range because of the environmental constraints present (such as in water supply), but then arrives at new stages or qualities of development discontinuously. The organizational change approach is also called the "evolving nature approach." According to this approach, successful efforts to constrain natural variability leads to self-simplification and fragility of the entire system. Thus, if ecosystem management is considered, the aim is to allow for a homeostatic development with respect to structure. Holling (1987) concludes that "Evolutionary change requires not only concepts of function but concepts of organization that concern the way elements are connected with subsystems" (p. 141). The latter refers to the relationship of a structural variable, that is, the organization of the case considered, to functions (see Figure 19.1).

Another reservoir of knowledge is the rules of biocybernetics as Vester formulated them. Cybernetics derives from the Greek word for steersman (κψβερvετεζ). The scientific field grew out of information theory and was first created by the mathematician Norbert Wiener (1948) as the science of communication and control in the animal and the machine. The feedback concept, taken from theories on control systems, may be conceived of as a core concept of this approach. Note that feedback is also elementary for the idea of homeostasis and is also inherent in the Brunswikian lens model via the functional arc feedback loop (see Figure 4.2). The latter feedback loop conceptualizes the rewarding and punishing of the system caused by the quality of the terminal focal variable. In this loop, evolution, based on feedback received, either rewards or penalizes the appropriateness/accuracy of the terminal focal variable, such as a visual image. The main emphasis of cybernetics is on circular mechanisms that allow complex systems to self-organize, maintain, and adapt themselves. Cybernetics clearly goes beyond classical science in two ways. First, cybernetics not only asks "What is the thing?" but also investigates "What is the thing for?" (Ashby, 1964). Thus, cybernetics has strong links to pragmatism and transdisciplinarity. On the other hand, cybernetics does not start from the assumption that every process is determined solely by its cause, that is, a factor residing in the past. Cybernetics postulates that living organisms' behavior involves striving toward a (better) future state that does not, as yet, exist.

Although we are aware that the original aspirations formulated by the research program of cybernetics did not meet all expectations, we consider Vester's biocybernetic rules (see Box 19.1) as prescriptive rules providing guidelines for an evaluation.

Obviously, BEPA is an assessment for sustainability. Sustainable development of a society means that subsequent generations will have the same opportunities as former ones had. Note that sustainability, in the sense of the capability of maintaining development rather than staying at the same level, also implies a dynamic equilibrium (see Scholz, Mieg, et al., 1998); for instance, nonrenewable resources that have been used by former

---

Box 19.1   Basic Biocybernetic Rules

---

1. Negative feedback must dominate positive feedback, as positive feedback endangers the system by pushing it above limits

2. System growth must be independent of system supply functions, as otherwise long-term stability is risked by making too many demands on limited resources

3. A system should be oriented towards functions not products, as a system shows more flexibility and adaptability when it is function-oriented

4. Using a coping strategy for incoming impacts according to the Jiu-Jitsu principle is better than responding antagonistically

5. There should be multiple use of products, functions and organizational structures, to increase energy, resource and information efficiency

6. Fluxes in solid, heat, and other waste products should obey recycling and closed loop waste management processes also in order to prevent irreversibilities

7. Symbiosis through mutual substitution (vicarious mediation) and diversity in the type of connections are desirable in order to establish internal robustness and minimize external dependencies

8. Biological design by feedback planning with the environment is essential, as endogene and exogene dynamics have to be both mastered and used for innovations

---

SOURCE: Vester, 1991, p. 84

---

generations must be replaced by later generations if they are supposed to have the same opportunities.

LESSONS TO BE LEARNED

▶ The Bio-Ecological Potential Analysis was constructed referring to evolutionary, developmental, and cybernetic system theories by people such as Darwin, Piaget, and Wiener. This reference is made in order to understand the prerequisites of a successful and sustainable case or system development.

▶   Most of the criteria of Bio-Ecological Potential Analysis (see Figure 19.2) —productivity, resilience, diversity, autonomy, and development rate— refer to fundamental principles of developmental and evolutionary theories.

THE METHOD IN DETAIL

BEPA is a method under construction and has not yet been fully developed or applied in complex cases. Lang (2001) provided a first application. Because of this, we can only sketch the different steps. In principle, although BEPA can be applied to areas of urban development, such as the ZZN case or rural areas, we believe that it can also be adjusted to analyze organizations, institutions, or companies.

The five evaluation criteria for BEPA are system productivity and performance, buffer capacity and resilience, change rates, well-structuredness evaluation, and dependence on other systems. These criteria can be assessed practically as follows.

System Productivity and Performance

If we consider an organismic system such as a landscape, one can theoretically record all processes, that is, activities, changes, and transformations in and of a system over a certain time range. We will call these processes "productivity." Productivity denotes what has changed or been exchanged objectively. We will distinguish "what is" from "what is considered and evaluated." Performance is the evaluation of a system's productivity with respect to the result of the productivity processes according to functional key variables. Thus, a crucial step of BEPA is to determine the functions that a system has to provide.

Let us consider the bio-ecological production of a small rural valley. What is a good measure for productivity? From an ecological point of view, biomass is often considered to measure the activity of a landscape. For the most part, we assume a positive correlation between biomass and

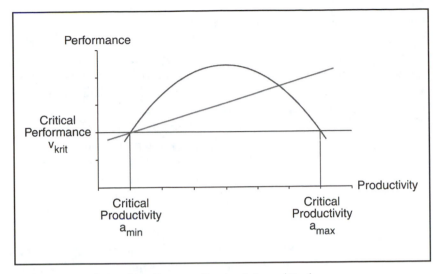

Figure 19.3 Relationships Between Productivity and Performance

NOTE: For the most part, a positive or U-shaped relationship is expected, but a linear relationship is also possible. The range between the lower critical productivity level and the upper critical productivity level is called the sustainability range.

performance (see the straight line in Figure 19.3). However, at least for biomass, a negative U-shaped relationship can be appropriate between productivity (i.e., the magnitude of biomass production) and performance (i.e., the evaluation of this aspect). Therefore, if we are considering systems with artificial inputs, such as fertilized agriculture or forest, a too-high biomass (e.g., due to overfertilization) can result in lower crop quality or lower soil quality and, therefore, in a lower short- or long-term performance (Kramer, Gussone, & Schober, 1988). This is illustrated in Figure 19.3. Note that the same holds true for human individuals. For instance, the activity level can be regarded as a measure of productivity. According to the Yerkes-Dodson law, the U-shaped relationship applies to the activity level-performance relationship (Yerkes & Dodson, 1908). It is a somewhat open question whether this also holds true for species richness or even aesthetics, but the simple rule "too much is too much" also holds true for design, as may be seen from some types of garishness.

Biomass as a productivity measure is significant for the assessment of anthropocentric as well as ecocentric landscape performance. Depending on the perspective, other functional key variables may serve as measures for landscape performance. From an anthropocentric perspective, aesthetics may be taken as a performance indicator, which, in general, relies only in part on biomass. However, from a biological view, for instance, species richness or biodiversity often is considered a functional key variable. Hector et al. (1999) showed that at a certain site, plant biodiversity seems to be positively correlated to biomass.

A crucial question is how to assess the sustainability range of a system. For this, the distinction between productivity and performance is crucial. Usually, sustainability is considered endangered if the performance is insufficient. However, a certain performance is given only if the productivity of the whole system is on a certain level. This is illustrated in Figure 19.3. Thus, the sustainability range is seen on the objective level.

In order to assess the lower and upper limit of the sustainability range, we will recommend comparative, historical, and complementary benchmarking. Comparative and historical benchmarking consist of comparing the performance with similar or former states, for instance, with reference to 1950, which, in Europe, is taken as an effective date for the start of progressive nature depletion (Pfister, 1995, 1998). The task of the case analyst is to define appropriate reference systems, scales, and measures. The idea of complementary benchmarking will be discussed later in the chapter on the modular superstructure.

There are many functional key variables that can be linked to the same system and that can be regarded as performance indicators. So far, we have considered two information functions, biodiversity and aesthetics. But in agriculture systems, the biomass of the yield can be seen as a production function, which, of course, often correlates with the total biomass. Depending on the case, carrier functions (e.g., tourism, human residents) or regulation functions (e.g., for soil erosion, groundwater recharge, biological control mechanisms, human health) also have to be taken as functional key variables. In planning projects, study teams are often in conflict with regard to which performances should be promoted, for instance, if conflicting societal needs are formulated toward a site. A common strategy to cope with this problem is to conduct a suitability analysis (McCharg, 1971; Steiner, 1991, p. 131) in which the degree of performance for different alternative productivities (e.g., agricultural, recreational, residential, commercial, and industrial purposes) is assessed and compared.

Similar considerations can be made with respect to enterprises. Here, productivity can be the number of pieces produced or the turnover per employee. Again, for this example, nonlinear or nonmonotone relationships between productivity and performance are plausible, for instance, if there are negative marginal costs.

LESSONS TO BE LEARNED

▶ Productivity, the total outcome of a system or case, has to be distinguished from performance. Performance is an assessment of productivity under a functional perspective. A precise definition of the function(s) is a prerequisite of BEPA.

▶ In general, there is no absolute scale for judging performance and choosing appropriate measures of productivity. In this case, one must make a comparative assessment by benchmarking.

▶ If there is more than one performance variable of interest, each should be synthesized through MAUT (see Chapter 11).

▶ If it is unclear which performance is best for a case or system, a suitability analysis is recommended.

Buffer Capacity and Resilience

Buffer capacity and resilience refer to the system's ability to sustain in the course of contextual or environmental change and stability. Resilience, as it has been formulated by Holling (1973),

> determines the persistence of relationships within a system and is a measure of the ability of these systems to absorb changes of state variables, driving variables, and parameters and still persist. . . . Stability, on the other hand is the ability of a system to return to an equilibrium state after disturbance. (p. 3)

Resilience is thus linked to a kind of absorption capacity with respect to environmental impacts and the capability of systems resulting in a (new) temporary equilibrium state. The balance between resilience and stability is the product of the system's evolutionary history and the fluctuations it has experienced. Or, to express it in opposite terms, resilience is a system's capability to prevent catastrophes as sudden, radical changes or breakdowns of a certain state. Heuristics for such changes were formally described by the mathematical catastrophy theory of Thom (1970) and Zeeman (1976).

Being exposed to diverse types of external pressures and stresses, the system must show resilience, resistance, and redundancy. Hence, one task of the study team is to determine which of the stress factors to which the case or system is exposed is the most important.

We will distinguish between two types of stresses. The first results from disturbance events caused by substantial anomalies in the availability of resources such as water floods, climate changes, and soil erosion. The second is the carrying capacity overload by xenobiotics or anthropogenic emissions such as organic chemical compounds (e.g., PCB), heavy metals, or anthropogenic nitrate from fertilizers.

In an enterprise, critical events with respect to resources are the loss of key people or major clients, unexpected new competitors, fundamental technological change, stock market disturbances, and so on. The carrying capacity of an enterprise can be endangered if the quantity or quality of one department's productivity is reduced by diseases, loss of motivation, or other reasons.

Measurement of a buffer capacity is difficult and relates to many ongoing discussions on environmental risk assessment. We will not go into details about this topic here. Although there are many possible arrangements, we suggest that an evaluation of buffer capacity should be organized along a risk assessment procedure. At first, undesirable states of case development have to be assessed (e.g., a critical load of toxicants, a critical height of flood water). Then, the buffer capacity can be measured in absolute, relative, or probabilistic terms. The absolute term is given by the distance to critical load, the relative term is the percentage of surmounting, and the probabilistic term establishes the likelihood that a certain critical load will be surmounted. The buffer capacity measures what a case/system in its current state can carry or bear. Aspects of flexibility will be subsumed to developmental flexibility.

We present a simplified version of the buffer capacity concept in Figure 19.4. The fictual dynamics of a system, say, a landscape, through the time course is displayed. The limits a_{min} and a_{max} denote the upper and lower limits of the sustainability range with respect to the overall system productivity, which is essential for the sociology of fauna and flora. The buffer capacity b_t represents the distance to the sustainability limits. Thus,

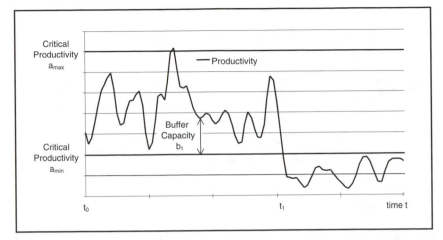

Figure 19.4 Illustration of the Buffer Capacity b_t

NOTE: When considering a case's or system's time course, b_t is a measure to assess the additional change in productivity that can be taken into account until a qualitative system change occurs. If productivity is below a critical threshold, we assume that the character of a system is changing (e.g., a steppe is turning into a desert).

buffer capacity refers fundamentally to the idea of keeping systems within their limits.

If we consider a certain ecosystem, such as a steppe being exposed to climate change, the system will turn into a desert if the humidity falls below a_{min} and turn into a forest if the humidity increases above a_{max}. In both cases, there will be a system change that will cause relentless changes for many plants and animals. We want to note that from an evolutionary point of view, ecologists often consider only the downgrading of a system as a negative respectively fundamental system change. This dynamic aspect of resilience will be dealt with in the next chapter as developmental flexibility.

LESSONS TO BE LEARNED

▶ Resilience is a system property and denotes in which way an external stress or internal changes affect the character of the system.

▶ The buffer capacity measures what a case/system in its current state can carry or bear.

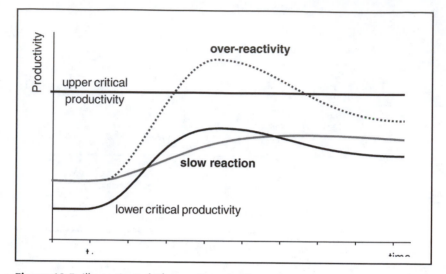

Figure 19.5 Illustration of Change Rates by Example

NOTE: The upper and lower bold lines denote the critical productivity. At time t_1, the lower critical performance is supposed to change, for example, due to external stress because of increased exposure to high-energy short waves. If the system reacts too slowly, it will be harmed. In some cases, overproduction or overreactivity can be harmful. This is presented by the dashed productivity function.

▶ An assessment requires the determination of stress factors and unwanted system states as well as a reference range. The buffer capacity can be measured in absolute, relative, or probabilistic terms.

Change Rates

We postulate that every system needs both change and stability. The stability has been subject to buffer capacity. We will now emphasize the dynamic aspects of the system. In general, an organismic system's rate of change should have a minimum and should not exceed a maximum (see Figure 19.5). We will illustrate this principle by presenting three examples.

The first example is with the flexibility of the buffer capacity and reveals the necessity of a system to adapt or assimilate to changing context. Presumably, most readers have experienced sunburn. The Western world has changed the human species to an indoor being. As a consequence, many of us, in our first days of summer vacation or when skiing, suffer if we are exposed to sunlight. The buffer capacity with respect to high-energy short waves becomes exhausted quickly, and the skin system is demolished. However, skin is a dynamic system. It has developed an assimilation schema in that it increases production of the pigment melanin and becomes thicker. This phenomenon clearly suggests a phylogenetic change in people's melanin production. For peoples living at a certain degree of latitude, this adjustment in production obviously got adapted to the sequential change of seasons and may not adjust to its maximum in one day. Note that there is also variance between people of the northern and people of the southern hemispheres. Nevertheless, the principle of limited change rates holds true for all skin types.

The second example is on mutualism and co-evolution and the balanced interrelationship between species or elements in a(n) (eco)system. In general terms, mutualisms are defined as couples of species that benefit from each other. The study of mutualism has been underrated and ignored in biology for a long time (see Begon, Townsend, & Harper, 1990). There are many examples and various types of mutualisms. For instance, one may distinguish between negative or antagonistic mutualisms, predator-prey, virus-host, or parasite-host relationships in which, presumably above all, one species profits from the other. We will not go into details here, but rather emphasize in general terms that (a) the reproductivity rate of one species depends on that of the other; (b) even in antagonistic relationships such as virus-host interactions, the virulence of the invader is arranged in such a way that it will not lead to complete extinction of the host; (c) mutualisms are believed to become unstable if the fluctuations become so big that the resilience of one species is overdemanded (May, 1981).[1]

This last statement is also supported by diverse findings and theories on viral diseases, which indicate that an organism hosts many viruses that are in a natural variance in the sense that there is variation in viral phenotype in a population of hosts. Clearly, the larger the population and the greater the geographic distance between the members of a host population, the greater the variance. Thus, if a virus is imported from a foreign host population that is far away, the rate of change of the immune system of the host population, which is required to overcome a virus, is too big, resulting in a viral disease with fever, and so on.

The third example is a heuristic from organizational change, although similar arguments can be found for ecological systems. It is a well-known phenomenon in business and organizational sciences that groups or companies become fragile when they grow or change too fast. Consider the case study ZZN. Originally, the whole transformation from a contaminated industrial site to a new quarter of Zurich was supposed to take 20 years. However, if an economic boom occurs, and the time is reduced to, say, 5 years, the quality control of planning soil remediation and construction could be cut below the critical value.

Although no general formula or thresholds can be defined, attention should be paid to overly rapid growth.

As we have shown by these examples, the rate of change in a system's adaptability is critical and should be adjusted to the necessities of the environmental change or to the inherent structural needs. Although no general rule exists for determining critical thresholds, various strategies can be used for assessing the critical range. One possibility is to investigate what must be changed if the environment changes and assess whether the (eco)systems can adapt sufficiently. Another is to investigate similar cases in which too many demands have been placed on a system's resilience.

LESSONS TO BE LEARNED

▶ Buffer capacity and change rates are salient system/case properties with respect to context, change, and environmental stress. Whereas buffer capacity denotes the system's ability to absorb and maintain its states in the case of context change and environmental change, the change rate indicates the system's ability to assimilate and adjust to new environmental demands.

▶ Change rates are not restricted to growth or increase of productivity; they can also be established by structural changes.

Well-Structuredness Evaluation

The well-structuredness evaluation assesses whether the case/system possesses the needed subunits and is organized in a robust way for providing a sufficient and sustainable performance, and whether the system performance can be improved by restructuring the system. Thus, well-structuredness evaluation deals with the capability, vulnerability, and potential of a case due to internal organization and interfaces. We will focus on whether the system has the necessary subunits, whether these are sufficient in size and numbers, and whether they are suitably connected. The well-structuredness evaluation does have some commonalities with the first three aspects of BEPA presented earlier. However, it goes beyond a black-box consideration and asks the study team to understand an appropriate structure for a good performance.

Given the structure, context, and function of an ecosystem, various subunits, such as habitats or local milieus, can be identified that are essential for the system's productivity. For an ecosystem, the internal resources are often separated spatially. For instance, for many animals, meadows and woods provide complementary functions, and both must have contingency and a minimum size for the animals to survive. We will focus on the question of size and structure of functional subunits as part of the BEPA because, as we know from conservation biology, large systems need and induce fragmentation, and small systems face the danger of extinction or the loss of their character.

Some basic issues should be considered when deciding how to define and measure the size and structure of subunits. First, functional subunits can be formed at any level of organization. There is no way to avoid subjectivity in the definition of levels and units, although there are sometimes natural categories, such as herds, families, habitats, or catchments. In any case, the criteria for determining subunits should be defined explicitly. Second, the significance of the various groups is understood only in relation to the behavior of the whole system. Third, as in biology, the role of the spatial arrangement of land is commonly overlooked (Forman, 1995). This also has to be acknowledged for seemingly objective systems, such as food webs. This is surprising, because it has been clearly acknowledged that the patches and corridors in an ecosystem play a key role in its sustainability (see Box 19.2). Fourth, on any level of an ecosystem, no long-term structural stability can be expected. This can be illustrated by the study of metapopulations, which is a set of colonies or local populations of a given animal in a given area that survive for a while, send out migrants, and eventually disappear. Thus, no general push-button solution for assessment of subunit size and structure exists. We recommend a

Box 19.2   The Evaluation of Well-Structuredness

Depending on context and function (see Figures 19.2 and 19.3), effective and efficient systems need appropriate organization, fragmentation, and connectivity. This holds true for landscape ecology (Forman, 1995), and groups and teams (see Chapter 16), but also for offices, buildings, cities, regions, cultures, and other organismic systems. The latter has been elaborated on comprehensively by Alexander, Ishikawa, and Silverstein (1995). For the evaluation of well-structuredness, we present some examples.

1. *Connectivity:* The evaluation of the connectivity depends on the relation between the objects. If an interaction is positive for both sides, a good connectivity (Pattern A) is required; if not, a low connectivity (Pattern B) has to be rated positively. For example, for land mosaics, there are mathematical indexes for measuring connectivity (Forman, 1995; Hawksworth, 1995).

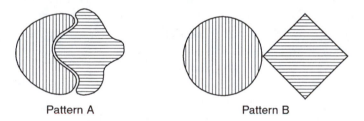

Pattern A   Pattern B

2. *Edginess:* Edges are the borders between systems. The assessment of edginess depends on the type of interactivity (supportive, competing, etc.) of interfering systems. If a system is endangered from the outside, the system of Pattern D is superior to that of Pattern C because it has a minimum edge length given a fixed size. Another issue of edge analysis is the crispness of the edges. Edges can be fuzzy, soft, or sharp and can have open and closed borders. Such descriptions can be found in biological textbooks.

Pattern C   Pattern D

3. *Networks:* Teams can be structured in completely different ways. Although there are general rules for the size, such as "the magic number 7 plus/minus 2 heuristic" (Miller, 1956), the type of organization has to be evaluated according to the type of task to be solved. Atoms (Pattern E) enhance the reliability if the same task is conducted by several individuals, such as data encoding. The egalitarian total information structure (Pattern I) is recommended for small groups for complex, ill-defined problems.

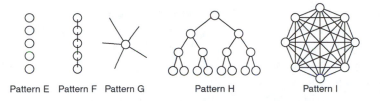

Pattern E   Pattern F   Pattern G   Pattern H   Pattern I

4. *Patterns:* Communities need structures for enfolding social quality and identification. Pattern J shows activity centers within a 10-minute walking distance. The outermost nodes (a and b) should be strong enough to prevent a contraction. The greens and parks shown in Pattern K should be distributed equally in a town within a 500-meter distance. Pattern L shows levels of intimacy in office planning.

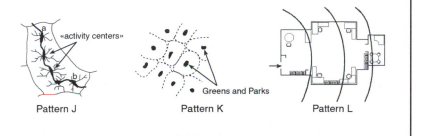

Pattern J   Pattern K   Pattern L

top-down procedure for this step of a BEPA, starting with determining those functions basic to survival and then focusing attention on others that are weak, in danger, or under pressure. An example of this is the determination of whether food and water supplies of vertebrates living in an ecosystem would be endangered by new roads or settlements. Various measures are developed to assess the gap formation, fragmentation, and shredding of an ecosystem (see Forman, 1995; and Box 19.2) and to evaluate mosaic and patch dynamics. Although measurement is desirable, and sophisticated mathematical indexes for assessing structure and mosaics have been developed, we recommend a semiquantitative approach.

We will illustrate a procedure for well-structuredness evaluation when referring to Noss and Csuti (1994) by suggesting a four-step procedure for ecosystem assessment.

1. *System size and key functions:* The first step of evaluation is on the core system and includes an assessment of the minimal critical size for the indispensable key functions. Conduct a system analysis. Determine the pattern of key functions and connections when considering food and resource chains, and relate these to the needs of native species. Then, classify key and characteristic habitats, and determine their major centers. Finally, consider connections to smaller habitats, and assess the quality of these connections.

2. *Border or edge analysis:* Provide a border or edge analysis (see also Box 19.2). Analyze disturbances, open fringes endangering invasions by antagonists, and any other opponents, such as new predators entering the system. Identify so-called ecological traps, which are places of high attraction that include essential risks or perils. Note that there are also internal edges created by gaps, which may endanger a system.

3. *Stress and niche analysis:* Are there fragments or cells being stressed by overpopulation or size? Are there fragments, niches, or patches that may provide for survival, renewal, or recolonization, as structure requires both change and stability?

4. *Networks and patterns:* Analyze migration routes and channels or corridors of information exchange. Are there isolated and, thus, endangered or inefficient subpopulations? Are networks organized in a way that will sustain, or will they transform (see Box 19.2, Pattern J)?

Other aspects, such as a hierarchy analysis, can be considered depending on the case being studied. We believe that a system may be assessed according to a 5-point scale with respect to each of these critical issues. The overall rating, then, has to reflect any low ratings on any individual dimensions.

LESSONS TO BE LEARNED

▶ The well-structuredness evaluation starts from an understanding of well-working systems and their organization. The analysis and evalu-

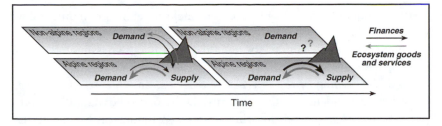

Figure 19.6 Input-Output Analysis as a Tool for Analyzing the Dependence of the Case on Other Systems

NOTE: In input-output analysis, both space and time can be disaggregated. For example, the return on investment in Phase A is planned for Phase B. The figure presents the two-dimensional disaggregation of time and space.

ation go beyond a black-box consideration and contribute to understanding and evaluating the robustness of a system.

▶ The well-structuredness evaluation should encompass the number, size, and arrangement of functional subunits. Critical issues are minimal size, isolatedness, and open/closed borders of the subunits.

Dependence on Other Systems

In this step, the ecosystem is considered a functional subunit of a larger configuration of systems. The first step is to consider the case/system in relation to other systems that are on the same or a higher level.

Some theoretical approaches, such as input/output analysis, have been developed for understanding the mutual relationships of complementary systems, such as city and countryside, or different countries, such as resource suppliers and consumers (Leontief, 1966). The core idea is thinking in demand and supply functions on ecosystem goods and services. Of interest is a disaggregation of both space (e.g., when considering cities and countrysides or alpine and nonalpine regions) and time. Regarding time, if, for example, the ZZN case (see Chapter 4) is considered before (System A) and after (System B) a contaminated soil remediation, the latter depends on the intensity of the remediation that is prepared in the former. The utility of the remediation for System B will compensate the costs for remediation in System A. Such a crude model of system dynamics can be justified if an assessment is required but lacks a detailed dynamic model (see Figure 19.6).

Once such complementary systems are identified, two issues have to be investigated:

1. *Self-dynamics of the interacting systems:* In which respects is the ecosystem dependent on other systems? Do structural dynamics or components in larger or neighboring systems promote or hinder future development?

2. *Feedback loops with interacting systems:* Is the case/system a key element of a larger system that depends on the system considered? Is the larger system sensitive to the system such that supportive, positive feedback loops are to be expected? Are there stabilizing or destabilizing external relationships?

The degree of being affected or independent on other systems is also called autonomy. Note that within our approach, neighboring and superposed systems create the context, and no pure autonomy can be expected for ecosystems, organisms, or complex cases because they are open systems.

LESSONS TO BE LEARNED

▶ Future development of a case/system can be promoted or hindered by developments in neighboring and superposed systems.

▶ Input-output analysis is considered an appropriate method to investigate dependence on other systems.

NOTE

1. In one approach to viral theory, for instance, the virulence of a viral infection and, consequently, the probability of its survival depend, in part, on a special type of self-pathology, which can be described as a self-mutation.

Part **IV**

VALIDATION
PERSPECTIVES

20

THE VALIDATION OF
EMBEDDED CASE STUDIES

THE RATIONALE

Throughout the entire course of a case study, the question arises of how to
evaluate the outcomes of the methods and the findings attained with
them. Typical questions are as follows:

- What are the criteria and means for judging the quality of the case
  study?
- Are the methods capable of measuring, representing, evaluating, and
  transforming the case according to the intention of the case study?
- Are better decisions made after applying the formative case
  methods?

These questions refer to the problem of validation. Note that the term
validation goes back to the Latin *valere*, which means to be strong,
healthy, appropriate, and powerful. There is no doubt that valid methods
and results are beneficial. However, the questions and issues just highlighted are austere and complex. A thorough answer would require a

separate volume, and that would take us into the core of the philosophy of science and its intriguing controversies.

Nevertheless, case study researchers must address the problem of validity. Yin (1994) highlights "four aspects of the quality of any design" that affect validity: "(a) construct validity, (b) internal validity (for explanatory or causal studies only), (c) external validity, and (d) reliability" (p. 18). Before moving on to the practical implications of the validity problem, we want to clarify the theoretical problems that are linked to these validation criteria in the context of embedded case studies. Readers who are interested only in practical aspects should go to the section "Validation of Embedded Case Studies: A Practical View."

This book has introduced a set of methods for case representation, evaluation, transition, and case study team methods. The objects of the case studies are complex, real-world cases that are investigated with respect to a theme and a functional perspective. These four types of methods each require different validation strategies. For the case study team methods and some of the case transition methods, the validation criterion is whether they have a positive effect on the outcomes of the case study. For the case representation, evaluation, and some of the transition methods, validity assessment of the overall outcome requires a mixed set of criteria derived from qualitative and quantitative research. We review how validity is addressed in quantitative and qualitative sciences after considering reliability and objectivity issues. Then, we take a closer look at how validation is addressed in the embedded case studies. The latter is central in our embedded case study approach and in the introduction of our methods.

Quality Criteria for Case Studies

The colloquial meaning of a valid argument is one that does not contain obvious errors in its internal logic. In mathematical logic, an inference or a mathematical sentence is valid or true if it is derived correctly according to the logical principles or theoretical fundamentals to which the inference belongs. In this sense, validation means verification. However, the truth of any proposition is impossible to demonstrate unless it is part of a closed system (Gödel, 1931). Most embedded cases are unstructured (see Table 2.1) and open systems. Logical standards of this type of validation are irrelevant for the overall validation of case studies. The validation criteria of mathematics refer only to the internal validity of some of the methods, such as System Dynamics, which is a minor piece of the overall validation.

For a long time, experimental sciences, and branches of social sciences as well, were influenced by the standards of physics and the natural sciences and by how leading philosophers reflected these standards. Sir Karl Popper was certainly the most influential. With respect to validation in the above etymological sense, he distinguished two etymological types of validation: verificationists and falsificationists.

> Verificationists . . . accept a scientific finding or belief only if it can be justified by positive evidence; that is to say, shown to be true, or at least, to be highly probable. In other words, they demand that we should accept a belief only if it can be verified, or probabilistically confirmed. . . . Falsificationists . . . say, roughly speaking, that what cannot (at present) in principle be overthrown by criticism (at present) is unworthy of being seriously considered. (Popper, 1969, p. 228)

The latter view, also called positivism or critical rationalism, dominated most branches of empirical sciences in the second half of the previous century. Thus, we are confronted with two fundamentally different approaches of validation. Within the social sciences, experimental psychology and hypothesis testing provide prototypes of falsificationism. As we have stressed, however, inductively attained synthesis statements are essential in case studies. These statements are usually not derived from the kind of crisp, theoretically grounded hypotheses that falsificationists demand (see Chapter 4, particularly the sections on the positivist Kant and inductive Hegel types of synthesis). Validation in embedded case studies falls, to a large extent, on the verificationist's side.

We find more pragmatic views on validation in applied natural sciences. Modeling of processes such as climate change and water transport in soil systems in the earth sciences, for example, works within limits that are acknowledged explicitly. "The verification and validation of numerical models of natural systems is impossible and confirmation by demonstration of agreement between observation and prediction . . . is inherently partial" (Oreskes, Shrader-Frechette, & Belitz, 1994, p. 641). Here, the goal of scientific modeling is not truth—which is acknowledged to be unobtainable—but empirical adequacy.

Reliability and Objectivity in Case Studies

We focus primarily on validity, but we are aware that reliability and objectivity are often given comparable emphasis. We have argued explicitly that despite their formative approach, case analyses are not objective. They are constrained by the study team, which is decisive. The outcomes of a case study depend on the study team's case understanding, its competence with the case study methods, its proficiency in finding the right graininess in analysis on the different epistemic levels, its motivation, and its intention.

In statistical terms, reliability measures the extent to which we can assume that a study will yield the same result if it were repeated. Reliability refers primarily to a special type of consistency. Quantitative reliability-consistency measures calculate the share of the measurements or findings that are due to errors, such as those caused by lasting or temporary features of the study. Thus, reliability is defined by the degree to which the findings are independent from accidental characteristics of the research. For example, if the case is a person, fatigue or illness may cause such accidental effects. If the case is an urban district, as in the Zurich North case, the study team has to take care that data gathering is not influenced by singular case events, such as a spectacular accident or festival activities.

Interobserver reliability "involves agreement among observers" (Aronson, 1990, p. 281). This concept overlaps with the notion of objectivity, because objectivity is often a measure of the independence of the outcomes of an inquiry from the people conducting the study. Many variants of reliability and many sophisticated quantitative reliability measures for tests and measurements have been formalized (see Bortz & Döring, 1995; Dick & Hagerty, 1971; Fekken, 2000). However, for the type of case study with which we are concerned in this volume, validity, rather than reliability or objectivity, is the core issue. The reason is that cases and the circumstances of their analysis are unique. Furthermore, the case is often affected and changed after a case study is performed. Nevertheless, we will postulate a weak type of reliability in the sense that there is a chance that a study team will end up with the same results if the same formative methods are applied. Or, to express it another way, the study has been arranged to "demonstrat[e] that the operation of a study—such as the data collection procedures—can be repeated with the same results" (Yin, 1994, p. 18).

Instead of asking for objectivity in a traditional way, we postulate that the results of a case study must convey both the findings of the study and the relationship of the study team to the case.

Validity Within Quantitative Research

We speak about quantitative research or quantitative case studies if quantitative (numerical) units represent the major data, findings, and arguments. Consider psychological tests like a professional aptitude test or an intelligence test. These tests produce a test score. The score provides a valid result if it is related to the entity that it intends or purports to measure or assess. The validity of a professional aptitude test or forecast might be assessed, for example, by correlating the test score with subsequent performance. The target is the prediction of an extra-test variable or reality (Aronson et al., 1990; Bortz & Döring, 1995). In quantitative approaches, a method is valid when there is a sufficiently high correlation between its results and the external criterion it was designed to measure. Construct, content, convergent, and external validity are dominant in quantitative approaches (see Box 20.1).

Criterion validity is a special way to assess validity and a subtype of convergent validity in quantitative research. It refers to the ability of an instrument or method to predict a relevant phenomenon or outcome. For example, the prospective annual income of a person may serve as a criterion for the validity of a professional aptitude test. Another variant of convergent validity (see Box 20.1) is discriminant validity. This concept refers to assessing the commonalities and the differences with respect to a set of traits that is considered to be indicative of the phenomenon of interest, such as professional performance. The main tool for these types of validity is multivariate correlation statistics.

These measures cannot be calculated meaningfully for the overall outcomes or the general results of an embedded case study. This also holds true for multiple-case studies, as we have already stressed in our introduction of multiple-case studies (see Chapter 2). A fatal flaw would be to investigate multiple-case studies with a quantitative, statistical approach. Instead, the appropriate "method of generalization is 'analytic generalization,' in which a previously developed theory is used as a template with which to compare the empirical results of the case study" (Yin, 1994, p. 31).

Box 20.1 Variants of Validity

There are many facets of validity defined in different sciences. The presented list refers strongly to psychology. In psychology, there is a wide range of research subjects and methodologies, ranging from physiological natural science experiments to clinical case studies of families and organizations.

Construct validity: This notion was first introduced by the American Psychological Association (APA, 1954; Cronbach & Meehl, 1955). This type of validity refers to the extent to which an instrument or method measures the theoretical entity ("the construct") that it was designed to measure. Construct validity is a kind of umbrella concept (Cronbach & Meehl, 1955).

Content validity: Content validity refers to the extent to which an instrument accurately reflects the investigator's conception of the construct being assessed.

Internal validity: In an experimental study, or causal, explanatory case study, internal validity is given if a causal statement can be made about the effects of (experimental) conditions manipulated or altered on dependent variables or other conditions.

External validity: External validity refers to the generality of a finding, such as an effect of a cause-impact relationship, and to what degree this finding or effect can be generalized to other measurements, variables, population, settings, situations, cases, and so on.

Convergent validity: Convergent validity is established when different measures were made to assess one issue using different methods, and the measures result in a high correlation.

This logic of replication should underlie not only multiple-case studies, but also the multiple uses of different case study methods on one and the same case.

Validity in Qualitative Research

No clear-cut line exists between qualitative and quantitative research. Statistical data can be found in ethnographic and holistic studies, and qualitative interpretations are common in quantitative studies. The difference is a matter of emphasis. "Quantitative researchers have pressed

Face validity: Face validity is a subtype of content validity. Face validity refers to the extent to which respondents and/or professional users regard an assessment instrument or a model as appropriate for the construct being assessed (Krueger & Kling, 2000, p. 150).

Ecological validity: This type of validity refers to the concept of probabilistic functionalism (see Figure 4.2). Ecological validity occurs if the proximal cues, that is, the information and variables sampled by the case study team, are appropriate to represent the case. "A high ecological validity means that that the cue is a good indicator of the distal variable (i.e. the information objectively present in an object or case such as size, number of persons etc.) in many situations" (Gigerenzer & Murray, 1987, p. 77). The question is, Has the appropriate information been sampled?

Functional validity: This type of validity also refers to the theory of probabilistic functionalism (see Figure 4.2). Within the frame of visual perception, this type of validity focuses on the question of how well the perceptual system and the subsequent information processing estimates distal stimuli. In general, functional validity refers to the adequacy and efficiency of (organismic) behavior or scientific study in goal attainment.

Consequential validity: The sum of the ethical implications of running a survey, test, or case study has been referred to as that test's consequential validity. In case studies, the consequences of using the results should be considered part of the study team's responsibility (Krueger & Kling, 1995; Messick, 1989).

for explanation and control; qualitative researchers have pressed for understanding the complex relationships among all that exists" (Stake, 1995, p. 37).

Qualitative inquiry focuses on verbal descriptions of phenomena. However, Taylor, Bogdan, and Walker (2000, p. 491) point out that qualitative methodology is more than a set of techniques for gathering and representing data. Theoretical perspectives and research strategies from symbolic interactionism to ethnomethodology and constructivism are linked to the qualitative approach. The presence of a central narrative is characteristic for any qualitative study. By narrative, we mean the expertise to arrange happenings and the dynamics of a story in a meaningful way. The novelistic case description of a Zurich North scenario (see Box 9.5) employs a strong narrative technique, even though it was fundamentally based on a quantitative Formative Scenario Analysis.

In his book titled *The Art of Case Study Research,* Robert Stake (1995), the most prominent representative of qualitative case study research, differentiates qualitative research as a subjective form of inquiry tied to the perspectives and often to the personal interests of the researcher (see Chapter 1 on intrinsic case studies). Quantitative and qualitative research can also be distinguished by their strategies for generalization: "Quantitative researchers regularly treat uniqueness of cases as 'error,' outside the system of explained science. Qualitative researchers treat the uniqueness of individual cases and contexts as important to understanding" (Stake, 1995, p. 39). Qualitative researchers share quantitative researchers' aspirations for achieving results that are reliable and valid (see Kirk & Miller, 1986). Their understanding of these quality criteria of research differs from the way these criteria are understood in the quantitative camp. Not surprisingly, qualitative researchers remain in their qualitative paradigm when they address validation methods and procedures (for a detailed discussion, see Peräkylä, 1998). For example, they often engage the empathy of the reader. We will introduce the method of validation by triangulation, which is central to the conception of embedded case studies and the integration of quantitative and qualitative knowledge offered in this book.

Stake (1995) introduces the metaphor of triangulation to denote methods for data collection and interpretation "which do not depend on mere intuition and good intention to 'get it right' " (p. 107). The core idea is that because there is no best view, researchers must rely on multiple perspectives or views on a case. Data source triangulation, for example, is attained if the phenomenon remains the same in other times and places or as the pattern of social interaction changes. With reference to Denzin (1989), Stake suggests that, by "choosing co-observers, panelists, or reviewers from alternative theoretical viewpoints, we approach theory triangulation" (Stake, 1995, p. 113).

This idea of qualitative validation is essential for our case study approach on many levels. We clarify this in our discussion of Brunswikian Probabilistic Functionalism, the epistemology underlying our approach to embedded case studies.

Validation Within Brunswikian
Probabilistic Functionalism

Throughout this book, we have introduced the methods of case representation, case evaluation, and case transition in the terminology of the Brunswikian Lens Model (see Chapter 2 and Figure 4.2). These methods also target the integration of qualitative and quantitative knowledge. According to the architecture of knowledge integration (see Figure 4.1), this integration should be performed on the medium level. In order to understand how case studies can be validated from a Brunswikian perspective, we compare the validity assessments that take place in embedded case studies with the validity assessments of models in the visual system.

The Brunswikian program of probabilistic functionalism focuses on the "relationship of the subject to the world—a relationship which philosophers and psychologists have always seen and considered essential" (Brunswik, 1934; McDonald & House, 1992). For example, if a psychological aptitude test is considered, the functional and the consequential validity (see Box 20.1 and Figure 20.1) have to be taken into account.

We will illustrate the different aspects of validity inherent in embedded case studies in four steps as we relate the discussion of the validity of probabilistic functionalism in the field of perception research to embedded case study work. The discussion of validity will follow Figure 20.1 on perception, which was Brunswik's research domain. The upper half of Figure 20.1 represents the epistemological model of the relationship between the subject and its environment. It entails what is theoretically assumed to be substantive but cannot necessarily be observed directly. The lower half of the figure shows the empirical model and presents what is observable and measurable. This distinction is basic in many branches of sciences. Even in atomic physics, measurements must be interpreted according to the theories. Geiger counters are calibrated according to the strong theory of half-life time of radioactive decay. Elstein, Shulman, and Sprafka (1978) consider this distinction as the dichotomy of "the *Ding an sich* and the *Ding für sich*—the thing-in-itself, the noumenon that is fundamentally unknowable, and the thing-as-perceived, the phenomenon we can know" (p. 37).

Figure 20.1 serves two purposes. On one hand, if the objects in the environment and the perceived object in the organism are the reference points, then behavioral predictability—the contingency between the

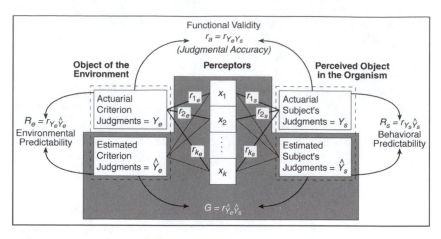

Figure 20.1 The Perception and Judgment Paradigm of Probabilistic Functionalism

NOTE: This paradigm has been modified and extended from Elstein et al. (1978). The left box represents a physical object of the environment and its true criterion values (e.g., the weight of a bear and the distance to a known plant next to it) that can become accessible by the perceptors (e.g., the visual impression of the height of the bear, and the distance to and the height of a known plant on the retina) in a probabilistic way. This relationship is expressed by the correlation coefficients and the bold lines. The subscript e indicates that the relationships between environmental distal cues and proximal cues are considered. At the right side, we find the subject's judgments. The cue utilization represents the way the subject is synthesizing the proximal cues x_1 to x_k to a judgment. The subscript s indicates that cue utilization is assumed to happen in the subject. The functional validity refers to the appropriateness and the accuracy of the subject's judgment (see text). The gray area represents the empirical assessment of the perceptual or judgmental process and its modeling. The relation between the actuarial criterion values and their empirical assessment establishes the environmental predictability. The difference between the subject's judgment and the predicted subject's judgment is a measure of the behavioral predictability.

estimated subject's judgment and the actual subject's judgment—is a measure of construct validity.

On the other hand, the empirical researcher's model (the gray area) can serve as a normative reference. In clinical reasoning and medical diagnosis, for example, the novice has to learn normative or prescriptive models. Students rely on such models when they learn to combine different laboratory data to diagnose liver diseases. The Brunswikian Lens Model defines a paradigm of multiple-cue probability learning that characterizes the case study team's activity. "Subjects must learn to make judgments based on the values of multiple cues to bear a probabilistic relationship to a

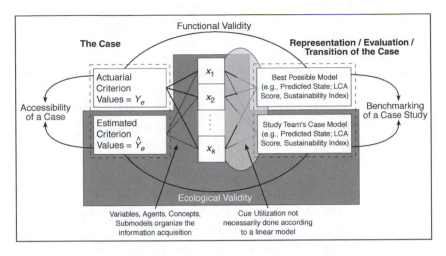

Figure 20.2 Validity Issues in Embedded Case Studies

NOTE: The left box of the figure presents a case. The right box is the representation, evaluation, or transition of the case according to a guiding question or topic by the study team or another research team. The study team's activities are sketched in the shaded area. The case is analytically decomposed by considering variables, agents, concepts, or submodels. Knowledge integration may not, in general, be conceptualized by the linear model, but by other processes. This is displayed by the gridlined lens. The lower part of the figure displays the best case study performed according to the intentions and goals of the study team. This provides a kind of benchmarking that can be used for the validation (see text).

criterion" (Elstein et al., 1978, p. 38). We turn now to the four steps through which validity is assessed in embedded case studies: (a) the validity and the initial and terminal focal variables, (b) cue sampling, (c) cue utilization, and (d) the functional validity of the products.

Step 1: Validity and the Initial and Terminal Focal Variables

Consider the gray area in Figure 20.2. On the left, we have the case as the object of the environment. Imagine yourself on a hiking trail in Alaska. Walking along the path, you unexpectedly see a single black bear a quarter mile ahead. In Brunswik's language, the bear is a real object that serves as an initial focal variable. To assess the danger, a quick judgment of the bear's weight may be in order, because a bear will not usually attack a person who is larger. Whether or not the weight of the bear is an appropriate terminal focal variable is obviously essential. In general, functional validity refers to the adequacy and efficiency of organismic behavior in goal attainment. Functional validity is shaped by the selection of an appropriate terminal focal variable. For example, we might expect the bear's eye color to have a lower functional validity than its weight. Even a highly accurate judgment would provide irrelevant information for danger assessment.

To construct an analog relationship for embedded case studies (see Figure 20.2 and Figure 4.2), we must first ask who takes the role of the perceiving subject (i.e., who will judge the bear's weight?). We presume that the study team will take this role and a best possible model provides the reference of modeling. The case then takes on the role of the object of the environment—the initial focal variable. The representation, evaluation, and transition of the case serve as the perceived object in the organism, or the terminal focal variable.

Just as we did when we saw the bear and we asked which variable would provide a good estimate for our danger, we have to answer the question, "What is to be perceived?" Their answer relies on a second question, "What is the analysis for?" This question refers to the research topic associated with the case. Case selection often depends on the theoretical and practical interests of the study team and their access to the case. For example, the Zurich North case was chosen because it provided insight into sustainable urban development. Sustainable urban development can be considered a general terminal focal variable analogous to the assessment of danger from the bear in the visual perception example. To clarify this relationship, we present examples of terminal focal variables from the Zurich North case for three case study methods:

- In Formative Scenario Analysis, the description of future states of the Zurich North site (see Figure 9.2) served as the terminal focal variable.
- In Multi-Attribute Utility Theory, the integral evaluation of a specific soil remediation technology (see Figure 11.4) took the role of the bear's weight.
- In Integrated Risk Assessment, the case agent's perceived risk for different soil remediation technologies (see Figure 12.4) can, for the most part, be interpreted in a manner similar to the weight judgment. Risk is a multifaceted issue, however, and the specific variant of risk inherent in the case agent must first be known.

The validity of the initial and terminal focal variables will be assessed mostly by face validation (see Box 20.1). The critical issue involves the experts at the beginning of the study who can judge the suitability of these variables.

Step 2: Cue Sampling Validity and Ecological Validity

The second question is, "Which cues are assessed by the organism or study team?" Gigerenzer and Murray (1987) state that Brunswik assumed that the "perceptual system identifies a subset of cues that [was] previously associated with the distal variable in the ever changing sample of cues available in the natural environment" (p. 76). "Uncertainty is a feature of the relationship between the organism and the distal environment" (Brunswik, 1955, p. 210). According to probabilistic functionalism, the organism is sampling information in a probabilistic way in order to end up with robust perceptions. In evolutionary terms, the response of the organism to this uncertainty in cue sampling is organized by vicarious mediation that goes back to the Bühlerian duplicity principle. This is

> the process by which perception makes at least two separate parameters from the stimulus array at the sensory surface of the organism (the proximal stimulus). . . . Via the combination of at least two . . . [kinds of] information (duplicity), the size of an object [e.g., the weight of the black bear] can be perceived as a constant while being perceived at varying distances. (McDonald & House, 1991, p. 161)

The organism is thus permanently learning to adjust its cue sampling capability by sampling the actual criterion values or the distal environmental information by its perceptors $x_1, \ldots, x_k$. "Only very late, in the Berkeley discussion and in two papers published posthumously, did Brunswik find the concise formula for his underlying conception of man: the perceptual being as an intuitive statistician" (Gigerenzer, 1987, p. 63).

This is the theory. But how can these theoretical considerations be used in practice? Consider the problem of estimating the bear's weight. The weight can be assessed by referring to different cues. When the bear is in the distance, the weight is probably assessed when comparing the perceptual cues from the bear to the cues from the stones, bushes, and tree trunks around him. This comparison allows us to assess the bear's weight. This information serves as criterion values or distal cues Y_e. According to the duplicity principle, at least one other distal cue (besides the visual information about the bear's size) will be taken into consideration. Cues such as the color of flowers next to the bear might be interesting, but they raise new problems. Approaching too close, and ignoring the weight estimation, might have some unwanted negative consequence. The election of the appropriate cue variable thus codetermines the judgmental accuracy that is a salient aspect of the functional validity of perception.

Brunswik used regression statistics for modeling the cue sampling. In Figure 20.1, this is expressed by the regression coefficients $r_{1e}, \ldots, r_{ke}$ between the actual environmental criterion values Y_e and the proximal cue in a perceptor x_k. In the terminology of the lens model, the size of the regression coefficients between the distal cues and the proximal cues determines the ecological validity. In this step, ecological validity is defined by whether a sufficient set of perceptors gets access to the (right) criterion values in an appropriate way. Ecological validity may be low for both internal and external reasons. Fog may distort our estimate of the bear's size (external reason). Faulty vision may also distort the assessment (internal reason).

According to the lens model, a model's validity is limited by the degree to which the object in the environment can be assessed. This is technically expressed by R_e, the correlation between the actual criterion values and the measurements or estimations of the environment.

The lower part of Figure 20.1 shows the empirical scientist's model of this process of information sampling. As expressed by $\hat{Y}$ and displayed by the dashed lines, the scientist may assume that different criteria (cues) are sampled by different perceptors. The term G in Figure 20.1 represents the judgmental process that is modeled by the empirical researcher using regression statistics.

Brunswik had already suggested the regression model. It is still widely embraced in social judgment theory (see Hammond et al., 1975) and arenas of applied decision making, such as medical diagnosis (see Elstein et al., 1978). The use of regression analysis within a Brunswikian lens framework was dubbed *bootstrapping* (Goldberg, 1968, 1971).

Case studies differ from visual perception in some important ways. First, the role of the scientist has somewhat changed. The study team's case model in Figure 20.2 takes the role of the subject's judgment in Figure 20.1. The goal of the case study team in applying research methods is to represent, evaluate, and transform the case. This is depicted in the shaded part of Figure 20.2. Because perceptors and proximal cues are usually not given, they have to be invented by the study team. Then, perceptors must be operationalized, and measurable variables have to be constructed. These variables are often called indicators. If an indicator has the function of measuring features of an object, say, the energy consumption in an urban study on sustainability, it can be interpreted as a distal variable.

This is just the kind of process that is followed in the construction of the impact variables in Formative Scenario Analysis (see Figure 9.2) that serve as perceptors. Interest groups in Area Development Negotiations (see Figure 13.1) and evaluation variables in Multi-Attribute Utility Theory (see Figure 11.2) can also serve as perceptors.

Another question is, "What is the reference for the study team's case model or outcome of method application?" What is the reference or benchmark for a validity assessment? For pragmatic reasons, we assume that there is a kind of best model with respect to the target value and to the constraints of the study.

Step 3: Validity in Cue Utilization and Synthesis

The question here is how the information can be integrated in the joint estimate or perception that forms the terminal focal variable. This has also been denoted as cue utilization, as depicted in the right-hand sections of Figures 20.1 and 20.2. Simple quantitative models, such as weighting, are often assumed. Brunswik suggested this himself. Within this book, we have also presented qualitative procedures for knowledge integration and synthesis. We assume that benchmarking works for cue utilization the same as it does for cue sampling.

To complete the overview of Figure 20.1, we clarify the role of the upper part of the diagram for validation issues. Researchers may try to model a judgmental process, such as a hiker's estimation of the bear's weight, using a linear model. One strategy for getting access to criterion values is to ask the subjects and then use the subjects' estimations of the initial focal variable for modeling (e.g., see Table 13.1, MAUD ONE). This is called bootstrapping in decision research (Goldberg, 1968, 1971). Dawes (1971), for instance, showed that university admissions committees' judgments could be predicted by using just three of the cue variables that were accessible to the board. These cue variables may not even have been used consciously by the board members (this was the idea of the MAUD TWO evaluation in Chapter 13). The admissions board example shows that, in general, researchers who can use environmental cues different from those used by the perceiving subject will end up with a good estimation.

Cue utilization in case studies can be arranged in a couple of ways. Some simple models of Integrated Risk Assessment (see Figure 12.2) or Multi-Attribute Utility Theory (see Figure 11.2) refer to a linear model. We also consider qualitative approaches to synthesis. In Formative Scenario Analysis, for example, the relationship between the perceptors and a representational change was suggested, leading to a qualitative, novelistic case description. In the Area Development Negotiation (see Figure 13.1), the synthesis was accomplished by a mediated, case-related negotiation and bargaining.

Step 4: Functional Validity

Now consider the perceptual task that a case study team faces. The degree of coincidence between the subject's judgment and the actual criterion values defines the judgmental accuracy. This is expressed in Figure 20.1 in terms of regression statistics by the equation $r_a = r_{Y_e Y_s}$. The better the subject's estimate, the higher the functional validity of the subject's performance.

Functional validity refers to the adequacy and the efficiency of the behavior of an organism or a case study team. In our framework, functional validity comprises more than just accuracy. The appropriateness of the initial focal variable is crucial for the functional validity. It matters whether we choose the bear's weight or eye color as the variable for assessing how dangerous our situation is. We have also argued that good functional validity also requires efficiency in cue sampling and cue utilization. Clearly, the arguments for functional validity are essentially the same as in the perceptual paradigm.

LESSONS TO BE LEARNED

▶ The references for the assessment of the validity of a case study are the initial and terminal focal variables.

▶ In general, cue sampling is imperfect, and ecological validity is limited. In the embedded case study methods, cue sampling must be organized by reference to disciplinary knowledge.

▶ Validation of the results of an embedded case study refers to the environmental predictability, ecological validity, cue utilization, and the difference between a best possible model and the subjects or study team's performance or model (see Figure 20.2).

VALIDATION OF EMBEDDED CASE STUDIES: A PRACTICAL VIEW

We will pragmatically suggest a set of six evaluation criteria. On the one hand, these criteria rely on the definitions of validity in different branches of science (see Box 20.1), on the theoretical considerations on validation in qualitative and quantitative research, and on probabilistic functionalism. On the other hand, we will refer to the experience gathered in almost 10 years of running large-scale embedded case studies.

Face Validation and Convergent Validity by the Study Team

The consensus of the study team about the main outcomes of a study is a common request for each qualitative study (see Bortz & Döring, 1995, p. 394). If there is clear dissent about core statements or messages, this may be taken as an indicator for a deficiency in the quality of a study. We call this the study team's content validity or face validity. If the team members' judgments are considered measurements, we can also speak of convergent validity. The study team's face and convergent validity can be assessed by a formal questionnaire with respect to salient issues of the case study.

There are many reasons for a lack of internal validity. In our experience, there are usually insufficiencies in case definition, target formation, or team communication. The latter is important because a case study requires that all team members know about the overall design of the study and how single pieces of information will be used.

Face Validation and Convergent Validity by the Case Members

The question here is how the people from the case judge the case study. The case studies should be highly acknowledged or at least respected by the people who are involved in or concerned by a case study. Validation by case members is also called communicative or dialogue validation (Bortz & Döring, 1995, p. 304).

Note that for any study, there are natural correlations between the knowledge about a study and the personal interests of the case members and the findings or recommendations of the study. Nevertheless, there are (statistical) means to filter the knowledge and interest level, for example, in a questionnaire evaluation on face and convergent validity assessed by the case members.

Face Validation by the Public

The question is how the public media judge the case study. There are different measures for positive feedback. The most objective data (in the sense that the data quality is least affected by the case study teams) are newspaper articles, radio and TV reports, or other public documents such as statements in municipal parliaments.

Note that these data are often biased and affected by political interests. Thus, in a content analysis, the source, intentions, and commitments of the sender of a public comment also have to be taken into account.

Validation Through Benchmarking by the Scientific World From a Disciplinary Point of View

This type of validation is concerned with how highly discipline-specialized scientists judge the case study. This dimension of validation means valuation from scientists who are not members of the study team or the case study community. Before we point out which types of validity are approached by these criteria, we will convey our experience with this type of validation. We have met two different, partly overlapping groups of discipline-oriented scientists with respect to this evaluation criterion.

First, there is the (discipline) scientist who becomes involved in the case study itself. In our experience, these scientists develop a typical attitude. Usually, they enter the study positively but then become confused. This is often due to the questions posed in the course of a study, because even the questions, which refer to specific disciplines, go beyond the scope of the knowledge and theories mastered by these scientists. In a further step, they usually assist in providing state-of-the-art textbook knowledge, which is the target of their involvement. In the end, the majority of them are satisfied with the results, although they have to acknowledge that their standard criterion of "maximal depth of disciplinary analysis" is not a dominant issue in case study work.

Second, there is a group of scientists that undertakes a formal review after the case study is finished. The task of this group is to find fundamental errors or inconsistencies in the written report and to appraise the scientific quality of the statements. Clearly, this evaluation should not be made according to the criteria applied in highly specialized journals, but rather to the standards that are to be fulfilled in popular, but scientifically sound, scientific outlets.

A validation of the results of an embedded case study by discipline-oriented scientists in general is related to the content validity of cue sampling (see Figure 20.2). This type of validation is indispensable for any study but should be done according to the sufficiency principle.

Validation by the Scientific World
From a Transdisciplinary Point of View

The question here is how pioneers in transdisciplinarity judge the case study. In the 1990s (see Gibbons et al., 1994), a discussion in the scientific world was initiated on how traditional disciplinary research and problem-oriented interdisciplinary research at the universities should be supplemented by scientific work that systematically goes beyond the sciences. The challenge for this research is to develop a sound, scientifically accepted methodology and to design strategies that keep the scientist in his or her neutral role and not substitute case action by the scientist's political program.

In recent years, checklists for evaluating the success of transdisciplinary research have been developed. According to these checklists, embedded case studies would be best shaped by joint goal formulation, problem analysis, and team formation and networking (Häberli & Grossenbacher-Mansuy, 1998; Häberli et al., 2001, p. 6; Scholz, 2000, pp. 14-15). These checklists focus on the embeddedness of the study and thus target the provision of "socially robust knowledge" (Gibbons & Nowotny, 2001, p. 67) on societally relevant issues. In this topic, reference is also made to a kind of convergent validity (see Box 20.1).

However, an evaluation from a transdisciplinary perspective should examine, beyond these applied perspectives, the exclusiveness of a problem-centered case study approach. Or, to put it in other terms, the question of whether the problem can be better investigated and promoted by disciplinary approaches should be answered.

Another fundamental question in this context is whether the knowledge integration is mastered in an adequate way. This issue affects many aspects, such as whether the graininess in defining and dealing with a set of variables (see cue sampling in Figure 20.2) is balanced or whether qualitative reasoning is put in the right place and suitably substantiated by quantitative arguments. Clearly, this requires a kind of expert review that again can be considered a type of face validation.

Case Impact Validation: Functional and Consequential Validity

Within this context, the question is whether the case study has positive impacts on the case. A general, applicable design for this type of evaluation is difficult, if not impossible, to find. Because the case has to be considered an open, complex, dynamic system, a retrospective analysis will not allow for a well-defined case impact analysis. For instance, if a new, groundbreaking idea has been developed in a case study discussion, there is no means to verify that this idea would not have been born without the study. Thus, a case impact validation must rely on subjective probability and evidence judgments, and therefore, this type of validation refers to the discussion on functional validity and consequential validity (see Box 20.1) as it has been presented in this concluding chapter.

REFERENCES

ABB. (1996). *Greater Zurich area: A central European business location*. Zürich: ABB Immobilien.

Abbott, A. (1992). What do cases do? Some notes on activity in sociological analysis. In C. C. Ragin & H. S. Becker (Eds.), *What is a case? Exploring the foundations of social inquiry* (pp. 53-82). Cambridge, UK: Cambridge University Press.

Abelson, D. E. (1996). *American think-tanks and their role in US foreign policy*. Basingstoke, UK: Macmillan.

Ahbe, S., Braunschweig, A., & Müller-Wenk, R. (1990). *Methodik für Ökobilanzen auf der Basis ökologischer Optimierung [A methodology for life cycle assessments on the basis of ecological optimization]* (Vol. Schriftenreihe Umwelt Nr. 133 [Series on Environment No. 133]). Bern: Bundesamt für Umwelt, Wald und Landschaft [Swiss Agency for the Environment, Forests and Landscape].

Aldenderfer, M. S., & Blashfield, R. K. (1984). *Cluster analysis*. Newbury Park, CA: Sage.

Alexander, C., Ishikawa, S., & Silverstein, M. (1995). *Eine Muster-Sprache: Städte—Gebäude—Konstruktion [A pattern-language: Towns—Buildings—Construction]*. Wien: Löcker.

American Psychological Association. (1954). *Technical recommendations for psychological tests and diagnostic techniques*. Washington, DC: Author.

Aronson, E., Ellsworth, P. C., Carlsmith, J. M., & Gonzoles, M. (1990). *Methods of research in social psychology* (2nd ed.). New York: McGraw-Hill.

Asch, S. E. (1956). Studies of independence and conformity: A minority of one against an unanimous majority. *Psychological Monographs, 70*(9), 177-190.

Ashby, W. R. (1964). *Introduction to cybernetics*. London: Chapman & Hall.

Axelrod, R. M. (1984). *The evolution of cooperation*. New York: Basic Books.

Ayres, R. U., Norberg-Bohm, V., Prince, J., Stigliani, W. M., & Yanowitz, J. (1989). *Industrial metabolism, the environment, and application of materials-balance: Principles for selected chemicals* (Vol. RR-89-011). Laxenburg: International Institute for Applied Systems Analysis.

Azapagic, A. (1996). *Environmental system analysis: The application of linear programming to life cycle assessment* (Vol. 1). Surrey, UK: University of Surrey, Centre of Environmental Strategy.

Baccini, P., & Bader, H. P. (1996). *Regionaler Stoffhaushalt. Erfassung, Bewertung und Steuerung [Regional Material Budget. Registration, evaluation and control]*. Heidelberg: Spektrum Akademischer Verlag.

Baccini, P., & Brunner, P. H. (1991). *Metabolism of the anthroposphere*. Berlin: Springer.

Baccini, P., & Oswald, F. (Eds.). (1998). *Netzstadt—Transdisziplinäre Methoden zum Umbau urbaner Systeme [Web City—Transdisciplinary methods for reconstructing urban systems]*. Zürich: vdf Hochschulverlag.

Bacow, L. S., & Wheeler, M. (1987). *Environmental dispute resolution*. New York: Plenum.

Baeriswyl, M., Nufer, A., Scholz, R. W., & Ewald, K. C. (1999). Intuition in der Landschaftsplanung: Anregungen zu einer ganzheitlichen Betrachtung mittels der Landschaftsidentität [Intuition in landscape planning: Suggestions for a holistic approach on the basis of landscape identity]. *Naturschutz und Landschaftsplanung [Nature protection and landscape planning]*, 2, 42-47.

Bales, R. F. (1950). *Interaction process analysis: A method for the study of small groups*. Cambridge, MA: Addison-Wesley.

Ballauf, T. (1971). Biologie [Biology]. In J. Ritter (Ed.), *Historisches Wörterbuch der Philosophie [Historic dictionary of philosophy]* (Vol. 1, pp. 944). Basel, Switzerland: Schwabe.

Barnes, L. B., Christensen, C. R., & Hansen, A. J. (1994). *Teaching and the case method*. Boston: Harvard Business School Press.

Barnthouse, L., Fava, J., Humphreys, K., Hunt, R., Laibson, L., Noesen, S., Norris, G., Owens, J., Todd, J., Vigon, B., Weitz, K., & Young, J. (1997). *Life cycle impact assessment: The state-of-the-art* (Report of the SETAC Life-Cycle Assessment (LCA) Impact Assessment Workgroup, SETAC LCA Advisory Group). Pensacola, FL: Society of Environmental Toxicology and Chemistry.

Baron, J. (1994). *Thinking and deciding* (2nd ed.). Cambridge, UK: Cambridge University Press.

Batelle-Institute. (1976). *Szenarien Chemische Fabrik [Scenarios chemical factory]*. Frankfurt: German Chemistry of Research and Technology.

Baumgartner, B., Kurath, M., Ranke, J., & Stauffacher, M. (1997). Stadtentwicklung. In R. W. Scholz, S. Bösch, H. A. Mieg, & J. Stünzi (Eds.), *Zentrum Zürich Nord—Stadt im Aufbruch. Bausteine für eine nachhaltige Stadtentwicklung. UNS-Fallstudie 1996 [City Center Zurich North—A city on the move. Building blocks for a sustainable urban development. ETH-UNS Case Study 1996]* (pp. 99-138). Zürich: vdf Hochschulverlag.

Bazerman, M. H. (1998). *Judgment in managerial decision making* (4th ed.). New York: John Wiley.

Bazerman, M. H., & Neale, M. A. (1993). *Negotiating rationally*. New York: Free Press.

Becker, H. S. (1992). Cases, causes, conjunctures, stories, and imagery. In C. C. Ragin & H. S. Becker (Eds.), *What is a case? Exploring the foundations of social inquiry* (pp. 205-216). Cambridge, UK: Cambridge University Press.

Begon, M., Townsend, C. R., & Harper, J. L. (1990). *Ecology individuals, populations and communities* (2nd ed.). Boston: Basil Blackwell.

Beins-Franke, A., & Heeb, J. (1995). *Begrünte Dächer [Green roofs]* (Vol. Schriftenreihe Umwelt Nr. 216 [Series on Environment No. 216]). Bern: Bundesamt für Umwelt, Wald und Landschaft [Swiss Agency for the Environment, Forests, and Landscape].

Berkowitz, L. (1962). *Aggression: A social psychological analysis*. New York: McGraw-Hill.

Berkowitz, L. (Ed.). (1975). *Advances in experimental social psychology* (Vol. 8). New York: Academic Press.

Bernhart, S. A. (1976). *Introduction to interpersonal communication*. New York: Cromwell.

Bhatnagar, R., & Kanal, L. N. (1992). Models of enquiry and formalisms for approximate reasoning. In L. A. Zadeh & J. Kacprzyk (Eds.), *Fuzzy logic for the management of uncertainty* (pp. 29-54). New York: Wiley.

Bignasca, F., Kruck, R., Maggi, R., Schellenbauer, P., & Schips, B. (1996). *Immobilienmarkt Zürich [The Zurich real estate market]*. Zürich: Zürcher Kantonalbank.

Bingham, G. (1986). *Resolving environmental disputes—A decade of experience*. Washington, DC: The Conservation Foundation.

Blair, G. M. (1993). *Starting to manage: The essential skill*. Bromley, UK: Chartwell-Bratt.

Blum, M., & Hofer, A. (1993). *KraftWerk 1—Projekt für das Sulzer-Escher Wyss-Areal [PowerStation 1—Project for the Sulzer-Escher Wyss area]*. Zürich: KraftWerk 1.

Blumberg, H. H., Hare, A. P., Kent, V., & Davies, M. F. (Eds.). (1983). *Small groups and social interaction* (Vol. 2). Chichester, UK: Wiley.

Boden, M. A. (1990). *The creative mind: Myths and mechanisms*. London: Weidenfeld and Nicholson.

Boos, M. (1992). *A typology of case studies*. München and Mering: Rainer Hampp Verlag.

Bortz, J., & Döring, N. (1995). *Forschungsmethoden und Evaluation [Research methods and evaluation]*. Heidelberg: Springer.

Bossel, H. (1994). *Modeling and simulation*. Wellesley, MA: Peters.

Boustead, I., & Hancock, G. F. (1979). *Handbook of industrial energy analysis*. Chichester, UK: Ellis Horwood.

Brachinger, H. W., & Weber, M. (1997). Risk as a primitive: A survey of measures of perceived risk. *Operations Research-Spectrum, 19*(4), 235-294.

Brauers, J., & Weber, M. (1988). A new method of scenario analysis for strategic planning. *Journal of Forecasting, 7,* 31-47.

Breidenbach, S. (1995). *Mediation: Struktur, Chancen und Risiken von Vermittlung im Konflikt [Mediation: Structure, potentialities and risks of mediation in conflicts]*. Köln: Schmidt.

Bretschger, L., Halbherr, P., Kilias, A., Koellventer, C., Meili, B., & Peter, R. (1995). *Wirschaftsstandort Zürich [Zurich: A place for business]*. Zürich: Regierungsrat des Kantons Zürich.

Bretz, R. (1998). SPOLD. *International Journal of Life Cycle Assessment, 3*(3), 119.

Breuer, R. (1990). Verhandlungslösungen aus der Sicht des deutschen Umweltschutzrechts [Negotiated solutions from the perspective of the German environmental protection law]. In W. Hoffmann-Riem & E. Schmidt-Assmann (Eds.), *Konfliktbewältigung durch Verhandlung [Conflict resolution through negotiation]* (Vol. 1, pp. 231-252). Baden-Baden: Nomos.

Bringezu, S. (2000). *Ressourcennutzung in Wirtschaftsräumen: Stoffstromanalysen für eine nachhaltige Raumentwicklung [Resource use in economic regions: Substance flow analysis for sustainable regional development]*. Berlin: Springer.

Bringezu, S., Fischer-Kowalski, M., Kleijn, R., & Viveka, P. (1997). *Regional and national material flow accounting: From paradigm to practice of sustainability (Proceedings of the ConAccount workshop, 21-23 January, 1997 in Leiden, The Netherlands)*. Wuppertal, Germany: Wuppertal Institute for Climate, Environment and Energy.

Brown, D. (1993). *Models in biology: Mathematics, statistics and computing*. Chichester, UK: Wiley.

Bruner, J. S., Goodnow, J. J., & Austin, G. A. (1956). *A study of thinking*. New York: Wiley.

Brunswik, E. (1934). *Wahrnehmung und Gegenstandswelt: Grundlegung einer Psychologie vom Gegenstand her [Perception and the world of objects: Fundamentals of object-driven psychology]*. Leipzig: Deuticke.

Brunswik, E. (1935). *Experimentelle Psychologie [Experimental psychology]*. Wien: Springer.

Brunswik, E. (1943). Organismic achievement and environmental probability. *Psychological Review, 50*(3), 255-272.

Brunswik, E. (1950). *The conceptual framework of psychology*. Chicago: University of Chicago Press.

Brunswik, E. (1956). *Perception and the representative design of psychological experiments*. Berkeley: University of California Press.

Brunswik, E. (1955). Representative design and probabilistic theory in a functional psychology. *Psychological Review, 62*, 193-217.

Buff-Keller, E., Gilgen, H., & Pfister, P. (1989). Geographische Fallstudie [Geographical case study]. *Geographica Helvetica, 1*, 29-37.

Bundesamt für Umwelt, Wald und Landschaft [Swiss Agency for Environmental Protection]. (Ed.). (1984). *Ökobilanzen von Packstoffen [Life cycle assessment of packaging material]* (Schriftenreihe Umwelt [Series on the Environment] Vol. 24). Bern: Author.

Bundesamt für Umwelt, Wald und Landschaft. (Ed.). (1998). *Ökobilanzen. Bewertung in Ökobilanzen mit der Methode der ökologischen Knappheit. Ökofactoren 1997 [Life cycle assessments. Impact assessment with the eco-logical scarcity method. Eco-factors 1997]* (Schriftenreihe Umwelt [Series on the Environment] Vol. 297). Bern: Author.

Campbell, E. T., & Stanley, J. C. (1963). *Experimental and quasi-experimental designs for research.* Boston: Houghton Mifflin.

Churchman, C. W. (1971). *The design of inquiring systems: Basic concepts of system and organization.* New York: Basic Books.

City of Zurich. (1995). *Privater Gestaltungsplan Escher Wyss-Gebiet [Private formation plan: Escher Wyss area].* Zurich: Author.

Claus, I., & Wiedemann, P. M. (Eds.). (1994). *Umweltkonflikte— Vermittlungsverfahren zu ihrer Lösung [Environmental conflicts: Mediation procedures for their resolution].* Taunusstein: Blottner.

Cohen, L. J. (1977). *The probable and the provable.* Oxford, UK: Clarendon.

Cohen, R. (1995). *Students resolving conflict: Peer mediation in schools.* Glenview, IL: Goodyear.

Cooke, R. M. (1991). *Experts in uncertainty.* New York: Oxford University Press.

Cottrell, L. S., & Dymond, R. F. (1949). The empathic responses: A neglected field of our research. *Psychiatry, 12,* 355-359.

Covello, V. T., & Merkhofer, M. W. (1993). *Risk assessment methods: Approaches for assessing health and environmental risks.* New York: Plenum.

Crawford, R. P. (1954). *The technique of creative thinking.* New York: Hawthorne.

Cronbach, L. J., & Meehl, P. E. (1955). Construct validity in psychological tests. *Psychological Bulletin, 52,* 281-302.

Crott, H. W., Gretzer, T., Hansmann, R., Mieg, H. A., & Scholz, R. W. (1999). Prozessanalyse von Gruppenentscheidungen zu Aspekten ökologischer Stadtplanung [Process analysis of group decisions with respect to certain aspects of ecological urban planning]. *Zeitschrift für Sozialpsychologie [Journal of Social Psychology], 30,* 77-91.

Crott, H. W., Scholz, R. W., Ksiensik, M. I., & Popp, M. (1983). *Koalitionsentscheidungen und Aufteilungsverhalten in Drei-Personen-Spielen: theoretische und experimentelle Untersuchung zu Konflikt, Macht und Anspruchsniveau [Decisions to form coalitions and to distribute pay-offs in three-person-games: Theoretical and empirical investigation of conflict, power and aspirational level]* (Vol. 1). Frankfurt am Main: Lang.

Darwin, C. (1859). *On the origin of species by means of natural selection, or the preservation of favoured races in the struggle for life.* London: Murray.

Dauscher, U. (1998). *Moderationsmethode und Zukunftswerkstatt [Method of mediation and future workshops]* (2nd ed.). Neuwied: Luchterhand.

Dawes, R. M. (1971). A case study of graduate admissions: Application of three principles of human decision making. *American Psychologist, 26,* 180-188.

Dean, B. V. (Ed.). (1985). *Project management: Methods and studies.* Amsterdam: Elsevier.

Decker, F. (1988). *Gruppen moderieren—eine Hexerei? Die neue Teamarbeit: Ein Leitfaden für Moderatoren zur Entwicklung und Förderung von Kleingruppen [Moderating groups—a sorcery? The new teamwork: A manual for moderators developing and supporting small groups].* München: Lexika.

de Finetti, B. (1974). *Theory of probability* (Vol. 1). London: Wiley.

de Groot, R. S. (1992). *Functions of nature: Evaluation of nature in environmental planning, management and decision making.* Amsterdam: Wolters-Noordhoff.

Denzin, N. (1989). *Interpretive biography.* Newbury Park, CA: Sage.

Denzin, N., & Lincoln, Y. (1994). *Handbook of qualitative research.* Thousand Oaks, CA: Sage.

DeTombe, D. J. (1999). Moments of support by a groupware brainstorming tool in handling complex technical policy problems. *European journal of operational research, 119,* 267-281.

Deutsch, G., & Springer, S. P. (1993). *Left brain, right brain* (4th ed.). New York: Freeman.

Deutsch, M. (1949). A theory of cooperation and competition. *Human Relations, 2,* 129-152.

Deutsch, M. (1973). *The resolution of conflict.* New Haven, CT: Yale University Press.

Devaney, R. L. (1989). *An introduction to chaotic dynamical systems.* Redwood City, CA: Addison-Wesley.

Dewey, J. (1966). *Democracy and education.* New York: The Free Press.

Dick, W., & Hagerty, N. (1971). *Topics in measurement: Reliability and validity.* New York: McGraw-Hill.

Dieudonné, J. (1985). *Geschichte der Mathematik 1700-1900 [History of mathematics, 1700-1900].* Braunschweig: Vieweg.

Dinkel, F., & Ros, M. (1996). The software tool EMIS. In S. Schaltegger (Ed.), *Life Cycle Assessment (LCA)—Quo vadis?* (pp. 81-91). Berlin: Birkhäuser.

Dörner, D., Kreuzig, H. W., Reither, F., & Stäudel, T. (1994). *Lohhausen-Vom Umgang mit Unbestimmtheit und Komplexität.* Bern: Huber.

Easley, J. (1983). The need for a cognitive ethnography of mathematics teaching. In M. Zweng, T. Green, J. Kilpatrick, H. Pollak, & M. Suydam (Eds.), *Fourth International Congress on Mathematical Education, Proceedings* (pp. 463-465). Boston: Birkhäuser.

Elstein, A. S., Shulman, L. S., & Sprafka, S. A. (1978). *Medical problem solving.* Cambridge, MA: Harvard University Press.

Enquete Commission of the German Bundestag "Protection of Man and Environment." (1994). *Die Industriegesellschaft gestalten. Perspektiven für einen nachhaltigen Umgang mit Stoff- und Materialströmen [Design of the industrial society. Perspectives for a sustainable treatment of substance and material fluxes].* Bonn: Economica.

Erlwanger, S. (1975). Case studies of children's conceptions of mathematics. *Journal of Children's Mathematical Behavior, 1,* 157-281.

Fekken, G. C. (2000). Reliability. In E. Kazdin (Ed.), *Encyclopedia of psychology* (Vol. 8, pp. 30-34). Oxford, UK: Oxford University Press.

Fine, T. L. (1973). *Theories of probability.* New York: Academic Press.

Finnveden, G., & Lindfors, L.-G. (1996). Life-cycle impact assessment and interpretation. In H. A. Udo de Haes & N. Wrisberg (Eds.), *Life cycle assessment: State-of-the-art and research priorities* (pp. 89-117). Bayreuth: Eco-Informa Press.

Fischhoff, B. (1987). Foreword. In S. R. Watson & D. M. Buede (Eds.), *Decision synthesis: The principles and practice of decision analysis.* Cambridge, UK: Cambridge University Press.

Fischhoff, B. (1996). The real world: What good is it? *Organizational Behavior and Human Decision Processes, 65*(3), 232-248.

Fischhoff, B., Bostrom, A., & Quadrel, M. J. (1993). Risk perception and communication. *Annual Review of Public Health, 14,* 183-203.

Fischhoff, B., Slovic, P., & Lichtenstein, S. (1981). Lay foibles and expert fables in judgments about risks. *Progress in Resource Management and Environmental Planning, 3,* 161-202.

Fischlin, A. (1991). Interactive modeling and simulation of environmental systems on workstations. In D. P. F. Moeller (Ed.), *Analysis of dynamic systems in medicine, biology, and ecology* (Vol. 275, pp. 131-145).

Fishbein, E. (1975). *The intuitive sources of probabilistic thinking in children.* Dordrecht: Reidel.

Fishburn, P. C. (1970). *Utility theory for decision making.* New York: Wiley.

Fishburn, P. C. (1982). *The foundations of expected utility.* Dordrecht: Reidel.

Fishburn, P. C. (1984). SSB utility theory: An economic perspective. *Mathematical and Social Science, 9,* 63-94.

Fishburn, P. C. (1988). *Nonlinear preference and utility theory.* Baltimore: Johns Hopkins University Press.

Fisher, R. (1981). *International mediation: A practitioner's guide.* New York: International Peace Academy.

Fisher, R., & Brown, S. (1988). *Getting together: Building a relationship that gets to yes.* Boston: Houghton Mifflin.

Fisher, R., & Ury, W. (1981). *Getting to yes: Negotiating agreement without giving in.* Boston: Houghton Mifflin.

Flavell, J. H., Botkin, P. T., Fry, C. L., Wright, J. W., & Jarvis, P. E. (1968). *The development of role-taking and communication skills in children.* New York: Wiley.

Forman, R. T. T. (1995). *Land mosaics: The ecology of landscapes and regions.* Cambridge, UK: Cambridge University Press.

Forrester, J. (1961). *Industrial dynamics.* Cambridge: MIT Press; and New York: Wiley.

Forrester, J. (1971). *World dynamics.* Cambridge, MA: Wright Allen.

Frazer, C. E. (1931). *The case method of instruction.* New York: McGraw-Hill.

Freimuth, J., & Straub, F. (Eds.). (1996). *Demokratisierung von Organisationen: Philosophie, Urspruenge und Perspektiven der Metaplan-Idee: fuer Eberhard Schnelle [Democratization of organizations: Philosophy, origins and perspectives of the Metaplan-idea].* Wiesbaden: Gabler.

Frischknecht, P. (1998). *Wegleitung des Studiengangs Umweltnaturwissenschaften [Guide to the curriculum in environmental sciences].* Zürich: ETH Zürich.

Frischknecht, R. (1998). *Life cycle inventory analysis for decision-making.* (PhD Thesis, ETH Zurich). Uster, Switzerland: ESU-Services.

Frischknecht, R., Hofstetter, P., Knoepfel, I., Dones, R., & Zollinger, E. (1995). *Ökoinventare für Energiesysteme [Life cycle inventories for energy systems]* (2nd ed.). Bern: Bundesamt für Energiewirtschaft [Swiss Federal Office for Energy Economy], ENET.

Frischknecht, R., & Kolm, P. (1995). Modellansatz und Algorithmus zur Berechnung von Ökobilanzen im Rahmen der Datenbank ECOINVENT [Modeling approach and algorithm for the calculation of life cycle assessments within the database ECOINVENT]. In M. Schmidt & A. Schorb (Eds.), *Stoffstromanalysen in Ökobilanzen und Ökoaudits [Material flow analyses in life cycle assessments and eco-audits].* Berlin: Springer.

Fromm, M. (1995). *Repertory Grid Methodik [Repertory grid method].* Weinheim: Deutscher Studien Verlag.

Fuller, G. (1991). *The negotiator's handbook.* Englewood Cliffs, NJ: Prentice Hall.

Funke, J. (1999). Komplexes Problemlösen: Ein Blick zurück und nach vorne [Complex problem solving—A look back and ahead]. *Psychologische Rundschau, 50,* 194-197.

Garnham, A., & Oakhill, J. (1994). *Thinking and reasoning.* Oxford, UK: Basil Blackwell.

Gassner, H., Lahl, U., & Holznagel, B. (1992). *Mediation—Verhandlungen als Mittel der Konsensfindung bei Umweltstreitigkeiten [Mediation—Negotiations as a means for creating consensus in environmental conflict situations].* Bonn: Economica.

Gay, P., Proops, J., & Speck, S. (1999). Optimal policy for materials flows: An integrated modelling approach. In R. Kleijn, S. Bringezu, M. Fischer-Kowalski, & V. Palm (Eds.), *Ecologizing societal metabolism: Designing scenarios for sustainable materials management. Proceedings of the ConAccount workshop, November 21st 1998 in Amsterdam, The Netherlands* (pp. 154-159). Leiden: Centre of Environmental Science (CML).

Gethmann, C. F. (1980). Methode, analytische/synthetische [Method, analytic/synthetic]. In J. Ritter & K. Gründer (Eds.), *Historisches Wörterbuch der Philosophie [Historical encyclopedia of philosophy]* (pp. 1331-1336). Basel: Schwabe.

Gibbons, M., Limoges, C., Nowotny, H., Schwartzmann, S., Scott, P., & Trow, M. (1994). *The new production of knowledge.* London: Sage.

Gibbons, M., & Nowotny, H. (2001). The potential of transdisciplinarity. In J. T. Klein, W. Grossenbacher-Mansuy, R. Häberli, A. Bill, R. W. Scholz, & M. Welti (Eds.), *Transdisciplinarity: Joint problem solving among science, technology, and society. An effective way for managing complexity* (pp. 67-80). Basel: Birkhäuser.

Gigerenzer, G. (1987). Survival of the fittest probabilist: Brunswik, Thurstone, and the two disciplines of psychology. In L. Krüger, G. Gigerenzer, & M. S. Morgan (Eds.), *The probabilistic revolution* (Vol. 2, pp. 49-72). Cambridge: MIT Press.

Gigerenzer, G., & Goldstein, D. G. (1996). Reasoning the fast and frugal way: Models of bounded rationality. *Psychological Review, 103*(4), 650-669.

Gigerenzer, G., & Murray, D. J. (1987). *Cognition as intuitive statistics.* Hillsdale, NJ: Lawrence Erlbaum.

Gödel, K. (1931). Über formal unterscheidbare Sätze der Principia Mathematica und verwandter Systeme I [About formal distinguishable theorems of the Principia Mathematica and related systems I]. *Monatshefte für Mathematik und Physik [Monthly Volumes on Mathematics and Physics], 38,* 173-198.

Godet, M. (1986). Introduction to "la prospective." Seven key ideas and one scenario method. *Futures, 18,* 134-157.

Godet, M. (1987). *Scenarios and strategic management.* London: Butterworth.

Goedkoop, M. (1995). *The Eco-Indicator 95. Final report* (9523). Utrecht and Bilthoven: Novem [Netherland's Agency for Energy and the Environment] and RIVM [National Institute of Public Health and Environmental Protection].

Goedkoop, M. (1998). The Eco-Indicator 98 explained. *International Journal of Life Cycle Assessment, 3*(6), 352-360.

Goffmann, E. (1959). *The presentation of self in everyday life.* Garden City, NY: Doubleday Anchor.

Goldberg, L. R. (1968). Simple models or simple processes? Some research on clinical judgments. *American Psychologist, 23,* 483-486.

Goldberg, L. R. (1971). Five models of clinical judgment: An empirical comparison between linear representations of the human inference process. *Organisation, Behavior and Human Performance, 6,* 458-479.

Götze, U. (1993). *Szenario-Technik in der stategischen Unternehmungsplanung [The Scenario Technique in strategic business planning]* (2nd ed.). Wiesbaden: Deutscher Universitäts-Verlag.

Greenbaum, T. L. (1998). *The handbook for focus group research* (2nd ed.). Thousand Oaks, CA: Sage.

Grissemann, H., & Weber, H. (1982). *Spezielle Rechenstörungen—Ursache und Therapie [Special types of dyscalculia—Causes and therapy].* Bern: Huber.

Guilford, J. P. (1967). *The nature of human intelligence.* New York: McGraw-Hill.

Haase, G. (1978). Zur Ableitung und Kennzeichnung von Naturpotentialen [To the derivation and indication of natural potentials]. *Petermanns Geographische Mitteilungen [Petermann's Geographical Reports], 122*(2), 113-125.

Häberli, R., Bill, A., Grossenbacher-Mansuy, W., Thompson Klein, J., Scholz, R. W., & Welti, M. (2001). Synthesis. In J. Thompson Klein, W. Grossenbacher-Mansuy, R. Häberli, A. Bill, R. W. Scholz, & M. Welti (Eds.), *Transdisciplinarity: Joint problem solving among science, technology, and society: An effective way for managing complexity* (pp. 6-22). Basel: Birkhäuser.

Häberli, R., & Grossenbacher-Mansuy, W. (1998). Transdisziplinarität zwischen Förderung und Überforderung. Erkenntnisse aus dem SPP Umwelt. [Transdisciplinarity between granting and overdemanding. Insights from the SPP environment]. *GAIA, 7,* 196-213.

Hacking, I. (1975). *The emergence of probability.* Cambridge, UK: Cambridge University Press.

Hackman, J. R., & Morris, C. G. (1975). Group tasks, group interaction process and group performance effectiveness: A review and proposed integration. In L. Berkowitz (Ed.), *Advances in experimental social psychology* (Vol. 8, pp. 45-99). New York: Academic Press.

Hadamard, J. (1945). *The psychology of invention in the mathematical field.* Princeton, NJ: Princeton University Press.

Haeckel, E. (1988). *Allgemeine Entwickelungsgeschichte der Organismen. Kritische Grundzüge der mechanischen Wissenschaft von den entstehenden Formen der Organismen begründet durch die Descendenz-Theorie [General theory of organismic development: Critical outline of the mechanical science of the developing forms of organisms based on the theory of descendence].* Photomechanischer Nachdruck. Berlin: de Gruyter. (Original work published 1866)

Hamel, J., Dufour, S., & Fortin, D. (1993). *Case study methods* (Vol. 32). London: Sage.

Hammond, K. R. (1990). Functionalism and illusionism: Can integration be usefully achieved? In R. M. Hogarth (Ed.), *Insights in decision making* (pp. 227-261). Chicago: University of Chicago Press.

Hammond, K., Hamm, R. M., Grassia, J., & Pearson, T. (1983). *Direct comparison of intuitive, quasi-rational, and analytical cognition.* Boulder: University of Colorado, Institute of Cognitive Science, Center for Research on Judgment and Policy.

Hammond, K. R., Steward, T. R., Brehmer, B., & Steinmann, D. O. (1975). Social judgment theory. In M. F. Kaplan & S. Schwartz (Eds.), *Human judgment and decision processes* (pp. 271-312). New York: Academic Press.

Hannon, B., & Ruth, M. (1994). *Dynamic modeling.* New York: Springer.

Hare, A. P. (1996). *Handbook of small group research* (2nd ed.). New York: Free Press.

Harrison, R. P. (1974). *Beyond words: An introduction to nonverbal communication.* Englewood Cliffs, NJ: Prentice Hall.

Hartung, J., Elpelt, B., & Klösener, K.-H. (1993). *Statistik. Lehr- und Handbuch der angewandten Statistik [Statistics. Textbook and manual for applied statistics].* München: Oldenbourg.

Hastie, R., & Park, B. (1986). The relationship between memory and judgment depends on whether the judgment is memory-based or on-line. *Psychological Review, 93,* 258-268.

Hauser, L. (2000, June). *Seitenwechsel [Changing sides].* Zurich: ProjekTATelier Lucie Hauser. Available: www.seitenwechsel.ch

Hawksworth, D. L. (1995). *Biodiversity measurement and estimation.* London: Chapman & Hall.

Hays, W. L. (1963). *Statistics.* London: Holt, Rinehart & Winston.

Hector, A., Schmid, B., Beierkuhnlein, C., Caldeira, M. C., Diemer, M., Dimitrakopoulos, P. G., Finn, J. A., Freitas, H., Giller, P. S., & Good, J. (1999). Plant diversity and productivity experiments in European grasslands. *Science, 286*(5), 1123-1127.

Heider, F. (1958). *The psychology of interpersonal relationships.* New York: Wiley.

Heijungs, R. (1992). *Environmental life cycle assessment of products: Backgrounds and guide* (Vol. 9266 resp. 9267). Leiden: Centre of Environmental Science.

Heijungs, R. (1994). A generic method for the identification of options for cleaner products. *Ecological Economics, 10,* 69-81.

Heijungs, R., & Hofstetter, P. (1996). Definitions of terms and symbols. In H. A. Udo de Haes (Ed.), *Towards a methodology for life cycle impact assessment* (pp. 31-37). Brussels: Society of Environmental Toxicology and Chemistry—Europe.

Heijungs, R., & Wegener Sleeswijk, A. (1999). The structure of impact assessment: Mutually independent dimensions as a function of modifiers. *International Journal of Life Cycle Assessment, 4*(1), 2-3.

Helmer, O. (1977). Problems in futures research, Delphi and causal cross-impact analysis. *Futures, 9,* 17-31.

Henseler, G., Bader, H.-P., Oehler, D., Scheidegger, R., & Baccini, P. (1995). *Methode und Anwendung der betrieblichen Stoffbuchhaltung. Ein Beitrag zur Methodenentwicklung in der ökologischen Beurteilung von Unternehmen [Method and application of substance bookkeeping in firms. A contribution to the development of methods for the ecological assessment of enterprises].* Zürich: vdf Hochschulverlag.

Henz, A. (1995). *Arbeiten, Wohnen Zusammenleben auf dem Escher Wyss-Areal, Zürich [Working, living and living together on the Escher-Wyss area in Zurich].* Zürich: ETH Zurich, Department of Architecture, Chair of Professor Henz.

Hochbaudepartement der Stadt Zürich [Zurich City Department of Building Construction]. (1996). *Ziele der Stadtentwicklung [Goals of urban development].* Zürich: Author.

Hoffmann-Riem, W., & Schmidt-Assmann, E. (1990a). *Konfliktbewältigung durch Verhandlungen—Informelle und mittlerunterstützte Verhandlungen in Verwaltungsverfahren [Resolving conflicts through negotiations—Informal and mediator-supported negotiations in administrative procedures]* (Vol. 1). Baden-Baden: Nomos.

Hoffmann-Riem, W., & Schmidt-Assmann, E. (1990b). *Konfliktbewältigung durch Verhandlungen—Konfliktmittlung in Verwaltungsverfahren [Resolving conflicts through negotiations—Conflict mediation in administrative procedures]* (Vol. 2). Baden-Baden: Nomos.

Hofstetter, P. (1998). *Perspectives in life cycle impact assessment: A structured approach to combine models of the technosphere, ecosphere, and valuesphere.* Dordrecht: Kluwer.

Hogan, R. (1969). Development of an empathy scale. *Journal of Consulting and Clinical Psychology, 33,* 307-316.

Holling, C. S. (1973). Resilience and stability in ecological systems. *Annual Review of Ecology and Systematics, 4,* 1-23.

Holling, C. S. (1987). Simplifying the complex: The paradigms of ecological function and structure. *European Journal of Operational Research, 30,* 139-146.

Hopcraft, J. E., & Ullman, J. D. (1979). *Introduction to automata theory, languages, and computation.* Reading, MA: Addison-Wesley.

Houston, W. R., & Howsam, R. B. (1974). CBTE: The ayes of Texas. *Phi Delta Kappa, 55*(5), 299-303.

Humphreys, P. C., & Wisudha, A. D. (1989). *Handling decision problems: A structuring language and interactive modules. Final report 1 Sep 87–3 Oct 89.* London: London School of Economics and Political Science.

Hussy, W. (1984). *Denkpsychologie [Psychology of thinking]* (Vol. 1). Stuttgart: Urban.

Ingham, J., Dunn, I. J., Heinzle, E., & Prenosil, J. E. (Eds.). (1994). *Chemical engineering dynamics: Modelling with PC simulation* (2nd ed.). Weinheim: VCH.

International Organization for Standardization. (1997). *ISO/DIS 14040: Environmental management—Life cycle assessment—Principles and framework.* Geneva: Author.

International Organization for Standardization. (1998a). *ISO/DIS 14041: Environmental management—Life cycle assessment—Goal and scope definition, life cycle inventory analysis.* Geneva: Author.

International Organization for Standardization. (1998b). *ISO/DIS 14042: Environmental management—Life cycle assessment—Life cycle impact assessment.* Geneva: Author.

International Organization for Standardization. (1998c). *ISO/DIS 14043: Environmental management—Life cycle assessment—Life cycle interpretation.* Geneva: Author.

Janis, I. L. (1982). *Groupthink: Psychological studies of policy decisions and fiascos* (2nd ed.). Boston: Houghton Mifflin.

Jantsch, E. (1980). *The self-organizing universe: Scientific and human implications of the emerging paradigm of evolution.* Oxford, UK: Pergamon.

Jarvik, M. E. (1951). Probability learning and a negative recency effect in the serial anticipation of alternative symbols. *Journal of Experimental Psychology, 4,* 291-297.

Johnson-Laird, P. N. (1983). *Mental models.* Cambridge, UK: Cambridge University Press.

Johnson-Laird, P. N., & Byrne, R. (1993). Author's response: Mental models or formal rules. *Behavioral and Brain Sciences, 16,* 368-376.

Jungermann, H. (1997). Reasons for uncertainty: From frequencies to stories. *Psychologische Beiträge, 39,* 126-139.

Jungermann, H., Rohrmann, B., & Wiedemann, P. M. (1991). *Risikokontroversen: Konzepte, Konflikte, Kommunikation [Risk controversies: Concepts, conflicts, communication]* (2nd ed.). Berlin: Springer.

Jungermann, H., & Slovic, P. (1993). Charakteristika individueller Risikowahrnehmung [Characteristics of individual risk perception]. In Bayerische Rück (Ed.), *Risiko ist ein Konstrukt [Risk is a construct]* (pp. 89-107). M<@252>nchen: Knesbeck.

Jungk, R. (1973). *Der Jahrtausendmensch: Bericht aus den Werkstätten der neuen Gesellschaft [Millennium person. Report from the workshops of a new society].* München: Bertelsmann.

Jungk, R., & Müllert, N. R. (1994). *Zukunftswerkstätten: mit Phantasie gegen Routine und Resignation [Futures workshops: With fantasy against routine and resignation].* München: Heyne.

Kahn, H., & Wiener, A. J. (1967). *The year 2000.* London: Macmillan.

Kahneman, D., Slovic, P., & Tversky, A. (Eds.). (1982). *Judgement under uncertainty: Heuristics and biases.* Cambridge, UK: Cambridge University Press.

Kahneman, D., & Tversky, A. (1979). Prospect theory: An analysis of decision under risk. *Econometrica, 47,* 263-291.

Kahneman, D., & Tversky, A. (1981). The framing of decisions and the psychology of choice. *Science, 211,* 453-458.

Kahneman, D., & Tversky, A. (1992). Advances in prospect theory: Cumulative representation of uncertainty. *Journal of Risk and Uncertainty, 5,* 297-323.

Kaplan, H. I., & Sadock, B. J. (1971). *Comprehensive group psychotherapy.* Baltimore: Williams & Wilkins.

Keeney, R. L., & Raiffa, H. (1976). *Decisions with multiple objectives: Preferences and value trade-offs.* New York: Wiley.

Kelly, G. A. (1955). *The psychology of personal constructs.* New York: Norton.

Kemeny, J. G., & Snell, J. L. (1962). *Mathematical models in the social sciences.* Cambridge: MIT Press.

Kerr, N., MacCoun, R. J., & Kramer, G. (1996a). Bias in judgment: Comparing individuals and groups. *Psychological Review, 103,* 687-719.

Kerr, N. L., MacCoun, R. J., & Kramer, G. P. (1996b). When are N heads better (or worse) than one? Biased judgment in individuals vs. groups. In E. Witte & J. H. Davis (Eds.), *Understanding group behavior, Vol. 1: Consensual action by small groups* (pp. 105-136). Hillsdale, NJ: Lawrence Erlbaum.

Kirk, J., & Miller, M. L. (1986). *Reliability and validity in qualitative research.* London: Sage.

Klebert, K., Schrader, E., & Straub, W. G. (1991). *Moderationsmethode: Gestaltung der Meinungs- und Willensbildung in Gruppen, die miteinander lernen und leben, arbeiten und spielen [Method of mediation: The shaping of opinion and decision processes in groups that share learning, living, working and playing].* (5th ed.). Hamburg: Windmühle.

Kleijn, R., Bringezu, S., Fischer-Kowalski, M., & Palm, V. (1999). *Ecologizing societal metabolism: Designing scenarios for sustainable materials management. Proceedings of the ConAccount workshop, November 21st 1998 in Amsterdam, The Netherlands.* Leiden: Centre of Environmental Science (CML).

Kleindorfer, P. R., Kunreuther, H. C., & Schoemaker, P. J. H. (1993). *Decision sciences: An integrative perspective.* Cambridge, UK: Cambridge University Press.

Knoepfel, P. (1995a). Von der konstitutionellen Konkordanz über administrative Konsenslösungen zum demokratischen Dezisionismus—zur Vielfalt von Verhandlungsarrangements in Konfliktlösungsverfahren der Schweiz [From constitutional concordance via administrative consensual solutions to democratic decisionism and the plurality of conflict resolution procedures in Switzerland]. In P. Knoepfel (Ed.), *Lösung von Umweltkonflikten durch Verhandlung—Beispiele aus dem In- und Ausland [The resolution of environmental conflicts through negotiation—Examples from Switzerland and other countries]* (Vol. 10, pp. 283-322). Basel: Helbing & Lichtenhahn.

Knoepfel, P. (Ed.). (1995b). *Lösung von Umweltkonflikten durch Verhandlung —Beispiele aus dem In- und Ausland [The resolution of environmental conflicts through negotiation<@151>Examples from Switzerland and other countries]* (1st ed., Vol. 10). Basel: Helbing & Lichtenhahn.

Koch, U., & Trüb, L. (1993). *Protokoll zur Zukunftswerkstatt: Kinder, Erwachsene und ältere Menschen—Wohnräume, Lebensräume [Protocol of the future workshop: Children, adolescents and elder people—Living rooms, living spaces].* Zürich: Schule für Gestaltung, Stadt Zürich.

Krackhardt, D., Blythe, J., & McGrath, C. (1994). Krackplot 3.0: An improved network drawing program. *Connections, 17*(2), 53-55.

Kramer, H., Gussone, H.-A., & Schober, R. (1988). *Waldwachstumslehre: Ökologische und anthropogene Einflüsse auf das Wachstum des Waldes, seine Massen- und Wertleistung und die Bestandessicherheit [Science of forest growth: Ecological and anthropogenic impacts on forest growth, mass and value development and stock security].* Hamburg: Parey.

Krohn, W., & Weingart, P. (1986). Tschernobyl—das größte anzunehmende Experiment [Chernobyl—The largest imaginable experiment]. *Kursbuch, 85,* 1-25.

Krueger, R. A. (1988). *Focus groups: A practical guide for applied research.* Newbury Park, CA: Sage.

Krueger, R. E., & Kling, C. (1995). Validity. In E. Kazdin (Ed.), *Encyclopedia of psychology* (Vol. 8, pp. 149-153). Oxford, UK: Oxford University Press.

Landgrebe, L. (1959). Von der Unmittelbarkeit der Erfahrung [About the immediacy of experience]. In R. Boehm (Ed.), *Edmund Husserl—Theorie der phänomenologischen Reduktion [Edmund Husserl—The theory of phenomenological reduction]* (Vol. 8, Pt. 2, pp. 252-259). Den Haag: Nijhoff.

Langdell, C. C. (1887). [Address to Harvard Law School]. *Harvard Graduate Magazine,* Cambridge, MA.

Langer, E. (1975). The illusion of control. *Journal of Personality and Social Psychology, 32,* 311-328.

Langer, E., & Roth, J. (1975). Heads I win, tails it's chance: The illusion of control as a function of sequence of outcomes in a purely chance task. *Journal of Personality and Social Psychology, 32,* 951-955.

Laplace, P.-S. (1921). *Essai philosophique sur les probabilités [Philosophical essay on probabilities]*. Paris: Gauthier-Villars. (Original work published 1816)

Laplace, P.-S. (1995). *Philosophical essay on probabilities* (translated from 5th French ed., 1825, with notes by Andrew I. Dale, Trans.). New York: Springer.

Laws, D. (1999). Representation of stakeholding interests. In L. E. Susskind, S. McKearnen, & J. Thomas-Larmer (Eds.), *The consensus building handbook: A comprehensive guide to reaching agreement* (pp. 241-286). Thousand Oaks, CA: Sage.

Le Play, F. (1855). *Les ouvriers européens [The European workers]*. Paris: Imprimerie impériale.

Leontief, W. (1966). *Input-output economics*. New York: Oxford University Press.

Leser, H., & Mosimann, T. (1997). *Landschaftsökologie. Ansatz, Modelle, Methodik, Anwendung [Landscape ecology. Basic approach, models, methodology, application]* (4th rev. ed.). Stuttgart: Ulmer.

Lévi-Strauss, C. (1955). *Tristes tropiques*. Paris: Librairie Plon.

Lewin, K. (1939). Field theory and experiment in social psychology. *American Journal of Sociology, 44*, 868-897.

Linstone, H., & Turoff, M. (Eds.). (1975). *The Delphi method: Techniques and applications*. Reading, MA: Addison-Wesley.

Lorenz, J. H. (1992). *Anschauung und Veranschaulichungsmittel im Mathematikunterricht [Perception and visualization tools in mathematics instruction]*. Göttingen: Hogrefe.

Lück, E. (1991). *Geschichte der Psychologie [History of psychology]*. Stuttgart: Kohlhammer.

Luhmann, N. (1996). Gefahr oder Risiko, Solidarität oder Konflikt [Danger or risk, solidarity or conflict]? In R. Königswieser, M. Haller, P. Maas, & H. Jarmai (Eds.), *Risiko-Dialog: Zukunft ohne Harmonieformel [Risk dialogue: Future without a harmony recipe]* (pp. 38-46). Köln: Deutscher Instituts-Verlag.

Luria, A. R. (1969). On the psychology of computational operations. In J. K. I. Wirzup (Ed.), *Soviet studies in the psychology of learning and teaching mathematics* (Vol. 1). Chicago: University of Chicago Press.

MacNulty, C. A. R. (1977). (Scenario) development for corporate planning. *Futures, 9*, 128-138.

Markowitsch, H. J. (1985). Der Fall H. M. im Dienste der Hirnforschung [The case of H. M. in the service of brain research]. *Naturwissenschaftliche Rundschau [Natural Science Review], 38*(10), 410-416.

Markowitsch, H. J. (1992). *Neuropsychologie des Gedächtnisses [Neuropsychology of the memory]*. Göttingen: Hogrefe.

May, R. M. (1981). *Theoretical ecology principles and applications* (2nd ed.). Oxford, UK: Basil Blackwell.

Mayer, R. E. (1992). *Thinking, problem solving, cognition*. New York: Freeman.

Mayo, E. (1933). *Human problems of an industrial civilization*. New York: McGraw-Hill.

Mazmanian, D. A., & Stanley-Jones, M. (1995). Reconceiving LULUs: Changing the nature and scope of locally unwanted land uses. In P. Knoepfel (Ed.), *Lösung von Umweltkonflikten durch Verhandlung—Beispiele aus dem In- und Ausland [The resolution of environmental conflicts through negotiation—Examples from Switzerland and other countries]* (Vol. 10, pp. 27-53). Basel: Helbing & Lichtenhahn.

McCharg, I. L. (1971). *Design with nature.* Garden City, NY: Natural History Press.

McDonald, M. J., & House, D. V. (1992). Positivist influences in "environment-behavior" studies: Egon Brunswik and contemporary social psychology. In C. W. Tolman (Ed.), *Positivism in psychology: Historical and contemporary problems* (pp. 155-184). New York: Springer.

McGrath, J. E. (1984). *Groups: Interaction and performance.* Englewood Cliffs, NJ: Prentice Hall.

Mead, M. (1923). *Coming of age in Samoa.* New York: Morrow.

Meadows, D. H., Meadows, D. L., & Randers, J. (1992). *Beyond the limits.* Post Mills, VT: Chelsea Green.

Meadows, D. L., Behrens, W. W., Meadows, D. H., Nail, R. F., Randers, J., & Zahn, E. K. O. (1974). *The dynamics of growth in a finite world.* Cambridge, MA: Productivity Press.

Meehl, P. E. (1966). *Clinical versus statistical prediction.* Minneapolis: University of Minnesota Press.

Memmert, C. (1993). *Über die Arbeit an der Zukunft: Die Praxis der Zukunftswerkstätten [About laboring over the future: The practice of futures workshops].* Unpublished doctoral dissertation, University of Bremen, Bremen, Germany.

Meredith, J. E., & Mantel, S. J. (1995). *Project management.* New York: Wiley.

Merriam-Webster, Inc. (1993). *Webster's third new international dictionary of the English language unabridged.* Springfield, MA: Author.

Messick, S. (1989). Validity. In R. Linn (Ed.), *Educational measurement* (3rd ed., pp. 13-103). New York: Macmillan.

Messick, S. (1995). Validity of psychological assessment: Validation of inference from person's responses and performances as scientific inquiry into score meaning. *American Psychologist, 50,* 741-749.

Mieg, H. A. (1996). Managing the interfaces between science, industry and society. In UNESCO (Ed.), *World Congress of Engineering Educators and Industry Leaders* (Vol. 1, pp. 529-533). Paris: UNESCO.

Mieg, H. A. (2000). University-based projects for local sustainable development: Designing expert roles and collective reasoning. *International Journal of Sustainability in Higher Education, 1,* 67-82.

Miller, G. A. (1956). The magic number seven plus minus two: Some limits on our capacity for processing information. *Psychological Review, 63,* 81-97.

Miller, J. G. (1978). *Living systems.* New York: McGraw-Hill.

Minx, M., & Mattrisch, G. (1996). Die Szenario-Technik—Werkzeug für den Umgang mit einer multiplen Zukunft [The scenario technique—A tool for coping with multiple futures]. In J. Gausenmeier (Ed.), *Paderborner scenario workshop* (pp. 96-103). Paderborn: Heinz Nixdorf Institut.

Missler-Behr, M. (1993). *Methoden der Szenarioanalyse [Methods of scenario analysis]*. Wiesbaden: Deutscher Universitäts-Verlag.

Moll, S., Hinterberger, F., Femia, A., & Bringezu, S. (1999). An input-output approach to analyse the total material requirement (TMR) of national economies. In R. Kleijn, S. Bringezu, M. Fischer-Kowalski, & V. Palm (Eds.), *Ecologizing societal metabolism: Designing scenarios for sustainable materials management. Proceedings of the ConAccount workshop, November 21st 1998 in Amsterdam, The Netherlands* (pp. 39-46). Leiden: Centre of Environmental Science (CML).

Möller, A., & Rolf, A. (1995). Methodische Ansätze zur Erstellung von Stoffstromanalysen unter besonderer Berücksichtigung von PetriNetzen [Methodological approaches to material flow analyses with special consideration of Petri nets]. In M. Schmidt & A. Schorb (Eds.), *Stoffstromanalysen in Ökobilanzen und Öko-Audits [Material flow analyses in life cycle assessments and eco-audits]* (pp. 33-58). Berlin: Springer.

Mood, A. M., Graybill, F. A., & Boes, D. C. (1974). *Introduction to the theory of statistics* (3rd ed.). Tokyo: McGraw-Hill Kokakusha.

Moore, C. M. (1987). *Group techniques for idea building.* Newbury Park, CA: Sage.

Moore, S. A. (1996). Defining "successful" environmental dispute resolution: Case studies from public land planning in the United States and Australia. *Environmental Impact Assessment Review, 16*(3), 151-169.

Moreno, J. L. (Ed.). (1960). *The sociometry reader.* Glencoe, IL: Free Press.

Müller-Herold, U., & Neuenschwander, M. (1992). Vom Reden zum Tun: Die Fallstudie in den Umweltnaturwissenschaften [From talking to action: The case study in environmental science]. *GAIA, 1,* 339-349.

Mumpower, J., Menkes, J., & Covello, T. (Eds.). (1986). *Risk evaluation and management.* New York: Plenum.

Murray, H. A. (1938). *Explorations in personality.* New York: Oxford University Press.

Nash, J. F. (1950). The bargaining problem. *Econometrica, 18,* 155-162.

Naveh, Z., & Liebermann, A. S. (1994). *Landscape ecology: Theory and application* (2nd ed.). New York: Springer.

Neale, M. A., & Bazerman, M. H. (1991). *Cognition and rationality in negotiation.* New York: Free Press.

Neef, E. (1966). Zur Frage des gebietswirtschaftlichen Potentials [On the question of area-specific potentials]. *Forschungen und Fortschritte [Research and progress], 40*(3), 65-70.

Nisbett, R. E., & Ross, L. (1980). *Human inference: Strategies and shortcomings of social judgement.* Englewood Cliffs, NJ: Prentice Hall.

Noss, R. F., & Csuti, B. (1994). Habitat fragmentation. In G. K. Meffe & R. C. Carroll (Eds.), *Principles of conservation biology* (pp. 237-264). Sunderland, MA: Sinauer.

Nothbaum, N. (1997). *Experten-Entscheidung unter Unsicherheit: Kognitive Didaktik und situative Rahmung bei der Erhebung von Verteilungswissen [Expert decisions under uncertainty: Cognitive didactics and situative framing in the determination of distributive knowledge].* Frankfurt am Main: Lang.

Nothbaum, N., Scholz, R. W., & May, T. W. (1996, September). *Die Akquisition von Verteilungswissen [The acquisition of distributive knowledge].* Paper presented at the 41. Jahrestagung der GMDS. Modellierung von Expositionsszenarien in der Umweltmedizin [41st Annual Meeting of the GMDS. The modeling of exposition scenarios in environmental medicine]. Bonn.

Oppenheim, L. (1977). *Ancient Mesopotamia.* Chicago: University of Chicago Press.

Oppermann, B., & Langer, K. (2000). *Umweltmediation in Theorie und Anwendung [Environmental mediation: Theory and application].* Stuttgart: Akademie für Technikfolgenabschätzung [Academy for Technology Assessment], Baden-Württemberg.

Oreskes, N., Shrader-Frechette, K., & Belitz, K. (1994, February 4). Verification, validation and confirmation of numerical models in the earth sciences. *Science, 263,* 641-646.

Osborn, A. F. (1963). *Applied imagination: Principles and procedures of creative problem-solving* (3rd ed.). New York: Wiley.

Otte, M. (1994). *Das Formale, das Soziale und das Subjektive [The formal, the social and the subjective].* Frankfurt am Main: Suhrkamp.

Peräkylä, A. (1998). Reliability and validity in research based on tapes and transcripts. In D. Silverman (Ed.), *Qualitative research* (pp. 201-220). London: Sage.

Petermann, F. (1989). *Einzelfallanalyse [Single case analysis].* München: Oldenbourg.

Pfister, C. (1995). Das 1950er Syndrom: Die umweltgeschichtliche Epochenschwelle zwischen Industriegesellschaft und Konsumgesellschaft [The syndrome of the 1950's: The epochal step in the environment's history from the industrial to the consumer society]. In C. Pfister (Ed.), *Das 1950er Syndrom: Der Weg in die Konsumgesellschaft [The syndrome of the 1950's: The path to the consumer society]* (pp. 51-95). Bern: Haupt.

Pfister, C. (1998). The syndrome of the 1950's in Switzerland: Cheap energy, mass consumption and the environment. In S. Strasser & M. Judt (Eds.), *Getting and spending, European and American consumer societies in the twentieth century* (pp. 359-378). Cambridge, UK: Cambridge University Press.

Piaget, J. (1923). *Le langage et la pensée chez l'enfant [The language and thought of the child].* Paris: Delachaux & Niestlé.

Piaget, J. (1924). *Le jugement et le raisonnement chez l'enfant.* Neuchâtel-Paris: Delachaux & Niestlé.

Piaget, J. (1932). *Le jugement moral chez l'enfant [The moral judgment of the child].* Paris: Alcan. [Trans. by Free Press, New York, 1965]

Piaget, J. (1936). *La naissance de l'intelligence chez l'enfant [The origin of intelligence in the child].* Paris: Delachaux & Niestlé.

Piaget, J. (1946). *La développement de la notion de temps chez l'enfant [The development of the notion of time in the child]*. Paris: Presses Universitaires de France.

Piaget, J. (1947). *La psychologie de l'intelligence [The psychology of intelligence]*. Paris: Colin.

Piaget, J. (1953). *The origin of intelligence in the child*. London: Routledge & Kegan.

Piaget, J. (1960). *The moral judgment of the child*. London: Routledge & Kegan.

Piaget, J. (1975). *L'équilibration des structures cognitives: Problème central du développement [The equilibration of the cognitive structures: The central problem of development]*. Paris: Presses Universitaires de France.

Piaget, J., & Inhelder, B. (1956). *The child's conception of space [La représentation de l'éspace chez l'enfant]*. London: Routledge & Kegan.

Piaget, J., & Szeminska, A. (1941). *La genèse du nombre chez l'enfant [The development of numbers in the child]*. Paris: Delachaux & Niestlé.

Poincare, H. (1948). Mathematical creation. *Scientific American, 179*, 54-57.

Pontrjagin, L. S. (1964). *The mathematical theory of optimal processes*. Oxford, UK: Pergamon.

Popper, K. R. (1969). *Conjectures and refutations: The growth of the scientific knowledge* (3rd ed.). London: Routledge and Kegan.

Pruitt, D. G., & Carnevale, P. J. (1993). *Negotiation in social conflict*. Pacific Grove, CA: Brooks.

Pruitt, D. G., & Johnson, D. F. (1970). Mediation as an aid to face saving in negotiation. *Journal of Personality and Social Psychology, 14*, 239-246.

Quinn, G. (1994). *Legal theory and the casebook method of instructions in the United States*. München: Hampp.

Raczynski, J. M., & Oberman, A. (1990). Cardiovascular surgery patients. In B. Spilker (Ed.), *Quality of life assessments in clinical trials* (pp. 295-322). New York: Raven Press.

Ragin, C. C. (1992). Cases of "What is a case?" In C. C. Ragin & H. S. Becker (Eds.), *What is a case? Exploring the foundations of social inquiry* (pp. 1-18). Cambridge, UK: Cambridge University Press.

Raiffa, H. (1968). *Decision analysis—Introductory lectures on choices under uncertainty*. Reading, MA: Addison-Wesley.

Reibnitz, v. U. (1992). *Szenario-Technik. Instrumente für die unternehmerische und persönliche Erfolgsplanung [Scenario technique: Instruments for the enterprising and personal success plan]* (2nd ed.). Wiesbaden: Gabler.

Remocker, A. J., & Storch, E. T. (1987). *Action speaks louder: A handbook of structured group techniques* (4th ed.). Edinburgh: Churchill Livingstone.

Renn, O. (1983). Technology, risk, and public perception. *Angewandte Systemanalyse/Applied Systems Analysis, 4*(2), 50-65.

Renn, O. (1992). Concepts of risk: A classification. In S. Krimsky & D. Golding (Eds.), *Social theories of risk* (pp. 179-197). Westport, CT: Praeger.

Renn, O., Webler, T., & Wiedemann, P. M. (Eds.). (1995). *Fairness and competence in citizen participation—Evaluating models for environmental discourse*. Dordrecht: Kluwer.

Rice, R. G., & Do, D. D. (1995). *Applied mathematics and modeling for chemical engineers.* New York: Wiley.

Richter, O., Diekkrüger, B., & Nörtersheuser, P. (1996). *Environmental fate modeling of pesticides from the laboratory to the field scale.* Weinheim: Vch.

Richter, O., & Söndgerath, D. (1990). *Parameter estimation in ecology: The link between data and models.* Weinheim: Vch.

Roberts, N., Andersen, D., Deal, R., Garet, M., & Shaffer, W. (1994). *Introduction to computer simulation: The system dynamics modeling approach* (1st ed.). Portland, OR: Productivity Press.

Röthlisberger, F., & Dickson, W. (1939). *Management and the worker.* Cambridge, MA: Harvard University Press.

Rohdenburg, H. (1989). Methods for the analysis of agro-ecosystems in Central Europe, with emphasis on geoecological aspects. *Catena, 16*(1), 1-57.

Ronstadt, R. (1993). *The art of case study analysis: A guide to the diagnosis of business situations.* Dana Point, CA: Lord.

Roth, U. (1996). Innerstädtische Umnutzung: Zentrum Zürich Nord [Inner-urban reuse of sites: City Center Zurich North]. *Schweizer Journal [Swiss Journal], 1,* 21-25.

Roy, B. (1991). The outranking approach and the foundations of ELECTRE methods. *Theory and Decision, 31,* 49-73.

Rudolph, D. (1993). Aufbau und Funktion von Fallgeschichten im Wandel der Zeit [The structure and function of case stories over time]. In U. Stuhr & F. W. Deneke (Eds.), *Die Fallgeschichte [The case story]* (pp. 17-31). Heidelberg: Asanger.

Ruoss, S., Siress, C., Stöckli, Kienast und Koeppel, Buchhofer Barbe AG, Büro ur Ueli Roth, & Hochbauamt der Stadt Zürich [Zurich City Department of Building Construction]. (1994). *Entwicklungsleitbild Zentrum Zürich Nord [Master Plan City Center Zurich North].* Zürich: Büro ur Ueli Roth.

Ruth, M., & Hannon, B. (1997). *Modeling dynamic economic systems.* New York: Springer.

Saaty, T. L. (1990). *The analytic hierarchy process* (2nd ed.). Pittburgh: RWS.

Sacks, O. (1973). *Zeit des Erwachens [Awakenings].* London: Picador.

Savage, L. J. (1972). *The foundations of statistics.* New York: Dover.

Schmidt, M., Möller, A., Hedemann, J., & Müller-Beischmidt, P. (1997). Environmental material flow analysis by network approach. In W. Geiger, A. Jaeschke, O. Rentz, E. Simon, T. Spengler, L. Zilliox, & T. Zundel (Eds.), *Umweltinformatik '97. 11. Intern. Symposium der Gesellschaft für Informatik (GI) in Strassburg 1997 [Environmental Informatics '97. 11th International Symposium of the Society for Informatics in Strasbourg 1997]* (pp. 768-779). Marburg: Metropolis.

Schmidt-Bleek, F. (1993). *Wieviel Umwelt braucht der Mensch? MIPS—Das Mass für ökologisches Wirtschaften [How much nature do people need? MIPS—The measure for an ecological economy].* Berlin: Birkhäuser.

Schnelle, E. (1979). *The Metaplan method: Communication tools for planning and learning groups* (Vol. 7). Quickborn, Germany: Metaplan.

Scholz, R. W. (1979). Team teaching: A way of co-operating which has no future? In H.-G. Steiner (Ed.), *Co-operation between science teachers and mathematics teachers: Conference proceedings* (Vol. 16, pp. 425-443). Bielefeld: Universität Bielefeld.

Scholz, R. W. (Ed.). (1983a). *Decision making under uncertainty.* Amsterdam: Elsevier.

Scholz, R. W. (1983b). Methodological problems of adequate modelling and conceptualization of teaching, learning and thinking processes related to mathematics. In M. Zweng, T. Green, J. Kilpatrick, H. Pollak, & M. Suydam (Eds.), *Fourth International Congress on Mathematical Education* (pp. 468-469). Boston: Birkhäuser.

Scholz, R. W. (1986). *Current issues in West German decision research.* Frankfurt am Main: Lang.

Scholz, R. W. (1987). *Cognitive strategies in stochastic thinking.* Dordrecht: Reidel.

Scholz, R. W. (1998). Umweltforschung zwischen Formalwissenschaft und Verständnis: Muss man den Formalismus beherrschen, um die Formalisten zu schlagen? [Environmental research between formalism and understanding: Do you have to master formalism to beat the formalists?]. In A. Daschkeit & W. Schröder (Eds.), *Umweltforschung quergedacht: Perspektiven integrativer Umweltforschung und -lehre [Cross thoughts of environmental research: Perspectives of integrative environmental research]* (pp. 309-328). Berlin: Springer.

Scholz, R. W. (2000). Mutual learning as a basic principle of transdisciplinarity. In R. W. Scholz, R. Häberli, A. Bill, & M. Welti (Eds.), *Transdisciplinarity: Joint problem-solving among science, technology and society. Workbook II: Mutual learning sessions* (pp. 13-17). Zürich: Haffmans Sachbuch.

Scholz, R. W., Bösch, S., Carlucci, L., & Oswald, J. (Eds.). (1999). *Nachhaltige Regionalentwicklung: Chancen der Region Klettgau. [Sustainable regional development: New opportunities in the Klettgau Region. ETH-UNS case study 1998].* Zürich: Rüegger.

Scholz, R. W., Bösch, S., Koller, T., Mieg, H. A., & Stünzi, J. (1996). *Industrieareal Sulzer-Escher Wyss—Umwelt und Bauen. Wertschöpfung durch Umnutzung. UNS-Fallstudie 1995 [Industrial area Sulzer-Escher Wyss—Environment and construction. Creation of values by reuse of land. ETH-UNS case study 1995].* Zürich: vdf Hochschulverlag.

Scholz, R. W., Bösch, S., Mieg, H. A., & Stünzi, J. (1997). *Zentrum Zürich Nord: Stadt im Aufbruch. Bausteine für eine nachhaltige Stadtentwicklung. UNS-Fallstudie 1996 [City Center Zurich North—A city on the move. Building blocks for a sustainable urban development. ETH-UNS case study 1996].* Zürich: vdf Hochschulverlag.

Scholz, R. W., Bösch, S., Mieg, H. A., & Stünzi, J. (Eds.). (1998). *Region Klettgau: Verantwortungsvoller Umgang mit Boden. UNS-Fallstudie 1997 [The Klettgau region: Responsible use of soil. ETH-UNS case study 1997].* Zürich: Rüegger.

Scholz, R. W., Flückiger, B., Schwarzenbach, R. C., Stauffacher, M., Mieg, H. A., & Neuenschwander, M. (1997). Environmental problem-solving ability: Profiles in application documents of research assistants. *Journal of Environmental Education, 28*(4), 37-44.

Scholz, R. W., Heitzer, A., May, T. W., Nothbaum, N., Stünzi, J., & Tietje, O. (1997). Datenqualität und Risikoanalysen: Das Risikohandlungsmodell zur Altlastenbearbeitung [Data quality and risk analyses. The risk action model of soil remediation]. In S. Schulte-Hostede, R. Freitag, A. Kettrup, & W. Fresenius (Eds.), *Altlastenbewertung: Datenanalyse und Gefahrenbewertung [Evaluation of soil remediation cases: Analysis of data and evaluation of risks]* (pp.<N>1-29). Landsberg: Ecomed-Verlag.

Scholz, R. W., Koller, T., Mieg, H. A., & Schmidlin, C. (1995). *Perspektive "Grosses Moos"—Wege zu einer nachhaltigen Landwirtschaft. UNS-Fallstudie 1994 [Paths towards sustainable agriculture in the region "Grosses Moos." ETH-UNS case study 1994].* Zürich: vdf Hochschulverlag.

Scholz, R. W., Mieg, H. A., Weber, O., & Stauffacher, M. (1998). Soziopsychologische Determinanten nachhaltigen Handelns. [Socio-psychological determinants of sustainable action]. *DISP [Documents and Information on Local, Regional, and Country Planning in Switzerland], 34*(133), 14-21.

Scholz, R. W., Popp, M., May, T. W., & Nothbaum, N. (1994). Risikoberechnungen zur Abwasserabgabe [Risk calculations for the sewage discharge fee]. In ATV Landesgruppe Baden-Württemberg (Ed.), *ATV-Landesgruppen-Tagungen 1993, Donaueschingen. [Meeting of the ATV-Regional Groups 1993]* (pp. 45-59). Hennef: Abwasser-technische Vereinigung, Landesgruppe Baden-Württemberg.

Scholz, R. W., & Zimmer, A. (1997). *Qualitative aspects of decision making.* Lengerich: Pabst.

Schultz, B. G. (1989). *Communicating in the small group: Theory and practice.* New York: Harper & Row.

Schulze, E. D., & Mooney, H. A. (1994). *Biodiversity and ecosystem function.* Berlin: Springer.

Schutz, A. (1971). The stranger: An essay in social psychology. In A. Broderson (Ed.), *Alfred Schutz: Collected papers: Vol. 2. Studies in social theory* (pp. 91-105). The Hague, Netherlands: Martinus Nijhoff.

Scoville, W. B., & Millner, B. (1957). Loss of recent memory in bilateral hippocampal lesions. *Journal of Neurology, Neurosurgery, and Psychiatry, 20*(11), 11-22.

Seiler, H.-J. (1995). Review of "planning cells": Problems of legitimation. In O. Renn, T. Webler, & P. M. Wiedemann (Eds.), *Fairness and competence in citizen participation* (pp. 141-156). Dordrecht: Kluwer.

Selten, R. (1983). Towards a theory of limited rationality. In R. W. Scholz (Ed.), *Decision making under uncertainty. Cognitive decision research—social interaction—development and epistemology* (revised papers of an international symposium; Bielefeld, November 10–12, 1982; pp. 409-412). Amsterdam: North-Holland.

Selten, R. (1990). Bounded rationality. *Journal of Institutional and Theoretical Economics, 146*, 649-658.

Shafer, G. A. (1976). *A mathematical theory of evidence.* Princeton, NJ: Princeton University Press.

Shanteau, J. (1988). Psychological characteristics and strategies of expert decision makers. *Acta Psychologica, 68*, 203-215.

Shubik, M. (Ed.). (1983). *Mathematics of conflict (Outcome of a conference on the theory of conflict; Seven Springs, Mt. Kisco—N.Y., November 1979).* Amsterdam: North-Holland.

Sidman, M., Soddard, L. T., & Mohr, J. P. (1968). Some additional quantitative observations of immediate memory in a patient with bilateral hippocampal lesions. *Neuropsychologica, 6*, 245.

Siegel, S., & Fouraker, L. E. (1960). *Bargaining and group decision making: Experiments in bilateral monopoly.* New York: McGraw-Hill.

Simon, H. (1979). *Models of thought.* New Haven, CT: Yale University Press.

Slovic, P. (1987). Perception of risk. *Science, 236*, 280-285.

Slovic, P. (2000). *Perception of risk.* London, UK: Earthscan.

Slovic, P., Fischhoff, B., & Lichtenstein, S. (1985). Characterizing perceived risk. In R. W. Kates, C. Hohenemser, & J. X. Kasperson (Eds.), *Perilous progress: Managing the hazards of technology.* Boulder, CO: Westview.

Smith, G. R. (1995). *Logical decisions for windows.* Denver-Evergreen: Msa Design, PdQ Printing.

Smith, J. A. (1991). *The idea brokers: Think tanks and the rise of the new policy elite.* New York: Free Press.

Smuts, J. C. (1926). *Holism and evolution.* New York: Viking.

Spilker, B. (Ed.). (1990). *Quality of life assessments in clinical trials.* New York: Raven.

Springer, S. P., & Deutsch, G. (1993). *Left brain, right brain* (4th ed.). New York: Freeman.

Stake, R. E. (1976). *The case method in social inquiry: The case study approach to educational program evaluation in Britain and "the colonies."* Urbana: University of Illinois, Center for Applied Research in Education.

Stake, R. E. (1995). *The art of case study research.* Thousand Oaks, CA: Sage.

Steiner, F. (1991). *The living landscape: An ecological approach to landscape planning.* New York: McGraw-Hill.

Steiner, H.–G. (1989). The nature of theoretical concepts in physics and mathematics: Implications for the fragility of knowledge in educational context. In *Proceedings of the 2nd Jerusalem Convention on Education: Science and mathematics education. Interaction between theory and practice* (pp. 387-396). Jerusalem.

Steiner, H.–G. (1990). Needed cooperation between science education and mathematics education. *Zeitschrift für Didaktik der Mathematik (ZDM), 22*, 194-197.

Steiner, I. D. (1983). Whatever happened to the touted revival of the group? In H. H. Blumberg, A. P. Hare, V. Kent, & M. F. Davies (Eds.), *Small groups and social interaction* (Vol. 2, pp. 539-548). Chichester, UK: Wiley.

Steins, G. (1998). Diagnostik von Empathie und Perspektivenübernahme: Eine Überprüfung des Zusammenhangs beider Konstrukte und Implikationen für die Messung [Diagnosis of empathy and perspective-taking: A verification of the link between the two constructs and implications for their measurement]. *Diagnostica, 44*(3), 117-129.

Steins, G., & Wicklund, R. A. (1996). Perspective-taking, conflict and press: Drawing an E on your forehead. *Basic and Applied Social Psychology, 18,* 319-346.

Sternberg, R. J. (1988). A three-facet model of creativity. In R. J. Sternberg (Ed.), *The nature of creativity: Contemporary psychological perspectives* (pp. 125-147). Cambridge, UK: Cambridge University Press.

Stoner, J. A. F. (1961). *A comparison of individual and group decision including risk.* Unpublished master's thesis, Massachusetts Institute of Technology School of Management.

Stuhr, U., & Deneke, F. W. (1993). *Die Fallgeschichte [The case story].* Heidelberg: Asanger.

Susskind, L. E. (1975). *The land use controversy in Massachusetts—Case studies and policy options.* Cambridge: MIT Press.

Susskind, L. E., Bacow, L. S., & Wheeler, M. (Eds.). (1984). *Resolving environmental regulatory disputes.* Cambridge, MA: Schenckman.

Susskind, L. E., & Madigan, D. (1984). New approaches to resolving disputes in the public sector. *Justice System Journal, 9*(2), 197-203.

Susskind, L. E., McKearnen, S., & Thomas-Larmer, J. (Eds.). (1999). *The consensus building handbook: A comprehensive guide to reaching agreement.* Thousand Oaks, CA: Sage.

Svenson, O. (1981). Are we less risky and more skillful than our fellow drivers are? *Acta Psychologica, 47,* 143-148.

Tack, W. (1983). Conditions of violating individual rationality. In R. W. Scholz (Ed.), *Decision making under uncertainty.* Amsterdam: Elsevier.

Tansley, A. G. (1935). The use and abuse of vegetation concepts and terms. *Ecology, 16,* 284-307.

Tavares, V. (1999). *Advanced models for project management.* Boston: Kluwer.

Taylor, S. J., Bogdan, R. C., & Walker, P. (2000). Qualitative research. In E. Kazdin (Ed.), *Encyclopedia of psychology* (Vol. 8, pp. 489-491). Oxford, UK: Oxford University Press.

Thibault, J. W., & Kelley, H. H. (1959). *The social psychology of groups.* New York: Wiley.

Thom, R. (1970). Topological models in biology. In C. H. Waddington (Ed.), *Towards a theoretical biology* (Vol. 3, pp. 89-116). Edinburgh: Edinburgh University Press.

Thompson, M., Ellis, R., & Wildavsky, A. (1990). *Cultural theory.* Boulder, CO: Westview.

Tietje, O., Scholz, R. W., Heitzer, A., & Weber, O. (1998). Mathematical evaluation criteria. In H. P. Blume, H. Eger, E. Fleischhauer, A. Hebel, C. Reij, & K. G. Steiner (Eds.), *Towards sustainable land use* (pp. 53-61). Bonn: Catena.

Tolman, E. C. (1948). Cognitive maps in rats and men. *Psychological Review, 55,* 189-208.

Towl, A. R. (1969). *To study administration by cases.* Boston: Harvard University Press.

Troll, G. (1971). Landscape ecology (geo-ecology) and bio-cenology: A terminology study. *Geoforum, 8,* 43-46.

Tukey, J. W. (1977). *Exploratory data analysis.* Reading, MA: Addison-Wesley.

Tukker, A., Jasser, A. S., & Kleijn, R. (1997). Material suppliers and industrial metabolism. *Environmental Science and Pollution Research, 4*(2), 113-120.

Tulving, E. (1972). Episodic and semantic memory. In E. Tulving & W. Donaldson (Eds.), *Organization of memory* (pp. 381-403). New York: Academic Press.

Udo de Haes, H. A. (Ed.). (1996). *Towards a methodology for life cycle impact assessment.* Brussels: Society of Environmental Toxicology and Chemistry—Europe.

Udo de Haes, H. A., & Owens, J. W. (1998). *Evolution and development of the conceptual framework and methodology of life-cycle impact assessment. Summary of SETAC (North America) and SETAC (Europe) Workgroups on Life Cycle Impact Assessment.* Pensacola, FL: Society of Environmental Toxicology and Chemistry.

Udo de Haes, H. A., van der Voet, E., & Kleijn, R. (1997). Substance flow analysis (SFA), an analytical tool for integrated chain management. In S. Bringezu, M. Fischer-Kowalski, R. Kleijn, & P. Viveka (Eds.), *Regional and national material flow accounting: From paradigm to practice of sustainability. Proceedings of the ConAccount workshop 21-23 January, 1997 in Leiden, The Netherlands.* Wuppertal, Germany: Wuppertal Institute for Climate, Environment and Energy.

Ury, W. (1993). *Getting past no: Negotiating your way from confrontation to cooperation.* New York: Bantam.

van der Kleijn, R., Huele, R., & Voet, E. (2000). Dynamic substance flow analysis: The delaying mechanism of stocks, with the case of PVC in Sweden. *Ecological Economics, 32*(2), 241-254.

van der Voet, E., van Oers, L., Guinee, J. B., & Udo de Haes, H. A. (1999). Using SFA indicators to support environmental policy. *Environmental Science and Pollution Research, 6*(1), 49-58.

Verhulst, F. (1990). *Nonlinear differential equations and dynamical systems.* Berlin: Springer.

Vester, F. (1978). *Denken—Lernen—Vergessen was geht in unserem Kopf vor, wie lernt das Gehirn, und wann lässt es uns im Stich? [Thinking, learning, forgetting: What happens in our mind, how the brain is learning, and when we can't rely on it].* München: Deutscher Taschenbuch Verlag.

Vester, F. (1991). *Ballungsgebiete in der Krise [Urban systems in crisis]* (Aktualisierte Neuausg. ed.). München: Dt. Taschenbuch-Verlag.

Vincke, P. (1992). *Multicriteria decision-aid.* Chichester, UK: Wiley.

Vlek, C., & Stallen, P.-J. (1981). Judging risks and benefits in the small and in the large. *Organizational Behavior and Human Performance, 28,* 235-271.

Vogel, D. (1978). *The Professional Teacher Preparation Program of the College of Education of the University of Houston: A case study* (Vol. 11). Bielefeld, Germany: Universität Bielefeld.

von Bertalanffy, L. (1968). *General system theory: Foundations, development, and applications*. New York: Braziller.

von Linder, C. (Ed.). (1986). *Von den Industriereportagen bis "Ganz unten." Berichte, Analysen, Meinungen und Dokumente [From the industrial reports to "Totally on the bottom." Reports, analyses, opinions, and documents]*. Köln: Kiepenheuer & Witsch.

von Neumann, J., & Morgenstern, O. (1943). *Theory of games and economic behavior*. Princeton, NJ: Princeton University Press.

von Nitsch, R. (1989). *Scenario Analysis. Ein neues Programm zur Unterstützung der Szenarioanalyse. [Scenario analysis. A new program to support scenario analysis]* (Report 89/6). Aachen: Rheinisch—Westfälische Technische Hochschule, Lehr- und Forschungsgebiet Allgemeine Betriebswirtschaftslehre.

von Winterfeldt, D. (1978). A decision aiding system for improving the environmental standard setting process. In K. Chikocki & A. Straszak (Eds.), *Systems analysis applications to complex programs* (pp. 119-124). Oxford, UK: Pergamon.

von Winterfeldt, D., & Edwards, W. (1986). *Decision analysis and behavioral research*. Cambridge, UK: Cambridge University Press.

Walley, P. (1991). *Statistical reasoning with imprecise probabilities*. London: Chapman & Hall.

Wallraff, G. (1991). *Industriereportagen. Als Arbeiter in deutschen Großbetrieben [Industrial reports. As a worker in large German companies]*. Köln: Kiepenheuer und Witsch.

Wallsten, T. S. (1990). Measuring vague uncertainties and understanding their use in decision making. In G. M. v. Furstenberg (Ed.), *Acting under uncertainty multidisciplinary conceptions* (pp. 377-398). Boston: Kluwer Academic.

Wallsten, T. S., & Whitfield, R. G. (1986). *Assessing the risks to young children of three effects associated with elevated blood-lead levels*. Argonne, IL: Argonne National Laboratory.

Weber, E. U., & Bottom, W. P. (1989). Axiomatic measures of perceived risk: Some tests and extensions. *Journal of Behavioral Decision Making, 2*, 113-132.

Weinbrenner, P., & Häcker, W. (1991). Zur Theorie und Praxis von Zukunftswerkstätten [Thoughts on theory and practice of future workshops]. In Bundeszentrale für politische Bildung [Federal Center for Political Education] (Ed.), *Methoden in der politischen Bildung—Handlungsorientierung [Methods in political education—Action-oriented methods]* (pp. 115-149). Bonn: Bundeszentrale für politische Bildung.

Weisz, H., Schandl, H., & Fischer-Kowalski, M. (1999). OMEN—An Operating Matrix for material interrelations between the Economy and Nature. How to make material balances consistent. In R. Kleijn, S. Bringezu, M. Fischer-

Kowalski, & V. Palm (Eds.), *Ecologizing societal metabolism: Designing scenarios for sustainable materials management. Proceedings of the ConAccount workshop, November 21st 1998 in Amsterdam, The Netherlands* (pp. 160-165). Leiden: Centre of Environmental Science (CML).

Westenberg, M. R. M., & Koele, P. (1994). Multi-attribute evaluation processes: Methodological and conceptual issues. *Acta Psychologica, 87*, 65-84.

Whyte, W. F. (1943). *Street corner society: The social structure of an Italian slum.* Chicago: University of Chicago Press.

Wicklund, R. A., & Steins, G. (1996). Person perception under pressure: When motivation brings about egocentrism. In P. M. Gollwitzer & J. A. Bargh (Eds.), *The psychology of action: Linking motivation and cognition to behavior* (pp. 511-528). New York: Guilford.

Wiener, N. (1948). *Cybernetics or control and communication in the animal and the machine.* Cambridge: MIT Press.

Wood, C. (1995). *Environmental impact assessment: A comparative review.* London: Longman.

Yates, J. F. (1990). *Judgement and decision-making.* Englewood Cliffs, NJ: Prentice Hall.

Yates, J. F., & Stone, E. R. (1992). The risk construct. In J. F. Yates (Ed.), *Risk-taking behavior* (pp. 1-25). Chichester, UK: Wiley.

Yerkes, R. M., & Dodson, J. D. (1908). The relation of strength of stimulus to rapidity of habit information. *Journal of Comparative Neurology and Psychology, 18*, 459-482.

Yin, R. K. (1989). *Case study research: Design and methods.* Newbury Park, CA: Sage.

Yin, R. K. (1993). *Applications of case study research.* London: Sage.

Yin, R. K. (1994). *Case study research: Design and methods* (2nd ed.). London: Sage.

Yoon, K. P., & Hwang, C.-L. (1995). *Multiple attribute decision making.* Thousand Oaks, CA: Sage.

Zadeh, L. A. (1978). Fuzzy sets as a basis for a theory of possibility. *Fuzzy Sets and Systems, 1*, 3-28.

Zeeman, E. C. (1976). Catastrophe theory. *Scientific American, 334*, 65-83.

Ziegler, A. (1993). Wer moderieren will, muss Mass nehmen und Mass geben: Kulturgeschichtliche Hinweise zum heutigen Verständnis der Moderation [Those wanting to mediate have to take and to give measure: Advice from cultural history about today's understanding of mediation]. In A. C. Wohlgemuth (Ed.), *Moderation in Organisationen: Problemlösungsmethode für Führungsleute und Berater [Mediation in organizations: A problem-solving method for leaders and consultants]* (pp. 17-51). Bern: Haupt.

Zillessen, H. (Ed.). (1998). *Mediation—Kooperatives Konfliktmanagement in der Umweltpolitik [Mediation—Cooperative conflict management in environmental policy-making].* Opladen, Germany: Westdeutscher Verlag.

Zonneveld, I. S. (1972). *Textbook of photointerpretation (Chapter 7: Use of aerial photo interpretation in geography and geomorphology)* (Vol. 7). Eschede, Germany: ITC.

Zonneveld, I. S. (1982). Land(scape) ecology, a science or a state of mind. In S. P. Tjallingii & A. A. de Veer (Eds.), *Perspectives in landscape ecology contributions to research, planning and management of our environment. Proceedings of the International Congress, Veldhoven, April 6-11, 1981*. Wageningen, The Netherlands: Centre for Agricultural Publishing and Documentation.

Zuber, J., Crott, H. W., & Werner, J. (1992). Choice shift and group polarisation: An analysis of the status of arguments and social decision schemes. *Journal of Personality and Social Psychology, 62*(1), 50-61.

INDEX

ABOUT THE AUTHORS

Roland W. Scholz is the Chair of Environmental Sciences: Natural and Social Science Interface at the Swiss Federal Institute of Technology (ETH Zurich, Switzerland), adjunct Professor of Psychology at the University of Zurich (Privatdozent), and head of the Organization and Decision Making Consultants (GOE Zurich). He has been visiting professor at the Department of Urban Studies and Planning at MIT (Boston, Massachusetts, USA) and was elected as the fifth holder of the King Carl XVI Gustaf's Professorship hosted at the Center of Environment and Sustainability of Chalmers University of Technology and Gothenborg University (Sweden). He graduated in mathematics, psychology, and educational sciences (Dipl.-Math., University of Marburg, Germany, 1976), social psychology (Dr. phil., 1979, University of Mannheim, Germany), and cognitive psychology (Dr. phil. habil., 1987, University of Mannheim, Germany). He specialized in decision sciences and systems analysis, particularly game theory, bargaining and negotiation, decision making under uncertainty, cognitive psychology, and organizational psychology. His current research is in environmental decision making. Current topics are complex environmental system analysis and complex problem solving. When running large-scale case regional industrial studies, he became aware that the integration of qualitative and quantitative knowledge can be managed successfully by a strong methodology. The methods presented in this book were adjusted or developed on the job in the annual transdisciplinary ETH-UNS case studies on sustainable development.

Olaf Tietje is Research Associate at the Chair of Environmental Sciences: Natural and Social Science Interface at the Swiss Federal Institute of Technology (ETH Zurich, Switzerland). He graduated in mathematics (Dipl.-Math., Technische Universität Braunschweig) and geo-ecology and system analysis (Dr. rer. nat., Technische Universität Braunschweig). He is an expert in stochastic modeling of dynamic processes in complex systems, such as water transport in soil or mobility systems. He is the head of a research group on environmental evaluation and mathematical modeling. The projects of this group deal with methods of technology evaluation, environmental impact assessment, life cycle assessment, and sustainable resource allocation. He participated in the ETH-UNS case studies to support the application of specific methods, such as life cycle assessment, multicriteria evaluation, risk management, system dynamics, and material flux analysis.